HORSES AND SADDLERY

Queen Victoria inspecting the 2nd Life Guards at Windsor in 1839.

HORSES
AND SADDLERY

An account of the animals
used by the British and Commonwealth Armies
from the Seventeenth Century
to the Present Day with a description
of their Equipment

BY
MAJOR G. TYLDEN

J. A. ALLEN & COMPANY
LONDON
In association with the
ARMY MUSEUMS OGILBY TRUST
1965

Designed and printed by W. S. Cowell Ltd
at their press in the Butter Market, Ipswich, England

TO R.M.T.
WHO LOVED A GOOD HORSE

The Army Museums Ogilby Trust

This Trust, which is responsible for the production of this book, was founded in 1954 by the late Colonel R. J. L. Ogilby, D.S.O., D.L., with the principal object of encouraging, equipping, caring for and maintaining existing Army and Regimental Museums. Since its formation the Trust in a number of ways has helped Regimental and other military Museums. As well as providing finance to enable them to purchase historical items of particular Regimental interest for the improvement of Regimental Collections, the Trust has itself purchased items of military historical importance, and it has provided an advisory service which is available to Museum Trustees and Curators.

The Trust has also endeavoured to foster interest in regimental and military tradition by sponsoring the publication of certain printed works and catalogues, of which this book is one. A number of copies of each book sponsored in this way have been distributed free of charge by the Trust to existing Army and Regimental Museums so as to provide them with authoritative works of reference. In addition, by making such books available to the general public, the Trust has endeavoured to stimulate and encourage interest in regimental and military tradition.

The Army Museums Ogilby Trust has its office in the Ministry of Defence at Northumberland House, Northumberland Avenue, London, W.C.2.

Foreword

by General Sir John Anderson, K.C.B., C.B.E., D.S.O.,
Chairman, Army Museums Ogilby Trust

To anyone joining a Cavalry Regiment or other mounted unit in even the early 1930's, the possibility of the horse disappearing from the British Army was but as a cloud no bigger than a man's hand, nor did the gradual realization of the facts prepare us for a change so complete or so swift. The momentum of mechanization, due to the knowledge that war was almost upon us, swept the Army horse and his accoutrements from their centuries-old place in the scene, and many things, which might have survived in less turbulent times, were scattered to the winds or left to the moths and the damp.

In the post-war Army very small, but fortunately very splendid, mounted units have been preserved. Much, however, has gone for ever and likewise the experts on such things, become rarer as the years go by. It is indeed fortunate, therefore, that Major Tylden, who is so admirably qualified for the task, should have felt inspired to compile this complete record and, had he not done so, much knowledge of the horse and his saddlery, and of other animals which served in war, would never have been recorded.

Major Tylden's scholarly, fascinating and admirably illustrated work on this wide subject, with its excursions into such varied subjects as equitation, tail-trimming, farriery and shoeing, and horse portraiture, will not only give the reader great pleasure but will also be a most valuable book of reference.

John Anderson.

General.

Contents

Plates and Figures

It has been found impossible to group the Plates described in Chapter Eight according to subjects as one Plate may show a type of remount, details of saddlery, 'furniture', and of a bridle and of a phase of the Cavalry seat. Another shows only a saddle: there is a series showing types of remounts only.

All the Figures are described in detail in the text.

xiv

Introduction

This book has been written to carry out the ideas of the late Colonel R. J. L. Ogilby, D.S.O., D.L., a Cavalryman of many years service, who decided in 1961 that if the subjects dealt with in it were not put down on paper there would comparatively soon be no one left who knew anything about them, much less be in a position to record them.

The original idea was to deal with the Army horse and the equipment used on him, but as research work progressed the scope of the book grew, until finally Colonel Ogilby decided that everything about the animals used by the Army should be included and that, among other details, the tools used in shoeing horses and mules should also be shown and described.

At least two General Officers of the present day have confirmed Colonel Ogilby's original contention by admitting that they had never been on a horse in the course of their service and presumably they are representative of a very large number of the officers who have served since the start of the last war.

The book has been written round the illustrations, which is in fact the only possible way of making the subject matter intelligible, and the line drawings in the text are designed to the same end. Both were selected to a great extent by Colonel Ogilby from a very large number collected by Brigadier R. G. Thurburn, C.B., C.B.E., Secretary to the Army Museums Ogilby Trust, whose advice and skill have contributed more than any other factor to making the book, it is hoped, a work of reference covering as much as can be found on the variety of subjects which came up for treatment.

The bulk of the evidence, especially on the complicated problems of the nineteenth century, has come from the library of the Army Museums Ogilby Trust and from that of the former War Office (now Ministry of Defence) Central and Army Library. The staff of the latter, under the direction of the Librarian, Mr D. W. King, have been unremitting during the four years spent in collecting material in unearthing every possible source which could be of use. Most of it had remained hidden in the voluminous and diverse records of the Ordnance, just as had the series of vital lectures delivered at Aldershot seventy years ago. The latter are in the library of the Army Museums Ogilby Trust.

The number of those who have helped with material is very large and to them the author can never be sufficiently thankful. First must be listed the officers responsible for the records of the various Corps concerned, who have contributed not only material and illustrations but have also helped with advice. They are as follows:

The late Major J. P. Kaestlin, M.B.E., M.A., Royal Artillery Institute Museum and Library.

Brigadier J. H. S. Lacey, O.B.E., Secretary of the Royal Engineers Institution.

Lieut Colonel A. G. Penna, O.B.E., formerly Curator of the Royal Army Service Corps Museum.

Brigadier J. Clabby, O.B.E., M.R.C.V.S., formerly Director Army Veterinary and Remount Services, the author of a book frequently mentioned, to whom the author is especially indebted for help.

The Curators of the Africana Museum, Johannesburg, of the Scottish United Services Museum, the Castle, Edinburgh, and the Librarian of the Royal Commonwealth Society have also helped very considerably.

It is to Mr W. A. Thorburn, of the Scottish United Services Museum, that the author is indebted for the photographs and detailed description of the seventeenth-century troop-saddle, which was the prototype of the British Army saddle, up to the middle of the eighteenth century and probably later.

The difficulty of finding details of troop saddles before the days of Ordnance publications has been very great and after much trouble had been taken by Mr F. J. Chandler of Marlborough and Messrs Jabez Cliff & Co. of Walsall a specimen of the first Hussar saddle of 1805 was also brought to light.

Mr Chandler has helped with research on many points, as has Mr A. W. Croft of Lambourn. To both these professional saddlers the author is indebted for the loan of trade catalogues dating back to the eighties of last century.

For details of Australian saddlery the author is indebted to Mr Robert Gray of South Australia and Mr P. H. Bullock of Sydney and in the case of New Zealand to Mrs Edith Tylden of Auckland and the City Librarian of the same city.

Important material on the saddlery, both riding and pack of the U.S.A. was collected by Dr R. C. Pearse of Durham, North Carolina, who also arranged for official publications to be made available.

The whole of the account of the saddlery used by the Canadian Defence Force came from Mr Charles H. Stewart, Librarian of the Department of National Defence Library at Ottawa. He collected evidence from every possible source, especially on pack-saddles.

More catalogues were lent by Mr B. T. Hinchley of Birmingham and finally we come to the members of the Society for Army Historical Research who have not already been mentioned. At the time of his death Colonel Ogilby had only just resigned the Chairmanship of the Council of the Society, and a very large amount of the detail in the book comes from the Society's Journal.

The Marquess of Cambridge not only supplied the photographs of the Royal Horse Artillery in 1861 but also lent books from his collection and is responsible for much of the account of the saddlery of the Household Cavalry.

Mr W. Y. Carman, the late Mr L. E. Buckell, Major N. P. Dawnay, Mr R. G. Harris, Mr C. C. P. Lawson, Mr John Mollo and Colonel H. C. B. Rogers all helped; Mr Buckell with constant criticism, Major Dawnay on illustrations, Mr Harris with illustrations and cuttings, Mr Lawson and Colonel Rogers in various ways, the latter with the loan of books, and Mr Mollo with the problems of the Hussar saddle of 1805, for which he drew the diagrams, and other help over this period. Mr Lawson's works have also provided a fund of authoritative information.

As regards some of the problems of the Indian Army, Mrs Westland, then of the staff of A.M.O.T., not only contributed photographs but also notes on a variety of points.

For details of the South African War of 1899–1902 the author is indebted to Brigadier Peter Young and to Dr H. H. Curson of Pretoria. The last-named contributed the notes on the Veterinary Corps of what was formerly the Union of South Africa Defence Force.

Thanks are also due to the following for permission to quote or use material from their works (see Bibliography): Lieut Colonel E. F. Bolton, D.S.O.; Mrs Lida Fleitman Bloodgood and Pelham Books Ltd; and Miss Preston, daughter of the author of *The Desert Mounted Corps* and Messrs Constable, the publishers; the Controller of Her Majesty's Stationery Office in respect of the *Manual of Horsemastership*, 1937, and other official publications listed in the Bibliography.

It has been difficult to avoid a certain amount of repetition, due to the various headings under which most of the subjects fall, as well as to explain points which are well known to many people but not always to those of this generation.

The author is alone responsible for the opinions expressed and the inclusion of the section on Artists and Photographers is his work and was not part of the original scheme of the book.

Acknowledgements to all those who have kindly given their permission for the use of illustrations are given under 'Illustrations'.

Finally, the full descriptions of the books referred to in the footnotes are given in the Bibliography.

G. TYLDEN 1965

CHAPTER ONE

The Development of British Regular Army Horses to the year 1902

The Rider must live only for his horse, which is his legs, his safety, his honour and his reward

THE OLD CAVALRY SOLDIER *c.* 1800[1]

THE old saying which heads this chapter contains the essence of what every good cavalryman had to learn before he knew his trade, from the earliest time when men rode horses to war. The saying needs no justification to the old hands, but so little is known and so much forgotten about the horse today that an explanation of what a good one can do and has done through the ages will not be out of place.

Of all the many and various animals domesticated and trained by man to do his bidding the most important, especially in warfare, was the horse. After the introduction of firearms he ranked in some countries as their equal as munition of war, and a warrior might part with neither without the permission of his chief, although the horse was the man's private property. Before that the war horse ranked first. This was because for centuries it was the mounted warriors, the knightly class and then the cavalry, that were the battle winners.

A modern writer, an experienced soldier,[2] has summed up the horse's capabilities in the following passage – 'The horse's versatility in performing many and various tasks has been known from time immemorial. He could be packed for one thing (Plate 48) and to this day he has no equal for riding. His back seems to have been made for a man's saddle. He was strong and could cover great distances. He could walk, trot, gallop, turn, halt and plunge at the slightest beckon of his master. He could jump, swim rivers, and pick his way down a mountain side with more skill and courage than any animal known. In battle he proved supreme, for warriors found in him unmatchable speed of movement. When packed he bore his load well. He was surefooted and could easily carry up to 250 lb. He performed hazardous marches across fields and valleys and hills that other animals could not have endured. Above all, he was the loyal companion.'

He also stood fire well, much better than the mule, though like his master he had his limitations. A memory of the old days is of a well-bred horse standing by his dead rider under sporadic machine gun fire. Like most of his kind when introduced to drill, to which he had been unaccustomed, he picked it up quickly.

The horse also stands cold, which would be too much for camels and mules and would kill dogs.[3] Even when half-starved and short of water he will still carry on until he cannot go another yard.

I

A modern estimate of the work a horse in good condition should do in a day, when forming part of a large body of cavalry, is from 20 to 25 miles. Most of this would be done at a walk, at an average pace of about four miles an hour. A march of 40 to 45 miles a day would constitute a forced march and might have to be done at a rate of 5 to 6 miles an hour, necessitating the occasional use of the trot, a pace averaging 8 miles an hour. The smaller the body of cavalry involved the quicker would the rate of marching be, and at the strength of a regiment a thirty miles march might be done at the rate of six miles an hour, thus giving the horse more time for rest. Whatever distance had to be covered cavalry had to be prepared to go into action at once and deliver a charge at the rate of twelve miles an hour, perhaps followed by a fast pursuit of a broken enemy.

According to Veterinary Surgeon Major General Sir F. Smith[4] so often quoted in this book, the mean weight of a cavalry remount should be 1,000 lb and the horse should be able to carry one-fifth of that amount, though in practice this was only too often exceeded.

There is no satisfactory relation between a horse's height and his weight-carrying capacity, hence the modern practice of buying remounts by weight, after classifying them according to the types required.

The height of a horse or mule is reckoned in 'hands', of four inches each, measured from the bottom of the hoof when the leg is upright to the top of the wither, the place where the front arch of the saddle goes and a little in front of it. Thus a 15·2 hands horse would be 5 feet 2 inches, and as most people know their own height, a rough estimate can be formed by standing alongside the horse immediately in front of the saddle. Plates 76–78 give excellent examples of height.

Although as a general rule remounts were not bought measuring less than 14 hands 2 inches, in many countries, where ponies smaller than this are the rule, Mounted Infantry especially have often made long and severe marches on ponies of 13 hands and even smaller. A great point of these ponies always was that they would work on a much smaller ration than the 10 lb of grain and the same weight of hay, which was the British Army ration for horses under 15 hands, and two pounds more of each for the larger remounts, per day. A pony of any of the hardy, well-bred breeds should go, if ridden by himself, 30 miles out from home, have a rest of an hour or more with a feed and water and do the return journey without being unduly tired, the round trip being done at the rate of 6 miles an hour. Despatch riders, well mounted and told to use extreme speed, have averaged much faster rates than this over rather shorter distances.

The capacity of the R.H.A. harness horse was about the same, when pulling guns and their waggons. That is to say the vehicles should be capable of keeping up with cavalry.[5]

The horse's usefulness as a pack animal is also very considerable and will be discussed later.

Two more points which affect the usefulness of the horse in war are the unsuitability of the horn of which the feet are composed to stand up to long distances, especially on hard stony road and tracks, without wearing down until complete inability to travel further is achieved and the animal must perforce be rested. The remedy is to attach a horseshoe, a three-quarter circle of iron to the foot, a complicated business which will be discussed in the section on Farriery. The second point is the very thick coat of hair which the horse grows in winter if transported to a country where the seasons are reversed in the hot weather. The advisability of removing the long hair or leaving it will be dealt with later.

Naturally horses vary as much in their dispositions and attributes as humans. One of the horse's most useful characteristics is his ability to see at night; only a few seem unable to do so. There are bad-tempered, intractable horses, sulky lazy ones, wildly excitable ones and those who make a practice of deliberately running away. Once bought as a remount, and many of the above traits are not at all easy or even possible for the buyer to detect, someone must break and accustom him to his new profession and someone must ride him and keep him in the ranks. But the generality of horses are such as the Old Cavalry Soldier, whose professional creed heads this chapter, loved and in whom he believed – implicitly.

The Provision of Remounts

There are two methods of providing horses and mules for an army; they can be bought in the open market either by officers or officials, or bred by the Government under the control of suitable officers.

In time of war there are a further two methods; animals can be impressed and either taken without payment or paid for at a fair rate, settled by the Government, or men who bring their own horses can be enlisted at higher rates of pay than those not doing so.

Mounted men who bring their own horses, whether paid out for them on joining or not, can usually be trusted to be good horsemasters; but this practice is, as a general rule, only satisfactory for a short campaign in or near the home country and need not be considered further. Forced impressment without payment lies outside the scope of this book; impressment on payment need impose no great hardship if properly carried out. There remain the two methods which begin this chapter.

As regards Great Britain there has never been any response to a suggestion that Government breeding studs should be established. For one thing hardly any Parliament has ever taken any serious interest in schemes of an expensive nature which concern the Army operating in peace time. The smaller the annual Vote can be kept the greater is the satisfaction of all political parties. The remount market was also always well liked by the large number of people who bred horses, especially in Ireland. Prices, if not high, were satisfactory and men breeding for the better class markets always had a number of young horses who were just not good enough for the purpose, but would sell well enough as remounts. The result was that in peace we could mount the Army in the open market and always did so.

A most unsatisfactory feature of this method was the constant drain on our home resources for stallions and mares suitable for breeding remounts caused by the high prices paid by agents of continental countries buying for their national studs. All the literature dealing with the subject has constant references to the export of valuable breeding stock to the Continent.

In India the position was different and the history of the Government studs maintained there will be dealt with in another section. In a separate section will be found notes on the continental systems.

Taking the question all in all we do not seem to have suffered to any great extent from our rather casual control of the export market or from adhering to the practice of buying direct from the breeder, at least in times of peace. But it took two wars before a proper organization for supplying horses in war time was set on foot in peace time.

There was a very considerable amount of buying and selling, not only of breeding stock but also of horses of remount types going on between this country and the Continent in peace time, and we also indented largely on the Canadian market in the latter half of the nineteenth century. This fitted in well enough with the average Britisher's ideas of leaving everything to the individual and allowing the open market to rule prices.

The bulk of the horse breeding was for many years somewhat loosely under the control of the big landowners and prosperous farmers. In every county there were men of these two classes breeding either thoroughbreds and hunters or some special breed of saddle or carriage horse. All these men contributed in one way and another to the supply of remounts and were many of them willing to spend money freely to further improvements. The heavy horse breeders, of shires and the like, also had their influence on draught horses, both for artillery and transport. But the important breed, the English thoroughbred, exercised more influence on remounts than the others. The main interest was in racing, either on the flat or over fences and it was the blood of the racehorse, originally coming from the East, that spread down to most types of remount as time went on.

The influence of the big breeders was always exercised in favour of encouragement by Parliament of any scheme for improving the type of remounts. Through the various Breed Societies who were responsible for the Horse Shows quite an amount of pressure could at times be brought to bear. Individual effort, however dispersed and disunited, did to a very great extent take the place of the centrally organized continental Government studs.

The Civil Wars

Before the general introduction of firearms, roughly speaking at the beginning of the seventeenth century, the remount most highly esteemed was the so-called Great Horse or Black Horse, as he was called later. Running well over 16 hands and massively built, he had been evolved in order to carry a man in full armour, a total weight of about 30 stone. He was also the horse used in the manège, where he was broken to every sort of controlled movement which could be of use in combat, horse against horse.[6] See colour plate, drum horses of the Household Cavalry.

How much the Great Horse was used in the Civil Wars it is not easy to say. He appears on the Great Seal of Charles I, a very fine horseman who was often painted mounted on one: Cromwell is shown on a Great Horse in the painting by Vandyke and there is extant a letter from him making an offer for 'A Black won in battle'. The price offered is '60 pieces' against '20 pieces' for cobs to mount 'Dragooners'[7] and there is no doubt what the Black would have been (see *ante*). Probably officers on both sides rode a Great Horse as what would have been later called a First Charger, but the authorities[8] consider that the bulk of the cavalry horses of both Royalists and Parliamentarians were much lighter.

Gervase Markham wrote in 1617 as follows: 'I do daily find in mine experience, that the vertue, goodness, boldness, swiftness and endurance of our true bred English horses is equal to any race of horses whatsoever. Some former writers, whether out of want of experience or to flatter novelties, have concluded that the English Horse is a great strong jade, deep-ribbed, sid-belled, with strong legges and good hoofs, yet fitter for the cart than either saddle or working employment. How false this is all English horsemen know. The true English horse, him I mean that is bred under a good clime, on firme ground, in a pure temperature, is of tall stature and large proportions; his head though not so fine as either the Barbarie's or the Turks, yet is lean, long and well fashioned; his crest is hie, only subject to thickness if he be stoned (a stallion not a gelding), but if he be gelded then it is firm and strong; his chyne is straight and broad; and all his limbs large, leane, flat and excellently jointed. For their endurance I have seen them suffer and execute as much and more than ever I noted of any foraine creation.'[9]

In other words a remount was a good specimen of an ordinary ride and drive utility horse, owing little or nothing to the blood of the Great Horse and probably with a small admixture of Arab and Barb (Barbarie and Turk) which had been imported in small numbers for some time. Presumably the officers would have favoured anything showing a dash of Eastern blood.

Newcastle, the apostle of the manège, writing in 1658,[10] considered that many breeds of English horses were well fitted for military purposes and from Ward[11] we know that Horse, Cuirassiers and Harquebusiers, should ride horses of 15 hands. Cuirassiers went out during the First Civil War, 1642–46; the Harquebusier we should call a heavy cavalryman. He wore a steel cap, a buff coat and long thigh boots, carried sword and pistol and later a carbine. He would have ridden heavy, though in those days he would not have carried much kit on his horse. According to Sir Walter Gilbey,[12] a first-class authority, we were breeding more light type horses than any other in the years immediately preceding the Civil Wars and the Great Horse had become the Shire Horse by about 1680. After that he became heavier and heavier and does not come into the remount class until modern times, when for a short period heavy guns were pulled by Shire horses or Shire crosses.

It is not easy to say what the troop horse of the Civil Wars period looked like. There is a monument to Sir Richard Astley, Bt. (1625–88), in Patshull Church near Wolverhampton which is considered by Brigadier P. Young[13] to have been made some years after the Civil War, which shows the uniform and equipment correctly. The horse furniture is certainly correct and the horses are of a type which one would expect from what has been written about them. All have long tails and manes laid on the off, small heads not markedly either coarse or Eastern type. They are short in front of the saddle, well coupled up with plenty of depth and strong rather short quarters. The officer is riding a stallion. They are definitely short and thick in the neck and are, generally speaking, what one would expect to find and are probably about 15 hands. They are entirely different from the big clumsy horses shown in Newcastle's book and in drawings of the early years of the century. How far this is due to the artist's imagination it is impossible to say.

The performance of the cavalry mounts of the period differs little from that expected of troop horses of the saddle breeds as distinct from the harness breeds used for a time in the eighteenth century by Heavy Cavalry. The following are the details of a fortnight's work by Royalist Horse in July, 1643, when there would be plenty of feed and the horses should have been in hard condition. Prince Maurice was commanding the Horse and Dragoons with General Sir Richard Hopton and Lieut General Lord Hertford's army of the West. After a period of marching at normal infantry pace the army arrived at Lansdown, near Bath on the 4th July and next day fought the indecisive battle of that name, remaining masters of the field of battle. During the fighting of the 5th July most of Maurice's command ran away and rode 60 miles to Oxford, the Royalist Headquarters. From the 7th to the 9th, Maurice with the remains of 1,500 horse, possibly 500 strong, was on rearguard covering the march of the army to Devizes, about 20 miles. His men were reported as not being in good heart. On the night of the 10th–11th Maurice left the army, which was on the point of being encircled by General Sir William Waller's Parliamentary army, and marched 44 miles straight to Oxford. On the 12th, Maurice collected 300 Horse, all that were fit, and rendezvoused with a strong force of Horse under Lieut General Lord Wilmot at Marlborough, 40 miles from Oxford. On the 13th, the Horse marched to Devizes, 14 miles, and fought the battle of Roundway Down, one of the most successful Cavalry victories of which there is a record. Maurice's 300 horse were described as being very tired. So from the evening of the 10th to midday on the 13th Maurice's troop horses had done over 90 miles and fought a general action at the finish.

There is nothing extraordinary in these marches – they have been cited as an example of what cavalry were normally called upon to do. It should be noted that a long night march can be very hard on both men and horses.

Roughly speaking the custom at this time was for a man presenting himself as a recruit for heavy cavalry, Horse, as they were called, to come with his own horse and to be paid more than Dragoons or Infantry. Dragoons also could bring their own cobs, valued at half the rate of a troop horse. Another method in favour with the Parliamentary Army was for 'well affected' persons to provide both horse and man. If they found both they received 2s 6d, if the horse only, 1s 4d a day. The

6

value of the horse was assessed and it was regarded as a loan for which repayment was promised, with interest at 8 per cent.

This form of subscription developed into a forced loan, horses being taken and valued by specially appointed committees. Thus, in 1643 a district would be assessed and have to provide a certain number of horses, which had to be collected and forwarded by the local authorities. Another plan was to confiscate horses owned by men belonging to the opposite party and this was done by both sides. By 1645 all horses had perforce to be bought, other means of providing them having broken down. Both the Troop Captain and the Trooper were responsible to the State for maintenance, at fixed rates, and for shoeing. The amounts paid were debited to the trooper on his pay sheet. All Government horses were branded and a trooper could keep his horse on disbandment by paying for it at a rate fixed at a reasonable figure.[14] A number of men not only brought their own horses but in some cases remounted themselves.

The royalists mounted their men by purchase and impressment and many of the officers and men provided remounts at the start of hostilities, just as did their opponents. In many cases the officers, drawn largely from the landowning classes, were not only very well mounted themselves but mounted their men as well.

At the commencement of the war the King would, by Proclamation, ask that 'horses, geldings, mares or naggs be sent in (from specified areas) to be used as Dragoon horses and with them saddles and bridles'.[15] A difficulty was artillery teams, for which horses with collars and traces and two carters to a team were impressed by both sides. If draught horses were in short supply oxen had to be impressed or bought, though they were not as satisfactory as horses. On the very indifferent roads of the time horses could barely keep up with infantry when moving the clumsy guns of the period and oxen are considerably slower. When possible oxen were sold and the money used to buy draught horses.[16]

In 1645 when the New Model Army was formed by Parliament practically all the horses were bought in the open market, remounts for Horse cost £7 10s od, for Dragoons, £4, and draught horses for artillery and baggage £6 apiece. After this prices rose slightly. Fit horses could also be seized in Royalist occupied territory.

In 1649 Charles I was beheaded and for ten years England was governed by the Commonwealth. Cromwell carried on the tradition of importing Eastern horses, both stallions and mares of Arab or Arab cross breeding.

Charles II

Charles II (1660–85), probably did as much for horse breeding as any king before or after him. His great interest was in racing, and it was through racing that the improvement of the saddle horse was so satisfactorily continued. Charles sent his Master of the Horse abroad to continue the policy of buying what were called Turks and Barbary horses. It has always been difficult to buy good class mares from Turkey, Syria, Arabia, Egypt and the African states along the Mediterranean, especially in Arabia, but Charles' efforts were successful and as is so well known it is to the mares he bought, entitled 'the King's Mares', that modern racehorses trace their descent on the dam's side. This may seem beside the point, but far from this being the case it was not only from the leading sires that the breed of horses benefited, but more from the rejects of the Turf. At this time and for many years, especially in the reign of Queen Anne, it was the custom for a horse to run in three or four heats of up to four miles in a day's racing. A horse that can do this is ideal for crossing with mares of riding stamp in order to get remounts. Far bigger weights were carried by much smaller horses than from the mid-eighteenth century onwards, and a cavalry or horse artillery remount requires the same qualities as these racehorses possessed in the highest degree – they could gallop far and fast carrying weight and their endurance was beyond question. The produce of Charles II's importations and those of the three succeeding reigns produced 'horses of full blood, three quarters blood or halfbred, suitable to carry burdens; by which means the English breed of horses is allowed to be the best and is greatly esteemed by all foreigners'.[17]

The Arab as bred in the Near East is not usually much over 14 hands 2 inches in height and Sir Walter Gilbey[12] gives the average heights of the English thoroughbred as follows: 14 hands in 1700, 14 hands 3 inches in 1800, and 15 hands 2½ inches in 1900. It will not be far from the mark if we take the average height of a troop horse, except those bought for Light Dragoons, from about 1750 to 1850, as 15 hands. The Black Horses ridden by Heavy Cavalry in the last half of the eighteenth century may have run bigger, as would those of the Household Cavalry. As a general rule the smaller the horse the greater the power of endurance on the short rations normally available in warfare and those interested in the subject will find it worked out fully in Sir Walter Gilbey's book *Small Horses in Warfare*.[12]

In the days of black powder and battlefields of restricted size it was natural for senior officers to ride a charger as tall as possible, as he gave his rider a few inches more command and made it easier for him to see what was taking place. There is a painting by John Wyck of Major General Randolph Egerton of the Life Guards, dated c.1672.[18] He rides a leggy Barb, a grey, and the artist has preserved for us an upstanding horse of about 15 hands or over with the small neat head of the Barb, a moderately good shoulder, a long back, well dropped hocks and a full tail. In the background are troopers riding strong chunky troop horses of very much the same type as those of Sir Richard Astley's troop in the Civil War, previously described. Mr Lawson[19] has given it as his opinion that Cromwell's men used horses of this type, the result of crossing local mares with Barbs.

In 1680 remounts available for service were in such short supply that the Life Guards had to hand over horses to the Tangier Horse, now the 1st Royal Dragoons, before they could be sent to Tangier as reinforcements.[20] The port was held by us from 1662 to 1684.

Throughout this reign and up to the end of the century it was still the custom for a trooper of Horse to bring his own troop horse on enlisting. If he could not do so the King provided him with a horse and if necessary stopped the price from his pay. It was never officially settled as to whether or not he was entitled to take his horse with him when he was discharged, the practice varying from regiment to regiment, but this was never allowed if the man had under a year's service. It was because the Horse originally found their own remounts that they received a higher rate of pay than Dragoons, who did not.

James II

James II (1685–88) raised several regiments of Horse and increased the Army considerably, but there does not appear to be any specific evidence on remounts during his reign.

William III

His successor, William III (1689–1702), was keenly alive to the importance of horse breeding. He took a personal interest in racing like Charles II, and imported two sires, a Turk and an Arab, which were among the best that were ever imported. He also brought over with him Dutchmen, who set to work to drain the fens on the East coast and they imported heavy black horses for the purpose. As already stated the Great Horse was also known as the Black Horse, so there must have been a considerable number of heavy type black stallions available to breeders and there were also a number of Oldenburg coach horses and mares imported; these were also black. It became the colour considered correct for cavalry and from this time onward more and more Regiments of Horse rode blacks, with exceptions like The Queen's Bays (2nd Dragoon Guards) and The Royal Scots Greys (2nd Dragoons). William himself is shown riding a heavy black charger with an obvious cross of the Great Horse in him. In 1692 the 2nd Troop of the Life Guards were all mounted on blacks.[21] Troop horses were still ridden with their tails left long, although docking the tail had been practised in England for a long time.

Anne

Anne (1702–14). The Queen continued the policy of importing horses of Eastern blood and took a great interest in racing. The policy of running races over long distances in heats with considerable weights up was continued, with, as before, satisfactory results in the class of stallions available to breeders of saddle horses and remounts. Most of the travelling was done on horseback and the market for a hardy stamp of roadster was a good one.

Lawson is of the opinion that at this period the cavalry was mounted on 'strong sturdy animals with high crests and small heads, lighter and more active than the heavy war horses of mediaeval times'. He considers that there would have been a considerable mixture of Barbs or stallions of Barb strain with English mares and that the latter would have been cob-like animals of about 14 hands. This description fits in well with Markham's of nearly a century earlier and especially with what is known of the continued import of horses of Eastern strains.

As is well known when Prince Eugene inspected the Duke of Marlborough's

9

cavalry in 1704 during the march to the Danube which culminated in the battle of Blenheim, he commented specially on the horses, equipments and uniforms. The British cavalry did magnificent work in this campaign. Markham's 'true English horse' with the lapse of time had not only borne out all of his eulogies but improved even more.

The illustration by James Ross, reproduced here (Plate 8) is one of four paintings called the Battle of Ramillies (1706) and was possibly painted in 1715. It is unlikely to have been painted to show that battle, but gives an excellent picture of Marlborough's army. The three officers in the foreground are appraising a grey charger, presumably belonging to the officer on the right of the group without a cuirass. The grey looks to be about 15 hands, a long (in the back) low well-bred type owing a great deal to Arab or Turkish blood – the terms were more or less synonymous – with a nice small, intelligent head and clean legs. In the middle distance is a gun team of farm horse type and in front of them mounted men. The gun horses have had their tails docked, not very short. Behind the three officers riding away is a Dragoon trooper with musket in a bucket under the off wallet or holster, a rolled cloak as a rear pack and his charger's tail docked short. Troopers' horses were not docked at the commencement of Marlborough's campaigns, but his Quartermaster-General, Cadogan, introduced the practice of leaving only two inches of the tail and later the hair was cut off as well.[22] About this time too, the horrible disfigurement of cropping the horses' ears short came into fashion and continued right through the century. All cavalry from an earlier date were taught to slash at the top of the headstall of the bridle in a mêlée in order to make the bit fall out of the horse's mouth and so make it impossible for the rider to steer him. Lawson is of the opinion that the cropping of the ears may have arisen in order to stop them being slashed.

At this time £12 was the price of a remount for Horse, and for a 'good squat Dragoon horse' £5 was paid in Ireland.[23] Greys for the 2nd Dragoons cost £15 and in Spain about £9 was paid for 'little Spanish jades' as remounts for the regiments serving there. Losses in that country were heavy and even heavier on the sea voyage, so much so that the Bays and Royal Dragoons went out dismounted and £6,500 was spent on Barbary horses, considered to be too expensive. The Blenheim campaign cost £6,725 for replacing losses in remounts. In 1706, £10,000 was spent on replacing officers' chargers and a like sum for horses of Horse and Dragoons killed or died of common distemper. At Malplaquet the cavalry lost only £2,000 worth of remounts.[24]

George I and II

George I (1714–27) and George II (1727–60). The black remount was now fully established as a mount for Horse and Dragoons. From 1729 the height was fixed at from 15 hands one inch for Horse and for Dragoons at 15 hands and not above. All were to be 'strong and well bodied'. In 1715 the 4th Dragoons, later Hussars, were all riding blacks. In other words they were practically mounted on the same type of horse as the Heavy Cavalry and this was by no means satisfactory to some of the survivors of Marlborough's campaigns. One of these men, Lieut General Hawley, wrote a scheme in 1728 for 'reraising a Regiment of Dragoons on the model of earlier days'. They were to ride what he called half-bred nags from 14 hands to 14 hands 2 inches. Nothing was done and in 1746 the height was fixed at 15 hands at most for Dragoons, the horses to be 'very Nimble kind of horses that can gallop, with short backs, broad fillets (or flat backs) for carrying of forage and small clean legs and as clear of hair as possible. The age was to be rising five but six year old would be better. The sergeants were to have a Lighter Nimbler kind of horse.'[25] These orders were issued and presumably written by the Commander-in-Chief, the Duke of Cumberland, and in 1745 a regiment, Kingston's Light Horse, was raised on the occasion of the Jacobite Rising of that year. They rode light horses of various colours with swish or nicked tails. On the disbandment of the Regiment in 1746 it was re-embodied as the Duke of Cumberland's Regiment. The horses were all chestnuts and the men were dressed and equipped as Heavy Dragoons. The Duke of Cumberland's Dragoons were disbanded in 1748. A painting by Morier shows a troop horse with a short docked tail, but not as short as the Cadogan dock. He is strongly built, appears to be about 15 hands, and does not differ very much from the painting by Morier, reproduced at Plate 58, of a trooper of the 1st Regiment of Horse, standing by his horse in 1751.

In 1746 there was a change in the status and nomenclature of the Horse Regiments and three of them became Dragoons, but with the addition of the word 'Guards'. Fortescue considers this was part of one of the general schemes of economy carried out from time to time. The change made little difference to the mounting of the cavalry, for Colonels of Dragoons had for some time been trying to mount their men as nearly as possible on the same type of remount as those of the Horse. This tendency on the part of commanding officers to make their troopers heavier and heavier by increasing the size of the horses was always very noticeable and persisted to the end of the period when the cavalry were mounted. The remaining Horse became Dragoon Guards in 1788 but by then the cavalry had been increased by the permanent addition of Light Dragoons (Plates 59 and 60).

It was the business of the Colonel of the Regiment to see to the mounting of other ranks, officers being supposed to provide themselves with horses. Losses of troop horses through negligence were chargeable to the Captain of each troop, who was allowed a special fund for this purpose and for recruiting. Abroad remounts were bought at current prices and in many cases no standard approximating to the official one could be observed. In Great Britain dealers brought horses for inspection at prices fixed by Government.

The following details are taken from Inspection Returns.[26] In 1753 the Bays were very well mounted, the Drum horses being greys; next year the Greys sergeants' horses had hunters' tails, docked but not short.

In 1753 we have a most interesting report on 'the 1st or Royal Dragoons, who are well mounted on black horses. The Sergeants' horses have hunters' tails. The horses are a lower size and lighter sort than other Dragoons *with a good deal of the saddle horse in them*; quarters not so heavy as the common run of black horses.' (The italics are the author's.) It is clear from this report that the generality of blacks bought as remounts approximated more to the heavy carriage horse than to a riding horse. Presumably the breeders had got the colour and the conformation from the imported black Dutch horses, from Oldenburg horses, imported for carriage work and also black, and from the black Shire stallions. There may have been a reason for this, for from about 1758 all European cavalry began to be issued with valises, round-shaped cases to fasten on behind the saddle and hold the man's kit and part of his equipment. 'The broad fillets for carrying forage', see above, were now to have more and more weight put on them, and as this went on increasing Colonels had to look more and more to the weight-carrying capacity of their remounts. This and the limitation as to colour made a difficult problem, never really solved.

Light Dragoons have already been mentioned. In 1756 a Troop was added to the establishment of regiments of Dragoon Guards and Dragoons. The Light Troops were mounted on 'well turned nimble road horses as nigh to the colour of the Regiment horses as can be got'.[27] The expression 'well turned' meant compact, short-backed strong cobs, which were not to be under 14 hands 3 inches. The tails had to be docked. This was just the sort of mount which a civilian, with a business which necessitated him making long trips on horseback, would keep in his stable. Consequently, there would have been plenty of material for the buyers of remounts to choose from. In 1759 the first complete regiments of Light Dragoons were raised, at first five and then two more in 1760. This experiment, which was a complete success, is noteworthy in the history of cavalry horses as making a move away from a special type and *colour* in the direction of using the more plentiful types of horses bred all over the country. Breeders were much more prone to breed remounts for the Army when they were assured of a plentiful market among civilians for any misfits they might turn up. Crossing sires of any established breed with mares whose breeding is largely a matter of conjecture is always a difficult and chancy business.

The last few months of George II's reign saw two notable exploits by British cavalry. There had been light cavalry in Continental armies for some time, but they were not expected to take their place in line of battle. That was the duty of Horse and Dragoons, as it was not thought that the lighter more 'nimble' mounts of the light horsemen, specially selected as they were for security duties, would have the weight and force to charge embattled troops, whether cavalry or infantry. This theory was completely exploded by our 15th Light Dragoons (later Hussars) who, at Emsdorff on the 16th July, 1760, charged through and over whatever came in their way. This practice succeeding generations of our Light Cavalry have made a commonplace. Another remarkable instance of the admirable type of remount of the period was seen at Warburg on the 31st July, 1760. Twenty-two squadrons of British heavy cavalry, including one of Household Cavalry, the Blues, made a forced march of two hours' duration, mainly at the trot, and without pausing, charged a force of all arms and utterly routed them. Both actions were fought against French troops, who had a very high reputation at the time. It is hardly necessary to stress that for heavy troop horses to have the stamina to carry out an approach march in the above manner is no small tribute to the breeders and to the men who bought them.

This chapter has so far taken the history of the British Army Horse from the decades before the Civil Wars of Charles I's time, which began in 1642, up to the accession of George III in October 1760.

The earlier period shows the rather confused methods practised at a time when the Great Horse of the days of full armour was giving way to a smaller, more active type. The Civil Wars showed the marching powers of the ordinary saddle horse of the day, who was not expected to carry too heavy a weight. From 1660 the history of the Army really begins and by Marlborough's day, early in the next century, the cavalry were all Heavies, though the Dragoons were still classed as lighter. Both types fought in line of battle, and Marlborough's victories owed not a little to the outstanding qualities of the remounts of his day. By modern ideas they were no doubt common looking, but did all that was asked of them in magnificent style, notably at Blenheim.

The succeeding period may be called the one of the black charger ridden by Horse and Dragoons alike, there being practically no difference between them. The introduction of Light Dragoons brought this period to an end.

George III

The long reign of George III, from 1760 to 1820, falls conveniently into two parts, firstly from its inception to the end of the century, and secondly the first twenty years of the nineteenth century, which saw the end of an epoch with the final defeat of Napoleon in 1815. The whole of the reign is marked by changes, by a general tightening up of everything pertaining to cavalry, the disappearance of the black colour* except for the Household Cavalry troop horses, and by two events which had a most important effect on the whole subject of remounts. The first was the commencement of riding fast to hounds, the second the speeding up of the mail service with the introduction of coaches travelling at seven miles an hour. Another important event was the beginning of scientific as opposed to rule-of-thumb methods in the veterinary service.

Another change, though started in the last reign, first became well known under George III. This was the development of the Hackney, not as we know him today as a high-stepping carriage horse, but as a most useful ride and drive, cut-and-come-again roadster, capable of performing great distances at a good pace. Not all roadsters were Hackneys, though many were bred from Hackney sires, but the

* Thus in 1811 the 3rd Dragoons (later Hussars) were 'mounted entirely on black horses for the last time', before proceeding to Spain on active service. Cassells' *Peninsula Portrait* p. 4.

13

type goes with the name for many years. The roadster at the end of the eighteenth century has been described as follows: 'they were strong, for they had to carry, besides the horseman in his heavy jack boots, leather breeches and broad-skirted coat, a heavy horseman's cloak, saddle bags, and holsters for a pair of pistols. They were tolerably swift, for a rider might owe his safety to his nag's pace. They had good shoulders and plenty before the pommel, capital legs and feet.'[28] If a shoulder firearm, ammunition pouch and sword are added, the description is an admirable one of a troop horse. A number of horse breeders preferred to use a thoroughbred sire rather than a Hackney, as giving more quality and pace, but the idea was the same and with an average height of 15 hands no better qualifications for remounts could be found than the above description.

In 1761 a distinguished cavalry officer and a very fine horseman, Henry Herbert, Earl of Pembroke, Colonel of the Royal Dragoons, published a Manual of Horsemanship in which he attacked the inhuman practices of docking the horses' tails and cropping their ears.[29] This had become a habit with many civilians since Marlborough's day and was still prevalent, though not to the same extent, in 1878. Pembroke preferred leaving the tail long, though he thought a switch or nag tail (see Plates 61 and 63) satisfactory. In 1764 an Army Order was issued ordering the horses' tails to be full except in the case of Light Dragoon Regiments. Another Army Order, of 1799, ordered all Heavy Cavalry, except the Household, to have nag tails. About 1850 long tails, squared off just below the hock, had been introduced and at last the troop horse had nature's provision against flies restored to him.

In 1764 different prices were still fixed for remounts intended for Horse and those for Dragoons, but in 1775 the Royal Dragoons were still mounted on blacks for all ranks, except for four trumpeters who rode greys, a common practice in most regiments. As this regiment always rode a smaller type of remount than other Dragoons, it is to be presumed that there was still a considerable amount of blacks procurable.

In 1773 two regiments, the Blues and the Bays (the 2nd Dragoon Guards) had riding schools, the only ones to be found in the United Kingdom.[30] In 1779 the 15th Light Dragoons had a troop mounted on chestnuts, another on blacks, one on browns and two on bays. All were described as 'small' and some were 14 hands three inches in height.[31]

In 1780 the modern method of fox hunting, when hounds are bred to run very fast indeed and a horse must have a really good turn of speed to live with them, was introduced. Prior to this men rode stoutly built horses, many of them cobs, schooled to jump almost from a standstill. The change brought with it a new type of hunter, a horse with a large admixture of thoroughbred blood, able to carry a weight of up to 16 stone over all sorts of fences at almost racing pace. Lighter men rode horses of a less heavy build and these Light Weight Hunters were very often clean thoroughbred. The Heavy Weight Hunter was the more expensive and breeders soon set to work to satisfy a demand which was growing every year. A very large proportion of the well-to-do upper and middle classes took to the new form of a sport which had always been popular, and this was especially the case with the powerful families who had so much to do with officering the cavalry and who had so much influence. Soon it was very much the thing for those who could afford it to keep a pack of hounds, which would be followed by all sorts of hard-riding men, from Members of Parliament to farmers' sons, often riding a young horse in the hopes of selling him.

Sport has always been one of the ruling passions of the British people and here was a novel form, which not only appealed to an ever-increasing number of horse owners, but provided increased profits for some, notably breeders and farmers, and employment for a large class of men of the status whence came a large majority of recruits for the mounted branches of the Army. A spate of literature, beginning in 1781 with Beckford's *Thoughts on Hunting*, and a very large number of coloured prints, from the important works of Alken and many others to the trade calendar of any number of firms, attested to the widespread interest in a sport, which had in former years been mainly of interest to country squires. As time went on people, whether they knew anything about horses or not, began consciously or unconsciously to associate the word 'hunter' with horses in the United Kingdom. The Irish breeders were not backward in breeding hunters of all the three types wanted, Heavy, Middle and Light Weight. The illustrations from 1800 onwards show the trend, ending with the latest types, as shown in War Office pamphlets of 1912 and 1927, when the Cavalry, Horse Artillery and Mounted Infantry remounts would all have made useful hunters and in the 1912 publication some of the Field Artillery gun teams as well (Plates 76 and 79–81).

There is no doubt that for service in Europe, provided he could be reasonably fed, the hunter would compare most favourably with all types of continental remounts. Especially in a rapid approach march followed by a charge he had no equal, and for pulling guns as fast as cavalry could travel there was nothing to match him. It is beside the point of this chapter that the superlative horsemastership and driving of the Royal Horse Artillery gave their horses every chance. (See among others Plate 31a for Field Artillery.)

Later on it will be seen how extremes of climate and lack of suitable, or, at times, any feed acted very much to the hunter type's disadvantage; although the gradual introduction of hunters of one type and another into the British Army worked as a general rule for nothing but good. The anxiety of foreign countries to secure sires and mares of the right stamp in order to reproduce remounts like ours is in itself a sufficient argument in favour of what became an established principle. The following story illustrates an Inspecting Officer's devotion to the ideal that all cavalry should be mounted on the hunter type. Some years ago, an Indian Cavalry Regiment[32] were for inspection. Unfortunately not all the remounts issued had been up to standard, so the Commanding Officer had recourse to stratagem. On the appointed day he put all the smartest troopers in the front rank, mounted on horses 'with bottoms like barmaids'. So impressed was the Inspecting General with the rear view of these horses that he never looked at the very indifferent remounts in the rear rank. The plan had succeeded!

It was, however, a long time before the Royal Horse Artillery were horsed with the type described officially as 'a well-bred drive and ride horse, able to gallop in a gun team and to move with cavalry'.

The Royal Horse Artillery were started in 1793 and this date coincides with the introduction of what were known as 'coach horses'. These had their origin in the vastly increased speed on the mail coaches from 1784 onwards, when an overall speed of seven miles an hour was attained. The coach horse has been described as being 'able to trot steadily on hard roads at eight miles an hour with a substantial load daily and for long distances without detriment to either bodily condition or soundness'.[33] Another writer[34] says 'the old coach horse was the modern lighter cart horse (as shown in the 1927 series of illustrations for Field Artillery, Plate 81). By 1820 he was perfection. In 1825 the nearest horses to the old type of fast coach horse were those of the R.H.A. But at great speed for long distances thoroughbreds would beat artillery horses.' Exactly what is meant by thoroughbreds is not clear, presumably the thoroughbred cross with heavy mares popular with modern artillerymen.

So by 1800 there were in existence in the United Kingdom two distinct new classes of remount coming into the market: the hunter type, light, medium and heavy, suitable for the different types of cavalry, and the so-called coaching type, which set a standard for the gun teams.

It is doubtful if the continental methods of scientific breeding by experts in Government studs have given better results than were reached in this country by our usual haphazard methods, which owe little to any official assistance directed towards the desired end!

It is necessary to go back to 1791 and note that in this year the Royal Veterinary College at Camden Town was started by a Frenchman, Charles Vial de St Bel or Sainbel.[35] The importance of this to the horse industry and especially to the mounted corps of the Army cannot be exaggerated. Prior to this, according to Sir Walter Gilbey, 'The English veterinary practitioners had followed principles which were hardly free from the taint of witchcraft and sorcery'.

All that there was to be said on the subject of the remounts in use in the fighting with the French Revolutionary troops in Northern France and Flanders in 1794[36] was fully brought out in the evidence collected from March 1796 by a Board of General Officers appointed by the Duke of York, the Commander-in-Chief, to enquire into the clothing, saddlery and equipment of the men of the cavalry. In the findings of the Board they pointed out 'that the breed of black horses formerly ridden by all heavy cavalry was either extinct or completely reformed, the animals of that description in the market being suitable only for draught and unfit to carry a soldier. But at the same time they reported that a new type of horse, bred chiefly for gentlemen's carriages, had been introduced, which was well fitted to take the place of the blacks for work in the ranks. Finally they urged that a veterinary surgeon should be attached to every regiment of cavalry in the service.'[37] Practically all the recommendations of the Board were adopted, and as a result five regiments, the 3rd, 5th and 6th Dragoon Guards and the 4th and 6th Dragoons, were allowed to ride brown, bay or chestnut horses. Officers were allowed to ride nag-tailed chargers, not under 15 hands, and if a man did not provide a charger himself the Colonel of the Regiment was to buy a suitable one at a price not over £50 and stop the cost from his pay. As three regiments, the 1st Dragoon Guards, 1st Dragoons and 3rd Dragoons were still riding blacks, it is to be inferred that nag-tailed remounts of that colour and presumably of the new type of carriage horse were readily available on the market.

It need hardly be said that the Colonels, whose business it was to see their regiments properly mounted, now had a much easier task than when only blacks were allowed for all heavy cavalry.

As regards Veterinary Surgeons, it was laid down in 1796 that they were to receive the King's Commission, and a Principal Veterinary Surgeon to the Army was also appointed. As will be seen, this officer was in time to occupy what had become one of the most important posts in the army.

These important reforms bring to a close that period of George III's reign which ended in 1800. With the abolition of the rigid colour scheme for the bulk of the cavalry the way was open for the introduction of faster types of remount bred for use rather than show.

George III and the Prince Regent (1800–20)

The century opened with the introduction of another type of remount. The Royal Artillery, who had hitherto used cart horses harnessed tandem to the guns which accompanied infantry in the field, now followed the example of the Royal Horse Artillery and used teams of six harnessed in pairs with the drivers mounted on the near side horses, instead of walking alongside as had been the custom. Illustrations show a heavier type of ride and drive horse than those used by the Royal Horse Artillery, and as the Field Batteries, as they were afterwards called, had to be able to trot on occasion, as when coming into action, the guns had to be horsed by teams of the type of strong light-van horses. These not only trotted fast, but on occasion could gallop for considerable distances.[38] (Plates 24 and 25.)

Remounts now consisted of special blacks for the Household Cavalry, just as they still do; of heavy cavalry troop horses of varying colours, greys being reserved for 2nd Dragoons (Scots Greys) and for trumpeters; of light cavalry troop horses for Light Dragoons (some regiments of these became Hussars mounted as before and later others were equipped as Lancers); of horses for the R.H.A. gun teams (see Plate 23a); and of those for the Field guns and the light waggons of the Royal Waggon Train (Plate 23b). Although many of Wellington's picked Staff Officers rode thoroughbreds in the Peninsular War (1808–14), the general run of cavalry chargers were of hunter type (Plates 61 and 63). Not included among the illustrations is the portrait of Captain William Tomkinson, 16th Light Dragoons' charger Bob, another typical hunter, who went through the Peninsula and lived to carry his master to hounds for years. Wellington kept seven chargers and eight hunters in such constant work that they were reported as having little flesh on their bones. He had his own pack of hounds in Spain, but obviously the whole of his stud of fifteen were used as chargers. The precise difference between chargers and hunters is not easy to define, presumably the former were better looking and possibly bigger. His favourite mount was Copenhagen, a thoroughbred who had won races, a chestnut standing 15 hands with any amount of endurance to match his pace.

Chargers for staff work were dear and could cost up to £75 apiece, in return for which the Government allowance for a horse was £35 only.[39]

The traditions of having hounds in the field and of being as well mounted as possible survived the Peninsular era and lasted on while cavalry rode horses. That is not meant to imply that all officers rode as expensive horses as the above price shows. General Sir Thomas Picton rode 'roadsters' of 15 hands, and this was the sort of charger ridden by many infantry officers who were entitled to one. Those who were not would have to pay anything from £10 to £25 for some sort of country-bred to ride on the line of march.

The following are Wellington's opinions on the remount question in 1813, by which time there was a certain amount of scarcity of horses of the right stamp in Great Britain. He wrote: 'a Dragoon horse costs 25 guineas, rising three and not fit for work or service for 1½ to 2 years. We prefer them here (in Spain) at 5 years, so it is not unreasonable to add to the sum about half as much again. Would it be extravagant to give £40 or 40 guineas for 5- and 6-year-old horses and mares for regiments on service and £45 or guineas for horses for artillery abroad? If not we must draft the 5- and 6-year olds from regiments at home and make a great effort to replace them by 2- and 3-year olds at the usual price. Old and worn-out horses if sent out are useless.'[40]

This last sentence probably referred among other things to an amazing occurrence in 1809 when the 14th Light Dragoons received 61 heavy horses, already cast as unfit for heavy dragoons from the Irish Commissariat.[41] Presumably these were some sort of harness animal.

The correct sort of remount for Light Dragoons was described by the Colonel Commandant of the 12th Light Dragoons in 1811 as 'active and fully master of 17 stone. Remember, Stout and good limbs – Stout backs – Good feet – Open in the counter – good shoulders and well up before. Deep-chested and not light carcassed, not too heavy in the hind quarters, but strong in the gammon and open between the jaws.' This is as good a description of a middle weight hunter, except that 17 stone is a load for a weight carrier, as one would wish to have. With great difficulty this zealous and experienced officer got together 150 suitable remounts, instead of 212 needed to complete establishment.[42]

Spain was a hard country for horses to campaign in. The local breeds ran small and as a rule were not plentiful. The roads or tracks were excruciatingly rough and stony and hard on feet and legs. The feed consisted mainly of maize, nutritious when harvested for horses doing slow work, palatable when eaten green, though only a limited amount can be fed at a time, and in winter the dry stalks make good feed for bullocks and satisfy a horse's cravings without doing him much good. Oats, the ideal feed, sent out from England, were often not to be obtained up country. Altogether the horses had a very rough time.

We are fortunate in having a straightforward account of exactly what service was like from the pen of Captain Tomkinson, as he then was.[43] On outpost in 1810 'we never offsaddle except in the evenings, merely to clean the horses and the men sleep in their appointments holding the reins. In 1812 February, the 16th Light Dragoons received a full allowance of corn (oats); after the starvation the horses have endured they will not come right till the Spring. They are so starved they eat the withered grass and swallow stones and die. Never were horses in such a bad state. 1813. – The horses now on green barley and get fat.' Under these conditions a regiment which had been reduced from 4 squadrons to 3 might show 300 men on parade (mounted), instead of 600. And a good many showed less.

It is to be noted that Wellington used the term 'Dragoon horse', meaning any cavalry remount light or heavy, 'Dragoon' being the generic term for any class of cavalryman for many years.

One lesson learned by many of our cavalry officers in the Peninsula, where the heaviest French cavalry we had to meet in the field were their Dragoons, medium cavalry and not always very well mounted while in Spain, was the tremendous impact of true heavy cavalry, big men on big horses, in a charge knee to knee. The charge of the Heavies at Salamanca on the 22nd July, 1812, was a case in point. Good as light cavalry might be, and not seldom have ours dealt successfully with opposing heavies, there was no doubt in the minds of men who had seen enough active service that the real heavy horseman must form an integral part of any force of all arms. As already stressed, the heavy weight hunter was the beau ideal of those responsible for mounting our cavalry. The experiences of the short Waterloo campaign of 1815 lay all in the same direction: given proper leading and a fair measure of fitness, the big, compact well-bred horse was a battle winner. Unfortunately, he was expensive to produce and so to buy, and needed considerably more feed than the lighter classes. After Waterloo there was no change affecting remounts: as already noted, the introduction of Lancers, copied from the French in 1816, merely meant that the Light Dragoon regiments converted kept to their own type of troop horse.

George IV and William IV

The most startling measures taken after Waterloo and during the reigns of George IV (1820–30), and William IV (1830–37), were the reduction of the R.H.A. batteries to a skeleton force and the Field batteries to an even smaller establishment. At the same time the Cavalry were allowed to deteriorate to such an extent that by 1836 the greater part of their troop horses are reported as being unfit for a campaign.[44] This form of economy has always been the rule after any big war or series of wars, with the result that horse breeders were apt to get discouraged and there inevitably followed a rise in prices and a scarcity of material when the next war broke out. Plate 24 shows a Royal Artillery leader of the period taken from a contemporary handbook. He shows more strength than quality.

Victoria

The next reign, Queen Victoria (1837–1901) saw such vast changes that it is impossible to epitomize them satisfactorily. The British Army fought in more than eighty wars during her reign, and although the last one, the South African War of 1899–1902, was not finished when she died in January 1901, a full description of that war is included in the section dealing with her reign.

In 1844 one of the most important Regulations issued by the War Office on the subject of remounts was published in Queen's Regulations. It was worded as follows: 'The number of British Cavalry in the British Army being small . . . it is of the utmost importance that this portion of the Army should be of the best description. That is that both Heavy and Light Cavalry should be equal to the Charge in Line as well as the Duties of Outposts. The Horses which are selected and trained for the Cavalry should therefore be of sufficient height and strength to be capable of performing the duties of that branch of the Service with the greatest efficiency.' The senior officers who were responsible for this order would all have been 'Wellington's men', in other words, veterans of the Peninsula. A study of 'The Military Opinions' of General Sir John Fox Burgoyne (1782–1871, Field Marshal from 1868),[45] who served as Chief Engineer under Wellington and again in 1854 in the Crimea, shows that in his opinion, shared by many other officers, there was much room for improvement in the cavalry not only in the Peninsula, but also in the Crimea. Though Burgoyne's book was published long after the Regulation quoted above, much of it refers to the Peninsula and could well be taken for some of the reason which led to the wording of the Regulation. Burgoyne wrote: 'The cavalry soldier of the British service is a large heavy man, heavily armed and heavily equipped, and rides probably not much under the weight of a man in armour of old times (man-at-arms 1440 A.D. about 21 stone; Light Cavalry 1813 with forage 21 stone; Heavy Cavalry about 22 stone, Author). He requires a horse of proportionate size and strength; the animal, besides being of that lengthy nature which is difficult to keep in condition, is so weighted as to be only fit for slow regular work, with an occasional trot to make good a manoeuvre, and a gallop for a charge; these efforts must be rare and of short duration . . . We have certainly among the regiments the denominations of heavy, light, lancer and hussar, but as regards the quality referred to, it is a denomination only; for there is little difference in man, horse and equipment; and the lightest are far from possessing the requisites of a really light cavalry.' Although in the main Burgoyne's ideas are probably correct enough, he rather spoilt the force of his argument by his admiration for the light cavalry of the King's German Legion in the Peninsula, who were noted for the excellence of their outpost work, as were, though he does not say so, the 14th and

16th Light Dragoons of our own service. This does not alter the fact that all our cavalry were badly overweighted. The Field Marshal was most anxious that small light men should be enlisted and formed into what he calls 'light, hardy active' cavalry, riding smaller horses than what he calls 'the cavalry of the reserve', in other words the existing regiments. We shall meet very much the same arguments later on in books by serving cavalry officers.

It is surely not unreasonable to regard the Regulation of 1844 as in some sort a charter for breeders, buyers and commanding officers, though how 'Heavy Cavalry were to be equal to the duties of outposts' if they were to ride the heavy weight remounts which needed so much feed and rest to keep them really fit it is difficult to see. Whatever the officers who helped to draft the Regulation may have meant, there is no doubt how the commanding officers took it. Every good cavalry-man from Coeur-de-Lion to Chauvel[46] has desired the same thing – to have his men mounted on horses big enough and fast enough to sweep away all opposition in one furious rush. The Victorian cavalry officers were of course entirely of the same opinion.

Ten years after the publication of the Regulation the Crimean War broke out and as if to point the moral the Commander-in-Chief, Lord Raglan, expressed his determination to 'keep my cavalry in a bandbox' or in other words use them as 'cavalry of the reserve'. Unfortunately, he had no Light Cavalry trained in security duties to do this most important part of a cavalryman's work.

By 1855 the strain on remounts, as is always the case when a war is not of the very shortest, had become serious. The practice was for the Colonel of a regiment to detail an officer to buy 3-year-olds in the open market, normally at fairs. In peace time he would usually have first choice, as those men who bought young horses, with a view to growing them out before selling, as well as the dealers, preferred to buy 4-year-olds. In war time these two classes would have no objection to buying 3-year-olds and the officer would also be in the market for 4-year-olds, which is the age preferred by the public. Competition would then be severe and the officer would have virtually had to take the culls, as prices would have been too high and above the Government allowance.

Consequently Government instructions were issued that horses from 5 to 9 years old were to be bought, £42 being allowed for artillery horses and £40 for cavalry troop horses. All were to be in hard, working condition. The price of 3-year-olds had been fixed at £26 5s od before the war and it was contended that young horses should still have been bought and allowed to graze on land bought or leased for the purpose. At 4 years old they would then have been issued to regiments.

The price of £26 5s od paid before the war included remounts for artillery and cavalry, except the Household Cavalry and the Greys. An artillery horse at 3 years should be 15 hands, at 4 years old 15 hands 2 inches, and at 5 years old 16 hands. The price paid for grown horses worked well enough, but as time went on the quality of remounts coming on the market had deteriorated and less satisfactory horses had to be taken. The average weight carried on service was 18 stone 11 lb, and light cavalry carried approximately the same as the heavies for 'recent regulations respecting recruiting were rapidly removing the distinction once so prominent between heavy and light dragoon horses'.[47] The officer detailed to buy horses had a serious risk to run – he was liable to have his purchases rejected at the headquarters of his Regiment, the responsibility being the Colonel's. In the case of Artillery and Transport, specially appointed officers were responsible for all purchases.

The remounts taken out to the East at the start of hostilities seem to have been of good quality, especially the artillery teams, though these had to be made up to strength from batteries remaining in England. (Plate 25.) There is a fine account by Sir Evelyn Wood[48] of his watching the Black Battery, later the 12th Field Battery, galloping into action at Inkerman on the 5th November, 1854. The unfortunate horses did not last long; there was virtually no feed available and some 5,000 artillery and cavalry horses dwindled to a little over 2,000 during the first winter. The horses became so thin that the high front arch of the Wood Arch Universal Pattern Saddle came right down on the withers. (See in the Chapter on Saddles.) (Plate 11.) The war made little difference to the price of remounts. In 1857 the average height of remounts was fixed at 15 hands and 2 inches; and dealers would supply officers' chargers at £50. The price of 4-year-olds was not to exceed £36 for R.A. and £30 for cavalry, and for 3-year-olds the relative prices were £30 and £26. These young horses were not, of course, expected to be otherwise than in fairly good condition, as they were not to be put to hard work for some time, in the case of the 3-year-olds, two years. As already mentioned the older horses bought during the Crimea were to be in hard condition, for it had been fully realized for a long time that to embark horses for immediate service in a foreign country in war time they must be put on shipboard in hard-working trim. Conditions on horse transports were never very good unless, as was the case in the next century, very great care was taken in the fitting out of the vessels selected. Even then horses could suffer severely in bad weather. Although there was no Remount Department in existence for some time, those responsible for buying remounts in the fifties thoroughly understood the necessity of buying only fit animals for shipment in time of war. Whether there is any record of their decision or not, the knowledge they possessed seems to have entirely disappeared by the end of the century, as will be seen in the account of the South African War. It is extraordinary that such a vital factor affecting the whole system of remount supply during hostilities should have been so completely forgotten in two generations. So much has been written, with absolute truth, about the gross mismanagement that characterized the Crimean War, including the well-authenticated accounts of the horses eating each others' tails, ropes and bits of leather, and gnawing at the spokes of the wheels of the vehicles, that it is only fair to stress that the old system of buying remounts at least delivered them at the ports of embarkation in proper fettle.

Post Crimea

The price of remounts after the Crimea has already been mentioned. It shows that there was no real scarcity in Great Britain of suitable horses. In Plate 26 we now come to a comparatively early example of the value of the camera in research work, often of more use, even if the photographs were badly taken, than the generality of drawings, however good. It is never easy to find illustrations giving the exact details which are wanted, so it is most fortunate that a complete set of photographs of the horses of an R.H.A. Battery in c.1861 have come down to us. We are much indebted to whoever had the idea of showing the horses of his Battery in such an admirable way. There are five photographs (Plates 26–28). The officer's charger, a nice-looking hunter up to a certain amount of weight comes first, a horse not quite up to taking his place in the team, as should have been the case with every horse in the battery.[44] The centre pair are not shown and there is little to choose between the pairs of wheelers and leaders. Perhaps the off-leader, a mare, is less well coupled up than the others. The off-wheeler is a fine big upstanding specimen, as indeed are all those shown. The tails are all squared well above the hocks. The weight behind the team at this date and for some time afterwards was about 37 cwt, well in excess of the 30 cwt considered sufficient for six horses to pull when keeping up with cavalry. Teams of eight were frequently used, but the extra power attained is not in proportion to the work done by each pair of a six-horse team. This shows the immense importance of correct buying for artillery as so little deviation from the high standard demanded could ever be permissible. Buying cavalry remounts was not as difficult, for at a pinch far smaller horses, if stoutly built, might be adequate enough, though the appearance of a regiment on parade would not have been all it should have been.

In 1864 transport horses for the Military Train, the forerunners of the R.A.S.C., cost £36 for an officer's charger and £30 for a draught horse. These would have been slower than artillery horses and less well bred. Presumably the Royal Engineers would have had the same type. Cavalry were still horsed by buying from dealers by Regimental Headquarters. Although in many cases this procedure worked well enough, especially when the commanding officer and whoever was his chief adviser really knew their job, it could also be unsatisfactory, for a great deal of money was changing hands and there could be loopholes in the case of a careless or stupid commanding officer. However the system survived for a considerable number of years. As is the case in most armies, War Departments can be, and often are, conservative to a degree.

Whether the remounts bought for the cavalry were altogether satisfactory or not, the artillery horses of the seventies were excellent. In 1878, in consequence of the possibility of war with Russia, the batteries in Great Britain next on the roster for foreign service were completed with men and horses to war strength. Owing to shortages of remounts in hard condition many of these batteries had to be horsed from others, not on the roster. In the words of an officer serving at the time, 'the

R.H.A. were never better horsed'.[50] He considered that the weight behind the teams was too heavy for mobility, and this was still the case five years later. The illustrations in the *Handbook for Field Service, Field Artillery 1883*, almost certainly done from photographs, show excellent types of horses.

The eighties were a time of many small wars, mostly in Africa, North and South, and for the first time Mounted Infantry were used to a considerable extent. After various experiments of no long duration they had been restarted in South Africa in 1877 with personnel drawn from each of the Regular Battalions stationed there, and it was not long before they were being regularly trained at Aldershot.

Although polo was first played in England from 1870 onwards, its adoption as one of the most important games in favour in the Army coincided quite nearly enough with the introduction of M.I. on a large scale, for the two to have considerable influence on each other. There are constant references to the effect that the ideal to keep in mind when buying M.I. cobs was the polo pony. The original height of the latter was 13 hands and 2 inches, and though many M.I. ponies were no bigger, the later height allowed for polo ponies, 14 hands and 2 inches, was ideal for M.I. work.

Plates 70, 71, and 73 show M.I. remounts pre-South African War, and Plate 78 in 1912.

So now as cavalry horses were tending to be more and more of a size, no matter for which class of cavalry they were intended, there was reintroduced a type of remount of very much the same pattern as those ridden by the Dragoons of the New Model Army of Parliament in the Civil Wars.

It was an officer serving with M.I. in the eighties who has left us an account of a practice common enough in the army during a campaign, which has gone more or less unnoticed, possibly because it contravenes what were popularly supposed to be the tenets of disciplined men of all ranks.

The one thing a mounted man dreaded when in the field was to be left dismounted; in fact, if this was due to his own negligence or carelessness there were frequent occasions when he might be crimed for losing or injuring his horse. From the officers' point of view a dismounted trooper meant the loss of a man in the fighting line, so they were equally concerned. If there were no spare mounts available, the first thing a soldier, especially a good soldier, thought about was where he could steal a horse – 'make' was the word usually applied to the deed. As long as the man could get away with it there were very few officers that would say or do anything except to see that the new arrival was suitably branded as soon as possible.

This is how this experienced officer[51] dealt with the problem and how he recorded his method; 'a certain amount of experience of human nature when connected with remount depots and mounted corps on active service had convinced me that the honestest mounted man becomes depraved on active service, when temptations assail him in the shape of horseflesh. One of the most elementary precautions to prevent loss of horseflesh is careful branding the instant a horse becomes (either honestly or the reverse) your property on active service.' So he took with him, when proceeding to the seat of war, a set of branding irons!

It is true that many a branded horse has changed owners on a dark night, especially if the stealer's unit would have been far away at daylight!

In 1887 the most important event in the history of remounts in the British Army took place. The old systems of the purchase of horses were abolished and the Remount Department was started as a separate establishment of the Army.[52] The importance of this step can hardly be exaggerated, for it meant that from this time onward there would be only one policy as regards the quality of the horses required, as to their treatment if bought as youngsters, and as to the policy to be pursued in peace for producing the extra number of remounts required on mobilization.

The Quartermaster-General was responsible for the remounts of the troops and dealt directly with the Inspector-General of Remounts. Under him was an Assistant Inspector, a Deputy Assistant Adjutant-General, four clerks and a copyist. This completed the Headquarters Staff. At Woolwich was an Assistant Inspector, a Staff Captain, two Veterinary Officers, a Quartermaster and 94 N.C.O.s and Men.

At Dublin was an Assistant Inspector, a Staff Captain, a Veterinary Officer, a Quartermaster and 36 N.C.O.s and Men.

The total cost of the establishment, including travelling expenses, was £16,460 per annum.

Every year some 2,500 horses and mares were bought at about 4 years old at about £40 apiece. They were supposed to have light work only, when issued after a few months at the Remount Depots, and not to be used on manoeuvres until they were 6 years old. The Depots were at Woolwich and Dublin respectively.

Under the orders of the Inspector-General three Colonels of cavalry or artillery with three veterinary surgeons travelled in the horse breeding districts and purchased horses from breeders or traders without the intervention of the middle man.

In 1888 a system of registration was started under the National Defence Act of that year. In a time of National Danger or when the Militia was being mobilized, the Government had the power to requisition all the horses, vehicles and means of transport in the country. In order to make full use of the type of horse required for the army, the owners of large quantities of horses, such as railway and omnibus companies, livery stable keepers, etc. were invited to register a percentage of their horses of their own free will. The Remount Department then examined and classified the horses and the owner signed a contract, binding himself in case of a Government declaration or of national danger, to supply within 48 hours on stipulated terms of prepayment a certain number of horses for military use, which had to be serviceable, sound and of defined breed and age. After the first needs of the troops had been met, horse depots were formed to take whatever replacements were bought. Ten shillings a year was paid to owners when the scheme was started.

Although this scheme did not turn out altogether satisfactorily, in the long run it was, at any rate, a great step forward to have made provisions for utilizing the equine resources of the whole country in the event of any national crisis.

As with all the Departments of the Army the great difficulty was to meet the many requirements of the service on the money allotted. Few, if any, peace-time Governments have been able to increase the grant for the Army unless war seemed really imminent. Nor was it in the least probable that the average politician would have any idea of the extent of the losses in horseflesh that were unavoidable, even in Europe, where in the Western and Central countries feed is usually plentiful and communications easy. The last war in Western Europe before the end of the nineteenth century was the Franco-German War of 1870–71, and there in eight months the Germans lost over a million horses. Including all the horses captured from the French at Metz and Sedan, the original number with which they had started the war was renewed three times. Presumably this includes not only deaths, but also casting of broken-down and useless horses.[53]

A note on the type of troop horses in the Prussian Army in 1886 may not be out of place. They were reported on as being 'of worse quality than the British, worse fed, groomed and equipped, but a long way better broken and they rally after a charge twice as fast as our men do'.[54]

The question of the time that would elapse in a normal war before it would be necessary to provide remounts for practically the whole of the cavalry was agitating the minds of many of those responsible for mounting the Army. The great authority on the whole question was the future Major General Sir F. Smith, K.C.M.G., in 1891 Veterinary Surgeon Major. At a meeting of the Aldershot Military Society he delivered a lecture from which the following is taken: 'I protest most solemnly against the crushing weight a horse has to carry, and leave it to the combatant authorities to decide in what way it can be reduced if Cavalry in the field is to remain efficient for any length of time; as matters stand at present it would not be a very difficult calculation to ascertain how many horses free from sore backs would remain to us, say out of our First Army Corps, after a three months campaign. In a future Continental War the cavalry will disappear in three months.'[55] That is to say if no remounts were bought and despatched to make good losses. Another cause of dissatisfaction was the absence of any Light Cavalry with the First Cavalry Division, only Heavy and medium Regiments being posted to it.[56]

Apart from the last objection, which did not really concern the Remount authorities at all, it is difficult to believe that Veterinary Surgeon Major Smith's remarks went for little or nothing. When, years later, he was to write the *Veterinary History of the War in South Africa*, of which he knew more than any other senior officer on the remount question, he was able to drive home the truth of his prophecy made eight years before that war broke out.

The South African War broke out in October, 1899, and the following is the position in Great Britain as regards remounts in the years immediately preceding it. In what may be termed an ordinary war, horseflesh, though always of great importance, was not of such vital import as a variety of other war material. In the South African War it is no exaggeration to say that remounts were to both combatants the lifeblood of the lengthy operations. Very few officers had foreseen this and their evidence, coming as it did from the ordinary run of field officers or those below them in rank, passed unnoticed, except by a small minority of those in high places. The question of the horseflesh of the fighting men of the two Republics with whom we were at war will be dealt with in the section on South Africa. It is sufficient to note that until the last stages their command of remounts was superior to ours both in numbers and quality for the work required.

The Remount Department was still buying as explained earlier. All purchases had to reach a standard of 15 hands and were usually sent to the Remount Depots for a time before issue, though in some cases they went direct to units. All were graded as saddle or draught horses immediately after being purchased.

In 1898–9 the intake amounted to 2,253 horses and mules, the great majority being the former. The prices paid were at £50 for Household Troops, 99 bought; at £39 15s 0d for Cavalry, 961 taken; Royal Artillery at £42, 891 bought; Royal Engineers, 42 bought at the same price as for R.A.; for Infantry Transport cadres, 32 at £40; Mounted Infantry, 39 at £30; Army Service Corps, 131 at £42 in Great Britain and 58 for those in the Colonies. There were 17,910 horses and mules on establishment, the ratio of remounts being 1:8.

In 1896–7 cast horses to the number of 1,204 were sold, this being 9·29 per cent. They averaged £9 3s 0d apiece at thirteen and a third years old.

There were 14,550 registered horses of whom 10,000 were draught horses. A large number of these registered draught horses were bred in Canada and had been bought for the Omnibus Companies in London. These made admirable Field Artillery horses and many of the batteries had them. (See Plate 94.)

A Cavalry Division with an Army Corps required 3,720 horses for the 8 regiments composing it; 720 for the 4 batteries R.H.A.; 1,950 for the 15 batteries R.F.A. and 7,316 for Details such as regimental transport.

It was decided to despatch an Army Corps to South Africa in the very early stages of the war, so the figures given should furnish a basis as to the number of replacements needed in the event of Veterinary Surgeon Major Smith's prophecy being correct, as it proved to be.

There are enough Plates to give an accurate picture of the types of remounts in use in the nineties just before the South African War. Plate 31 shows the wheelers of a Field Battery, from a photograph taken at Sandhurst c.1898. Plate 35 shows a team in a pontoon equipment of the Royal Engineers and Plate 37 a team of their Balloon Section. The Sappers had used balloons in S.A. in 1884 and were to do so again in 1899. Plates 72–74 are taken from a once well-known book[57] by Lieut Colonel Alderson, an infantry officer with a long record of service in M.I. and a keen hunting man. He selected the types as being as representative as possible. The first two photographs show two chargers, bought privately, as so many officers did, for £40 at 6 years old for the medium weight charger, No. 1 and £50 for the Irish-bred light weight charger as a 5-year-old. Both had won a number of Point-to-points, in those days ridden over untouched fences in a selected section of a hunting country. The next is a mare, a plain looking cavalry troop horse, 15 years old, a

27

great age for a horse to remain sound doing the work she had, with 11 years service without a day's sickness or lameness. The next is a good sort of Mounted Infantry trooper, a cut-and-come-again looking cob. The last two are respectively a Horse Artillery leader and an Army Service Corps draught horse, a good strong commoner. Plate No. 71, not in this series, shows another type of M.I. remount. The price at which an officer might buy chargers from the Remount Department was £63 for Household Cavalry and £52 for the other arms – the horse had to be kept for five years.[58]

A short reference to the introduction of Polo into the army has already been made. During the South African War a number of officers took their polo ponies out as chargers. They were a great success in the field, so much so that an expert on the class needed in South Africa reported as follows from that country during hostilities: 'What is wanted is a good strong, well made, hardy polo pony type, an Irish hunter in miniature, but which need not be fast enough to play an International polo game'. This was the ideal mount for all ranks. The reference to the Irish hunters (see above for Alderson's number two) is because that country had such a well-deserved name for good quality hunters. The above gives a correct idea of the influence of hunting and polo on good judges of remounts. Plate 96 shows a Basuto pony; he was played at polo, but was not fast enough for polo in England.

So serious were the losses that at times the Remount Department was hard put to it to keep up an adequate supply, partly because the Government policy was so vacillating that the officers sent abroad, all over the world in fact, were constantly receiving contradictory orders, and on one occasion were withdrawn altogether for some time and then sent out again. In all, horses were sent to the seat of war from the following countries:

Great Britain	80,000	this does not include
	7,000	bought by the Imperial Yeomanry Committee
Australasia	23,028	separate figures for New Zealand not given
Canada	14,621	
South Africa	160,000	
India	5,611	
U.S.A.	110,000	
Rhodesia	3,220	bought from the U.S.A. by the B.S.A. Company
Hungary	64,157	
Argentina	26,544	
Total	494,181 [59]	

The figures given in Sir F. Smith's book[60] for casualties is a daily loss of 336 horses, the total for the war being 326,000 horses. Another estimate is 7.8 per cent per month.[61] Sir F. Smith's account of why these heavy losses occurred makes interesting reading. One of the most surprising facts is that there were no reserve veterinary stores sent to South Africa, with the result that when the supply taken with the Field Army was exhausted there was nothing left with which the Veterinary Officers could treat sick horses. The next difficulty, a most serious one, was an outbreak of glanders at Cape Town, brought by infected imports. Glandered animals must be destroyed and all suspected cases tested. This not only carried off valuable remounts, but entailed heavy work and a certain amount of delay at the ports where Vets were not too plentiful.

The English horses suffered very severely from the heat. By November, when they were arriving at the commencement of a South African summer, which is very hot indeed, they had grown their heavy winter coats. There was no question of clipping them, as they were standing out at night and the summer rains can be very cold. The saddle blanket would have hardly been sufficient on a cold night and besides this in the case of most of the regiments there would have been little time to clip them. Owing to the exigencies of the service the horses were often kept saddled up all day and sometimes far into the night; for one thing it took two men to lift the fully loaded saddle on to a big English horse and thus saddling up took a considerable amount of time, a serious thing in an emergency. Water is also very scarce in most of the country covered by the cavalry in the first eighteen months of the war, but all these difficulties were dwarfed by one insurmountable obstacle. This was nothing less (on the evidence of the future Sir F. Smith) than the fixed determination of the Commander-in-Chief, Lord Roberts, who took the field himself, to keep the whole of the cavalry horses on the feed ration proper for a pony. No doubt this saved a considerable amount of transport, but the consequences were disastrous. This step Lord Roberts insisted on adhering to in the teeth of an official pronouncement by the Principal Veterinary Officer as to what must happen if this diet was adhered to. Nor was there any chance of the horses getting a bite of grass during a halt, for the men were not allowed to dismount without orders, or to take out the bits to allow of the horses grazing. As a matter of fact, many of the thick-necked English horses could not get their heads down to graze without breaking the breastplate.

Sir F. Smith was of the opinion that had the cavalry division been able to proceed out of a walk, which they could not do, during the pursuit of the main Republican Army of the West just before they abandoned Bloemfontein, we would have captured the Presidents of the two Republics, in which case, he was inclined to think, the Republicans might have made peace. Whether this conclusion is tenable is of no moment, but the fact that the whole of the mounted troops of Lord Roberts' main striking force were completely out of action after about two months' activity was a very serious matter, and allowed the Republicans to pull themselves together after the crushing reverses dealt by the Commander-in-Chief. He had achieved a brilliant stroke and taken a most unsatisfactory defensive war on our side over to an offensive one from which we never swerved. It is surely an extraordinary thing that a veteran of so many campaigns should be so shortsighted as to take away the whole of the striking power of his mounted arm by such complete disregard of the advice of his Chief Veterinary Officer, a man who knew the technique of his profession and was better qualified to judge on what was, after all, a very simple matter than anyone else under Lord Roberts' command. Another serious miscalculation was due to the failure of the Remount Department's officers in charge of the depots for debilitated and lame horses to grasp the fact that a trained troop horse, however badly over-worked, would build up with good food, rest and proper treatment until fit to be issued again. This type of remount would then be of more use 'than a dozen soft untrained remounts off shipboard'. Instead of which these overworked horses were nearly all shot. In 1900 a Veterinary Officer was placed in charge of every Remount Depot and the destruction of horses which not only could have been saved, but were so well worth saving, ended.

In the section on the Crimean War it was stressed that to be satisfactory re-mounts must be shipped in working condition. Conditions on shipboard, unless a boat has been efficiently fitted for the job, and there is an adequate number of men trained to look after the horses on board, can be extremely hard on the horses from causes unavoidable in any long sea voyage. It follows that when landed the horses want careful feeding and a good rest. During the second half of the three-years war, when Lord Kitchener had succeeded as Commander-in-Chief, the field force, by now enormously increased in mounted men, had to be broken up into small mobile columns, whose business it was to deal with the very large guerilla bands into which the Republicans had been split up. Endless pursuits by day and night of a most elusive and highly-skilled enemy wore out the remounts at short notice. Because Lord Kitchener would stand no delay at all, as soon as horses reached the Depots straight from the ship, they were despatched by train to whatever column was to be completed to strength, untrucked, saddled, and taken on long marches. The result-ing waste of horseflesh was little short of appalling. In many cases the animals were fed with grain to which they were unaccustomed, ridden beyond the pace which suited them best – this was unavoidable – with the result that many became casual-ties after only a few hours marching.

A typical case of the remount situation as affecting a first-class cavalry regi-ment, officered by some of the best horse-masters in the service, was that of the Inniskilling Dragoons. Among their officers were Major Rimington[62] who had a long experience of horses in many parts of the world, and the future Lord Allenby, whose reputation as a Cavalry Commander needs no explanatory remarks. The Veterinary Surgeon attached to the regiment, Lieut A. S. Head, kept a scrupulous day-to-day account of everything which concerned his own department and pub-lished it.[63] After describing the full kit carried (see in the chapter on saddlery), he adds that the front rank, as was the case in all heavy cavalry, carried the lance, and both ranks from 20 lb to 30 lb of oats according to circumstances, and 150 rounds – about 20 stone in all.[64] The regiment detrained up country on the Coles-burg front, where General French faced superior forces of Orange Free State Republicans. Neither side could win a decisive advantage for some time and the regiment took part in more or less normal operations with no long forced marches.

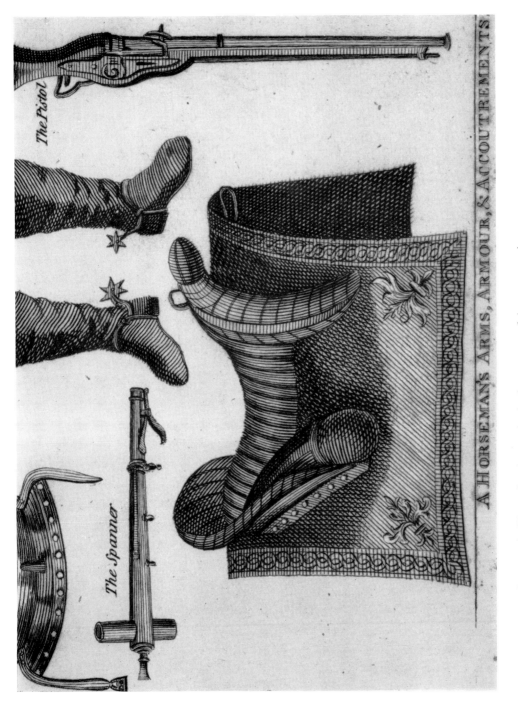

The Pistol

The Spanner

A HORSEMAN'S ARMS, ARMOUR, & ACCOUTREMENTS

D

PLATE I   The Equipment of a Heavy Cavalryman in the first quarter of the seventeenth century.

Guard your Cock

PLATE 2 The Heavy Cavalryman of the early seventeenth century.

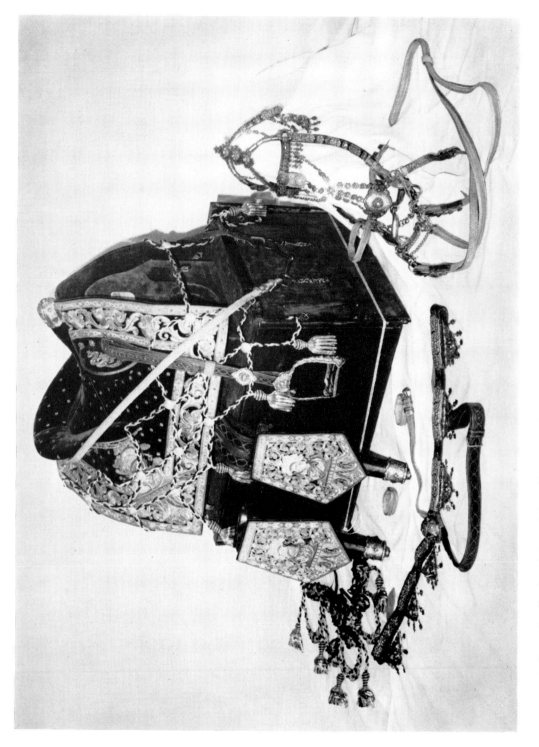

PLATE 3   A General Officer's saddlery of the mid-seventeenth century.

PLATE 4   Seventeenth-century saddle: front view.

PLATE 5   Seventeenth-century saddle: side view. For details see Figure 4.

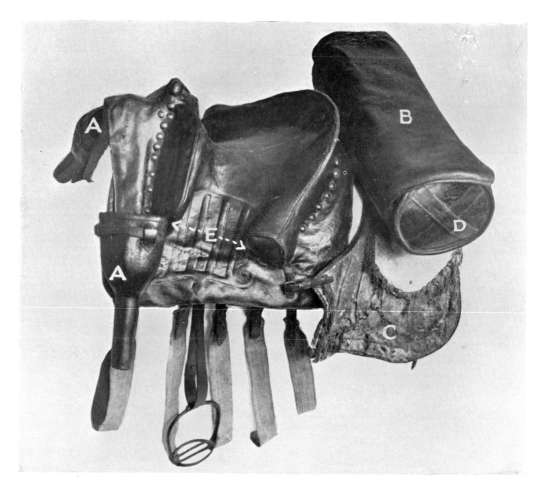

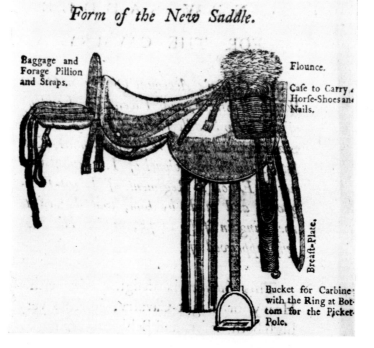

Form of the New Saddle.

Baggage and
Forage Pillion
and Straps.

Flounce.

Case to Carry
Horse-Shoes and
Nails.

Breast-Plate.

Bucket for Carbine
with the Ring at Bot-
tom for the Picket-
Pole.

PLATE 8   A painting by James Ross showing a scene from Marlborough's campaigns.

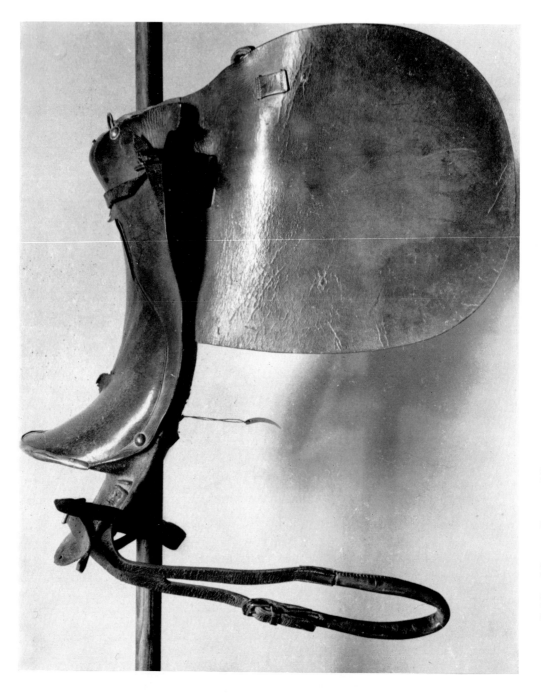

PLATE 9   Saddle of Cornet Gape, 2nd Dragoons, used at Waterloo in 1815, showing bullet holes inflicted by enemy action.

PLATE 10   Cornet Gape's saddle.

a)

PLATE 11
The Light Cavalry Universal Pattern saddle of 1805.
See also Figures 6 and 7.

b)

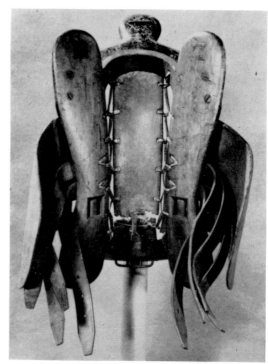

c)

 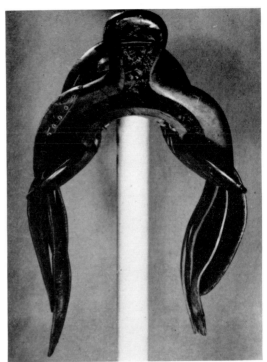

d)   e)

f)

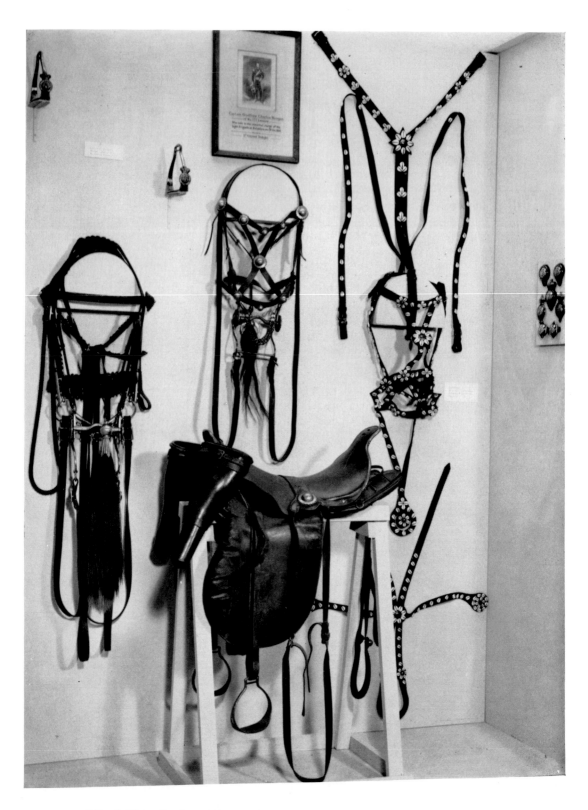

PLATE 12　Officer's Light Cavalry saddlery used in the charge of the Light Brigade at Balaclava in 1854.

PLATE 13(a) Heavy Cavalry Officer's saddle used by Cornet Richard Glyn,
1st Royal Dragoons, at Balaclava, 1854.

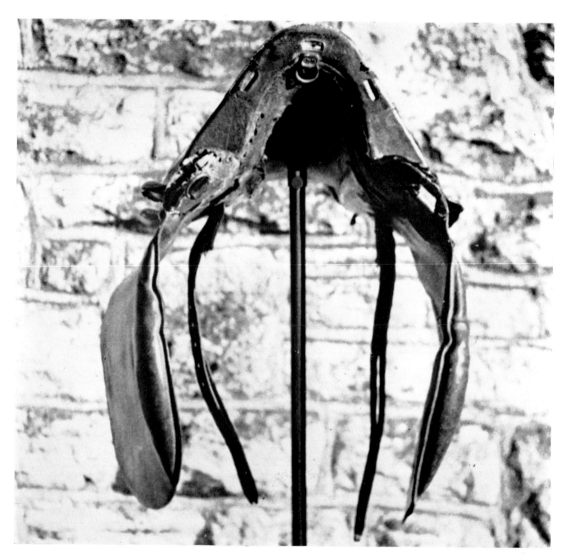

PLATE 13(b)   Heavy Cavalry saddle used by Cornet Glyn at Balaclava, 1854.

PLATE 14   Staff Pattern saddle of 1884. The officer is the future Field Marshal Lord Methuen.

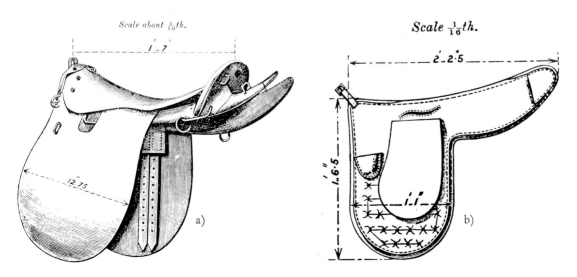

PLATE 15   Household Cavalry Troop saddle of 1885 with details.

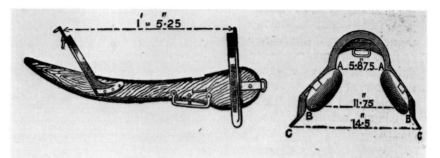

Seat.

It is removable, and is provided with buckles and straps for attaching it to the tree. A ring is attached to the front of the seat to take the breastplate strap.

Seat on.

Seat off.

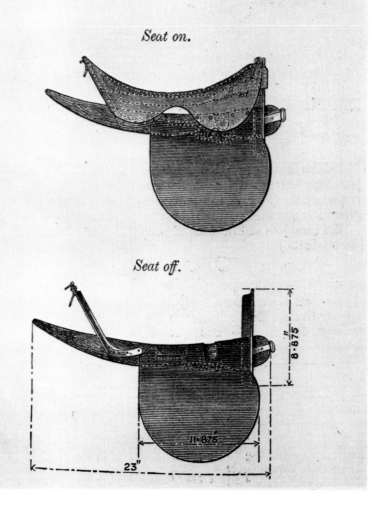

PLATE 16   The Universal Pattern Removable Iron Angle Arch Troop saddle of 1885.

The strength in horses in November, 1899 was 406, all English, in fair condition, except that they contracted mange, which became a scourge in South Africa. In three months fighting 31 horses were killed in action, 20 shot for bullet wounds and 9 died. Less one squadron detached to the Cavalry Division, the Regiment marched 200 miles from Colesburg to Bloemfontein from the 6th March to the 17th April. They covered 47 miles on reconnaissance in one day and lost altogether 3 horses shot owing to exhaustion, 8 were sick and 12 had sore backs. The detached squadron lost about the same and noted, as did the rest of the regiment, that the horses were usually saddled from dark to dark. In May, 1900, they received recently shipped Argentine ponies, very soft, unused to eating oats and many with sore backs. Some died from exhaustion. The regiment then had 447 horses. (Argentine Remount: see Plate 98.) There is nothing special to note about the foregoing; the losses are given in detail as some guide to losses under normal conditions. During Lord Roberts' advance from Bloemfontein to Pretoria from the 6th May to the 6th June conditions were not normal. It became colder and colder with heavy frost on some nights, there was very little water, no grazing, the nosebags were worn out and leaked badly, letting the oats out, and in the last stages the horses could hardly walk. Horses were dying all the time, 70 were abandoned with their saddlery and of those left by the whole force thousands died in the Veterinary Hospitals. The regiments that took part in the fighting before the taking of Bloemfontein had lost just as heavily, so their totals were even higher than those of the Inniskillings.

After the fall of Pretoria the regiment was engaged at Diamond Hill, north of that town. They took 196 horses still able to work into action, but all were completely exhausted. They were still being kept under the saddle till nightfall. In June, the regiment was 'remounted up to 556 horses, mostly Hungarians, flat catchers, of whom not 10 per cent lasted'. The expression 'flat catcher' denotes a horse possessed of good looks with hardly any other desirable qualities. Hence in peace time he would usually be sold to a man who knew next to nothing about horses. The Austrian and Hungarian Remount Officers, highly skilled men, had obviously seen to it that no remounts fit for their own army were offered to the British buyers. Anyone who had the misfortune to be issued with one of these horses would have endorsed every word that Lieut Head wrote about them. He goes on to give the following details: 'In two days trek of 20 miles each, 31 Hungarians died, 20 were abandoned and 72 sent to hospital. Rather more than three horses fell out every mile.' Casualties were replaced partially by the issue of 59 remounts who had recovered their condition in the Veterinary Hospitals. In the next trek of 120 miles, no less than 64 horses died or had to be destroyed, and 130, mostly Hungarians, were sent to hospital. Losses then fell off, and in October 93 Colonial ponies were received, who did good service. The fact was that Colonial ponies were at a premium as everyone wanted them and occasional captures from the enemy were eagerly snapped up. In January, 1901, the regiment was remounted to 406, mostly on North Americans. As a rule these horses did well and were liked. An order now came out that if a horse had a sore back the trooper was crimed and had to march as an infantryman till the horse recovered. In April transport was provided on which horse rugs were carried. Each weighed 12 lb and made a very great difference indeed to the condition of the horses as the winters from April to September are bitterly cold on the high veldt. For a long time the mounted troops had been split up into columns of varying sizes and employed in anti-guerilla warfare. The immobility of the infantry, mostly employed in guarding blockhouse lines, made it possible to provide extra transport for the mounted units. (See Plates 14, 96, and 97 for Colonial ponies.) In July the troop horses were almost all Colonials, any remaining Hungarians having been exchanged for them. On the 9th November the last English troop horse left was shot in action. He belonged to a trumpeter and had never been sick or sorry. Not many English horses survived the ordeal of the first year. The author knew one, a stocky well-built horse, bought out of a butcher's cart, who was ridden by the same man for 18 months in the ranks and for the rest of the war as an officer's charger. The old horse returned to England, having never been unfit for duty. The Inniskillings were lucky enough to have escaped being issued with Russian ponies. They were better than the Hungarians, but too slow for any but slow harness work. For the remainder of the war the regiment had work which was possible for the horses, now properly fed and rugged at night in the winter. The summary of the losses in horseflesh is as follows:

Strength on landing	406
Remounts received	3,061
Picked up in the veldt	222
Transfers	601
Total of horses issued	4,290
Sent to veterinary hospitals	1,600
Missing	201
Returned to depots	202
Abandoned	201
Destroyed	595
Died	482
Transferred	469
Total expended	3,750

On the 30th June, 1902, there remained 540 remounts with the regiment. Lieut Head's estimate of the distance covered was 6,116 miles in a straight line. He considered that 'reconnaissance and scouting would probably double this, making the total distance covered 12,232 miles'; and that 'On this liberal basis one horse was used up for every $3\frac{1}{2}$ miles covered'. He concludes 'I hope next time we shall do better'. It is doubtful if men who have taken part in operations of this sort will disagree with the above figures showing mileage. No South African road or any other unfenced waggon track is ever straight for more than a few hundred yards and troops on widely spaced flanking duties can easily cover double the distance marched by the main body.

We certainly did very much better as regards horseflesh in the next war of 1914–18; but the losses sustained by the South Africans in German East Africa, now Tanganyika, were far heavier, though from very different causes. (See in the section on South Africa.)

The above account should give a good idea of how and why a cavalry force could be reduced to impotence, if the logistics governing that branch of the service had not been meticulously worked out in peace time, and if a sufficiency of men trained to organize and run remount depots and veterinary hospitals was not available from the first outbreak of war. As a rule the ordinary officer of the fighting units had no wish to be posted to remount work, and even if he had, however fine a horseman and good judge of a horse he might be, he was not necessarily competent at a job for which he had not been trained. Perhaps the most important part of Lieut Head's survey is the way it brings out the uselessness of putting horses in bad condition, straight off shipboard and not acclimatized to the country or to the food, into hard work.

The report of the Committee on the Supply of Remounts, 1902, raised many points of interest. The evidence stressed the fact that to get a grass-fed horse into condition for ordinary work three months was necessary, and that another month would be necessary to get him fit for hunting, presumably three days a fortnight, which was the usual amount demanded of a hunter. It was also stated that it would take six months at least to get a grass-fed horse in good enough condition to send out to South Africa as a remount. There is also an interesting account of the number of horses fit for remounts imported into England at this time from the Continent and sold as English-bred. The difficulty of buying at the Government price of £40 a head the class of horse required was stressed by several witnesses. There is little doubt that the publication of the evidence and findings of this Committee, though they recommended no very drastic changes, did much to clear the air and exerted considerable influence on the Government with respect to establishing altogether better methods of dealing with remounts in large quantities than had been the case in 1899.

Before going on to the next period it is advisable to examine Plates 66 to 69. Drawn in the nineties by R. Simkin, the well-known military artist, they show a rather stereotyped ideal of what officers' first chargers should look like. They differ in quite a few ways from those in Alderson's set of remounts (see *post*), and from the next set to be discussed. All the same, until after the South African War they give a fair idea of the type of charger aimed at, if not often attained.

33

REFERENCES

1   Aldershot Lectures, Veterinary Surgeon G. Fleming. 1889.
2   Parrino, *Introduction to Pack Transport etc.*, p. 24.
3   Maxwell, *History of King Edward's Own Lancers, Probyn's Horse*, pp. 82, 83.
4   Aldershot Lectures, 1891, p. 25. *Animal Management*, p. 136.
5   *Animal Management*, as 4.
6   Gilbey, *The Great Horse*.
7   Gilbey, as 6, p. 42, quoting Carlyle, *Letters and Speeches of Oliver Cromwell*.
8   Sidney, *Book of the Horse*, chapter on 'The English Horse in 1600'; Baldock, *Cromwell as a Soldier*, p. 28; Firth, *Cromwell's Army*, p. 242.
9   Markham, Gervase, *Soldier's Accidence*.
10 Newcastle, *Horsemanship*.
11 Ward, *Animadversions of War*, 1649.
12 Gilbey, *Horses Past and Present*, pp. 32–7; *Horse Breeding in England and India*, p. 14, and *Small Horses in Warfare*, pp. 10, 18 and 19.
13 *Journal of the Society for Army Historical Research* (JAHR), Volume xxxviii, p. 12.
14 Firth as 8.
15 Stevens, *The King's Wagon-Master General*, p. 14.
16 As 15; Hogg, *English Artillery, 1326–1716*, p. 25.
17 As 12. *Horses Past and Present*, p. 44.
18 JAHR. Volume xxxii, p. 108.
19 Lawson, *History of the Uniforms of the British Army*. Volume 1.
20 Routh, *Tangier*, p. 320.
21 JAHR, Volume xxxvi, p. 109.
22 See in the section on 'Tails'.
23 JAHR, Volume xxxvi, *Queen Anne's Army*, by Atkinson.
24 As 23.
25 JAHR, Volume xxiii, p. 98.
26 JAHR, Volume iii, pp. 231 *et seq.*
27 Rogers, *Mounted Troops of the British Army*, p. 117 and Royal Warrant P.R.O. W.O. 26/23 (40, 305).
28 Sidney, *Book of the Horse.*
29 Pembroke, Earl of, *Military Equitation or a Method of Teaching Soldiers to Ride*; JAHR, Volume xvi, p. 102, ill. of 1767.
30 Fortescue, Volume iii, p. 543.
31 JAHR, Volume xxii, p. 216.
32 Doubtless apocryphal!
33 *History of the Army Veterinary Corps, 1796–1919*, p. 63.
34 Miles, *Farriery*, pp. 168, 169; Gilbey, *Horses Past and Present*, p. 80.
35 Gilbey, *Horses Past and Present*, p. 38.
36 Fortescue, Volume iv, p. 908.
37 As 36.
38 Whinyates, *From Corunna to Sevastopol*, p. 11.
39 JAHR, Volume xxxvi, *Waterloo Arthur*, pp. 125, 126.
40 Brett-James, *Wellington at War*, p. 263.
41 JAHR, Volume xxvii, p. 182, under date 1809.
42 Stewart, *XIIth Royal Lancers*, pp. 58 and 79.
43 Tomkinson, *Diary of a Cavalry Officer*, p. 24.
44 Gilbey, *Horse Breeding in England and India*, pp. 19, 20.
45 Burgoyne, *Military Opinions*, p. 435 *et seq.*, and pp. 417, 418.

46 Lieut General Sir H. C. Chauvel, K.C.B. Commanded the Desert Mounted Corps in Allenby's Campaigns of 1917–18 in Palestine.
47 Aide Memoire to the Military Sciences, Volume II, p. 271.
48 Wood, Field Marshal, *The Crimea in 1854 and 1894.*
49 Agriculture and Fisheries, Board of. Figure 3, caption: See Plate 76. Preston, *The Desert Mounted Corps*, p. 324.
50 Aldershot Lectures, 1895, Major W. G. Knox, R.H.A.
51 Parr, *Recollections and Correspondence*, p. 170.
52 Sessions, pp. 14, 15; see also *Report of the Committee on Remounts.*
53 Sidney, *Book of the Horse*, p. 127.
54 Parr, p. 229.
55 Aldershot Lectures, 1891, p. 37.
56 Aldershot Lectures, 1891. *The Development of Modern Cavalry*, Major W. C. James.
57 Alderson, *Pink and Scarlet.*
58 Grierson. He wrote under the pseudonym of *A Lieutenant Colonel in the British Army*, pp. 245, 246, and 248.
59 Times *History of the War in South Africa*, Vol. VI. Chapter VI, p. 418.
60 *A Veterinary History of the War in South Africa.*
61 Statistics of the Military Effort of the British Empire, 1914–20.
62 Rimington, *The Horse in the Late War.*
63 Head, *Wear and Tear of Horses.*
64 As 63, page 2. See also Champion & Wilton, Equipment Book under date 1901.

CHAPTER TWO

British Regular Army Horses to 1918. Remounts in India, the Commonwealth, North & South America, & on the Continent

THE South African War of 1899–1902 made little or no difference to the types of remount required in Great Britain. Although it had taught the Army and the nation a great deal of value, it had been in many ways an exceptional war, and though the weight-carrying well-bred cavalry horse had not fared well on the very poor treatment meted out to him, he was still considered by men of great experience as the beau idéal of a troop horse. Indeed, Colonel Rimington[1] stated that the English troop horse, *if given enough to eat*, had been the best remount we had in South Africa. Under the existing conditions he made it clear that every man who could get hold of a Colonial pony did so, and with this he was entirely in agreement. He rode a Basuto pony himself.

The ruling question after 1902, on which senior officers held widely differing opinions, was whether cavalry should still be trained in the use of the *arme blanche*, and as of old consider it their principal weapon, or whether they should be trained solely as mounted riflemen. On this depended to a great extent the type of remount they would require. Although the consensus of opinion gradually veered towards a transposition of the importance of the weapon to be used, there were occasions during the next war when mounted riflemen were issued with swords and used them to great effect.[2] However, the tradition of mounting the army on horses of hunter type continued to influence those responsible for the purchase of remounts and as a general rule those bred from thoroughbred sires were considered the most desirable. The correctness of this will become apparent in due course. There was, however, a school who thought that the thoroughbred got too many misfits when crossed with hunter mares also sired by thoroughbreds. Among these was Sir Walter Gilbey, who preferred to use hunter stallions. He also makes the point that on the Continent a very good stamp of remount was being bred from Hackney sires, bought in England, and that Continental buyers snapped up any useful looking mares that came on the market in this country.

In 1900 it was decided to increase the number of Horse and Field Batteries as well as horsing a number of heavier guns. In all, 54 new batteries were raised, requiring a total of 3,132 horses. The standard set for Royal Artillery remounts was a high one. (Plate 76.)

In June 1909 the Board of Agriculture and Fisheries issued a brochure entitled *Types of Horses Suitable for Army Remounts*. This was reissued in a revised form in 1912 and the illustrations are reproduced in this book as Plates 75–8. Just as the Simkin drawings (Plates 66–9) of officers' chargers represent perfection as depicted by an artist of great experience, so the photographs collected by Lieut Colonel Alderson in 1899 show his ideas as to the ordinary run of useful remounts of that date, and this official publication of 1912 also shows horses in use but in this case they are obviously the best possible to select as guides for the breeder – and the buyer. Captions will be found under the photographs, and the following is a guide:

No. 1. 2nd Life Guards, trooper, black like all the Household Cavalry with minor exceptions. Height 16 hands, cost £65 as a 4-year-old; these remounts are always more expensive than other cavalry horses. A real nice-looking heavy-weight with plenty of bone.

No. 2. 9th Lancers. Noted as being of hunter stamp. Height 15·2 hands, cost £40 in Ireland, a black gelding. A thousand like this one were required yearly.

No. 3. R.H.A. Height 15·2 hands, bought in Ireland for £42 as a 4-year-old. Capable of pulling anywhere in a gun team, the standard being that of the wheelers.

No. 4. Royal Field Artillery. A bay gelding, 14 years old, height 15·3 hands, 'can gallop, and looks as if he ought to have spent his life as a hunter'. Cost £42; his place in the team is a leader.

Writing in 1962 Brigadier J. Clabby, O.B.E., Director of Veterinary and Remount Services, to whom the author is very greatly indebted for help and advice, gave it as his opinion that 'in practice there might have been very little to choose between a good gunner leader and a point-to-point horse'. This was written apropos of the 1912 brochure, which the Brigadier had lent for purposes of reproduction.

Nos. 7 and 8. Royal Engineers and Army Service Corps. Draught horses of the type known as 'the Parcel Vanner', must be able to trot with a good load but do not require as much pace as the R.A. remounts. Heights up to 16 and 15·3½ hands respectively. The R.E. remount is 12 years old and 15·3 hands in height. The A.S.C. draught horse is described as a good stamp of slow mover; age 8 years; height 15·2½ hands.

There is not all that much difference between the Field Artillery and Royal Engineer remounts, and twenty years earlier the latter would probably have been taken for Artillery. The annual requirements for remounts for the R.A., R.E., and A.S.C., were 1,360.

Nos. 9 and 10 are Mounted Infantry cobs and Plates 70 and 71 show the changes since the nineties. The two men, one dismounted, dated 1890, are riding quite a different class of horse, not very different to those in use by Light Cavalry. The other Plate showing a Sergeant of the Gordon Highlanders in 1896 on a much smaller cob is much more like the typical M.I. cob or Galloway of 1912.

No. 9 is a 12-year-old who had done 7 years' hard work without a day's rest; his height is 14·2½ hands and No. 10, the piebald, is 9 years old and 14·1½ hands high. The standard for polo ponies at this time was 14·2 hands, so ponies going over this measurement were available for M.I. at a very much smaller price than if they could be played as polo ponies. Annually 140 of these cobs were required.

The brochure just described does not deal adequately with the Royal Engineers.

In 1904, 1905, the R.E. remounts, both draught and riding, compared very favourably with those issued to the R.F.A. and there was very little difference between the two types. My informant, ex-Troop Sergeant Major F. Banning, who served in 'B' (the Bridging) Troop says their horses were all chestnuts and all their names began with a 'B'. As mentioned before, the desire of all ranks, in any smart unit, was always to turn out with horses all of the same colour. The effect is as good as anyone can wish.

FIRST WORLD WAR

This brings us up to the commencement of the First World War, the last of so many in which British horsed Artillery and Cavalry were to play their part. As regards the principal campaign of the many waged, that in Northern France and Flanders was the only one in which the regular regiments of the British Army took part in large numbers. Magnificently mounted and kept in hand for the final breakthrough and pursuit of the German Army, the whole character of the war, dominated as it was to such a great extent by the machine gun, gave no opportunities for any action of this nature. On the contrary, the fighting powers of the cavalryman were only utilized, and that to a very full extent, in trench warfare in the role of infantrymen.

There were certain occasions, especially in the very early days of the war, when the *arme blanche* was used with conspicuous success, but only by small bodies and there were a few more later on towards the end of the war. In these affairs, especially those in the early period, the English troop horse of hunter type never showed to greater advantage.

It might perhaps be thought that in trench warfare the horses would not have suffered very severely. This was not the case, although the losses were anything but serious compared with other wars. Indifferent forage and constant exposure to the cold were nearly as serious when a unit was at rest as when it was in the front line. The frequent calls made on the cavalry to move from one part of the line to another also came hard on the horses. Apart from enemy action, some of the marches in winter on roads covered with ice and blocked with other troops told severely on their condition and it was noted[3] that they recovered much more slowly than the men from fatigue. The provision of oats and forage imposed a severe strain on shipping resources, more weight of oats and hay being shipped to the France and Flanders area than of ammunition, the total weight of horse feed being nearly 5,500,000 tons. In December, 1916, due to the action of enemy submarines, the horses were receiving only 7 lb of feed a day, which was not sufficient.

The number of animals on establishment in August, 1914, before the outbreak of war was 25,000.[4] This was raised on mobilization to 165,000 horses, purchased by impressment, which ceased to be used afterwards, except in a few cases. The highest total of animals, including mules, with the Army on the Continent was reached in June 1917, when 460,000 were on charge. The losses were also the highest, due to a very cold spring and the Somme offensive; they were 28 per cent. The total number of replacements, including mules and all classes of horses and ponies, was 377,312.

The Army Remount Service during this war fully vindicated the shortcomings of their branch of the Service during the South African War of 1899–1902, as the losses show. They started the war with 121 officers and 230 other ranks, and in 1917 had 423 officers and 20,560 other ranks. No officers of other branches were withdrawn from military service in order to staff the Purchasing Commissions sent to Canada and to North and South America. In all 468,323 horses were bought in Great Britain up to 1920, sixteen months after the close of hostilities in France on the 11th November, 1918. In four years 17 per cent of the working horse population of Great Britain was mobilized for the war effort. Serving in a climate differing hardly at all from that to which they were accustomed, for the most part well fed and not overworked to any great extent, the home-bred horses did well. Of these the number of riding horses bought in the United Kingdom from the 5th August, 1914, when mobilization began, to the 31st December, 1918, was 174,665. By November 1918, the Canadian Commission had shipped from North America 428,608 horses and 275,097 mules. From South America came 6,000 horses and 1,500 mules; the latter went to East Africa.

The total losses in the British Army in France and Flanders and in England were 256,204, compared with a loss of 541,714 in the French Army.

The percentage of losses sustained on shipboard among animals shipped to Great Britain and other countries was 3·23 compared with a loss of 3·98 per cent during the South African War of 1899–1902, when there were no submarines to attack convoys and ships moved independently.

Owing to submarine action during the 1914–18 war, shipment of horses from Australia to Egypt had to be stopped (later, direct shipment from America to the Mediterranean also had to be discontinued).

In all a total of 417,685 horses and 209,618 mules were imported from Canada, the U.S.A., Argentine, Uruguay, India, and Spain. The South African figures will be found in the section on that country.

When the bulk of the Australian and New Zealand contingents were transferred from the Mediterranean to Europe, the Imperial Government undertook to supply them with horses and did the same for the Canadian contingents. In March 1916, the Remount Department added to their responsibilities the supply of horses needed for the Belgian Army; they also supplied some 18,000 animals to American Divisions in France. When the Food Production Department of the Board of Agriculture was started, they required a number of horses for work on the land. The Remount Department bought 6,792 horses for the Board and 3,200 Army horses, which were no longer suitable for military purposes, were transferred. Draught horses were also lent to the Department of Draught Horses, and were conditioned by them at their prisoners-of-war ploughing camps. The horses were then returned to the Remount Depots when fit and replaced by others.[5]

The majority of the light draught remounts came from America and turned out extremely well. (See under the section on North America, p. 70.) The trouble with the home-bred light draught horses was that they were often the result of crossing dissimilar animals, such as the heavy Clydesdales and Shire horses with fast light draught Hackneys. These cross-breds have neither the stamina or quality of the true coach horse and were not fit for Field Artillery work. Their casualties from disease and lameness were heavy. In contrast to this the heavy draught horses were very useful under the conditions obtaining in trench warfare.

Although a heavy draught horse requires twice as much feed as a mule, a pair of Shires will do the work of four mules, though at a walk only.[6] These cart horses, as they are commonly called, had been used before the war to pull the big 60-pounder guns and continued to do so until some time after peace.

The chief Remount Depots were situated at points near the ports of Bristol, Liverpool and Southampton. The one at Romsey, served by Southampton, had a staff of Headquarters and 10 squadrons, there being 21 personnel at H.Q. and 201 for each squadron. There was stabling accommodation for 5,000 animals and the personnel included 40 Rough Riders, all animals being carefully trained for the work they had to do. A very serious difficulty in all the Depots was the transfer of men fit for active service to fighting units and their replacement by men of low category, inferior physique, and generally with no previous knowledge of horses. During the last two years of the war the turnover of men was continuous and during the six months 1st January to 30th June, 1918, 2,534 of all ranks were sent to other units and 816 were released for various civilian activities; that is to say, the personnel was changed at the rate of 40 per cent per annum. Horses and mules are not like machines and a man with a knowledge of, and sympathy with, them is worth anything when handling and breaking horses, especially in quick time, for transference to a seat of war, where everything may have to be sacrificed to speed and where there is no place for a frightened half-broken animal. The difficulty of running a Remount Depot with only a small percentage of trained men is very great indeed.[7] The Director of Remounts in August, 1914, Major General Sir W. H. Birkbeck, K.C.B., might well congratulate himself and his staff on their magnificent work in the long-drawn-out war.

As regards the other theatres of war the supply of animals for the Mesopotamian campaigns was carried out by the Indian Government, and for the South West and East African campaigns by the South African Government, with the exception of a small reinforcement from Buenos Aires.

Perhaps the most interesting campaign from the remount point of view was the one waged in Palestine towards the end of hostilities, which resulted in the complete defeat of the Turkish Army, stiffened by German Staff Officers and German and Austrian units.[8]

Except that there were no British Regular Cavalry present, the make-up of the

Desert Mounted Corps bore certain resemblances to conditions in South Africa, sixteen and seventeen years before. In both cases personnel came from various parts of the British Empire and were mounted on remounts from as many. The great difference lay in the organization of the Remount Service, which was as near perfection as possible in Egypt, the base for the operations in Palestine, in contradistinction to the lamentable state of affairs in South Africa in the past.

The General Officer Commanding in Egypt in 1917, when the operations with which this account deals commenced, was General Allenby, later Field Marshal. A cavalryman of very considerable experience, he made the greatest possible use of his mounted troops. It is a bad country for horses, distances are great, water is very scarce indeed, the going is atrocious in many areas and both the troop horses and transport animals were constantly being extended to the limit of their strength.

Owing to shipping difficulties no remounts arrived in Egypt after May or June, 1917. When the stock of remounts in Palestine was exhausted casualties had to be replaced by horses which had been sent to the Remount Hospitals on account of either wounds or sickness and reissued when fit for work. Thus there was no constant influx of fresh animals and the Remount Officers and Veterinary Surgeons had to do their best and be successful or else let the war effort down. This never happened, yet so close was the margin that at the beginning of September, 1918, there was scarcely a single fit horse left behind the fighting troops.

General Allenby disposed of about 20,000 mounted men rising to 25,000, and in August, 1917, there were nearly 32,000 riding horses in Egypt. On the 31st August, 1918, there were nearly 2,000 more, but a number of these would not have been available for the cavalry of the Desert Mounted Corps.

This consisted at first of what was known as the Desert Column under the command of Sir Philip Chetwode, comprising the Australian and New Zealand Mounted Division and the Fifth Mounted Brigade, Yeomanry, who formed part of the Territorial Force in Great Britain.

When reorganized under Lieut General Sir H. G. Chauvel, K.C.B., and renamed the Desert Mounted Corps, the force consisted of ten Brigades, forming a corps of three Divisions, including two Indian formations. In April 1918, a portion of the Yeomanry was set to France and replaced by Indian Cavalry regiments. The artillery consisted of R.H.A. Territorial Batteries, and a French unit, Régiment Mixte de Cavalerie, was also attached to the Corps. They were mounted on goodlooking Barbs, cross-bred Arabs from North Africa, who could not stay the pace with the big English and Australian horses on the forced marches which were such a frequent feature of Chauvel's operations. Captured ponies belonging to Arabs were of no use and were sold locally, for good prices. Some of the stronger ponies were issued to infantry as 'cobs' but there were not many of them.

The British formations brought their horses with them from Great Britain. These did very well, though it was considered that the Australian and New Zealand horses did better (see under Australia). Nearly all the remounts that reached

Egypt were either Australians or Canadians. The latter were employed in the transport and were a success. (Plates 91, 92 and 94.)

There is no doubt that the horses suffered severely at times, working as they were on an average number of waterings per animal of only one every thirty-six hours. This was in the 1917 advance, later on horses were able to be watered once a day. At one place where water was quite insufficient an officer attached to the Camel Transport thought he could make out the lie of an underground supply. He rode along, not very hopefully, and in due course found the place where a strong stream had been opened out but allowed to run away. The Royal Engineers dammed the stream and it provided water for a large number of animals. The discoverer was mentioned in despatches, so vital was the find.[9]

In many cases the wells were 150 feet or more deep, the pumping apparatus had been destroyed by the enemy, and the horses had to be watered by letting down canvas buckets on a piece of telephone wire. This method might make it possible to water the horses of one troop, approximately 40, in an hour. No one who has not had experience of watering in this manner can really grasp what it means to have to carry it out in the dark after a long march. On one occasion it took a Yeomanry unit the whole night to water, most of the horses had been 84 hours without any, were carrying an average weight of 21 stone, and subsisting on less than half the normal amount of forage.

Besides the difficulty of water, long marches were the rule and from the 29th October to the 1st November, 1917, the cavalry divisions covered nearly 170 miles. One of the batteries with the Australian Mounted Division had only been able to water three times in the past nine days, the actual intervals between waterings being 68, 72, and 76 hours respectively. Yet the battery lost only eight horses from exhaustion, not counting those killed in action or evacuated as wounded.

On the 16th November, out of the three regiments of one of the Mounted Brigades only 690 men and horses were reported as fit for duty, the losses being due to sickness and casualties among both men and horses. There was, surprisingly enough, not much disease among the horses; there were a few cases of anthrax, and towards the end of the war one Cavalry Division had to destroy thirty or forty horses for laminitis, or 'fever in the feet', caused by a very fast approach march.

So much of the condition of horses on active service depends on the horse-mastership of the troopers themselves. This most valuable quality can be learnt, but is difficult for officers and N.C.O.s to teach unless the men are keen. In a dozen little ways, whether he is a good horseman or not, a man can look after his horse and bring him through conditions such as extreme heat or cold and long marches in, at any rate, moderate condition. The Yeomanry trooper in the South African War, mentioned in the section on the campaign, was one of the most inveterate thieves of any form of horse feed that ever existed, and so have many of the best horse-masters always been. These men do not want telling how to make things as easy as possible for 'the old 'oss'. They have learnt by experience and a genuine sympathy with horses. In this respect conditions with the Desert Mounted Corps

42

became exceptionally good. Not all of the Yeomen knew much about horses before they joined up and had to learn, and the Colonials were mostly men who had done their work on the big ranges in Australasia with plenty of spare horses. In Palestine there were none and it takes time for a man to learn to ride the same horse day after day and watch his condition like a trainer does with his string. The small losses and the great distances covered are enough to show that the troop horses of the Corps had as good attention from the individual troopers as could be. For one thing there was hardly ever a sore back in the whole force, a certain proof of good horse-mastership.

As regards the artillery and draught horses of the transport, the difficulties were much more serious than among the riding horses. Like the rest of the re-mounts they had been in Egypt for a long time before 1917, eating fodder heavily impregnated with sand, which is so harmful to a horse's stomach even when it does not cause sand colic. Marches of 40, 50, and 60 miles were comparatively common and there was one of 90 miles. It is not possible for the heavier type of draught horse to cover such distances except at a slow rate, and this meant they would be a day's march behind the cavalry. Only the lighter type of draught horse was any use at this sort of work and, as already stated, they were not bred in sufficient numbers in Great Britain, although they were in Canada. They had to put up with the same extremes of great heat and once in a way with snow, but their work was far harder and more distressing than that of the cavalry troop horses, especially in desert country. So severe was it that in the opinion of the author of *The Desert Mounted Corps*, Lieut Colonel the Hon. R. M. P. Preston, D.S.O.,[8] probably 90 per cent of the draught horses of the artillery and transport had strained their hearts to some extent during the advance across Sinai. He was present at upwards of 20 post-mortems on draught horses that had died, and in every case there was an enlarge-ment of the heart greater than could have possibly been accounted for by the age of the horse. In one instance the wall of the heart was ruptured right through. Colonel Preston's book has been used for almost the whole of this section. It is an exception to the fact that the average senior Staff Officer, however brilliantly he may write of the strategical and tactical problems of a campaign in which he has played a prominent part, hardly ever deals fully and in great clarity with the prob-lems of the remounts employed and their share in the operations. Yet, as in this instance, horseflesh can play a most important role. Fortunately, for the research worker, Colonel Preston's knowledge of, and interest in, horses extended to every detail which concerned not only those of his own arm, the Royal Artillery, but of any type with which he had been brought in contact.

He was of the opinion, held by many other experts, that provided a horse is adequately exercised while being conditioned, he cannot be too fat and round at the start of a campaign. A really fat horse finished a hard spell of work in better con-dition than one who had started looking harder and more muscular. This is especially the case when water is scarce.

Experiments carried out by the Royal Army Veterinary Corps and by unit commanders proved that a horse does better on two waterings a day than on three and drinks more water on the two waterings. In this connection it may be noted that horses work well enough on one watering a day, even when marching hard, in countries where water is not available oftener, such as in parts of Africa.

A point which Colonel Preston drove home is the fact that, however well horsed and however good the driving is, artillery cannot keep up with cavalry when the latter are moving really fast. An artillery draught horse has to carry nearly the same weight as a cavalry trooper and do his share in dragging along 'over hill and dale, through bush, through briar' a clumsy mass of steel weighing a ton-and-a-half.

The illustrations in this book should show how much knowledge and experience is required of Remount Officers who buy artillery, especially horse artillery, remounts and how high the Royal Regiment must set the standard. In his book Colonel Preston emphasized once again the desirability of every horse issued to a battery being fit to take its place if need be, in the teams. In 1917 in Palestine even officers' chargers were sometimes worked in the teams in order to give the over-taxed horses some rest. Colonel Preston was no advocate of the heavy-weight hunter type of remount for any class of troops; his reasons will be found in the section on Australasian remounts.

It is of great interest to note that the *arme blanche* was freely used by the units of the Desert Mounted Corps with very great success. Then the value of a cavalry remount that could really gallop for the last couple of hundred yards was clearly brought out.

The total strength of the animals in all areas with which the Remount Service had to deal was at its highest in 1917, when there were 896,931 on charge; by 1919, 210,000 remained, and by 31st March, 1920, when the operations in the Black Sea against the Russian Bolshevists terminated, only 110,708 remained.

The Royal Army Veterinary Corps and the Remount Department could hardly have done better work, and came out of the war with vastly increased prestige. As already stated, the mistakes of 1899–1902 in South Africa had been amply vindicated.

POST FIRST WORLD WAR

The difficulty experienced by all branches of the British Army was that it was impossible to persuade the Government to lay down a modern policy of mechanization or to do more than fiddle with the subject. In 1929 the first two Cavalry regiments, the 11th Hussars and 12th Royal Lancers, were converted into armoured car units, and in the next few years mechanization was being extended to both artillery and more cavalry units. In July, 1927, the War Office issued a similar brochure to the one published by the Board of Agriculture and Fisheries in 1912 (see Plates 79–81 for the 1927 publication). In the description of the types specially wanted are the following specifications: 'The two types of horses required are the cavalry or hunter type of horse and the light active draught horse which can trot on'.

There are three photographs only (Plates 79–81), showing a cavalry trooper, a Royal Horse Artillery remount and a horse for Field Artillery and other light draught. Descriptions are also given of officers' chargers – 'they should be well-bred horses of the hunter type, active, well ribbed up, short in the back with plenty of bone and good head and shoulders', and of Household Cavalry troopers – 'these must have quality and at the same time be able to carry weight and be good looking. The price paid for these horses is higher than that paid for the ordinary cavalry troop horse. The colour required is black, minimum height at 4 years, 15·3, and at 5 years, 16 hands.'

The photograph of the cavalry trooper, a horse not to exceed 15·3 hands at over 4 years and to be of the hunter stamp, looks perhaps a trifle long in the back compared with the R.H.A. 'ride and drive' horse. He should be of the same height as the trooper and weigh from 1,200 to 1,300 lb. In Plate 34 the R.H.A. teams of the King's Troop in 1961 show the same characteristics.

The Field Artillery and other light draught remount is described as 'the best type of active light vanner, height as for R.H.A. but somewhat heavier'.

The photographs in the Manual of Horsemastership, published in 1937,[10] show R.A.S.C. light vanners in harness considerably lighter than the one shown in the brochure. Plates 36, a, b and c, taken from *Engineer Training* Vol. I, 1929, show an officer, Lieut J. Marsh, R.E., on an Infantry Officer's type of charger. The mare is described as 'going like a bomb' after her rider started the R.E. Drag in 1928 in the best tradition of the British Army. These and the following notes were sent by Brigadier J. H. S. Lacey, R.E., who served between 1929 and 1934 in the 1st Field Squadron, R.E., when it was a mounted unit, and as a R.E. Equitation Officer at the R.E. Mounted Depot, Aldershot, after attending an Equitation Course at the Army School at Weedon. The Sapper, mounted, in marching order is riding a trooper, a useful horse, and the two photographs showing the Driver differ very little from the R.F.A. and light vanner in the brochure. Neither they nor the troop horse are as heavy as Nos. 7 and 8, R.E. and A.S.C. of the 1907 brochure. The Sappers also had 'round chubby little cobs' used as packs, who trotted level with the troop horses. There were also pack ponies led by a man on foot. One of these in a photograph of 1920[11] looks to be a short, stuggy rather plain type.

The changes in the number of types of remount required were due in the case of the heavy R.A.S.C. type to the introduction of motor lorries, with a capacity for surmounting difficult terrain which increased every few years. The disappearance of the M.I. cob was due to the very great improvement in the shooting of the cavalry. The armoured car and the tank had come to stay and the disappearance of mounted troops became more of a certainty every day.

In the section on the Desert Mounted Corps mention was made of the horse-mastership of two types of auxiliary artillery and cavalry. Writing in 1926 on a different subject, an officer of Canadian Regular Cavalry[12] commented as follows: 'The standard of horse-mastership in the British Regular Army is second to none, and that in our own (Canadian) Regular Cavalry is not far behind'.

The years 1940–1 saw the end of the horse as the motive power for cavalry and artillery but not, as it turned out, for transport and more especially for pack. Forecasts by experienced officers lend strength to the belief that pack animals will still play a vital role in the event of wars of normal type being waged in mountainous areas. Except in certain unhealthy parts of the East, where disease takes a heavy toll in imported animals, the horse and mule are no longer exposed to heavy battle casualties and losses from long and arduous marches at a fast pace. But they are exposed to air attack and it is unfortunately only half true to say that mechanization 'has eradicated one of man's greatest friends from the horrors of war'.[13] This had been what men had hoped would happen before the Second World War broke out.

Note

Approximate Weights carried by Troop Horses in the Armies of the World during the period 1890 to 1900.

Austria-Hungary	from 20 to 21 stone	
Belgium	14 stone 7 lb	
France – Heavy	21 stone	Cuirassiers
Medium	18 stone	Dragoons
Light	16 stone 10 lb	Hussars and Chasseurs à Cheval
Germany	23 stone to 18 stone 7 lb	according to class
Great Britain	19 stone 8 lb	in peace time
	20 stone 1 lb	in the field in 1901
Italy	18 stone	
Russia	20 stone to 18 stone	according to class
United States of America	16 stone	

These weights are mostly taken from Carter's *Horses, Saddles and Bridles*, published in 1902. This American Cavalry Officer was in complete agreement with Major General Rosenberg, Inspector General of the Prussian Cavalry, who wrote in 1888 that 'Cavalry carrying more than 15 stone 10 lb are fit for nothing. Weight ruins horses and multiplies empty files.' This statement was quoted and considered correct by Major General Sir F. Smith of the Army Veterinary Corps in 1891.

Although included in the chapter on Saddles, the above notes have been repeated here to emphasize the difference between theory and practice which obtained all over Europe at the height of the maintenance of large bodies of cavalry, considered absolutely essential to the successful prosecution of a great war.

REMOUNTS IN INDIA FROM 1781

From the time when the Honourable East India Company raised the first cavalry regiments in Madras in 1781, the want of size in so many of the numerous local breeds and the lack of interest taken in horse breeding by the large majority of the people made it essential to establish Government breeding establishments. These were expensive to run, largely owing to so much of the science of crossing local mares with imported stallions being at first mainly guess-work. The first thing that a British officer had to do when posted to Indian Cavalry was to disabuse himself of nearly all he had learnt about remounts in the United Kingdom.

Before describing the work done by the Department of Army Remounts and Horse-breeding as they eventually became, it will be as well to go into the different breeds with which they had to deal.

The Country-bred mare

'The majority of country-bred mares may be said to range in height from 13·2 hands to 14·2 and some few are found as high as 15 hands, and in weight from 6 to 8 cwt (a modern Horse Artillery horse was expected to weigh 10 cwt or over). They are as a rule remarkably well bred, rather light in barrel, not evenly put together, often of an angular and ragged appearance, with small but steel-like bone of joints and limbs, and measuring from $6\frac{1}{4}$ to $7\frac{1}{4}$ inches under the knee at the top of the shank bone. They have wonderful powers of endurance under either tropical sun heat or intense cold, with a light weight, say from 10 to 12 stones in saddle or light draught, and after the hardest day's work are never off their feed but always ready for it; moreover they will continue work on the scantiest of feed.'[14] (Plate 90.) Stallions and geldings ran about the same height and in the early days those measuring 14·2 were considered the best that could be bought for British Cavalry.

Stud-bred Remounts

Varied very much, originally were fit for British Cavalry, but cost too much. Later in the twentieth century stud breds from 15 to 16 hands of excellent quality were produced.

Dekhani

Horses from the Deccan were bought in Hyderabad from early days and were liked for Native Cavalry, as were the Kathiawar and Cutch remounts from the Malabar Coast.

The Kathiawar

Ran from 14 to 15 hands and were brown, bay, grey, piebald and skewbald with some cream. Lady Wentworth, the leading authority, stated that they were also spotted and splashed with white, a coloration which came from the Tanghar ponies of Tibet. They were as a rule hot — 'impetuous' is the word used.

The Marwari

From Rajputana, were about the same height as the last breed described. They were carefully bred and held in great esteem by the Rajputs.

Two other breeds specially mentioned[15] as having been kept pure were the *Baluchi* and the *Unmool*, the latter, bred in the Northern Punjab, having been held

F

in high esteem. The last four breeds were noted as sufficiently established and carefully bred to be able to be used as stallions under the Government Remount breeding scheme of the eighties. In all, thirteen breeds were stated to exist in India.

The imported breeds were as follows:

The Arab

The Kehilan or Thoroughbred, bred in Arabia for, it is stated, over 5,000 years, kept absolutely pure and the pedigrees known and to be trusted. (Plates 83 and 86.) It is well known that from the Arab stallions and mares imported into England during the seventeenth and eighteenth centuries was developed the English Thoroughbred. The latter has inherited from the Arab foundation stock their bravery, their staying power, except in strains developed almost entirely for short distance racing, their paces, their looks and their suitability as sires, but the English Thoroughbred became much faster and bigger than the Arab. Nearly all the breeds of Asia have been successfully crossed with the Arab. In spite of their small size (they seldom stand over 14·2 hands on an average), and the size of British cavalrymen and the weight of even a light field gun, the Arab has carried the one and pulled the other with outstanding success, helped by his pluck and tremendous stamina. For good looks he has no equal, nor has he any for kindness of disposition. His early upbringing, when as a foal he is fed his small ration of barley in the tent of his breeder, frequently makes him a charming companion, a fact which needs no stressing to those who have known and owned him. He is apt to stumble at a walk, probably from boredom; his other paces are perfect. The Arabs expected their ponies to do twenty days fast travelling on eight feeds of barley when raiding an enemy tribe. They would presumably have ridden light, yet the Arab has proved capable of carrying 15 stone and over with apparent ease. So many books have been written and so many proved facts are available that it is unnecessary to say more about him, except that an Arab's bone is of the hardest and his feet, in hot countries, like iron.

The Gulf Arab or Shirazi

Bred on the Persian Gulf, these Arabs are not as highly esteemed by the tribesmen as those bred in the interior. Plate 87 shows a Gulf Arab, who ended his days as a Government Stallion used for getting pack ponies.

The Persian or Persian Arab

Was very highly thought of as a remount both for Artillery and British Cavalry. He has been described as of great beauty and quality, high spirited, speedy and courageous, and as a typical Oriental. In other words, he has the Arab qualities without the pure breeding. Probably fresh Arab blood was constantly being introduced. They stood from 14·2 to 15·2 hands, and in the fifties cost £55 a head (550 rupees) in Bombay. Horses from Afghanistan, including ponies from Herat, are also mentioned among the importations of Remounts. It is not clear what these were, but the breed from beyond Afghanistan, the *Turcoman* horses, once had a very high reputation, both as artillery and cavalry remounts. With Persians and Arabs these horses were used for stud purposes in India with great success.

The Turcoman or Turkestan

Horses known to the Russians as *Argamac* and extensively used by their mounted arms after they got a firm grip on the country in the eighties, have been described as 'the only horses in Asia which come up to our English standards as a horse rather than a pony'. A further quotation[16] states 'the Turcoman horses appear quite thoroughbred and on one occasion General Valentine Baker (who travelled in Turkestan *c.*1873) saw a perfectly thoroughbred dun horse full 17 hands high. These horses always stand in the open air, carefully clothed in thick felt rugs and hoods, the latter so heavy that the manes are worn away and hogged. The horse I brought to England had no mane, but since his arrival it has grown freely. A high-class Turcoman horse is always followed by a pony carrying his heavy clothing'. They average 15 hands and over, some being 16 hands. They were considered to have been bred from the Arab, according to one modern authority, originally crossed with the old Mongolian pony strain, but not very much seems to be known of their origin. The two Plates, 85a and b, show the characteristics of the breed – a straight or a Roman nose, the face not dished like an Arab's, a ewe neck and a tail well set on. They travelled tremendous distances on very little feed and their endurance was very great. They were specially fed and galloped 18 miles a day before a foray. Another reference says their ears are peculiar, small, pointed and turning inwards. In the seventies a high-class Turcoman entire might fetch as much as £400 to £500 sterling. They are said to be as gentle as the Arab and just as courageous, but quieter and more sedate.

Those who remember Kipling's Horse Artillery leader, Snarleyow, in the poem of that name, may be interested in Sir George McMunn's theory[17] that this horse may have been a Turcoman entire.

Their value as Artillery remounts was as great as that of their best entires for breeding Cavalry troop horses.

Non-indigenous Breeds

A few English Thoroughbreds were ridden by senior officers as chargers in the early days; a well-known example being the black ridden by Brigadier General Thomas Pakenham Vandeleur at Laswarree in 1803. Vandeleur was killed on the horse's back and the thoroughbred kept his place at the head of the Brigade. Plate 82 shows a charger of this type. Otherwise the British breeds were imported for stud purposes only, the *Thoroughbred* being the most used at first. Later the *Hackney* and *Norfolk Trotter* were introduced in considerable numbers with success. The most numerous imports were of Australasian horses, known officially as *Walers*, from the Colony of New South Wales, whence most of them came. The thorough-breds from the Colony were also used at stud, but it was as Artillery and Cavalry remounts that the Waler got his most deservedly high reputation.

Before the time of the Waler, *The Cape Horse* had a high reputation in India for all purposes. The discovery of diamonds in South Africa *c.*1871 led to a decline in the export of horses, as the local markets paid very high prices and from the early seventies onwards not many were sent to India.

Both Walers and Cape Horses will be described under their own countries.

Remounts

When the Honourable East India Company found it to be absolutely essential to raise a force of cavalry, in order to be able to make headway against the masses of irregular horsemen which formed part of the armies of the Indian rulers in the territories surrounding their possessions, they were faced with the problem of buying remounts. The Indian irregular light horseman rode very light indeed and the small country-breds served his turn well enough. Indian Cavalry, trained on the European model so as to be able to charge in line, needed the best and strongest troop horses procurable and plenty of them. To think of organizing Horse Artillery was out of the question, at least as late as 1797,[18] and the only alternative – not adopted – was to have the guns bullock-drawn with the horse teams only hooked in for action.

In 1791 Sir Eyre Coote disposed of only 830 sabres belonging to the Nawab of Arcot, with whom he had to face 40,000 horsemen of Hyder Ali's army, who would practically all be available to raid into our territory round Madras. Horses were dear and scarce.

In 1785 four regiments of Indian cavalry were raised in Madras and by 1795 there were the same number in Bengal; there were none in Bombay.[19] At the same time as the Madras regiments were raised a Remount officer, Lieut Colonel D. Campbell, was appointed and opened up a line of supply southward from Madras and another from Hyderabad and the Deccan. A horse market was opened in Madras. Three years before, in 1782, the first British cavalry arrived in Madras, Burgoyne's 23rd Light Dragoons, later better known as the 19th Light Dragoons. By 1789 Campbell had travelled 2,000 miles in 30 months and bought 1,675 horses, and in the same year Colonel Floyd was buying for the British regiment 14·2 hand ponies at double the price Campbell was paying for remounts for Native cavalry. A few Arabs were picked up in Travancore and eagerly accepted. This is an early mention of the Arab being bought for cavalry in India.

From 1787 to 1794 Lieut Torin (afterwards Officer Commanding 1st Madras Light Cavalry) bought horses in Cutch and Kathiawar in conjunction with the Malabar coast purchasing agency.

In 1794 the H.E.I.C. established the Stud Department[20] with a branch in each of the three Presidencies, Bengal, Bombay and Madras. By 1808 only the branch in Bengal remained, the other two not having turned out a satisfactory type of horse.

To return to Madras; there is a good example of the Indian point of view as to what a big officer's charger should look like. Between 1792 and 1796 the champion swordsman in single combat, sword mounted versus sword mounted, was Captain Thomas Dallas, 1st Madras Light Cavalry, well known to our Mysorean enemies. They were accustomed to describe him as 'a gigantic figure on a black horse of enormous size'. Dallas stood 6 feet and his stallion 14·3½ hands! Posted to Hyderabad, he was instrumental in buying 1,474 remounts.

Madras was responsible for two studs in 1795, one in the island of Delft, started by the Portuguese and one at Ganjam on the East Coast. Neither survived long. One of the great difficulties Remount Officers had to contend with was the constant risk of losing shiploads of horses to pirates, who were very active off the coasts of India. A cargo of picked horses was a valuable capture and they were saleable to any Indian ruler at a good price. Shipwreck was another hazard. If cargoes had to be landed on an open beach, such as at Mangalore, the horses were transferred to small Arab dhows, which were capsized in shallow water and the remounts driven ashore. At this date officers on appointment paid 600 rupees for a charger.

In 1799 when Seringapatam was stormed, out of 3,000 captured troop horses, 500 were kept and the remainder handed over to the Hyderabad cavalry, from whom eventually four regiments were formed as part of the H.E.I.C.'s forces. Their country-breds must have had plenty of stamina, for they are credited with marching sixty miles in a night without leaving a horse behind.[21]

Between 1802 and 1806 the Depot at Mangalore issued 3,986 remounts from 2½ to 8 years old and in the following two years a further 2,500.

In 1803 during Wellesley's Assaye campaign he disposed of eight regiments of cavalry, including one British, the 19th Light Dragoons, a total of 1,800 sabres. They were constantly employed and their troop horses ran from 13 to 15 hands in height. The artillery were ox-drawn, there being still no remounts of sufficient size and weight to horse the guns.

The Cavalry Agent in Bengal had purchased, early in 1797, enough remounts 'submitted to and approved by a Committee of Cavalry Officers'[22] to mount the 27th Light Dragoons, when they reached Fort William, Calcutta, in that year. They had to draw another 50 from Native Cavalry and were mounted at Cawnpore. In 1803 during the campaign when the battle of Laswarree was fought, the 8th Light Dragoons, described as 'stout heavy fellows, too much so for Light Dragoons', were mounted on 'beautiful white horses' by the Nabob of Lucknow.[23] Heavy fellows though they were, these country-breds (possibly from Arab stallions) carried them well enough.

In 1810 the future Remount Department was started and took over the purchasing. At this time and up to the Second Afghan War of 1879, the horses from the Deccan had a high reputation, but in 1880 the area was cleaned out even of breeding stock, so great was the wastage in Afghanistan. The breed never recovered.

In 1810 it is not too much to say that the remount position in India took a great step forward. In that year Lieut St. J. Blacker, 1st Madras Light Cavalry, was sent to the Persian Gulf to buy Arabs, described as '14·2 high, short limbed, boney, full chested, broad across the loins, round sided and deep barrelled'.[24] (See Plates Nos. 83, 86, 87.) Up to 1813 he bought 584, of whom 402 were picked for cavalry. The Board that passed them said 'Arab horses appear to be infinitely better calculated for the service than the generality of those procured at Cutch and those which are from 14·1 to 14·2 hands upwards in height are better adapted for heavy weights and to undergo fatigue'. The Governor-in-Council acquiesced. This is believed to be the first occasion on which Arab horses were obtained by organized efforts. Or, it would seem, any imports from other countries.

At about this date the 1st Madras Light Cavalry furnished a return of the best 12 horses in each troop – a total of 72 per regiment – after hard marching for long periods on short rations. Some were only 13·2 hands in height, there were 21 over 14·2 and 51 below. General Sir J. Doveton, an officer of great campaigning experience, preferred the Kathiawar, running from 14·1 to 14·3 hands, as having been justly famed for centuries for speed and stamina. It has already been mentioned that in 1808 of the three Presidency Studs only that in Bengal was left. About that time the H.E.I.C. engaged the services of William Moorcroft, who had been joint head of what is now the Royal College of Veterinary Surgeons, to superintend the stud in Bengal and breeding operations generally. He became, in effect, the first Director of Remount and Veterinary Services in India. At Pusa in Bihar he succeeded in producing a much better stamp of remount than had yet been bred in India. They went in batches to cavalry regiments and each officer was allowed to pick one as a charger at the price of 800 rupees, considered very high indeed.[25]

Moorcroft had been using English and Arab stallions, on what scale is not stated, and considered them unsuitable for breeding remounts from the local mares. He had heard of the Turcoman breeds in Central Asia and went there in 1812 and again in 1819. He made a treaty with the Government of Ladak which threw open the trade of Central Asia into Hindostan. He never returned from beyond the passes and there are various accounts of the manner of his death in about 1825. This is the first mention of the possibility of importing Turcomans into India.

According to General Outram[26] in the 1830's the horses bought at the Cape of Good Hope were superior to the stud-breds (see under South Africa). They were sufficiently well known for the Viceroy of India to present a pair of stallions, Thoroughbreds, to Runjeet Singh, the ruler of the Punjab. Welterweight British officers rode Cape horses and there is no doubt that these had a high and deservedly high reputation at this time and for some long period afterwards. The mounting of the 10th Hussars in 1847 – there was no regiment from whom they could take over horses, as was the rule – gives a fair picture of the remount at this time[27] and gives us a definite line on the types on issue. Remounts came in slowly; there were none to be had in Bombay, it being August, as Arabs, at that time the majority of those bought in this place, did not usually arrive until October. The supply of Cape horses was exhausted and it was not until the middle of March that the first batch of remounts arrived at Kirkee, where the Regiment was stationed. The intake consisted of 150 Arabs and Persians, some purebred, some halfbred, of both types and 50 Cape horses. Nearly all the Arabs were entires, always a nuisance on horse lines and in stables, as they fight so much, but though the men at first preferred the larger Cape horses, which would have averaged about 15 hands, they soon became well satisfied with the Arabs.

From 1850 an officer of the Indian Army, Captain Apperly, was posted to New South Wales, in Australia; he bought Walers up to £20 a head, had them broken and shipped them to India. He was not replaced after the Indian Mutiny. In 1851 Nolan (see under Saddles), who was in India with the 15th Hussars, wrote that 'the Arabs, Turcomans and Persians were unrivalled'. He had an excellent working acquaintance with British, Hungarian and Austrian remounts before he made this statement. In the following year, when the Punjab Frontier Force Cavalry was in process of being raised and mounted regimentally, as were all the Indian Cavalry except the Madras regiments, on what was known as the Silladar system, their Commanding Officers were buying remounts in Afghanistan and Persia, at an average price of £25. Most of them showed Arab blood.

Two English regiments, the 12th Lancers and the 10th Hussars, took horses to the Crimea from India in 1855. The 12th had Arab geldings, greys, described as 'quiet, useful little animals' and the 10th mostly Arab stallions. Both regiments considered their troop horses a great success.

The Mutiny of 1857–8 imposed a heavy strain on the remount system. The Cape sent as many as could be bought. Hayes[28] says that the better-class Arabs and Persians were excellent and 'pulled guns and carried British cavalry successfully'. When the 17th Lancers arrived at Kirkee in December 1857, they found all sorts of remounts arriving slowly in batches. They included Arab stallions, a few Cape mares, a collection of 'long-tailed nondescripts', and some Australian Walers. This is an early note on the issue of Walers in India[29] to British Cavalry.

Sir John Fortescue, in his account of the campaigns in Central India, describes the work as endless pursuits of fugitive columns of mutineers who needed forces of all arms to deal with them. The marching was severe and the evidence shows that while the Cape and Australian horses could not stand the strain, the Arabs kept going. Though they sometimes showed leg-weariness, they were never off their feed.[30]

The newly raised Indian Cavalry regiments mounted themselves as best they could, men enlisted bringing country-breds or any other horse they could lay their hands on. Contemporary sketches done in the field, notably those by Colonel Hope Crealock,[31] show a preponderance of Arab type, various sorts of ponies ridden by junior Staff Officers and in the case of senior officers nearly always Arabs, as had been the case from at least the forties. Several of the very senior officers took a favourite Arab home with them and kept him till he died or had to be put down.

The 9th Lancers rode Arabs throughout (see Plate 83), and in 1860 handed over a hundred of them to Probyn's Horse,[32] one of the regiments raised in 1857. In 1864 this regiment started a stud farm in the Punjab, christened Probynabad, where remounts were to be bred for the regiment. The first stallions used were all Arabs and the first foal was dropped in August 1865. Two stud-bred stallions were bought next and in 1878 the Remount Department lent the stud a Thoroughbred. In 1880 a Turcoman stallion was presented to the regiment. Russian influence in Turkestan was already making itself felt and in a short time they were to control and monopolize the export of these famous horses, which they used for their own artillery. Originally presented to the Ameer of Afghanistan by the Khan of Bokhara, this stallion came to the regiment by devious ways. He was a great success at stud and his stock, especially from the first cross with Thoroughbreds, were described as 'magnificent'. Successful as the stud undoubtedly was in breeding remounts, by 1913 it was not supplying the whole of the regiment with the amount of horses required annually and the cost must have been considerable. As will appear, in India at any rate, there was little difference between small studs like this and the big Government studs when it came to producing quantity as well as quality. Later on the Government partially solved the problem.

In 1876 the Stud Department, which in Bengal had succeeded in supplying 'both Cavalry and Artillery with a remarkably fine class of stud-bred remounts for many years', and had 'accomplished a certain measure of success' but at a cost out of proportion to the results, was abolished.[33] Before dealing with the Departments it will be as well to see what the requirements of the Army of India, which since the Mutiny were all directly under the Crown and reorganized in 1861, really were.

The total quantity of remounts required annually for Horse and Field Artillery, British and Native Cavalry was 4,630, including a reserve of 1,000. This excludes the Indian regiments raised on the Silladar system, who found themselves in horses and all equipment, except firearms and ammunition, until 1921.

A Government Notice dated 15th February, 1881,[34] gives details of the various classes, etc. required. It runs as follows: 'With reference to the advertisement of the 3rd March, 1880 – It is hereby notified that the Government of India are prepared to purchase about nine hundred (900) horses suitable for Army purposes during the year 1881–2, classed as follows:

Class I – Walers		771
Medium Cavalry and Hussars	246	
Field Artillery	253	
Horse Artillery	272	
Class II – Countrybreds		69

As many as possible full-grown horses; the remainder young stock between $2\frac{1}{2}$ and $3\frac{1}{2}$ years old.

Class III – Persians and Arabs		60
Medium Cavalry and Hussars	40	
Field Artillery	20	
Horse Artillery	—	
Total		900

'The purchases will be made by remount agents at the stations Calcutta, Bombay, Allahabad, Cawnpore, Lucknow, Agra, Morar, Meerut, Bareilly, Umballa, Lahore, Mooltan, Sialkot, Rawal Pindi and Peshawar.

'Except under special circumstances, purchases will be made in Calcutta only between the 15th September and 28th February.

'Horses and mares of all breeds will be received, but they must be within the prescribed ages, 4 to 7 years, except as regards country-breds. It is to be distinctly understood that in regard to classes I and III remounts 3 years old and mares in foal will not be purchased.

'After the expiration of three (3) years from the 1st June, 1879, greys will not be purchased for Horse or Field Artillery.

'The average price of a remount has been fixed at Rupees 550 (Rs 550). Every horse presented for purchase will be valued separately and higher or lower prices may be given, provided that the averages of the purchases does not exceed that limit.'

This notice was issued not long after the close of the Second Afghan War and shows the very strong trend towards the Waler. No doubt the country had been scoured for remounts of any kind, for the wastage in Afghanistan had been heavy,[35] also no horses were available from South Africa, but the swing over to the Australian horse market is none the less remarkable, and continued. Since the start of the Mutiny, British medium cavalry regiments, as well as Lancers, who had served in India for some time, had been taking turns of duty there, and the Waler had been found fully as suitable for them as for Hussars, the light cavalry of the British Army. The Heavies did not yet serve in India, and were not to do so until many years later. Persians and Arabs were no longer bought for Horse Artillery; and it is possible that Australia may have been sending over a type of horse suitable for the R.H.A. Various photographs show Artillery with all-white or grey teams in 1880, though it is obvious that in the days when the limbers might be exposed to direct fire even a pair of greys would provide a good aiming mark for the enemy. The old soldier's saying 'never stop near a white stone, an officer, or a white horse if you can help it' has a great deal to commend it. But in a country that once produced so many greys as India, it was difficult for Remounts to avoid buying them. In the above notice a definite term is put to the practice as far as both types of Artillery are concerned.

To return to the reorganization of the Remount Department in 1876; as already mentioned, the new organization consisted of two separate Departments,

'Army Remounts' and 'Horse Breeding Operations'. The Department of Army Remounts was concerned with the selection and purchase of Australian and Persian horses in the local markets and of as many suitable country-breds as might be procurable.

The term 'country-bred' seems to have been very elastic. Thus in 1879 a Gunner subaltern[36] bought 'the second best country-bred in India, stud-bred and very nearly thoroughbred, who won races and was a first-class pigsticker'. This was the class of remount that the organization of 1876 was not anxious to produce in large numbers, as it was found in India that a tendency to breed for speed was not in line with Service requirements! The Department of Horse Breeding Operations was subordinated to that of Army Remounts, not always with the best results.

The Remount Department's business was the immediate supply of remounts to the army, and it was natural that they should buy as cheaply as they could; the Horse Breeding Department had in view the general improvement of the horse population with a view to producing suitable remounts on what may be called a long-term policy. The two Departments thus worked on widely different lines and the chances given the breeder of selling quickly militated against his keeping suitable mares for breeding.

The Breeding Department instituted what was called the 'Diffused System'. Three hundred stallions were bought in 1876, the purpose being to gain greater size *and power* in the produce of country-bred mares. By 1886 the Indian Stud was composed of 90 English Thoroughbreds, 159 Hackneys and Norfolk Trotters, 146 Arabs, 10 Stud-bred horses, 6 Australian Thoroughbreds, 2 Turcoman stallions and 1 Persian. The Hackneys and Trotters, following on the French ideas, were presumably to breed Field Artillery remounts and the class known as Light Vanners. The arguments between the two schools of experts, those who preferred the Thoroughbred cross, and those who wanted something with more substance, went on continuously. The one school wanted to grade up with Hackneys and Trotters and put the progeny to the Thoroughbred, the other preferred to have as many first-cross foals from the racehorse as possible. It may be said at once that the figures showing the Percentage of Prizes won by each Class according to the number of Stallions employed,[37] dealing with the years 1886 to 1892, show the Hackney sires as coming out easily first, the Australians second and the English third. One difficulty was that the 300 stallions were scattered all over the horse-breeding districts in charge of natives, and though they were only supposed to serve carefully selected and branded mares, the temptation to oblige the owners of other mares was a serious one.

Meanwhile the Waler continued to be imported in very considerable numbers – the average for ten years, 1890 to 1900, being 1,625. The artillery were almost entirely horsed with Walers and a few country-breds.

In Stewart's *History of the XIIth Royal Lancers* is an account[38] of what the Waler could do in the way of marching under conditions of extreme heat. The feed issued was bran and maize (or Indian corn) with hay. Maize is not a good feed for horses doing fast work, it is fattening and apt to affect the feet. The regiment was mounted mostly on Walers, with one Persian and at least one of the officers rode an Arab. In drill order the 12th marched from Bangalore to Mysore and back next day. Only one horse fell out, the distance covered being 171 miles in 51 hours. The weight on the horses was, of course, considerably reduced by the men not being in marching order. This test was neither meant to be nor to be taken as a serious one. The fact that it was held does, however, go to prove that the Waler had moved up into first place as a remount for medium cavalry. That Australasian horses, transported to India, ever had the stamina and toughness of the Arabs whom they replaced is beside the point. The Arab would and did live and work on the sooty thatch pulled off the roofs of native huts on the N.W. Frontier,[39] but he lacked the weight-carrying capacity, the stride, and the height that made the Waler so suitable for cavalry work as it was before the days of smokeless powder. Also, though from the official point of view it was of no account, the Arab was gradually being replaced on the polo ground by bigger, faster ponies. This is not meant to infer that polo had the same effect on breeding in India as hunting had in Great Britain, but to quote the opinion of experts[40] 'the temptation to produce a racing or polo pony in Northern India is a factor which must be reckoned with'. Englishmen will always pay for their sport and it did not take the native breeders long to discover this fundamental fact. The result was that under the Diffused System a breeder with a certain number of branded mares, eligible for free services from the Government stallions (there were nearly 20,000 of these mares), tended to send their mares to a Thoroughbred, whether or not the Horse Breeding Department considered them as more suitable for crossing with a Hackney, for instance. If the result was a leggy, well-bred looking colt, he might race! If he was the right size for polo he might also fetch more than the price of a remount!

However, just as the old Bengal Stud had turned out a number of many useful remounts for both cavalry and artillery, so the Diffused System did the same. But in neither case were the results commensurate with the expense, and the aim and object of the studs, which was to build up a national Indian breed of horses, was far from being achieved.

In 1900 a Commission was appointed to go into the whole question. Their main recommendations were that more supervision and method were needed, especially in order to prevent stallions being sent to districts where there were not enough suitable country-breds to be served. They also objected to the way in which no proper care was exercised in seeing whether or not a mare was likely to nick well with a stallion of a certain breed. In future the efforts of the Breeding Department were directed to be concentrated as far as possible on the Kathiawar, Marwar, Baluchistan and the Northern Punjab breeds, and that the best stallions from these types should be bought by Government. Later on the Arab was used at the Studs to breed pack ponies, which were coming more and more in demand.

The Commission, which sat into 1901, inspected a very large number of horses and mules, and took evidence on a very wide scale.

Since 1881 the Remounts Department had been buying a certain number of young horses and running them at various Depots; from 1889 the number bought was 1,000 a year with a minimum age of 6 months. This policy was also approved. It is obviously impossible to pass any sort of balanced judgement on a horse-breeding scheme until it has been operating for a considerable number of years. A remount is of no value in the ranks under five years old, and young horses who have not been well fed as yearlings often develop slowly and are not fit to stand severe work before they are six. So evidence as to the success of a particular cross may take a long time to collect.

As regards the methods instituted by the Commission, we are fortunate in having the following conclusions drawn by an officer of great experience both of Indian conditions and of horses generally. The late Major General Sir George McMunn, in an article published in 1934 on 'Soldiering in India Today',[41] had this to say:

'Scientific horse-breeding on a scheme which has not been tinkered with has been in progress since 1900 and horses three parts English or three parts Arab can be obtained at any height from 15 to 16 hands. These are really high-grade horses and turn out very successfully.'

Further on in the same article Sir George says: 'the small Waler issued to Indian Cavalry often makes an excellent polo pony!'

The only comment which seems necessary is to point out the excellent showing made by Indian Cavalry, especially in Palestine in 1918, mounted on many of these stud-breds.

THE CAPE HORSE

The above was the name commonly used to describe the horse or pony bred in most of the territory of the present-day South African Republic and in the High Commission Territory of Basutoland, still under the Union Jack. Carelessly as horse breeding has been carried on in the past in the latter country, the Basuto have, with a considerable amount of help from the British officials, evolved a type of pony which still has a deservedly high reputation.

The Cape horse has had many ups and downs. Horse sickness, a virulent and in the old days almost always fatal disease, used to make breeding anything but easy, and excessive drains on the horse population have also taken heavy toll. Horses were not indigenous to South Africa and from 1653 to 1796, when the Cape of Good Hope was first captured by the British, the Cape horse was largely of Arab and Eastern origin. At least one shipload of horses *en route* from Spain to South America was captured and taken into Cape Town, ponies were brought from Batavia, an important Dutch possession, and by 1769 Cape horses were being exported to India as remounts. They are described as being 'plentiful but not very handsome'.[42] By 1796 'a fairly good saddle or harness horse' was common,[43] the average price being £8 or £9 apiece. The 8th Light Dragoons, who served during the Third Kaffir War of 1799–1802, seem to have been well mounted.

In 1806 the future General Sir Robert Wilson, at that time serving in the 20th Light Dragoons, did not consider the Cape horse generally as of good quality, though he was very pleased with a Troop of his Regiment, who were mounted on roans 'of great beauty'.[44] These would have been requisitioned from the townspeople and valued by a Board, which put the high price of £26 a head on them. The roan or skimmel (in Afrikaans) colour has always been very much liked at the Cape and is believed to have come from some of the Spanish blood. In 1807 'some Spanish breeding horses and mares captured and landed at Cape Town were blue roans and red roans of medium height, broad chested and possessing great powers of endurance'.[45] For many years very few South Africans rode mares, so the latter were always bred from as much as possible. In 1811 the English Thoroughbred began to be imported in considerable numbers and their progeny from the Eastern blood already in the country soon produced an excellent type of ride and drive animal, eminently suited for light cavalry remounts, but rather on the light side for artillery, so that teams of eight were often used for even as light guns as 6-pounders.

From 1817 to 1870 the only mounted corps stationed permanently at the Cape was a local regiment, the Cape Corps, from 1827 the Cape Mounted Riflemen.[46] During this period only two cavalry regiments, the 7th Dragoon Guards from 1843 to 1848, and the 12th Lancers, from 1851 to 1853, served at the Cape. Both were well mounted, though the big Dragoon Guards troopers looked underhorsed on the 15-hand Cape remounts. Their performance under the heavy weight they had to carry was, however, outstanding, and, as one of the few cavalry charges ever delivered in South Africa proved,[47] there was no doubt as to the quality of the South African horse and his ability as a troop horse.

Colonel Valentine Baker, so often mentioned in this book,[48] served as a subaltern in the 12th Lancers in the Kaffir War of 1850–52. He rode a Cape horse, took him to India, to the Crimea and finally to England. He wrote of the breed as follows: 'the Cape horse is, in my opinion, the beau idéal of a light cavalry horse; strong, compact, hardy and temperate and bearing the change to any climate without deteriorating. He is a small, coarse-looking cross-made animal, but wonderfully hardy and enduring.' This was written after Baker had collected experiences of many types of remount in the countries mentioned.

The Cape Mounted Riflemen, small-boned coloured men, weighing considerably less than any British cavalrymen, were admirably suited with remounts bred in the North of the Cape Colony in the Colesberg District. Many were branded with the initials of one of the biggest breeders, and had over 14 years service before being cast. They cost £25 apiece and were seldom over 14·2 hands, were rather low in the shoulder and had drooping quarters. They were described as capable of undergoing great fatigue.[49] General Brabant (1839–1914), of the Cape Regular Forces called them 'the best military animal in the world'. He also stated that in spite of the men being light-weights, they rode from 20 to 22 stone in marching order with rations and forage!

From the eighteen-thirties onwards the exports of remounts to India continued and in 1857–8 during the Indian Mutiny, the Cape Mounted Riflemen were almost all employed in collecting remounts and delivering them at the ports for shipment. The standard was rising, for in 1859 the Madras Horse Artillery had 'several teams of Cape horses, hardy and enduring', and up to 1866 the best batteries in Scinde were horsed from the Cape.[50]

There followed a bad horse sickness year and, as already noted, in the early seventies the discovery of diamonds led to the absorption of any horse that could be made to go in harness for the transportation of men and women to Kimberley, where the main finds had been made. The demand for horseflesh continued to rise and was met at the cost of seriously reducing the standard. From 1878 the supply of horses had increased sufficiently to furnish some remounts for the series of small wars which took place from 1877 to 1881.

The following is a contemporary description of the situation in South Africa in August, 1878.[51] 'Having been at H.Q., which is at Kingwilliamstown, during most of the campaign (against the Coast Kaffirs) which has now come to an end, I have had opportunities of seeing some thousands of horses sent down for remount purposes for artillery, mounted infantry and volunteers. The neighbourhood of King-williamstown is not a horse-producing country, so most of the remounts were bought between the North of the Colony and the Orange Free State (then a Republic). Mounted Infantry and Volunteer horses were purchased at a price up to £25, but £21 was the average. They were all ponies, from 13·2 to 14 hands, capable of doing hard work on very little food in all kinds of climate. This class of horse would be quite unfit to carry the men of an English cavalry regiment, as they could neither carry the weight of a man in marching order nor move at the pace required.' (Plates 97 and 14.) This report goes on to say that a 15-hand horse was a rarity and that it was thought impossible to horse a battery of Royal Artillery. Actually the officer charged with mounting a newly arrived battery collected a useful lot of horses, all over 15 hands, at an average price of £25, although he had to cover a large stretch of country in the process. It was considered quite impossible to collect 5,000 or 6,000 artillery and cavalry remounts as had been done in 1857–8, largely because the average horse breeder took no trouble at all in mating suitable stallions with his mares.

A year after this was written 1,800 English remounts were sent to Natal during the Zulu War. Between 1879 and 1884 four regiments came from England, all bringing horses, and three from India, of whom one came mounted, one brought no remounts and one is uncertain. All the Royal Artillery Batteries brought their own horses.[52] (Plate 30.)

The deterioration in the type of horse to be bought in South Africa as a possible remount shows up plainly enough. Gone were the heavy-weight officers' chargers and the Horse Artillery teams that had done such good work in India. But when Cecil Rhodes was preparing to move his Pioneer Column into what became Rhodesia, he turned to a hitherto untapped source of mounted infantry remounts, the Basuto pony. Bred under the hardest of conditions in a mountainous country

60

about the size of Belgium, originally from horses of Arab stock, stolen or bought in the Cape Colony, from the sixties onwards the Basuto pony received a strong infusion of Thoroughbred blood from some of the best sires imported into South Africa. By 1881 they were becoming well known as a very hardy, stocky type of 13·2 to 14·2 hands riding pony, up to a surprising amount of weight, sure-footed and able to exist on very short rations. In 1890 some 200 were bought in Basutoland for Rhodes's Pioneers[53] and Major General the Hon. Paul Methuen (later Field Marshal Lord Methuen) who was sent by Lord Loch, High Commissioner at the Cape, to inspect them, reported as follows: 'The horses obtained for the Pioneer Column were the best working stamp of horse that has probably ever been got together for military work in South Africa'. He had commanded a regiment of Irregular Horse in 1885 (see Plate 14), and so had plenty of experience to draw on. (Basuto Pony: see Plate 96).

Here is the other side of the picture; in 1891 and 1892 Captain M. H. Hayes, who was collecting material for his book on *The Horse*, worked in South Africa and in a series of lectures delivered at Aldershot gave his opinion on the remount situation there as he found it. The lecture was printed at Aldershot under the title of 'The Horse for Military Purposes'. He was of the opinion that horse breeding in South Africa was in a state of neglect and that in consequence not even remounts for Indian Cavalry could be found there. The 11th Hussars, who arrived from India in 1890 without horses, and were the only cavalry in the country, found that in Natal they could not obtain sufficient remounts at £40 each. It was not difficult in Natal to draw on the Orange Free State, where horses should have been plentiful, but the Commanding Officer's report on the horses he received was to the effect that they were altogether too slow for the normal rate of manoeuvring at a fast pace. Four more regiments came from India to Natal between 1895 and 1898 and three of them brought horses with them. In 1898 remounts were imported from the Argentine and were a success. This was the position immediately before the South African War of 1899–1902. Plate 98 shows an Argentine remount.

That war has been dealt with at some length in the section on remounts from Great Britain and there is no doubt that *under the conditions normally prevalent in South Africa*, where there is a drought in some large areas every two-and-a-half years,[54] Lord Methuen's liking for the local breeds was much sounder than Captain Hayes's summing up from the point of view of cavalry working on the lines in use by continental armies, including our own.

Plates Nos. 14 and 97 show South African ponies; the one showing two Transvaal Police, serving on the Swaziland border, is the most typical of all. In a lecture given shortly after the War, in 1904, by General Rimington, 6th Inniskilling Dragoons, who had a long and extensive acquaintance with British, Argentine and South African horseflesh, he had this to say of the latter type.[55]

'At the beginning of the War I calculate there were about 70,000 mounted Boers in the field, who averaged three horses each. These horses were more useful than any imported horses, however good, for enduring the fatigues of a campaign in South Africa. They had each about three riding horses – that makes up 210,000 horses – so that I think I may fairly say that we were unprepared and mistaken in our estimate of there being no horses in South Africa. Certainly, towards the end of the war, everyone who could get a Colonial pony rode it in preference to any other.' He also notes that we spent one tenth of the cost of the War on horseflesh, the total amount being twenty-two millions for remounts and presumably mules also. On returning to the Cape horse the General brings out the salient points of the breed: 'they are the survival of the fittest, for often a foal has to travel long distances when only a few days old. If the foal cannot keep up he dies. Those who survive have to put up with great changes of temperature, and winter feed of any quality was often not available for the mares and young stock. There are practically no diseases in the country that affect the wind; if a young horse has not learnt to avoid holes, of which there are plenty and to spare, he is schooled or lunged on ground full of them. With a certain amount of grazing and up to 10 lb of grain a day he will work hard with very little rest and keep fit.' General Rimington ends with a saying common in Ireland when describing a good tough sort of horse – 'You could not kill him with a hatchet'.

Valentine Baker's remarks quoted earlier refer. He would surely have agreed with every word of Rimington's lecture.

In the schedule of the number of horses bought in various countries the total of 'Cape Horses' is given at 160,000. This does not include very large numbers captured either direct from the enemy or rounded up on the farms. The fact is that South Africa was normally in those days a valuable reservoir of Mounted Riflemen or Mounted Infantry remounts; although the wastage was so great that in the four years following the end of the War in 1902 there was a serious shortage of remounts bred in the country fit for service. During those years, and for the succeeding period to 1914, large numbers of very suitable thoroughbred stallions and a smaller number of Arabs from the Crabbet Park Stud were imported from Great Britain, and by 1914 the country was well stocked with an excellent type of remount, mostly under 15 hands and showing a considerable amount of breeding.

At the start of the First World War in August, 1914, the newly created South African Defence Force had on mobilization an establishment of 8,000 horses and mules; this had increased to 160,000 by January, 1916, after sixteen months during which two campaigns, both local, had been successfully concluded. The first, in which 30,000 men, mostly mounted, were engaged, dealt with an internal insurrection which, with German assistance from South West Africa, aimed at the overthrow of the pro-British South African Government and the establishment of an independent state. The marching was severe and in about six weeks, the duration of hostilities, the horses of both sides were practically unfit for further work, a veterinary report on one brigade of three regiments showing only 14 per cent as fit. Losses had been small and two months rest on good grazing set the bulk of the troop horses on their feet again.[56]

A campaign against the German Colony in South West Africa had been in progress for some time and by March, 1915, the General Officer Commanding and Prime Minister of the Union, General Botha, had about 50,000 men under arms on German Territory, of whom the main part were mounted. In the earlier stages of the campaign marches were long and feed not plentiful. There were outbreaks of epizootics, including glanders and mange, but remounts were plentiful. In the final advance to the north of the territory, which ended with the surrender of the entire German force on 9th July, the marches from waterhole to waterhole were necessarily long, but transport and supply were admirably conducted and the horses stood up extremely well with hardly any losses.

The losses in the whole of the Defence Force from August, 1914 to January, 1916, were 8·12 per cent or 5·72 per cent per annum. Little enough, considering the distances covered.

In 1916 the Union of South Africa sent two Divisions of all arms to the campaign in progress for the capture of the German Colony in East Africa, later known as Tanganyika. Conditions in this tropical country told severely against both horses and mules and the ten Regiments of Mounted Rifles from South Africa suffered appalling losses in horseflesh. The sickness among the men was also very serious.

In all, 22,655 horses and mules were shipped from South Africa to East Africa. The losses to October 1916, that is, in ten months, were staggering and amounted to a mortality of about 98 per cent.

Of 31,000 horses there remained 827 at the end of the year.
Of 33,000 mules there remained 879 at the end of the year.
Of 24,000 donkeys there remained 1,402 at the end of the year.

Deaths were chiefly due to trypanosomiasis and horse sickness.[57]

It has been said of this campaign that 'there is no parallel instance of such colossal wastage of animals in any campaign'.[58] Whether this is correct or not, it is obvious that losses could not mount much higher.

In the Second World War the Defence Force was undecided as to the policy to be carried out as regards mounted troops. In June, 1940, the purchase of animals was commenced and by October 5,591 horses and 2,279 mules had been bought. Later, in 1944, equines to the number of 15,762 were bought for the Indian Government. From 1942 to 1945 the Indian Army took 22,016 mules.[59]

Recruiting for the Commandos, for which the South African authorities had bought the horses mentioned above, was quite good and although they never left the Union, but were dismounted, broken up, and transferred to other units, the policy probably netted a number of badly needed men, who might otherwise not have volunteered.

It is only fair to say that the South African horsebreeder has taken his share in breeding remounts for the British Army as well as for the forces of his own country.

AUSTRALASIA

It is natural that any country which has bred horses fit for remounts should at one time or another have put forward the claim that their cavalry and horse artillery are the best horsed for war conditions of any. The evidence does not usually go beyond campaigns carried on in country similar to that in which the horses were bred, though in the case of the British Army this is not so. In fact this book deals largely with the performance of remounts bred in the British Commonwealth and shipped to many and various parts of the world for war service. So far we have dealt with the claims of the Arab, supported by the strongest evidence, and with a claim on behalf of the Cape horse during a short period, quite well authenticated. We now come to the rather conflicting claims of the Waler, a name used roughly for all horses bred in Australia and New Zealand.

There can be little doubt not only that the Arab, in spite of his lack of size, has been pre-eminent over the centuries, not only as a light cavalry charger, but also in transmitting to both the breeds mentioned most of their best qualities, and though both owed a very great deal to the English Thoroughbred, he again owed his place to his forbear, the Arab.

The principal horse-breeding colonies of Australia and New Zealand were New South Wales, from which the name Waler comes, Queensland, Victoria and Southern Australia. The sires used were to a great extent thoroughbred and in the section on Remounts in India we have already seen how dependent the Indian Government was on Australia for mounting artillery and cavalry, both British and Indian. In fact, in the seventies and eighties the Waler was the most important remount in India. Writing in 1892 Captain Hayes[60] sums up as follows: 'Australasian horses are eminently fitted for Army Service'. By the time of the South African War of 1899 artillery in India were almost entirely horsed from Australia and the Waler's name stood high as a remount.

The original Walers which the first Australian contingents brought over to South Africa in 1900 were very well reported on, but the later importations were not satisfactory. The Waler was mainly grass or hay-fed in his own country and the bigger type did not do well on the short rations available in South Africa.[61] A report by the Assistant Inspector of Remounts in South Africa describes the type sent to that country as 'light on the leg, ewe-necked and angular. Has undeniable quality and was expected to prove hardy, wiry and untiring. This type has not done well in South Africa.' The small cobs, known in Australia as 'nuggets', were excellent, but the larger type both from New Zealand and Australia lacked recuperative powers, though another report spoke well of them.[62] This report has a description of the small Waler, written before the South African War, which leaves no doubt how useful he was. 'The "nugget" was a "big little" animal, a symmetrical, typical English three-quarter-bred hunter of 16 hands to 16·2, focused into a height of 13·2 or 13·3 hands with slightly lower withers. These horses have combined stamina, courage and speed; their paces, when on a long ride, are a jog and a canter. They are in Australian parlance "cut-and-come-again" customers. The smartest stock horses, those in use for drafting cattle, are also small and handy and well up to twelve stone.' Plates 91 and 92 refer, though the New Zealand horse shown is not typical of the normal run of well-bred stock horses in that country.

Besides supplying horses for their own contingents, for the Imperial Government and a few for the Imperial Yeomanry, who had their own buyers, Australia also supplied a small number of artillery and mounted infantry horses at £30 and £12, respectively, for the British Force operating in China in 1900. A new complication arose in connection with this campaign, for the German Army sent buyers to Australia for horses to mount their troops in China. However, the number was too small to affect prices as might well have been the case.[63]

Although on the whole the evidence on the Waler in the South African War is conflicting, diaries and private letters which appeared in book form or in the Press show a definite liking for the Waler, always the smaller type, as a troop horse, especially for Mounted Infantry.

During the First World War 28,000 horses were shipped from Australia and New Zealand to France and Egypt, and the Government of India also bought in Australasia on behalf of the British Government. When the bulk of the Australian and New Zealand forces were transferred to Europe the Imperial Government took over the supply of horses.[64] In all about 5,000 Walers were landed in France. The last horses shipped to Egypt from Australia arrived in May or June 1917, and though a further 8,000 were bought in Australia, they had to be kept there for want of shipping.[65]

In the section on British-bred Remounts very considerable use was made of the evidence contained in Lieut Colonel Preston's book *The Desert Mounted Corps*, which describes in detail the campaigns which resulted in the capture of Palestine in 1917–18. The author took the greatest interest in the whole question of remounts, cavalry, artillery and transport, and especially in the Walers who formed the majority of the horses in the Desert Corps. He stated categorically that these hardy Australian remounts made the finest cavalry mounts in the world and produced a quantity of evidence in support of his contention.

It appears that for many years the Australians had been buying up the well-bred failures on the English Turf. Colonel Preston does not give any date, but it is known to the author of this book that this policy had already begun by 1898, on what scale is uncertain. These sires were bought cheap and were intended to breed saddle horses for the up-country stations, where the stockmen required a small number of fast, useful horses for each man. The writings of the late Will Ogilvie, an expert in horse-flesh with a very great liking for the Waler, leave no doubt of the quality of these horses between the two great wars, or of their habit of bucking! In 1914, when there was talk of our cavalry breaking the German lines, Will Ogilvie wrote the following: 'And first of them all, before night, shall the Waler, with foam on his Muzzle, Drink deep of the Rhine'.

The up-country breeders were not primarily interested in breeding race horses; what they wished to produce in numbers were not only saddle horses, but compact harness horses from the same sires. The foundation stock of mares was good and tough, and in Colonel Preston's opinion no other part of the world could show as good a type of all-round purpose remounts. The Australasians had no liking at all for the weight-carrying English hunter class of cavalry trooper, which they thought looked like a cart horse! The result of their ideas was a compact animal, rather on the light side according to English ideas, in other words 'a little horse' (Preston), hard as nails, with beautifully clean legs and feet who proved successfully the old saying 'an ounce of blood is worth a pound of bone'! The average Australian weighed about 12 stone, making a weight on the horse in marching order of about 21 stone.

The Australian cavalry draught horse ran from 15 hands to 15·2 in height, was short backed, well coupled and showing breeding. They did admirable work in Palestine, both as artillery horses and transport animals.

The great point of the Australasian horses as remounts was their ability to do the hardest work on less than half rations of feed and to recover their fitness with amazing rapidity, when given a short rest on full feeds and plenty of water. With these qualities the Waler also showed himself fully capable of charging with great speed and dash at the end of a long trek, and when the Australians were issued with swords their horses gave them plenty of opportunities for making use of them.[66]

A pleasing sidelight on the Australians and New Zealanders comes from Colonel Preston, where he says that 'they have the same almost instinctive love of horses as the Irish'.

CANADA

During the first half of the nineteenth century cavalry regiments proceeding to Canada took their own horses from Great Britain and in some cases brought them back at the end of their tour of duty. The sea voyage being comparatively short allows of horses being shipped without undue loss of condition and since the introduction of steam there have always been very considerable imports of excellent draught horses to this country from Canada.

A large proportion of these light draught horses were bought by the big omnibus companies, especially in London, and were very successful. It was largely these 'bus' horses that pulled the guns of the Royal Artillery in the South African War of 1899–1902 doing 40 miles a day on short rations. There is a considerable proportion of trotting blood in most Canadian horses and they were at that time usually rather long in the back.[67]

The remounts brought over by the Canadian Contingents during this war were a very good type of saddle horse, hardy and thrifty, and the interest taken in Canada as a possibly continuous source of supply, especially in the event of war, was reflected in the minutes of the Report of the Committee on Remounts which took evidence in 1902.[68] The Hon. Sydney A. Fisher, Minister of Agriculture in the Canadian Government, had been instrumental in drawing up a Report to the Imperial Government as to the possibility of a purchasing scheme for remounts for the British Army being set up on a permanent basis, and gave evidence at some length before the Committee. Mr Fisher explained that the Canadian, generally speaking, 'was not a riding man and so there were not a great many horses in the country broken to the saddle. There were, however, plenty of unbroken horses fit for the saddle and in a few months 25,000 to 30,000 could be procured.' At that time Canada was exporting to Great Britain 15,000 to 16,000 horses a year, mainly 'bus and van horses, and included were a number of carriage and saddle horses. A draught horse in working condition 5 to 6 years old, weighing about 1,300 lb, 15.3 to 16 hands in height, could be delivered at the ship for £30. The only large breeding studs were in the west, on some of the big ranches, and on one of these Thoroughbred stallions had been in use. In the west many more people rode than in the east, but that does not detract from Mr Fisher's evidence as given above.

The Remount Commission which bought horses in Canada secured 14,600 horses in 1900, 1901 and 1902, there being something like a million light-bred horses in the country. The reason that so few were bought was partly because there were not enough broken horses and partly because of the comparative scarcity of sufficiently well-bred horses of saddle type. As regards the remounts sent to South Africa they were an unqualified success, and as a general rule they were preferred to horses from the United States. This was also the case in the States, where it was well known that a horse with a Canadian brand sold better than the local product.[69]

Unfortunately, the official publications[70] do not give separate figures for Canada and the United States of the remounts shipped to Great Britain by the Purchasing Commission sent to Canada in 1914 and operating there until the end of the First World War. Canada supplied no mules and the total of horses was 428,608 from the two countries.

In January 1915, the Imperial Government took over the supply of horses for the Canadian Contingents in Europe. The Canadian Light Draught horses were again very much liked, those with a Percheron strain being especially commented on. They were, as a rule, tractable and easy to handle and break.

It has been found impracticable to deal with the Canadian remount contribution to the First World War separately, so mixed is it with the North American effort and especially with the remounts bought in the United States. The simplest solution arrived at was to treat the whole question under the heading of the following section devoted to the United States of America. All that is written in that section on the period 1914 to 1918 should be read as referring generally to Canada as well.

UNITED STATES OF AMERICA TO 1914

To be strictly accurate this section starts with a brief account of the horses to be found in the country before the Declaration of Independence in 1776. Practice in North America had naturally been the same as in England, a typical import having been an English Thoroughbred, Janus, who stood at stud in Virginia and North Carolina between 1756 and 1780. Races were of great length in those days and Janus could get four miles. He was 14.2 hands in height, a fair aggregate in those days. His stock all turned out to be sprinters. Earlier saddle horses of various breeds, English (not thoroughbred) from Spain, France, Africa, and the East had all gone to produce an all-round riding, and later driving, utility animal.[71] This refers to the Eastern States before the migration to the West had started. In other words any horses bought or captured would have made useful light cavalry remounts for the British Army engaged in the War of Independence against the Americans from 1775 to 1783. The only two Regular Cavalry regiments engaged were the 16th and 17th Light Dragoons, who took their own horses with them. As an instance of the sort of 'remounts' which could possibly be picked up, in 1780 in the South 16 'blood horses', including two Arab stallions and 28 mares and fillies, were captured at one particular stud.[72]

Just as must always be the case, the advent of road making, however unscientific at first, leads to a gradual change over from the saddle to the light cart and carriage, so in the United States by the end of last century the predominant breed of horse was the light trapper. In the East many showed Hackney or Trotter and Pacer (the standard Breed) blood, and were lacking in hardiness.[73] When the British Foreign Remount Commission sent buyers to the States in 1900 they[74] divided the saddle horses roughly into three groups for commercial purposes, the Eastern horse, the Western horse and the Texan.

The Easterners were nearly all bred from parents brought up in Kentucky and Virginia or imported within the nineteenth century from Europe.

The Western horse was bred in the North West, principally in the Washington Mountains and Wyoming. He gets his own living throughout the year at an altitude of from 5,000 to 10,000 feet with, in winter, snow on the ground and a temperature of below zero. Those who cannot stand up to this severe test die of starvation. Rough looking though he is he can move at speed over the worst and most treacherous terrain and for endurance he has few equals.

The Texan is a pony, bred on the plains of Western America,[75] and is otherwise known as a Mustang or Bronco. By English standards he is ugly, with small bone and sloping loins and looks to be up to no weight, yet he carries a heavy Mexican saddle weighing 40 to 50 lb with a hard-riding cowboy on top, not by any means always a light-weight.[76] Another name for this animal is the Indian Pony, but all are of the same type and are descended from the horses brought from Spain by Cortez and his successors to what is now Mexico. Running wild they spread North and increased in numbers very rapidly. They are about 14·2 and weigh from 600 to 800 lb. Whole regiments of United States Cavalry have from time to time been mounted on these 'little bronco horses',[77] as active as cats and of great endurance. The weight on the American Cavalry horse was about 16 to 20 stone, according to the amount of rations carried.

The specifications laid down by the British Commission in 1900 were, for all saddle horses, age 5 to 9 years, height from 14 to 15 hands. Many of the Western horses were decidedly queer tempered and were brought in for sale more or less broken to the saddle, an elastic term permitting of various interpretations.

The procedure adopted in the States was to have each remount offered for sale saddled, bridled and ridden by an experienced 'cowboy' under the eye of one of the purchasing officers. If considered satisfactory the horse was then vetted, accepted, described by the Veterinary Officer and last of all branded. Arrangements were made for contractors to provide sufficient land, with any buildings necessary, to lay on water and make all arrangements for feeding the horses until they were ready for shipment. The very large numbers of horses and mules bought had all to be tested for glanders. Shipping had to be hired and properly fitted up, one great difficulty being to take on suitable hands to look after the stock on the voyage.

Up to the end of 1901 over 76,000 horses and over 67,000 mules had been bought and shipped from the States. As already noted they were a success in South Africa. The following section deals with the great changes in the type of horse used commercially in the twelve years after the end of the war in South Africa. There is no doubt that a great deal had been learnt in every way by the Remount and Veterinary Departments working in America during the three years they were there from 1900 to 1902.

THE UNITED STATES OF AMERICA, 1914–18

As we have seen the contribution of the United States during the South African War was very considerable, especially as regards mules. The horses sent over were almost all riding horses. By 1914 the position of the horse market in North America had changed very considerably. The vast unfenced ranches of the West were more or less broken up and the 'cowboy', the man who lived in the heavy stock saddle and 'rode the range', as the expression went, was becoming less and less a necessity of North American farming. The turn over from the saddle horse, the bronco of today's fiction, to the light draught horse was gradual, but very complete by 1914. Naturally it was helped by the advent of the internal combustion engine, as used in cars and lorries. But the shocking roads and the difficulties of adapting machinery to farm use as far as the smaller man was concerned, made the employment of the light draught horse, and to some extent the heavier animal, a very real factor in the horse-breeding world of North America. As the light draught animal was in 1914 the only answer to the problem of the transport of Field Artillery and other comparatively light vehicles and as in other Allied countries the numbers of this type of animal were much less, indeed hardly comparable, to those bred in North America, it was to that country that our remount buyers, most carefully selected experts with very great knowledge, turned their attention first.

The number of animals bought by the Buying Commission in North America has already been given. It will be convenient to reiterate this in a rough estimate. They are as follows: 7–800,000 bought and shipped from North America as compared with 4–500,000 bought in Great Britain. To make the North American effort more understandable it has been roughly computed that by the end of hostilities all the British Armies in the field disposed of close on a million horses and mules. Compare this with another rough estimate, that from 1899 to 1902 during the South African War the average strength of horses and mules employed was about 150,000. Well may Captain Sidney Galtry[78] write in unequivocal terms of 'the vast contribution made to the world's war horse supply by North America' between 1914 and 1918, for in all it accounted for two-thirds of the horses and all the mules. The types offered for sale to our buyers, who were already at work in North America in 1914, were three in number and all were classified by the British Army in their usual all-embracing, but not necessarily polite, way as 'Yanks'. It will be convenient, if needful, to do as the fighting men did. No offence was meant and surely none was taken by the soldiers of the United States.

The first and by far the smallest type was the riding horse, in other words the cavalry trooper. Even in the days of which we are treating cavalry horses did not exist in sufficient numbers for modern requirements. There was not the demand.[79] American Cavalry were mounted on any type procurable and well mounted, but their numbers were too few to warrant special breeding of the types required. A comment on the American riding horse, as offered in 1914, is that he was apt to be straight in the shoulder, though this was atoned for in some measure by the loping gait so characteristic and so comfortable for long-distance treks. The numbers bought were inconsiderable compared with those of the other two types.

The second type was the heavy artillery or transport horse. Breeding this type in any considerable number was altogether a recent venture and animals of the weight required were not easy to find. In parenthesis it should be noted that all animals were bought by weight as in 1899 to 1902.

There were two classifications, horses with a minimum weight of 1,400 lb and those with a minimum of 1,500 lb. Both Canadian and American breeders very much disapproved of hair on a horse's legs, with the result that their heavy horses never look as heavy as the British types, all of which normally have hair, feather it is called, below the knee. The first purchases of this type were not thought heavy enough, but by March 1918 our buyers were being offered animals which compared favourably with our heavy cart-horses in Great Britain. The States of Iowa and Illinois produced most of this class, with Canada competing well. Most were sired by the Percheron (see *post*) with the Shire horse[80] running him close. Percheron sires had been used on ranches in Texas since 1886 and possibly earlier.

We now come to the third and by far the most important class of horse bought in North America, the light draught or light artillery animal, who horsed all the Field guns of the British Army in France with all their transport. Twenty of these were bought to every one of the other two types. In the section on the Waler in the Palestine Campaigns will be found a description of the gun horses bred from English thoroughbred sires in Australasia. Mention is also made there of the excellent Canadian gun horses on issue. As regards the Australasian gun teams and their magnificent achievements in the desert it must be made plain that the light draught horses from North America had no connection at all with the British or American bred thoroughbred, as eligible for the Stud book. They were bred on entirely different lines and no comparison will be made between them in this book. Both were excellent, and those anxious to come to a decision can only judge each case on what they consider its merits.

The fact that the horse most suitable of all those bred in North America for light artillery work was also the 'commercial equine of the country', and that after the export of thousands of animals of this type between 1914 and 1918 the high standard was still maintained, should be sufficient proof of the necessity of the early presence of our Buying Commission in the country. First come was always best served in the average horse market, in which both breeders and middlemen were always considered extremely good business men. They were told that our require-ments were an animal of from 15·2 to 16 hands, weighing about 1,200 lb, short in the back, strong in the neck and quarters and with as much quality as was procur-able. It is not easy to define the term 'quality'; roughly speaking it may be held to mean that a horse does not have that nondescript look which is the result of un-scientific and unsatisfactory crossing of too widely differing types. Plates 33 and 101 refer, and Plate 2 should also be studied in connection with the term 'non-descript'. Some notes on this point will be found on page 40 of this chapter. It is sufficient to note that in Great Britain the light draught horse had not anything approaching the importance which the type had in North America.

Colour was no longer of importance. By 1914 camouflage was beginning to come into the deservedly high place it will presumably continue to hold, and the amount required to alter the rather startling visibility of a team of greys was more or less insignificant. Needless to say, this lightened the work of the buyers con-siderably. The most usual colours were black, grey, steel grey, sometimes bay and occasionally chestnut. Brigadier General T. R. F. Bate was responsible for much of the following matter extracted from Captain Galtry's book.

Just as in the case of the heavy horses, the States of Iowa and Illinois and the Dominion of Canada were the best areas breeding the light draught horses. Strains of the following heavy breeds were predominant and sires could come from Shires, Clydesdales, Belgian, Norman and Percheron studs.[81] According to Galtry's book, and to most of the expert Royal Artillery officers in France, the Percheron cross with suitable mares gave the best results. The first and last im-pressions produced by looking carefully at their progeny were of thickness and sturdiness of physique.

Plate 100 shows an American Percheron sire and 101 one of his progeny from a 'common' mare, the right-hand drawing showing the future Field Gun horse as he looked on disembarkation at an English port, and the left-hand as he was when shipped to France. These two drawings are by Lionel Edwards. The following description of the Percheron by R. S. Summerhays[82] fits well with the two Plates in this book. Mr Summerhays writes as follows: 'the horse is of low draught, having a short and compact body of tremendous depth, with quarters of outstanding size. Exceptionally short-legged, the horse carries great bone, and it is surprising that so heavy a horse can be so active, for that is indeed what it is.' A sire should be 17 hands, have depth of chest equal to half his height and weigh in breeding con-dition about a ton. The best mares usually stand from 16·2 to 16·3 hands and weigh from 1,750 to 2,000 lb. This description refers to clean-bred mares of the Percheron breed, not to the produce of a sire of the same breed from ordinary mares

The requirements for the light artillery horse, bred as just described, were height 15·2 to 16 hands, weight about 1,200 lb. Compare Plate 101 with Plate 76, figure 4, a Light Artillery horse bred in Great Britain with a considerable amount of thoroughbred blood, stemming originally from the Arab. These home-bred Artillery horses should weigh about 1,200 to 1,300 lb and stand about 15·2 hands. There was, therefore, little difference in weight between the 'Yanks' and the horses bred more or less of hunter stamp, which the Percheron and other heavy sires certainly were not. It might be possible to differentiate between the two types by claiming that the hunter type would be the faster on galloping ground and the light draught 'Yanks' the better in continuous heavy going as on the Western Front. Both seem to have had about the same amount of bottom. Glancing back to the South African War of 1899–1902 we find the Canadian-bred ex-bus horses did extremely well there. Comparisons are no doubt odious in the case of horses as in anything else, and this particular one would seem to bristle with difficulties.

One fact which does emerge from the urgent and vital need to buy as many of these invaluable 'Yanks' as possible, is that unless the types of animals required by the Army in very large numbers in time of war are those in common use for the commercial needs of the country, they must either be imported or bred, however expensively, by the Government of the country.

EGYPT   THE EGYPTIAN 'SYRIAN' TROOP PONY

Known as 'Syrian Arabs' or simply 'Syrians', these 14-hand ponies were the mounts of the Egyptian Cavalry in the eighties, when we took over the training and organization of the Egyptian Army. Bred anywhere in Syria or Lower Egypt, with a very large proportion of Arab blood, these ponies, like the Basuto (see under South Africa), were extraordinarily well fitted to be remounts for Light Cavalry and Mounted Infantry. In the case of both breeds a sturdy trooper with his kit might have been thought to look altogether too much for the pony he was riding. The following account, written by the Officer Commanding the 19th Hussars, Lieut Colonel Barrow, gives a good idea of what these cross-bred Arabs could do. Barrow commanded the Regiment during the Gordon Relief Expedition of 1885. We had already had some experience of these ponies in 1882, when the Mounted Infantry had them in the Tel-el-Kebir campaign. The future Major General Sir Henry Hallam Parr,[83] who commanded the Mounted Infantry, commented that the Syrian ponies, who were all entires, fought continuously on the horse lines, but 'were beautiful walkers and quite different from the Bombay Arabs, who kick every stone which is within their reach'. It is needless to stress the importance of remounts who are really good walkers. A regiment mounted on horses or ponies that could do 4½ miles an hour at a walk, many could do considerably more, not only outpaced a unit riding slow walkers, as so many of the big English cavalry chargers used to be, but took less out of their mounts and their riders. The regulation pace is 4 miles an hour.[84] Plate 102 shows the 'Syrian Arabs' with Egyptian troopers, taken c.1896, and fully bears out the description given of 'small Syrian horses'. Barrow's report, slightly condensed, is as follows: 'the Arab stallions were on an average 14 hands; age 8 to 9 years, some 15 per cent over 12 years; bought by the Egyptian Government in Syria and Lower Egypt at an average price of £18 apiece'. Three hundred and fifty of these ponies were issued to the 19th Hussars in November 1884; about half of them had been through the campaign in the Eastern Sudan with the regiment in February and March and had returned to Egypt 'in a very exhausted state'. Ten per cent had been at Tel-el-Kebir. When taken over in November 1884 all but 10 per cent were in fair marching condition. The first march made by the regiment was one of 360 miles, the average distance covered daily being 16 miles. The horses received 8 lb of grain and 10 lb of ahouna stalk. The latter is one of the millets grown all over Africa; the grain is very nourishing and the stalks, even when dry, make a useful bulk ration, just as do the stalks of maize.

This was the ration ordered, but in practice the horses seldom received more than 6 lb of grain and 10 lb of stalk. At this point the main body halted for 18 days, while a reconnaissance party of 50 covered 100 miles in 63 hours, rested for 15 hours, and made the return journey in 63 hours. Six of the horses did the 100 miles in 46 hours, and the last 50 miles in 7½ hours. During 141 hours of marching the horses were ridden for 83 hours. These 50 horses had three days rest on rejoining before following the main body, who left with the relieving force on the desert march which ended abruptly on the news of the death of General Gordon. The total strength of the regiment was 135 all ranks and 155 horses. On this march the 19th, charged with all the scouting duties and described by the officer commanding the Force as 'some of the finest Light Cavalry in the world', covered 31 miles a day, exclusive of one day's halt. For 55 hours they were without water and had only 1 lb of grain. The average forage ration for the first ten days was 5 to 6 lb of grain and 2 gallons of water. Under the above conditions they did patrol and outpost duty, averaging 8 miles a day, during the halt when the expedition was coming to an abrupt end, when they *recovered from the effects of the march.* The whole of the first 75 miles of the return journey was done on 4 lb of grain and 3 gallons of water a day; after this water was plentiful and the daily ration of grain was 8 lb. After two weeks rest at the advanced base on the Nile from which the march had started, the horses marched strong and well to the main base and after two months rest were in as good condition as when they had started on the expedition.[85] The weight carried averaged 14 stone and the care and highly skilled horsemastership exhibited by all ranks can have seldom been equalled and never surpassed. Every minute detail which it was possible to carry out to save the horses was done. The combination of these tough ponies and officers like Colonel Barrow and the future Field Marshal Lord Ypres with the type of other rank in the regiment had accomplished wonders. For the period during which the 19th Hussars were in North Africa the reduction of weight carried was as remarkable as it was effective.

In 1890 we have details of these 'Egyptian' ponies from the pen of Major

Miller in his book on Modern Polo.[86] The 17th Lancer troopers rode *c.* 18 stone 7 lb and the height of the 'Syrians', as Miller calls them, was 14·2 hands. In 1898 the 21st Lancers were again mounted on these ponies for the campaign which ended in the capture of Omdurman. The ponies did well enough, but there was no marching to really test their powers of endurance.[87] Readers will probably recall Sir Winston Churchill's well-known account of these ponies in the charge of the 21st Lancers at Omdurman. It is amazing that these small ponies should have done so extremely well in a role normally associated with a big-striding weight-carrying troop horse. The so-called 'Barbs' ridden by French Light Cavalry in North Africa were of the same type and many instances of their endurance under heavy weights on long marches have been recorded.

Wherever the progeny of the Arab is found, there will appear his gallant bearing, his endurance and his outstanding ability as a war horse, be he and his graded descendants as unlike the popular conception of a war horse as can be imagined.

NIGERIA

From about 1897 to 1959 there were Mounted Infantry units in Nigeria, and from *c.*1914, a battalion. They were mounted locally and Captain (later Lieut Colonel) E. F. Bolton of the Queen's Royal Regiment has recorded the seven different types from which remounts were drawn. They were the Sulibawa, whose origin was probably Arab, and who were introduced by one of the kings of the Mandigo Fulani from the far North West of the Sahara. They show good quality, average 15 hands and are cleanly built. The second type are the Asbin or Bagazzam, probably a cross between the Arab and the Barb. They are capable of great endurance, but badly fed and weedy. Similar to this breed are the Damagaram introduced from that locality.

The Hausa is the type most frequently met with, except in the extreme North of Nigeria. They are probably the result of crossing the Asbin with some breed without any history.

The Bornu run about 15 hands, are large and rawboned, leggy and of nondescript colour at times. The head is coarse with a Roman nose and they show strong signs of an admixture of Asbin blood.

The Pagan is probably the result of Asbin-Hausa crosses. The ponies run about 13·2 hands and are small and sturdy.

South of Lake Chad the Borau breed is found; they have short bodies and are greyish white in colour. The Emirs in the Northern Provinces take pride in being well mounted and import sires from the French Sahara. The Sarkin Mussulmin of Sokoto breeds a good type of Asbin. Captain Bolton considered that horses suitable for trekking, polo and racing could be bought. He wrote his book *Horse Management in West Africa*, in 1931.

ARGENTINE

In the chapter on the South African War of 1899–1902 a good deal was said about the non-success of the Argentine horses imported for cavalry, and to a much lesser extent, for artillery. As a matter of fact, both Mounted Infantry and all classes of Mounted Rifles drew Argentines if available. There were also notes on the polo ponies belonging to a few officers and on the earlier imports of Cavalry Remounts on a small scale, prior to the war. Major Rimington was quoted as saying that these latter types were a success. They had every chance. They were properly acclimatized, carefully fed and gradually conditioned to put to work. The polo ponies were, and are, 'a type of cow-pony probably evolved from a cross of Spanish Andalusian, Arab and Thoroughbred blood on native South American stock. Characterized by great hardiness, agility, with a short dish-faced head, crested neck and heavy shoulders.'[88] Plate 98 refers, as explained; this is a good type and possibly a misfit from some breeder trying to produce polo ponies. But the above description does well enough for him; only the ponies which have been a success at polo were without this horse's faults of action and temper.

The ordinary Argentine as bred and used on the ranches was of a much rougher type. These, presumably carefully picked and sent to Natal for British Cavalry in the years preceding the South African War of 1899–1902, did well enough, but as already stated they were well handled and treated on arrival and had every chance.

Very different was the fate of the unlucky animals bought and shipped during that war. The gaucho, the cowboy of the Argentine, like his American confrère, expects to change his mount several times during a day's herding. The horses of each man are herded in small self-contained troops each with a bell mare who leads and round whom the troop graze. They are grass fed and unused to grain when worked in their native state. It follows that one of these horses will be apt to miss the familiar mare and his mates with whom he has grown up. Divorced from his familiar surrounding, hustled on to a ship, disembarked, railed up country, and very indifferently fed and watered *en route*, at any rate in the earlier stages of the war, he found himself tied on to a picquet line, offered oats or perhaps maize, to which he was not used, saddled up and kept for long hours without off-saddling, seldom watered and expected to gallop fast for considerable distances. He did not respond at all kindly to the treatment he received. His rider, a cavalry trooper or mounted infantryman used to English or Irish horses, thought the often clumsy, ewe-necked charger he was riding was sulky, as Argentines are apt to be, lazy, spiritless and faint hearted. In this he was not far wrong and experience with Argentines in peace time went far to explain the soldier's reactions. Even when properly fed and treated the Argentine is apt to be sluggish and take little interest in his work; in fact he is constitutionally a member of what used to be called the 'sooner' type of horse, who would much sooner be heading homeward than in any other direction. In slow, steady draught the Argentines did well enough, but as remounts opposed to the South African locally bred product they were not a success.

GOVERNMENT REMOUNT STUDS IN EUROPEAN COUNTRIES

As already explained the British Government left the breeding of horses for use in the British Army to private enterprise and indeed went so far as to allow foreign

75

armies to buy remounts in this country, and in what is now Eire, even up to the outbreak of war with ourselves. This extraordinary practice obtained as late as the period preceding the Second World War. However, we ourselves also at times availed ourselves of foreign markets and especially during the South African War of 1899–1902 large numbers of Continental-bred remounts were shipped to Great Britain and sold to Remount Officers. These did not come from the large Government studs maintained by the Great Powers of Europe, indeed their Remount officials saw to it that any extensive purchases made by our Remount Department did not come from any stock which might be of any use to their own governments. The two powers concerned were Russia and Austria-Hungary and a short account of the types bought from these countries between 1899 and 1902 is appended with notes on their and other countries' methods of what might be termed mass production of remounts. As will appear their methods differed vastly from those employed in this country.

Russia

This country maintained towards the close of last century seven breeding establishments totalling 2,500 stallions, mares and foals, and private enterprise was also encouraged in every way. The following types of stallions were in use: English thoroughbreds, some 300 head, for which large prices were paid; trotters, presumably more or less of hackney type and including special trotting breeds carefully bred by private enterprise; hunters, including half-bred English thoroughbreds and draught horses, the latter being in a minority.

Besides the breeding establishments, which furnished all the horses for the heavier type of cavalry, there were 1,100 stallions standing, as the expression goes, at depots all over the country and used to serve selected mares belonging to private owners. Much Arab blood is used throughout Russia and at the time of the South African War some 7,000 horses were required annually for their cavalry. When the buyers from the British Army visited Russia during the South African War they were only permitted to purchase a considerable number of strong, coarsely bred and built cobs, lacking in spirit, pace and the conformation for troop horses, but possessed of stamina and an ability to live under rough conditions. They could not be pushed beyond their natural very slow paces.

The issue of these cobs to mounted men, operating as mounted riflemen against the Afrikaner Commandos riding the excellent ponies shown in Plate 97, was as useless as it was extravagant and stupid. The Russian cobs made very useful pairs harnessed to the two-wheeled light carts of the country on which medical stores, officers' kit and mess utensils were frequently transported. A mounted man, operating on the flanks of a column with probably a screen of mounted enemy troops probing for weak spots, was perfectly helpless at any pace faster than a slow trot and in the event of a hurried retirement was certain to be hit or captured.

No illustration of these cobs has been included; they were simply and solely a class of slow working animal for which the well-mounted Russian Army had no use.

Hungary

The system prevalent in Hungary did not differ so very widely from that already described in the last section dealing with Russia. There were four State breeding farms, over 2,800 stallions operating from 18 central depots. The annual estimates in the years preceding the South African War were in the neighbourhood of £233,000 a year. Although the stallions in use included a number of English thoroughbreds and Norfolk Trotters, which we should have classed as hackneys, the Hungarian authorities did not set as high a value on the English thoroughbred as on their own strains developed for breeding cavalry remounts. They liked a very considerable infusion of Arab blood and claimed to have the best light cavalry troop horses in the world.

We bought a number of remounts in Hungary during the early stages of the South African War and although a few did well and were liked, as a general rule the Hungarians were not satisfactory at all as remounts. They were good-looking attractive horses, but seemed to have no bottom and little stamina. Obviously, the authorities in Hungary were as wise as those in Russia and saw to it that we got no remounts which would have been of any use to their own cavalry.

It may be of interest to note that the trend among both the Government studs and private breeders in both France and Germany was away from the English Thoroughbred and towards the Hackney and other harness breeds produced in the two countries. The French made more use of Arabs and Arab-Thoroughbred cross-stallions than the Germans, and liked the trotting breeds especially for breeding artillery horses. France spent £308,000 and Germany £190,000 a year on their horse breeding, though in the case of France this was offset by about £100,000 a year derived from a tax on the pari-mutuel, the betting organization.

The average price paid for remounts bought from private owners in Germany in the first years of this century was about £47 a head. In Russia it was considered that a remount had cost about £37 when fit to take his place in the ranks.

The above notes should give a rough idea of what Continental nations were doing to provide the very large number of remounts required annually by their large conscript armies. They appear to have been more successful than we were in India, where we laboured under such great difficulties of climate and the lack of an intelligent class of private horse breeders. Somehow or other, in spite of our allowing other nations to compete at times with our own Remount officers in our own country, we succeeded in mounting our small army in peace time and our vastly expanded forces in war time without having recourse to the very large drain imposed by breeding Army horses departmentally instead of depending on the individual breeder. Truly we were a horse-loving nation.

CHINA

This account of the China Pony, written specially by Colonel P. Cleasby-Thompson, late Lancashire Fusiliers, is included as a postscript to the section dealing with foreign remounts.

'The First Battalion the Lancashire Fusiliers on its arrival at Tientsin and Peking in North China in 1937 was required to convert its Vickers Machine Gun transport from limber to pack.

'Mongol ponies, mostly greys and standing round 13·2 hands, were bought through a White Russian dealer, Mr. Sokoloff. Pack ponies cost approx. £3–£5 each and selected ponies for chargers a maximum of £10.

'The Machine Gun Platoon and certain Battalion tactical transport became pack. The China pony has great stamina and lived on next to nothing. They were usually hard mouthed, hammer-headed, long necked and long bodied animals. They were, of course, the mounts of the "Golden Hordes" of Genghis Khan and Timur.

'Officers used to play polo, hunt, and race their ponies, which had quite a turn of speed. The Lancashire Fusiliers handed over their ponies to the Durham Light Infantry in 1939. The illustration (Plate 99) shows Lieut P. Cleasby-Thompson, Machine Gun Platoon, British Embassy Guard, Peking, as he then was, on a 13·3 "China" pony.'

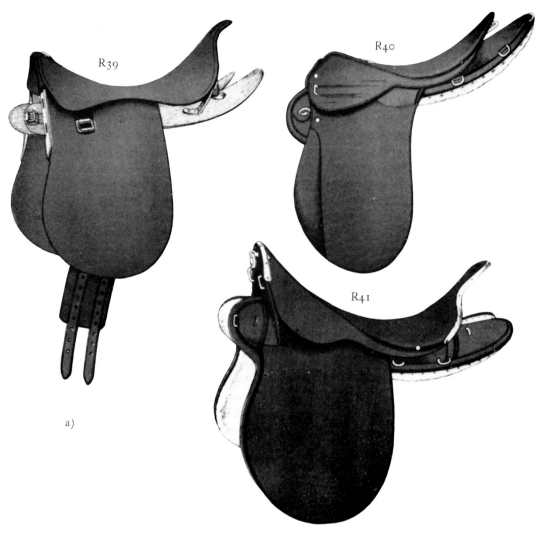

R39

R40

R41

a)

Cape Fan   Military Steel Arch

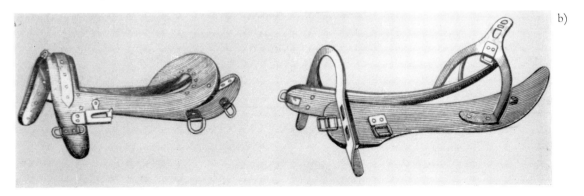

b)

PLATE 17   Universal Patterns of 1890, the first Steel Arch Pattern and R40, the development of the Staff Pattern of 1884.

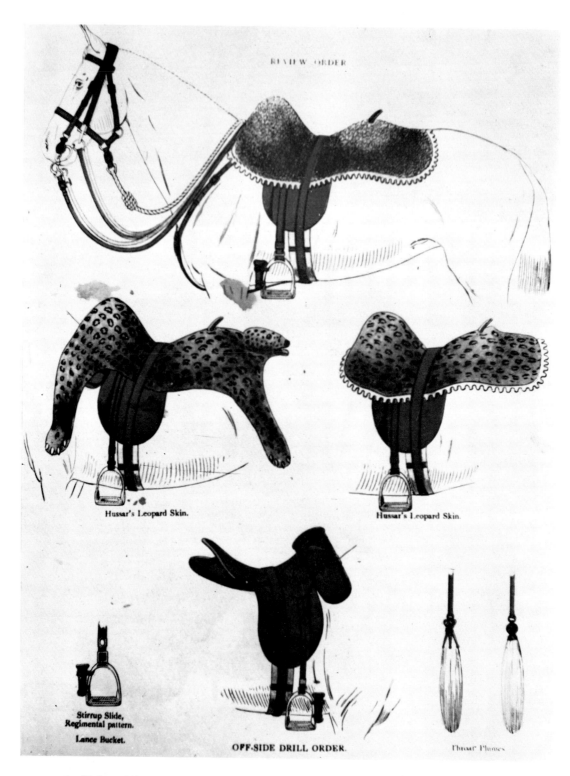

Hussar's Leopard Skin.

Hussar's Leopard Skin.

Stirrup Slide,
Regimental pattern.

Lance Bucket.

OFF-SIDE DRILL ORDER.

Throat Plumes

PLATE 18   Universal Pattern Steel Arch officer's saddle of 1890, complete.

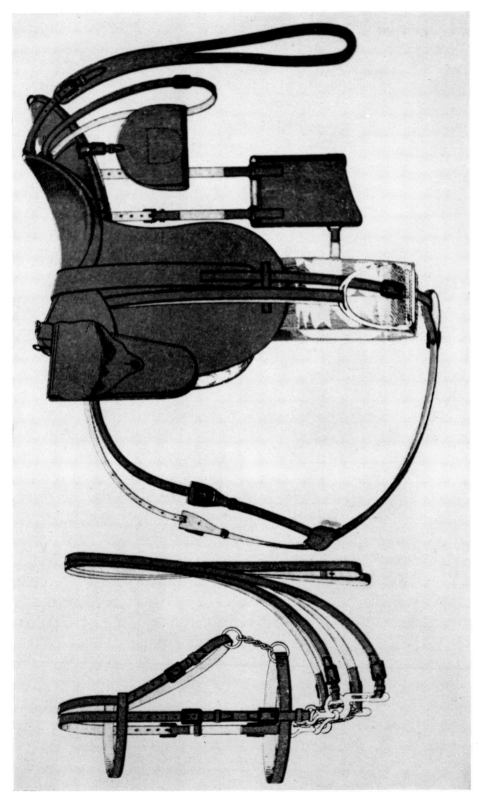

PLATE 19   Staff, Yeomanry and Colonial Pattern saddle of *c*.1904, with the butt rifle bucket introduced in 1884.

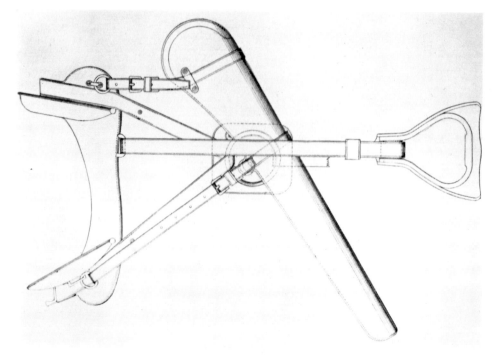

PLATE 21   The McClellan Universal Pattern American Cavalry saddle.

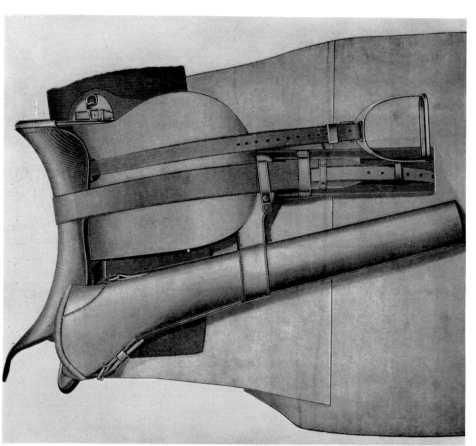

PLATE 20   The Universal Pattern Steel Arch saddle of 1902 with the deep rifle bucket.

PLATE 22   The First Aid Nursing Yeomanry riding with the side-saddle of today (Figure 14) as in 1909.

PLATE 23(a)   The Royal Horse Artillery, Peninsular period.

PLATE 23(b)   The Royal Waggon Train during the Peninsular and Waterloo campaigns.

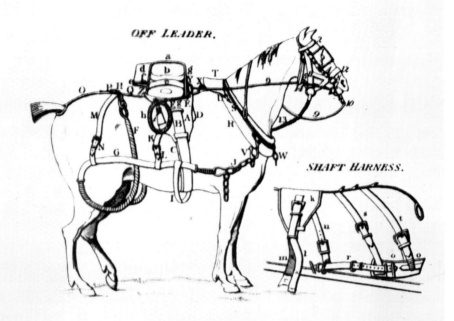

OFF LEADER.

SHAFT HARNESS.

OFF LEADER		
A	Pad or Off Saddle	
B	Surcingle	
C	Girth of the Pad	
D	Pannel of Do	
E	Pad Staples	
F	Trace	
G	Pipe of Do	
H	Hook of Do	
I	Belly Band of Do	
J	Trace Lines	
K	Bearing Strap	
L	Buckling Piece of Do	
M	Hip Strap	
N	Buckling Piece of Do	
O	Crupper	
P	Crupper Ring	
Q	Buckling Piece of Crupper	
R	Collar	
S	The Hames	

T	The Housing
U	The Housing Strap
V	Shoulder Link or Hook
W	Breast Chains or Links
X	Wither Strap
Y	Bearing Hook
Z	Cantle of Pad
a	Oil Deck
b	Horse Cloth
c	Saddle Bag
d	Tin Canteen
e	Do Strap
f	Buckle of Do
g	Baggage Strap
h	Forage Cord
i	Nose Bag

THE BRIDLE.

1	Winker
2	Front or Brow Band
3	Cheek

4	Cheek Billets
5	Throat Lash
6	Bearing Rein
7	Bit
8	Cheek of Do
9	Leading Rein
10	Bar of the Bit
11	Head Collar
12	Nose Band
13	Collar Chain
14	Jowl Strap

SHAFT HARNESS.

k	Pad or off Saddle
l	Back Band
m	Shaft Tugs
n	Bearing Strap
o	Breeching
r	Strap of Breeching
s	Loin Strap
t	Hip Strap

PLATE 24   Royal Artillery Harness, 1840.

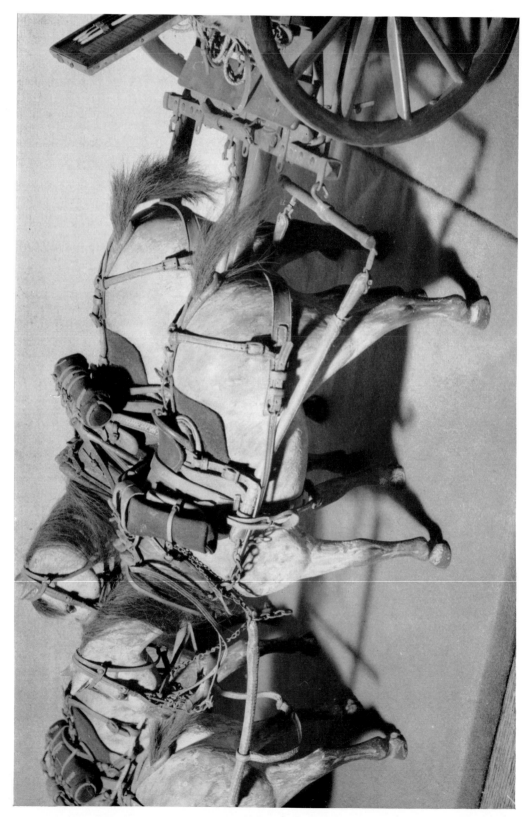

PLATE 25   Royal Artillery Harness, 1853.

PLATE 26(a)   Officer's charger, Royal Horse Artillery, *c*.1861.

PLATE 26(b)   Off wheeler, gun team, Royal Horse Artillery, *c*.1861.

PLATE 27(a) Near wheeler, gun team, Royal Horse Artillery, *c.*1861.

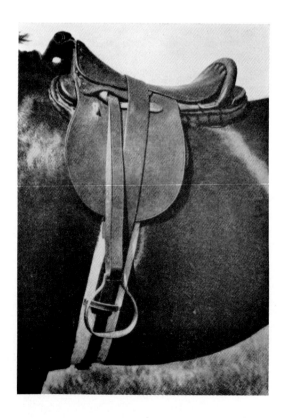

PLATE 27(b) Driver's saddle, Royal Horse Artillery, *c.*1861.

PLATE 28(a)   Near leader, gun team, Royal Horse Artillery, *c*.1861.

PLATE 28(b)   Off leader, gun team, Royal Horse Artillery, *c*.1861.

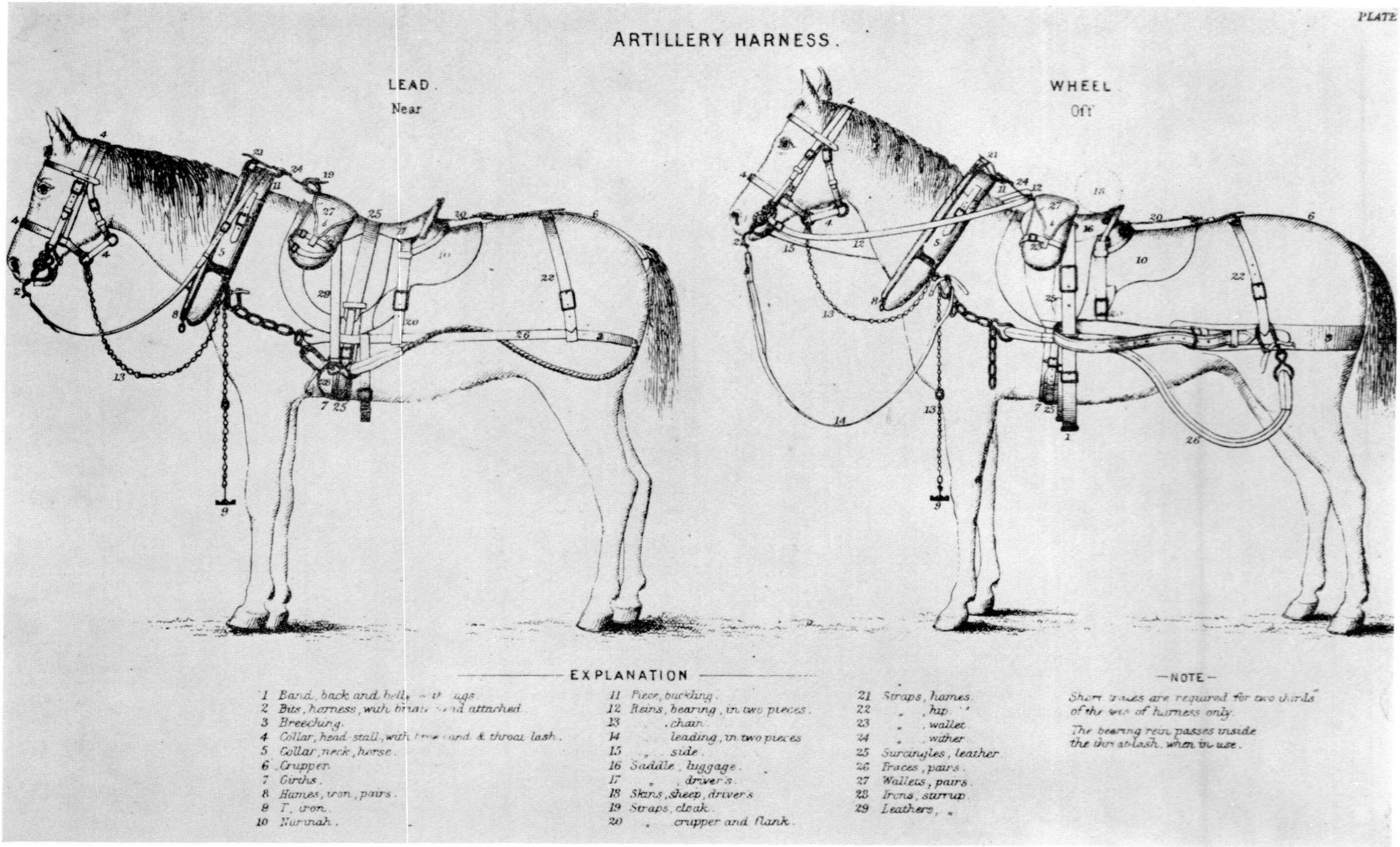

ARTILLERY HARNESS.

LEAD. Near

WHEEL. Off

PLATE 29 Royal Horse and Field Artillery harness of 1883.

─── EXPLANATION ───

1 Bard, back and belly ... it ... legs
2 Bits harness, with bivat...id attached
3 Breeching.
4 Collar head stall, with rem and & throat lash.
5 Collar, neck horse.
6 Crupper.
7 Girths.
8 Hames iron, pairs
9 T. iron.
10 Nurnah.

11 Piece bucking.
12 Reins, bearing, in two pieces.
13   „   chain.
14   „   leading, in two pieces
15   „   side.
16 Saddle, baggage
17   „   drivers.
18 Skens, sheep, drivers
19 Straps, cloak.
20   „   crupper and flank.

21 Straps, harness
22   „   hip.
23   „   wallet.
24   „   wither.
25 Surcingles, leather
26 Traces, pairs.
27 Wallets, pairs
28 Irons, stirrup
29 Leathers, „

─── NOTE ───

Short traces are required for two girls of the wn of harness only

The bearing rein passes inside the thin splash. when in use.

a)

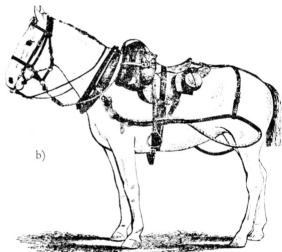

PLATE 30(a, b, c)
All Royal Horse and Field
Artillery harness of 1883.

b)

c)

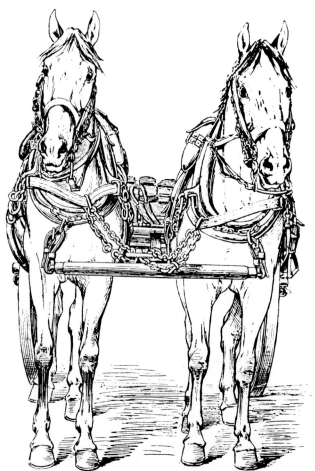

PLATE 31(a, b)   Royal Artillery harness in 1892.

a)

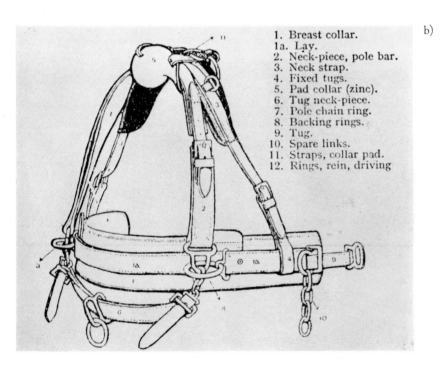

b)

1. Breast collar.
1a. Lay.
2. Neck-piece, pole bar.
3. Neck strap.
4. Fixed tugs.
5. Pad collar (zinc).
6. Tug neck-piece.
7. Pole chain ring.
8. Backing rings.
9. Tug.
10. Spare links.
11. Straps, collar pad.
12. Rings, rein, driving

PLATE 32   Universal Pattern used in the First World War.

PLATE 33   First World War: Royal Artillery gun team, bred in the U.S.A.

PLATE 34(a), (b)   The King's Troop Royal Horse Artillery in 1961.

REFERENCES

1   Rimington, *The Horse in the Late War.*
2   Preston, *Desert Mounted Corps.* The Australian Light Horse were issued with swords in 1918.
3   Stewart, *History of the XIIth R. Lancers*, p. 287 and *passim.*
4   Statistics of the 'Military Effort of the British Empire'.
5   As 4. See Jessel, *The Romsey Remount Depot.*
6   *History of the Veterinary Services in the First World War*, p. 63.
7   Jessel, *The Romsey Remount Depot.*
8   Preston, *The Desert Mounted Corps.*
9   Note from Captain B. T. Hinchley, of the Camel Transport Corps, 1917.
10 *Manual of Horsemastership*, plates I, II, and III.
11 Photograph in the Collection of Colonel H. C. B. Rogers.
12 Timmins, Major R. S., D.S.O., Royal Canadian Dragoons, 'Notes on the Phillips Pack Saddle', *Canadian Defence Quarterly*, 1926.
13 Fitch, *Queer Horses and Queer People*, page 48.
14 Gilbey, *Horsebreeding in England & India*, p. 53, quoting Veterinary Colonel J. H. B. Hallen.
15 As 14, p. 64.
16 Sidney, *Book of the Horse*, quoting Colonel Valentine Baker, *Clouds in the East*, c.1877. See also *Armies of Today*, 1891, published Osgood & Milvane, p. 252, for 'a Russian General' giving the name Argamac to the Turcoman Horses.
17 *Blackwood's Magazine*, Aug. 1927, pp. 149–150. 'Some Kipling Origins.'
18 Whinyates, *From Corunna to Sevastopol*, Appendix 2, pp. 282, 283.
19 *Cavalry Journal*, 1927, 1929. Sidmouth, Major Viscount, 'Notes on the Recruiting of the Madras Cavalry in the Days of the Company Bahadur'.
20 Gilbey as 14, p. 52.
21 Donovan Jackson, *India's Army*, p. 80.
22 JAHR, Volume XXXIII, p. 181
23 Grant's *British Battles*, p. 188, under Laswarree.
24 As 19.
25 Donovan Jackson, *India's Army*, p. 472.
26 Goldsmid, *James Outram*, Volume I, p. 170.
27 Rogers, *Mounted Troops*, p. 200.
28 Aldershot Lectures, 1892, Captain M. H. Hayes.
29 Parry, *Death or Glory Boys*, p. 228.
30 JAHR, Volume XXXII, p. 108.
31 Crealock, Lieut Colonel H. Hope, Portfolio of Sketches published by Hogarth, London, 1861.
32 Maxwell, *History of the XIth, King Edward's Own Horse*, p. 28.
33 Gilbey, *Horsebreeding in England and India*, p. 52.
34 Cape of Good Hope Government Gazette, 1881, No. 482.
35 Aldershot Lectures 1891, Veterinary Major F. Smith.
36 Royal Artillery Institution Journal, Volume L, No. 12, p. 468.
37 Gilbey, *Horsebreeding in England & India*, p. 57.
38 Stewart, *History of XIIth R. Lancers*, pp. 163–4.
39 Note from Major 'Kitty' Apthorp, Royal Irish Regt.
40 Gilbey, *Horsebreeding in England & India*, p. 58.
41 Royal Artillery Institution Journal, Volume L, No. 12, p. 503.
42 Theal, *History of South Africa Before 1795*, Volume III, p. 100.
43 Theal, *History of South Africa Since 1795*, Volume I, p. 66.
44 Colburne, *United Services Magazine*, November 1876, Part III, pp. 345–8.

45 Thornton, *Origin and History of the Basuto Pony*, 1937, pp. 1 and 2.
46 JAHR, Volume XVII, p. 227.
47 On the 8th June, 1846, at the Gwanga River, Eastern Cape Colony, by the 7th Dragoon Guards and the Cape Mounted Riflemen.
48 Stewart, *History of the XIIth Royal Lancers*, p. 146.
49 Brabant, *Autobiography*.
50 Cunynghame, *My Command in South Africa*, p. 36.
51 Sidney, *Book of the Horse*, chapter on 'Cape Horses'.
52 Theal, sup. cit. Volume X, p. 333. Dr H. H. Curson of Pretoria. 'Type Script List of Cavalry Units Posted to South Africa'.
53 As 45.
54 *The Farmers Weekly*, published at Bloemfontein, Republic of South Africa, issue of 30.1.1946, Historical Survey of Droughts.
55 As 1.
56 Notes in the author's collection from figures supplied by the Veterinary Officer in charge of the brigade.
57 History of the Veterinary Services in the Great War.
58 As 57, p. 425.
59 Marriott, *Source History of the South African Veterinary Corps & Remount Corps* 1919 *to* 1946.
60 Aldershot Lectures, 1892.
61 As 1; Sessions, pp. 200–1.
62 Gilbey, *Small Horses in Warfare*, pp. 28–9.
63 Sessions, p. 199.
64 Jessel, *Story of the Romsey Remount Depot*, quoting 'The Remount Service'.
65 Preston, *Desert Mounted Corps*, p. 317.
66 As 65.
67 As 1.
68 *Report of the Committee on Remounts*, 1902, p. 8.
69 Sessions, pp. 203, 204.
70 As 64.
71 Summerhays, *The Observers Book of Horses & Ponies*.
72 Parry, *Death or Glory Boys*, p. 79.
73 Summerhays & Sessions, p. 140.
74 Sessions, p. 140.
75 Bloodgood & Santini, *The Horseman's Dictionary*.
76 Sessions, p. 140.
77 Carter, *Horses, Saddles & Bridles*.
78 Galtry, *The Horse & the War*, pp. 19 and 27.
79 Carter, sup. cit.
80 Galtry, p. 34; Fores *Sporting Notes*, 1887, 1888, p. 163. The latter gives a date for the import of Percheron sires into Texas.
81 As 78.
82 As 71.
83 Parr, p. 171.
84 *Manual of Horsemastership*, 1937; Bloodgood & Santini under 'Gait'.
85 Gilbey, *Small Horses in Warfare*, pp. 6–10. Burn *Notes on Transport*, etc.
86 Miller, *Modern Polo*, 1902, pp. 196–8.
87 Churchill, *My Early Life*.
88 Bloodgood & Santini under 'Criollo'.

CHAPTER THREE

British Army Horses to the Present Day. Details of all animals used by the British & Commonwealth Armies at all times & their Equipment

THE circumstances under which the Second World War, which began in 1939, was fought makes it convenient to deal with the remount question as a whole, rather than to have separate chapters on the different types of animals used. The horse was no longer the paramount consideration; the mule and any other pack animal available and considered suitable took the place of importance so long held by the horse and this state of affairs still continues in 1965, when the British Army, always as of old operating anywhere, may at any time be again dependent on the pack mule or even the donkey.

The publication of Brigadier Clabby's anxiously awaited *History of the Royal Army Veterinary Corps*,[1] has been a prime factor in writing this chapter.

At the outbreak of war in 1939 the Veterinary and Remount Services were separate, the Army had been extensively mechanized, and the horse strength of the Army in Great Britain was only 2,600. In India there were still a very considerable number of horsed cavalry regiments and animal transport units; but generally speaking the idea that mechanization had ousted animals from being used in wartime had been widely, if incorrectly, accepted; though not by those serving in the Army who had a realistic appreciation of what might and did happen. However complete and efficient mechanization can be and however adequately modern aircraft can supply troops in all sorts of terrain, either by making use of landing grounds or by dropping men, animals and materials by parachute, the fact remains that over a large portion of the earth's surface the infantryman, the P.B.I. as he is known in our Army, must finish the job on his feet and must rely on the pack animal, which can creep or crawl almost anywhere a man can go and bring up ammunition, supplies and whatever else must be used in the fighting line.

So, as of old, the Veterinary and Remount Corps were, and still are, of vital use and in January, 1941 the two services were combined, with most excellent results.

In Great Britain the number of pack horses or cobs and of light draught horses was not very large, but exceeded the number of mules, bought in America. The peak strength was reached in December, 1943, with 4,428 horses and 1,022 mules, the latter going to the Royal Artillery and to six mule companies of the Royal Indian Army Service Corps. These figures are given to emphasize the idea so prevalent in many uninformed circles that mechanization had completely eliminated animals from active participation in warfare. This was very far from being the case and in due course, as will appear, pack animals, principally mules, took the place previously held by riding animals, in other words horses, cobs and ponies; only the last two being normally used as being handier for pack work. Horsed vehicles were still in use to a limited extent and it would be correct to say that this war reduced the breeding of horses to an enormous extent, especially in Europe, and to a great measure in North America as well.

The process of eliminating horsed units was a gradual one. In 1929 the British Army in Great Britain still had 2,600 horses, while in India there were over 24,000 horses, 26,000 mules, 13,000 head of cattle and 5,000 camels, the total being just over 70,000.

Although it was realized in the British Army and in the German and Italian forces that pack animals were going to be a necessity, it was not easy to decide to what extent they should be made available. The German Army, especially, felt the need of accumulating as many as possible and imported horses in numbers from Ireland and elsewhere. In 1938 their equine establishment was over the 100,000 mark.

As far as the War Office was concerned there was considerable reluctance to rely on mechanized units only as far as action in the Near East, which was a well understood certainty, was concerned. The author will, it is hoped, be forgiven for recalling a personal experience of the first months of 1940. In company with a number of other 'dug out' officers of the Defence Force of the Union of South Africa, he was privileged to listen to a long lecture from a distinguished officer of the First World War on the necessity of employing horsed units in Africa, as had been the case in the past. The amazement and surprise of a number of young officers of the South African Air Force, who were also attending the lecture, may be imagined. As stated in the section on Remounts in South Africa, horsed units were duly raised in that country, but never used.

In Great Britain, although it had been decided that by 1939 only the Household Cavalry, two line regiments of cavalry and one battery Royal Horse Artillery were to be retained mounted at home and that abroad mounted units were to exist only in India and Hong Kong, the decision was radically altered in 1939. It was decided to despatch a Cavalry Division, the First, to Palestine, which meant that in September, 9,000 remounts had to be bought by the few remount officers available, a return to a state of affairs so typical of the history of remounts as dealt with in this book. A quotation from an authoritative report made some years later may not be out of place; it runs 'this is not the place to query the reason for such action, but obviously it was entirely unexpected'. So unexpected was it that the results were, to quote again from the above account, 'to put it mildly, unsatisfactory'. It was laid down, it can safely be said in the teeth of a very large amount of previous experience, that any horse over five years old, fit for one month's service in the field, could be bought. This regulation was not wisely applied, with the result that horses over 15 years old, the age at which a remount was cast in peace time, were bought and even mares in foal included. The Director of Veterinary Services not unnaturally intervened and the regulations were altered, but much harm had been done and the veterinary hospitals inevitably received considerable numbers of totally unsatisfactory animals.

Apart from the Composite Household Cavalry Regiment and the Royals and Scots Greys, the last two being already abroad, the Division was formed by eight Yeomanry Regiments. These were composed of excellent material, but the number of men enlisting who had any real experience of working with horses under the conditions likely to be met with in the Near East was not large and although a number of excellent ex-Regular Cavalry reservists, both N.C.O.s and men, were drafted into the Yeomanry, the standard of horse management was not high. There was also a considerable shortage of trained men available to the Remount and Veterinary Services as farriers and saddlers, as well as of men used to working with animals at all and this in spite of the use of Reservists not fit for active service as combatants. As of old, no one in high places appears to have thought out the complexity of the problem of raising a division of cavalry and staffing the necessary Veterinary and Remount Services at the shortest possible notice. Yet in spite of bad weather and many difficulties on shipboard the officers and men of the two branches succeeded in transporting the entire range of animals belonging to the division across the Mediterranean with a casualty rate of only 1·6 per cent died or destroyed and only 722 admitted to and treated in the Veterinary hospitals. This, it was stated 'compares favourably with the percentage of losses during transporation during the First World War'.

The unfortunate results of hasty and unskilled buying showed only too clearly in the Palestine and Transjordan campaigns in 1939 and 1940. To quote again from the above report: 'the old story was clearly illustrated that unsuitable horses, especially in the hands of half-trained men, are more trouble than they are worth, and that soft English horses need a great deal of acclimatization before they are fit for work in the East'. So much for the attempt at putting the clock back insisted on by the War Office.

The amount of animals allotted to the British Expeditionary Force in France in 1939 and 1940 consisted of six mule transport companies sent from the Middle East and India with a total strength of about 2,700. They were wanted to convey ammunition and supplies to forward positions, as had been done during the First World War. In spite of the severe winter experienced, the mules from India did well and the sick rate was very low. There were few facilities available for roughing the shoes by means of frost nails, as is always done under icy conditions, and the mules slipped badly on the frozen *pavé* of the French roads. One company was captured when the German blitzkrieg started and the others reached the beaches at Dunkirk, but were unable to evacuate the mules, as there was no room on the ships.

The campaign in North West Europe in 1944–5 was also not remarkable for the number of remounts used. There were two Mountain Regiments, Royal Artillery, with mules bought in America, six Indian Army and four Royal Army Service Corps pack companies. The latter were issued with surplus cavalry horses and cobs bought in the United Kingdom. With a Norwegian contingent the total number of animals was 3,700. A horse transport service was also organized from captured enemy vehicles and animals with civilian drivers, locally enrolled. Harness and farriers' tools were flown out from England.

About this time considerable use was made of horsed transport in England for short hauls, 400 vehicles and 600 horses being employed.

We now return to the Middle East, where, after the campaign against the Vichy French in Syria in 1941, large numbers of enemy animals were taken over at the same time as the British Cavalry units were being mechanized. The cavalry horses not considered suitable for light draught were destroyed, in accordance with an undertaking given in Parliament that the scandal caused by the sale of British remounts on the open market in Egypt after the First World War might not be repeated. The treatment then of a very large proportion of these unfortunate animals at the hands of African owners was nothing short of terrible, although what little could be done by private enterprise partially mitigated a position which was felt to be intolerable by everyone who took any interest in the sufferings of animals. But private subscription was not an adequate way of dealing with the situation. It should, however, be noted that a considerable number of remounts were shot at some of the remount depots, when it was certain that under post-war conditions in 1918 hardly any horses were to be shipped to Great Britain. No such action was necessary after the Second World War.

In 1941 the British Army took over from the Vichy French 1,200 horses and 3,200 mules. The light draught horses among them were of good type, as were the heavy draught and Mountain Artillery mules and these were utilized. The French cavalry remounts, Syrians and Barbs, were of a low standard.

By October 1942, horsed transport companies accounted for 2,800 horses and mules and were a useful addition to the motor transport available. There were also in the Middle East six Cypriot pack transport companies, fifteen Indian mule companies and one mountain artillery patrol; a total of over 6,500 horses, 9,600 mules and 1,700 camels.

The mule can stand a great deal and twice during the war mules were shipped from Palestine to India and from Basra to Kantara during the hottest months of the year with no casualties at all on shipboard. The credit goes to a very great degree to the skill of the Royal Army Veterinary Corps officers who were in charge on the voyage, and to the experienced men with them, but there is no doubt that in this respect the mule is far tougher than the horse.

During the fighting against the Italians in Abyssinia in 1940–1, thousands of camels and mules were employed, firstly to help the Abyssinians, who had rebelled against their Italian conquerors, and later as organized pack units with the 4th and 5th Indian Divisions. Brigadier Clabby, who was present in the rank of Captain, for a time combined both medical and veterinary duties in the absence of R.A.M.C. personnel. In his book, already mentioned as so very extensively used in writing this chapter, he records that the two Cypriot Transport Companies, Nos. 1 and 2, whose personnel had escaped from Dunkirk and served in Abyssinia, were equipped with 800 mules, 'or rather jennets', bought in Cyprus. (In the section on mules these crosses of a horse stallion on a she-ass are described as 'hinneys', the term 'jennet', according to the *Oxford English Dictionary*, being used for a species of small Spanish horse. In common parlance it is very usual to reverse the verdict of the o.e.d. and other dictionaries.) The animals employed in this campaign were immunized against African horse sickness, a deadly complaint, carried by mosquitoes, which spread widely during the Second World War and had for years been the bane of the southern portion of the Continent. In 1943 and 1944 the disease raged in Egypt and Palestine until all Army animals could be immunized. It was noted that the mule was less affected by horse sickness than the horse, as had been the case in South Africa.

When the First Army landed in North Africa in 1943 the cadres of two pack transport companies accompanied, without animals. As an instance of the difficulties experienced in requisitioning suitable animals in a foreign country it may be noted that some 20,000 animals were examined in Algeria before sufficient suitable ones were found to equip the two companies. Generally speaking the campaigns in North Africa were conducted purely by mechanized formations, but with the transference of the Allied war effort to Sicily and Italy very different conditions were encountered. In both areas, as emphasized in *R.A.S.C. Training*, published in 1922, Part III, 'there remain and always will remain such theatres as those supplied by the Austro-Italian front (etc., etc.) where pack transport, both for guns and supplies must be employed'. In Sicily, as in North Africa, the British Army decided to rely on local impressment for both animals and saddlery, nor were trained men of transport companies sent as had been done in North Africa. Eventually three companies were sent with animals, otherwise all pack transport was requisitioned locally and staffed from the fighting units.

In Sicily, being a country in which the muleteer and his charges are part of the economy, there were enough mules and equipment to make the experiment in improvisation a success, though a rather costly one, and this in spite of the fact that the Germans had removed a large number of mules before we landed. The operation was of very short duration, the casualties in 14 days being, however, as high as 50 per cent in animals and equipment.

In the Italian Campaign pack transport was not needed until the autumn of 1943, when it was urgently required by all formations until the end of the operations in May, 1945. The original request made by 15 Army Group to Allied Force and Middle East Headquarters was that up to a total of 4,500 animals should be shipped at once and, if unavoidable, that a reduction of 1,000 vehicles a month could be accepted. In other words wheeled transport of any type must, if in any way possible, be replaced by pack animals. By 1945 the Field Units accounted for over 1,000 horses and 11,754 mules, with a further 500 horses and 8,850 mules in the Veterinary and Remount units.

Enough has been written to indicate the scope of the work involved, which can be studied in the fascinating detailed account published in Brigadier Clabby's book. Among the many facets dealt with, not the least interesting is the intensively successful co-operation between the Veterinary and Remount Services, now, as already explained, combined.

The bulk of the animals required were bought in the Middle East and in Persia, Iraq and India. The supply from North Africa was limited.

As the Official History sums up the situation: 'the Italian campaign is the only one in which considerable numbers of pack and other animal transport were used and where there was an organized combined veterinary and remount service working over a considerable period. . . . The campaign is therefore of particular interest from the veterinary and remount aspect, as it is impossible to say that armies in future will not find themselves fighting in areas where motor transport must be supplemented by pack transport.' Although this was written in 1954 the British Army is still using pack transport in various areas and seems likely to continue doing so.

Brigadier Clabby has given us a most deeply interesting account of an inspired plan set afoot by authority, which operated in the British Army of occupation in Italy and Austria in the months immediately following the end of the War. The emphasis was upon the enjoyment of life after the long, to many seemingly unending, series of campaigns in so many parts of the world. There were a large number of good quality captured German cavalry chargers and troop horses available as well as many others, and there were in all about 3,000 riding horses attached to various units for recreational purposes. Among them were some 200 registered race horses, thoroughbreds, mostly German, with a few Hungarians. It is pleasant to record that an English horse, belonging to the 1st Cavalry Division, a bay gelding of about 16 hands 2 inches named Ramle could show a clean pair of heels to all others on a racecourse. Equitation units supplied 'useful and enjoyable instruction on equitation and in the techniques for cross-country riding and racing, together with the theory and practice of animal management', and Brigadier Clabby goes on to say, 'Never since the beginning of the war had the Army been so horseminded', and that 'the enthusiasm for recreational riding was a notable memory for those of us in the R.A.V.C.' The full story must be studied in his book.

The Army had also learnt to appreciate the many virtues of the mule during the fighting in the mountains in Italy, and though the Second World War had been the first of the wars in which mechanization had played a really tremendous role, it did leave in the British Army a memory of the virtues of the animals which had served past generations so faithfully and well. In all some 85,000 animals were handed over by the German Armies when the final surrender took place.

We now turn to the invasion of France, which was almost entirely a mechanized campaign on an enormous scale. There were, however, horse-transport companies raised from captured horses and equipment, except harness and farriery tools which were flown over from England. In all about 1,000 horses were utilized.

INDIA AND BURMA

In India the Veterinary and Remount Directorates were not amalgamated as was done in Great Britain and in other Overseas Commands in 1941, but remained separate until after the war. Up to the end of 1941 little use was made of animal transport as mechanization progressed in the Indian Army. At the outbreak of war the animal strength of the Army in India was some 24,000 horses, 26,000 mules, 13,000 cattle and 5,000 camels. As already noted, animal transport companies were sent to France in 1939 and a contingent of 620 mules in the spring of 1940. Animals were also sent to the Sudan and Aden in 1940 and detachments of mules to the Middle East in 1941. In the same year mule and camel companies were sent to Iraq, but expansion did not really start until 1942.

From 1940 the Army Remount Department had been buying animals from India; mules for East Africa, the Middle East and Burma, and camels for the Aden garrison, where the Bikanir Camel Corps, an Indian State Force unit, was sent. (See Plate 88.)

Mules were bought in South Africa, the Argentine and the United States of America for use in India. The U.S.A. furnished 1,960 mountain artillery mules, a most important contribution, and 1,516 'Class II equipment mules', presumably pack animals. From South Africa between 1942 and 1945 over 22,000 mules and 10,015 donkeys were shipped to India. The latter possibly went to Burma, where on the formation of Brigadier O. C. Wingate's Long Range Penetration Group, known as the Chindits, in 1943, a special demand was made for small mules and ponies. Many animals of this type were bought in the bazaars and the hilly districts of India with but little success, as they were either too small to take even the smallest size of Army pack saddle, or their backs had been too much injured to stand any reasonable weight at all. There is no evidence that any donkeys except a very few went to Wingate's Force. The operations of this force should be of great interest to anyone concerned with the subject of animals used in war. A point stressed by the commander is the danger and difficulties experienced by the muleteers, in this case Gurkha recruits untrained in animal management, which called for such fighting qualities as to make it incumbent for them 'to be as good or better fighting men than their comrades in an infantry company'. Wingate added that so great was the physical effort demanded of the muleteer in these operations in impossibly difficult country, where the forces engaged were working entirely detached from any base and supplied by air, that double pay for him was in fact underpayment! This very remarkable statement by a very distinguished officer surely conveys as fine a tribute to the men in charge of the pack mules of these desperate, dedicated columns which he commanded as can be imagined. The mule was as, or perhaps even more, vital to the success of our troops than ever was the cavalryman's charger in the days before mechanization.

Very remarkable new techniques in the handling of animals were initiated during the operations of Wingate's force. For the first time mules were forwarded to the operational base, not by road, but by Dakota aircraft and by gliders specially adapted for the purpose. This was the first time that mules were sent by air. Perhaps even more interesting was the very great success attained by the skilled experts of the R.A.V.C. who operated on the horses and mules destined for Wingate's force and removed the vocal cords under a general anaesthetic, thereby muting them and preventing them giving away the positions of our troops to the Japanese, who were in very superior numbers and naturally desperately anxious to eliminate forces operating in their rear. Between 1943 and 1945 over 5,600 animals were muted with a casualty list of only 43 deaths. In ten days after the operation a mule was again fit to carry his pack and no decrease was noted in the staying power of these muted animals. A more complete success of the methods of modern surgery as applied to the everyday needs of warfare can hardly be imagined.

Altogether over 500 horses and over 3,000 mules were employed with Special Formations operating in Burma and of these 2,216 were flown in. A few animal casualties were also flown out. Of those flown in there were 120 bullocks, a donkey and a goat. Personnel going in by air with animals were carefully trained in the technique of the process. As an experiment in 1945 mules were dropped by parachute from Dakota aircraft. They were narcotized and fastened to a padded wooden platform fitted with statichutes to keep it level. No ill effects were observed, but the official account states that the operation may not be worth repeating. However this may be, there can be no doubt that the value of being able to supply a force, whether isolated by the difficulties of the terrain or by enemy action, by air can hardly be exaggerated.

Brigadier Clabby's summing up of the transport situation as regards animals is to the effect that rail was successful and that mules lost little or no condition even when eight days in the trucks. Air transport was excellent and that in operation behind the enemy lines, mules survived much better than Indian-bred ponies, but South African ponies did well. All animals stood fire remarkably well. There is no doubt that the mule was the ideal 'remount' under these most adverse conditions. The only criticism of the mule was to the effect that although he stood shell fire well, he was apt at times to dislike coming under small arms fire. In a long campaign under the most trying circumstances he had proved absolutely invaluable and fully borne out the very high opinion expressed by Major Parrino, of the U.S.A. Mountain Artillery Service, in his book on Pack Transport quoted in the chapter on Mules.

GREAT BRITAIN

The history of remounts in the British Service after the Second World War must obviously be that of a branch which was declining more and more as mechanization became practically complete. As already stated the mule, and occasionally the donkey, were the only solution possible for getting the infantryman's arms, ammunition and supplies to him in certain areas.

As regards the horse, he still holds a very limited place as a feature of that ceremonial which is so much a part of the national life on certain momentous occasions. The three regiments of Household Cavalry, now reduced to two with only a comparatively small quota of mounted men, and the King's Troop Royal Horse Artillery (see Plate 34 for the latter and Plates 66 and 67 for the Household Cavalry) were remounted after the war, partly on their old horses, which had been functioning with horse transport, and partly with fresh intakes. The Household Cavalry have had difficulty in securing the traditional black troop horses which they have always ridden and have been fortunate enough to be presented with two fresh intakes, one by the Royal Family of Holland and the other from a detachment of the Royal Canadian Police, who came over a few years ago to take part in the Royal Military Tournament and purposely brought only black remounts. The Metropolitan Police also have mounted detachments.

The Coronation of Queen Elizabeth in 1953 brought the horse into prominence, if only for a short time. Senior officers of the three fighting services, the Prime Minister's escort and the processional marshals all had to be provided with mounts and extremely well-broken ones, well accustomed to the many and various noises to be encountered on such occasions. Eighty additional animals were added to the establishment at Melton Mowbray Remount Depot (see Plate 57) and familiarized with whatever unusual conditions they might have to face, with, it is needless to add, the greatest success.

Melton Mowbray is still very much in evidence. About eighty horses a year pass through the Depot, mostly troop horses for the Household Cavalry and the King's Troop R.H.A. Most of these are bought in England or in Eire, and they, as well as the future riding instructors of the British Army, are in the words of Brigadier Clabby 'trained together by the traditional Weedon methods', Weedon, as is well known, having been *the* Equitation School of the Army.

The students, drawn from the officers and men of the horsed units mentioned above, from the Brigade of Guards, the Royal Army Service Corps, and the Royal Corps of Military Police, are each given three horses to look after. Of these one is trained, one half trained and the third unbroken. Attached are also a School of Farriery and one of Saddlers. The Training Area is also used by the War Dog Training School. (See under section on dogs.)

This concludes the chapters on Horses, and has taken the story from the rather shadowy account of the Great Horse of the days of armour, who does just come into the period covered by this book, through the various vicissitudes of the types of horses used by the British Army to the more or less standardized hunter type of the last hundred years. Today it is easy enough to meet a General Officer who has never, at any rate officially, been on a horse, but the tradition of the once widely bred hunter type so highly esteemed in the Army lives on, though on a small scale only and the product can still be seen at shows and bought, though at a price which would have staggered the men of the past.

The hard-swearing, even harder-fighting, General Picton of Peninsula and

Waterloo days could still, if he cared to pay the price, buy a strong active 15-hand charger which would carry him through the hottest fire of his day and be able to have the legs of any foreign cavalryman who might be unwise enough to pursue him too close in to his veterans.

MULES

(See Plates 39 to 41 and 44 to 47)

For either packing or draught purposes the mule is the most useful of all animals. Mules have been ridden in warfare with success, indeed individuals have gone so far as to prefer riding one on trek and changing to a pony or horse when action was imminent.[2] But this is not common and as a general rule the mule's lack of pace makes him far inferior for mounted infantry, to say nothing of cavalry, to the pony or horse. Although the mule, unless carefully trained, does not stand fire anything like as well as the horse and is not as efficient on slippery ground, he makes an excellent artillery team animal, pulling well and steadily on the longest marches on short rations and scanty water. He is at his very best in a pack or mountain battery where his sure-footedness, skill in choosing footholds and sagacity in the handling of the very awkward loads furnished by the various parts of the ordnance, on any sort of terrain make him an object of the greatest respect to the men who work with and understand his peculiarities.

The mule is the result of a cross between a male donkey and a mare. A female donkey bred to a stallion results in a 'hinny', a light animal once highly esteemed as a mount for men and women who had to travel long distances. Here we are concerned with the mule only. A modern work by an American Artillery officer of great experience of pack artillery[3] gives the following details: 'experienced breeders state that a very desirable 'mule' mare is one having about one-fourth draft blood and three-fourths light-horse blood. A mare of this breeding will weigh between 1,100 and 1,500 lb and produce good sized mules, with style, action and stamina.' Today, with the far greater demand for mules than for horses, it would presumably pay better to put the class of mare described to a donkey jack rather than to a stallion.

It should be noted that mules do not propagate their species.

The account quoted above lays down the correct measurements of the donkey jack to be used on the mare as follows: weight 1,200 lb, height 15 hands 3 inches, with a girth of 70 inches, and an overall length of 84 inches. In the U.S.A., one of the greatest mule-producing areas in the world, the most favoured type of animal is known as the Missouri mule, though why this name is mainly used is not clear to the authority quoted above. He should stand from 14 hands 3 inches to 16 hands, weigh on an average about 1,200 lb, and resemble the horse as far as possible. He should have a broad chest, smaller legs and larger buttocks than the horse, should have an even gait (at a walk understood) with as little swaying or rocking motion as possible, a comparatively straight back, much stronger than that of a horse and for Army use be capable of carrying well over 300 lb. With this load he should be able to travel up to 30 miles in a day. The mule is generally longer lived than the horse and thrives on much worse food; he will not normally overeat and he stands weather conditions at extreme limits very well.

The loads as given above are presumably those in use in the U.S.A. Pack Artillery with the big 16-hands mule and have been quoted in order to show what can be achieved. The practice in the British Army is to prefer smaller animals and smaller loads.

Thus in 1887 the Official Manual on Transport[4] gives the correct average size of a pack battery mule as 14 hands, with a weight of 8 cwt. Six years old was considered about the average age required. Mules should not stand under 12 hands 2 inches for ordinary transport work, be 56 inches in girth and not be bought at under 4 years old. A 15-hand mule should not be over 1,000 lb in weight and should do 20 miles a day, carrying from 100 to 160 lb plus the saddle, according to the state of the terrain and the amount of feed available. About 5 lb of grain and 15 lb of dry fodder was given daily.

Writing of the big Missouri mules bought for the South African War of 1899–1902 a Remount Officer[5] stated that they had great bone, strength, and compactness and had the power to do an incredible amount of work.

As a draught animal the mule was replaced in the Near East in 1916 with the Desert Mounted Corps by the horse, as the natural pace of the former is slower than that of the latter. The historian of the Corps,[6] however, considered the mule as admirable for Field Artillery teams and for infantry transport. He wrote as follows: 'their hardihood, soundness, freedom from disease, patience and docility are marked. Left to themselves they can march indefinitely, but rapidly lose condition when pushed beyond their natural gait.' It is, however, only fair to say that the mule teams used by the South African Artillery in German South West Africa in 1915 with the Horse Artillery field piece kept up well with the ponies of the Mounted Brigades, fast walking though the latter were.

The above criticism of the mule as a harness animal was no doubt true under the circumstances of the very fast, long marches put in by the Desert Mounted Corps, but on the Western Front where 'perhaps a quarter of a million mules were used' (the figure is that given in Galtry's *The Horse and the War*), many experienced officers preferred the mule to the horse for all purposes, partly because of the former's toughness and powers of resistance to bad conditions. The life of a mule at the Front between 1914 and 1918 was also normally longer than that of a horse.

The authority just quoted gives the prevalent colours of the mule; the dominant note being brown with a fair percentage of bays, chestnuts, greys and duns and an occasional smoky blue. Most of the duns and chestnuts have a strongly defined black line running along the neck and back to the tail with dark zebra-like bars about the shoulders, knees and hocks. There are a few with white legs, and occasionally white mules are met with. Mules work in all shapes and a weedy mule is not necessarily as much of a misfit in a team as a horse of the same type would be. Mules, however, are not as easy to work with as horses, as they have more unpleasant tricks, and though not, according to those who know them well, really vicious, they are apt to be unpleasant to the unwary. This is said to be due to the so-called suspicious nature of the mule, but whether this is the case or not, the mule undoubtedly has acquired a bad character in a general way of speaking, probably undeservedly. It has been said that men of coloured races can get better work out of mules than Europeans, though many white soldiers who have worked with them like and respect their mules.

It is as a pack artillery animal, as already stated, that the mule is best known to the Army generally and in the British service for this work the medium-sized mule is preferred. A Pack Battery (they used to be called Mountain Batteries), is not only incredibly efficient on the steepest hillside but also very fast indeed on the flat, out-marching most other troops at a walk.[7]

In the Second World War the mule was much more used than the horse and has been dealt with in the section dealing with that subject. In 1965 as these lines are being written, the mule is still an integral and important part of the mechanized British Army.

In conclusion may be quoted the rather unkind definition of a muleteer given in the o.e.d. . . . . 'Muleteers are typical Bourbons, they learn nothing and they forget nothing.' Perhaps officers and men who have had difficulties with civilians hired with their mules may agree!

DONKEYS

The donkey is, for his size, an excellent pack animal and has served the British Army well in this capacity in Africa, including South and Central, Somaliland and Egypt, as well as in India. In South Africa, especially in the West and in all areas where tsetse fly and horse sickness are prevalent, he also worked well in harness, and on one occasion in Palestine was used to a limited extent under the saddle.[8]

Donkeys are normally grey, though there are white varieties and the grey donkey has a black dorsal and shoulder stripe. According to a well-known tradition,[9] this stripe was given after the service rendered on Palm Sunday (see Matthew, Chapter XXI, verse 5).

In height the donkey seldom exceeds 13 hands – this being a fairly common size in South Africa – and at the other end of the scale is the Indian grey donkey, running from 8 hands to about 10 hands 2 inches. Animals under 9 hands 2 inches are not taken in India for service and they should have a girth of from 47 inches to as small as 41. They should be from 3 to 8 years old. The pack carried varies from 130 lb in South Africa to 100 lb elsewhere; the pace is $2\frac{1}{2}$ miles an hour and 15 miles is about the limit of a day's march.[10]

Donkeys will subsist on almost any sort of grazing; failing this in South Africa a ration of 8 lb of grain a day was given to draught animals. In India, in war time, the ration was half that amount with 13 lb of dry or 20 lb of green fodder; this was for pack donkeys.

Plate number 51 shows a small donkey in Palestine in 1918 with the simplest kind of equipment of twisted rope or fibre, used with a piece of sacking. The native pattern of saddle is known as a 'sunka'.[11] It consists of a straw bolster with supple sticks or canes, doubled in the centre with the sides tied close together. The bend of the bolster goes in front of the withers, so that these and the spines of the backbone lie in the space between the doubled portions, on which the load goes. There is a thick layer of blanket underneath. This arrangement in the hands of a man who thoroughly understands it works quite well, but is inferior to a regulation pack saddle in a small size. R.A.S.C. Regulations laid down 9 hands as the minimum size to be used and a saddle must be smaller than the smallest mule saddle to fit this type of donkey. In draught the South African donkey compares not unfavourably with the ox, though sixteen donkeys will not take more than about half the load of the same number of oxen. Although on the level the chains (see Plate 39) do not appear to be taut the waggon moves along all the same. Donkey waggons have always been a great feature in the dry, arid, regions of the Western part of South Africa and during the conquest of the German Colony of South West Africa in 1915 by the troops of the Union of South Africa (now the Republic of the same name), a large proportion of the transport during the initial stage of the campaign consisted of them. There used to be a common saying, typical of the widespread belief in the toughness of the donkey, that one hardly ever saw a dead one. In the long waterless marches from the coast of German South West Africa to the more fertile inland belt, the waterholes were very far apart, and the water in them was not too plentiful. On one occasion a convoy after a long trek reached the next watering place only to find the supply exhausted by the preceding convoy. The loads were dumped and the empty waggons taken on to the next water hole, which was supposed to have a good supply. On arrival it was again found that there was no water, so the spans in the empty waggons were taken back to the water where the loads had been dumped in the hope that the water hole would have filled up in the meantime. On the march back even the tough little desert-bred donkeys succumbed and died in harness. It would, of course, have been fatal to have unharnessed them as they could have become quite unmanageable, as really thirsty animals, and men too, quickly become. This is no doubt an extreme instance; normally a donkey will stand up to incredible hardships and survive.

Though, as already stated, the donkey is usually employed as a pack animal, he did on one important occasion fulfil with success the role of a cavalry troop horse, on the march only. During the final gruelling marches which preceded the collapse of Turkish resistance in Palestine in 1918, Allenby's Desert Mounted Corps were extremely short of remounts and it was decided that the non-combatants of the mounted units would have to make shift with the best of the donkeys available in lieu of troop horses. Loaded with big men with their kits the donkeys made the grade and if they did not reach camp with the troops were never far behind![12] On a former occasion ammunition and stores had to be delivered to the forward echelons of the Desert Corps and waggon transport was not available. Two hundred donkeys were collected from cooks, batmen and any other possible sources, loaded and, after a twenty-mile night march, returned to base with the loss of only a few donkeys who had strayed.[13]

In 1937, during the unrest in Palestine, the 2nd Battalion Royal Ulster Rifles were operating mainly in the hills. They had been furnished with the small local donkeys to pack their mortars, light machine guns, wireless sets, reserve ammunition and water and rations. The difficulty was to get the slow-moving donkeys to the areas where the Battalion had to de-bus before taking to the hills. This was solved by fitting civilian lorries with crates along the sides into which the donkeys were inducted by way of the tailboards of the lorries. They took quite kindly to the operation and were duly unloaded and saddled up wherever the troops were operating. Needless to say, the lorries were christened 'donkvans'. Surely this was as neat a bit of improvization as even the British Army has put into operation![14]

Regular cavalry operating on the North West Frontier in India found donkeys most convenient for carrying odds and ends such as farriers' and saddlers' tools etc., and corps such as the Bechuanaland Border Police (1885–95), operating on the border of what has since become Rhodesia, had all the men's kits carried on donkeys, who lived on the bush and rough grass and saved the troop ponies having to carry too much weight.

Probably the most serious mortality which ever took place among donkeys employed in large numbers was in the campaign against the Germans by South African troops and battalions of the King's African Rifles in the First World War. Of 24,000 donkeys, shipped to East Africa or bought locally, only 1,402 survived the fighting. The circumstances were no doubt exceptional, but it has seldom been the case that donkeys have suffered as severely as horses and mules, as they did in this instance.[15]

In the Second World War over 10,000 donkeys were shipped to India from South Africa for the Burma Campaign. But they do not seem to have been used to the same extent as formerly, possibly because of the small load carried and the difficulty of procuring saddles small enough to fit.[16]

ANIMALS, OTHER THAN HORSES, MULES AND DONKEYS, USED BY THE BRITISH ARMY; WITH AN ACCOUNT OF THE SADDLERY AND HARNESS USED

This section has details of saddlery, harness and equipment used by elephants, camels, oxen or bullocks, reindeer, dogs and yaks, all of which have been pressed into the service of the British Army at various times. There are also notes on war dogs, as well as a mention of the buffalo.

Plates refer as follows:

Elephants 42 and 43. Camels 49 and 50 and riding 88. Bullocks 43; only Indian bullocks are shown. Reindeer 54. Dog teams 53. Yaks 52. War dogs 55.

The elephant, once used in line of battle in a role more or less equivalent to that of the tank, though with a much greater degree of vulnerability, was valuable in comparatively modern armies as a pack animal carrying about 800 lb of supplies or a light gun, and as a transport animal pulling heavy artillery. Elephants were extremely useful in cases where other forms of transport were in difficulties and either unable to proceed or unwilling to make further efforts. They were also invaluable for helping guns or waggons stuck at narrow corners on mountain roads, when they would push from behind with their heads. They could keep up well with the ordinary army train and, if they could be suitably fed, were generally of great use. They required each a specially trained mahout or driver, and were especially valuable in jungle country, but needed considerable quantities of bulk food and would not stand hostile fire. Hence an elephant battery had bullock teams to take the guns into and out of action under enemy fire. They were not satisfactory in continuous draught. For the Indian Army only female elephants were bought at between 20 and 30 years of age and a first-class animal should have stood 8 feet high, all those below this measurement being second class. The Indian Army Regulations state that elephants of the first class should carry up to 1,200 lb and of the second class up to 960 lb. This is considerably in excess of the service load already quoted from Steel's *Indian Veterinary Manuals, I*, taken from Burn's *Notes on Transport*.

Plate 42 shows the saddle used for heavy ordnance in the Abyssinian Campaign of 1868, which was described as being 'almost all that could be desired, except that breechings and breast ropes should have been fitted'. They are shown fitted to what was presumably the next saddle designed.

The drawing which follows is of an elephant pack saddle designed by Mr Sanderson about 1885. He was very well known as Superintendent of Elephant Keddahs at Dacca.

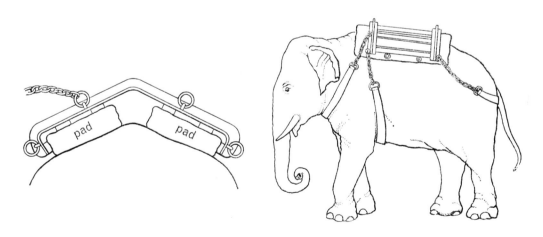

FIGURE I   Elephant with pack-saddle and diagram of the tree and panels.
From Burn's *Notes on Transport and on Camel Corps*, page 106.

This baggage saddle, adopted by the Commissariat Department in India, is described by the inventor as follows:[17] 'it consists of two pads or pillows, entirely detached, each 4 feet long, 15 inches wide and 6 inches thick. These are of blanket covered with waterproof tarpaulin, encased in stout sacking. One is placed on each side of the spine and there retained by two connecting arches of T-iron. No saddle cloth is required underneath. The spine is entirely free along its whole length and for a width of 15 inches for the circulation of air. The load rests entirely on the upper part of the ribs. The breast strap and crupper hook into rings on the saddle, and do not come into play except in steep ground. The girth hooks onto the saddle on the off side, and is drawn tight on the near side by a rope 6 feet long. Girth, breastplate and crupper can be drawn tight without removing the load. The complete weight is 140 lb. The saddle pads cannot become wet and therefore increase in weight. Owing to the broadness of the base, 200 lb may be placed on one side of the centre without any counterbalancing weight, without affecting the equilibrium. The stability is such that an elephant has been loaded with 1,200 lb and marched on level ground for miles without girth, breastplate or crupper, and without the saddle shifting. It is specially adapted for hilly countries. With foot boards attached it is convenient for riding. A cradle could be made and fitted to it for the conveyance of guns, mortars and their carriages. The pad formed of layers of Meerut blanket weighs 60 lb, the iron frame 80 lb. The loading rope is 22 yards long and ⅞ inch in diameter.'

The ordinary gear in use by the Royal Artillery in Abyssinia (see Plate 42) consisted of a quilted cloth 1½ inches thick, reaching halfway down the sides and from the nape of the neck to the croup. On this went a pad, 6 feet long, 5 feet broad and 9 inches thick, formed of stout sacking packed with dry grass. In some parts of India another pad went over this. A long rope passed twice round the body, round the neck as a breast strap and under the tail as a crupper. The weight complete is 200 lb.

This type of equipment was defective because the load rested on the spine, the rope went slack when the load was put on, and in steep ground the load shifted and had to be taken off in order to tighten the ropes. Also the centre of gravity of the load was too high.

These two types of pack-saddle as used for elephants are an excellent example of the pad without a tree normally evolved in all countries where loads are carried on animals, and of the European (including North American) more scientifically constructed saddle with a tree. The main difference, and a most important one, is that in the latter type the weight does not rest directly on the spine. The drawing of the cross elevation of Sanderson's saddle shows this clearly. The principle is the same for all types of saddle.

The notes on pack-saddle for elephants in the 1911 edition of Army Service Corps Training Part III are as follows: 'the best form of pack-saddle for the elephant is one constructed on somewhat similar lines to those of the mule saddle and fitted with a girth, breast plate and crupper, which does not pass round the tail, but hangs immediately below the buttock. In many parts of India, however, a quilted cloth about $1\frac{1}{2}$ inches thick is placed over the elephant's back, surmounted by a pad of stout sacking stuffed with dry grass, about 5 feet long, 6 feet broad and 9 inches thick. The whole is girthed by a long rope passing twice round the body, round the neck as a breast strap, and under the tail as a crupper. This primitive method presents many disadvantages; the load rests on the spine, the pad is apt to slip on steep ground, the ropes frequently gall the animal, in wet weather the pad gets soaked and its weight doubled and the cloth retains the sweat and favours galling'. Plate 43 shows two elephants harnessed to a 40-pr Rifled Muzzle Loader, the weight of the gun without the carriage being some 34 cwt. By conformation a pack animal rather than one used for draught, the elephant when in harness 'loses much of the relative advantage his weight, strength and size give him'. Breast harness presses in a most unsatisfactory way on the upper part of the chest, the most delicate part of the animal's construction. Indeed, Major Burn, who has been so frequently quoted, stated that 'a mule or bullock in a cart is for transport purposes, as far as load is concerned, the equal of the elephant'. The Plate shows the bullock team which took over the gun when coming into action, for as already stated elephants will not stand fire though bullocks do.

THE CAMEL

God made the Horse but a Committee made the Camel—ANON.

This animal has for centuries occupied a valuable place in the list of animals suitable for pack transport. Camels have also proved most useful as remounts for mounted riflemen and have also been worked in harness with success. Although a camel pulls double the load he can carry on his back he is far more suitable as a pack animal, with the proviso, which attaches to all pack transport, that he shall be looked after by men who understand him. There are two classes of camel, the type with the single hump and the Bactrian with two humps, bred and used throughout Central Asia and inured to cold. Although the British Army had some experience of this type in the Crimea and Afghanistan, it was not sufficient to make it worth while including Bactrian camels in this book.

The single-humped camel is bred in Arabia, Northern Africa, Egypt, Abyssinia, Somaliland and India, and has been used in South Africa as a riding camel by police and in Australia by civilians. Specialized breeding has produced two types; the riding camel, called Sowari in India (Plate 88), and Hagheen in Egypt, comparable to the thoroughbred horse. All camels have a stride of from 6 to 7 feet at the walk and at this pace do from 2 to $2\frac{1}{2}$ miles an hour, the riding camel being, however, able to travel up to 12 miles an hour, carrying a load of 250 lb for 30 miles daily for long periods. The riding camel's best pace is a 'jog' of 5 or 6 miles an hour.

There are many breeds of baggage camel, those bred in different countries each having their own slight peculiarities and doing best under climatic conditions as near as possible like those to which they are accustomed. Thus those bred in Egypt in the Nile Delta are big, soft creatures unsuited to desert conditions. Those bred in the desert are as useful there as the Sudanese types, of which there are seven, bred by as many different tribes. The Bisharin and Kababish are well known, the former being light and looking well bred, used to light loads only and capable of great endurance.

A transport camel under good conditions should carry from 250 to 450 lb for 20 miles a day, should not be under 6 years of age and can work on up to the age of 15 if the teeth remain good. They should not work more than 8 hours a day and if possible be grazed for at least 6 hours eating thorn bushes as well as any other vegetation obtainable. If there is no grazing, camels in war time have been fed at a rate of from 6 lb of grain in various forms and 40 lb of fodder. If possible camels should be watered daily, although Indian camels will carry on if watered every other day, Arab and Desert breeds every two or three days, and Somali camels will carry on if only watered once in four days. The camel has a foot adapted to soft sand and does not travel at all well on muddy or slippery ground. He stands fire well, more especially when kneeling down, as when being loaded. He cannot cross narrow ditches and must have some form of portable bridge on which to traverse them. He swims well. He is extremely difficult for the average white man to work with, but is capable of great endurance and will carry on till he drops.[18] Camels are unintelligent and have almost uniformly had a 'bad press' from war correspondents and the like.

Transport camels are excellent for Pack Artillery, and pack, mountain and camel guns — different names for the same type of ordnance — are very suitable as loads.

As a camel saddle must not touch the hump on the back at all, more stuffing is needed at the ends than in the middle, and as the weight-bearing surface lies mainly in front of the hump each camel requires his own saddle carefully fitted. Otherwise the main principles are roughly the same as in other animals' saddles. There are high horns at both pommel and cantle and though Service riding saddles have stirrups fitted normally, it is more usual to ride with the legs crossed in front of the horn at the pommel. It was a very common practice to have riding saddles made to take two men as in Plate 88, the rear man being much lower on the camel's back. A single saddle weighs about 30 lb; a double one of the Indian pattern 65 lb, and the British Army type $73\frac{1}{32}$ lb.

In 1843–5, Sir Charles Napier had a corps formed of from 500 to 600 Native Infantry under British officers mounted on camels and operating in Scinde. Four camel guns were attached and each camel carried two men, the weight on the camel being about 360 lb inclusive. The illustration in Burn's *Notes on Transport* shows both men facing forward, using stirrups and carrying only their arms and ammunition.[19]

In 1858, during the final stages of the Indian Mutiny, the 92nd Gordon Highlanders had 150 men on camels, also with double saddles. An Indian driver sat in front, armed with sword and lance. He was in charge of the camel and in action the animals were parked in the kneeling position and defended by the drivers.

The rear seat, on which the Highlander sat, was padded up as high as the front one. This small unit of Mounted Infantry was extremely effective. They were issued with a good type of riding camel and could cover 30 miles a day for 6 consecutive days. Their Commanding Officer, Major Bethune, considered that, as already stated, 6 miles an hour was the easiest pace of his men's mounts. On one occasion the unit marched for 42 hours out of 48, coming into action at the end. This Camel Corps is also illustrated in Burn's book.

In 1884 four regiments formed from detachments of picked men, both cavalry and infantry, were equipped as a Camel Corps in Upper Egypt for the expedition sent to relieve Khartoum, where General Gordon was besieged. Single saddles were used and there were no native drivers with the riding camels. The wooden saddle was covered with red leather,[20] and many were badly made. They had panels and the seat was padded with the man's blanket and the canvas of a small bivouac tent. The man rode with stirrups and on the saddle were wallets holding grain, water-bags, the rifle in the deep Namaqua bucket,[21] spare ammunition and the man's kit. The men's camels were of baggage type, they were half-starved and kept short of water, sore backs were the rule rather than the exception and the corps was not a success. In fact no one understood the proper way to work with camels.

Very different was the experience of a Camel Corps five companies strong, raised for the operations round Suakin in the Sudan in 1885. There were five infantrymen and one native driver to three camels, riding double. Without the saddle and saddlebags the weight carried was 418½ lb, but the marches were not long and the camels were well fed and watered. Besides their arms and seventy rounds of ammunition, the men had on the camels blankets, great coats if needed and one day's rations. Everything else wanted was carried on baggage camels. The use of native drivers ensured that they were properly looked after, for the British soldier co-operated well with these men.

The Egyptian Camel Corps, under British officers until Egypt became independent, are shown riding with stirrups in the eighteen eighties,[22] though photographs taken during the First World War show them riding with the feet crossed in front of the pommel, as do those of British officers with their own men on camels, though other ranks are shown using stirrups.

As regards artillery the equipment of the Mountain Battery R.A. which served with the Gordon Relief Column in 1884 was typical. They had the 7-pounder steel screw gun, with the two parts of the gun itself each making a load, the carriage and wheels three more loads, with three ammunition camels to each sub-division of one gun and there was one native to every two camels. The officers, an Egyptian officer and interpreter, the N.C.O.s and the trumpeters rode riding camels and the gunners baggage camels. The pack saddles weighed 120 lb complete, the gun and carriage loads from 200 lb to 226 lb, and the ammunition loads 220 lb each. These loads were considered too heavy, although not above the average as already given.

In the Afghan War of 1839 a strong beast was given a load of 400 lb, a weak one, one of 320 lb; overloading, unless discipline was very strict, was common.

The next Afghan War, that of from 1878 to 1881, was notorious for the mortality among transport animals, described by the future Major General Sir F. Smith as follows:[23] 'Hecatombs of transport animals were sacrificed to ignorance. There was a shameful neglect and ignorance of saddle fitting.' Another cause was that the rules for only buying camels of the proper age were not enforced. Smith added that we did as badly in Egypt in 1884. From September 1880 to September 1881 during the Afghan War, 2,000 camels were bought in Persia, about 6,000 in Afghanistan and 25,000 in India.

The following is a description of camel gear as used in Bengal in 1885.[19] The panels, known as 'pulan', were made of taut stuffed with straw, they were secured to a wooden frame by ropes and the weight was about 42 lb. The breastplate, girths and crupper were of rope and worn loose. The loading rope weighed 8 lb and the blanket or 'jhool' and saddle bag about 16 lb each. The panel was open like a horse collar so as to clear the top of the hump well, with a clear opening in the middle of from 9 to 15 inches. Numnahs were preferred to sheepskins under the saddle.

The pack-saddles used in Egypt did not differ much from the Indian pattern; the modern type used in the latter country have the arches so arranged that they are joined by a wooden peg (kokra) which allows of their being opened or closed as needed.[24]

General Service Patterns: Egyptian Pattern Mark I, 1900.[25] The two wooden arches of the tree are connected at the top by an iron rod and at the lower parts by wooden sidebars strengthened by plates. There are rings and thongs for the girth and breast straps. The panels have bag hide backs, are lined with coarse canvas faced with camel hair cloth and stuffed with horse hair. The sizes are 28½ inches by 16 inches and each panel has a V-shaped channel with the broad side at the top. When used for the conveyance of wounded men it is fitted with cacolets similar to the G.S. pattern. This is an iron-framed adjustable chair, a pair weighing 56 lb, hung one on each side of the saddle with the seats facing forward. The straps holding the footboard are 58 inches long.

These cacolets are used on practically all types of pack-saddles and are shown on camel saddles of the 1915 pattern, made in Egypt to Ordnance specifications; see Plates 49 for cacolets, and 50 for the saddle with nets, loading ropes and girths. The camel in the background in the first Plate shows two men in the sitting type of cacolet and the one in the foreground the cacolet for wounded men lying down, with a shade over the man's head.

These contrivances were in use by the French in the Crimea. The sitting type is shown in the *Manual of Horsemastership*, etc., 1937, Plate VI, page 59, fitted on the Mark V Universal Pattern on a pack horse. They are reasonably comfortable, which the lying down pattern when used on a camel is said not to be. Indeed, Captain B. T. Hinchley, who served with the Camel Transport Corps in the Near East during the 1914–18 War and kindly supplied the photographs for the two plates, states that they could be hideously uncomfortable. His description of the saddle in Plate 50 runs as follows: 'these saddles were entirely native, made in

Alexandria and the neighbouring districts, of hessian and straw with a wooden frame. No modification was required for carrying water tanks. These latter held ten gallons each and were made by Buller's of Tipton. The Egyptians called them "fantasis".' The author of the history of *The Desert Mounted Corps* wrote of camel transport in Palestine as being 'useless and dangerous in mountainous country!'

In India in 1910 the correct type of camel pack-saddle was still under consideration. There were a variety of patterns both in general use and in mobilization stores. The commonest pattern had a wooden front arch only, made of two stout pieces of wood bolted together with a wooden key and lashed with string. The key was intended to act in the same way as a hinge and to allow the opening or closing of the gap at the top of the two halves of the arch, according to the condition of the camel. The space between the tops, which should never be less than 6 inches when open, must be closed as the animal gets thinner to keep the arch off the withers. There are three sidebars of male bamboo, lashed to the arch and the upper one to the top of the pad and the other two spaced down the depth of it. The pad is of goat's hair, lined with blanket and stuffed with straw or grass. The back of each pad is joined to the other at the rear making a point 10 to 12 inches above the back. There is no ironwork, the whole saddle being lashed together with rope and string made of goat's or camel's hair. The loading rope is 60 feet long and the whole saddle is very primitive and should be used only by skilled men.[24]

The modern form of G.S. Camel Saddle as used in 1937[25] is known as the improved Baladi Pattern. The line drawing at Figure 2 is taken from Plate XVI of *Manual of Horsemastership* 1937. The shape of the arches of the trees is shown here. They are of the heavy pattern, the light-burden saddle differing only in the measurements.

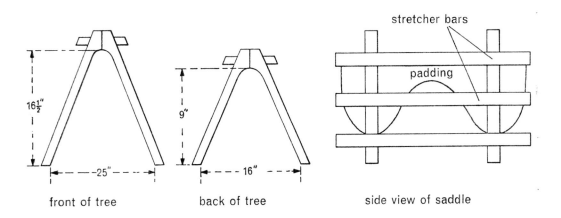

front of tree   back of tree   side view of saddle

FIGURE 2   Camel saddle, diagrams of the tree.

It is made up of the two arches, called trees, two cross poles, two or four side bars, two front and one back pads, one double girth with lateral straps, a breast-plate and, in hilly countries, a tail strap. The side poles, fastened high on the tree, and side bars are of teak, and should be strong enough to stand up to the camel rolling unexpectedly, and the front and back trees (see Figure 2) of Douglas fir or pine. The pads or panels are made of strong cotton, strengthened with a kind of hemp sacking and have pockets for packing the rice straw used as padding. They are laced to the trees. The large size weighs about 80 lb, the smaller 56 lb, and it has only one instead of two side bars on each side.

For fitting cacolets, of two types, one for sitting and one for lying down wounded men, iron frames with brackets are clamped to the sides of the larger saddle. Plate 49. The plate shows a camel girthed up with the girths tight, not loose as in 1885. As already stated the main weight-bearing surface of the camel lies in front of the hump but it is small and the centre of the load has to be carried further back and the surface over the loins utilized. The pads take the weight front and rear with the load resting on the side bars and side poles. The illustration of the Havildar of the Bikanir Camel Corps (Plate 88), though showing a double riding saddle, should make the above description clearer, to the extent of showing how a camel carries a saddle.

As is usually the case with pack animals it is necessary to hire animals with their owners or drivers furnished with their own saddlery. Very often these saddles have to be strengthened with metal plates on the front arch; stretcher bars may be added and the pads lashed by thongs passing through the woodwork.

THE OX OR BULLOCK

Generally known as a bullock in India, the ox has always been a valuable transport animal either in draught or under pack. They should not be bought at under 4 years of age, and provided the teeth are not too worn down, can work well up to 11 or 12 years old if grazing is indifferent, and up to 16 or 17 if it is good.[26] But few 'transport riders', the men who did the work of the railways with their ox-wagons in the old days, would work an ox over 12 years old. Oxen will work for 7 or 8 hours a day, travel best at night, and can average 20 miles or more a day. Their pace is from 2 to $2\frac{1}{2}$ miles an hour, although the celebrated Mysore trotting bullocks of the early days of the nineteenth century would walk 4 and trot 6 miles an hour.[27] As a pack animal an ox will carry from 150 to 200 lb, the lighter load being enough in mountainous country. In a two-wheeled cart a pair of oxen will draw 800 to 960 lb and in a waggon in spans or teams of sixteen up to 5,000 lb.

Although an ox can be ridden, and there was a farmer in the Shires in the old days who rode an ox to hounds, his loose skin makes saddling difficult and constant care is needed to keep the load in place. Infantry officers who rode pack oxen in the Kaffir War of 1835 in South Africa did not find them satisfactory.[28]

Oxen were used to a limited extent by the Cape Mounted Riflemen Artillery

Troop in Basutoland in 1879.[29] The 150 lb mountain gun made a fair load and was easily carried by a small compact ox. This was an exceptional case; the great use made of pack bullocks was in India from 1780 onwards, when there was usually a pack bullock to nearly every fighting man.[30] Like all other animals the bullock pays for being looked after by experts and it was the Brinjarry caste, the hereditary bullock packers of India, who furnished Colonel Wellesley, the future Duke of Wellington, with the best transport he had from about 1803 onwards in Southern India. His despatches are full of references to them and to the pack bullocks bought by the Government, and the numbers available were considerable. Thus, in January 1803, there were in Mysore 32,000 loaded Brinjarry bullocks. All were to be fitted with bags for carrying rice and the carriage bullocks – presumably baggage is meant – were to have saddles. Wellesley's meticulous care for every detail does not seem to have gone as far as describing the type of saddles used. Drawings of a later date show a heavy pad with a loop round the hump so characteristic of the Indian breed and a large saddle bag on each side.

From his Supplementary Despatches we learn that Wellesley had the Government drivers taught how to load their bullocks as well as how to drive them, or rather not over-drive them. They were not to be taken out of a walk unless ordered and they carried everything, ammunition, entrenching tools, treasure and tents. A cavalry regiment had to have 1,000 bullocks to carry a month's supply of grass, in other words bulk fodder, for the horses.

We used pack bullocks in India for a long time and in Abyssinia in 1868, where they were not a great success.

It is as a draught animal that the Indian bullock and the South African ox excelled. Wellesley's artillery in 1803 were all drawn by bullocks, and, as horses suitable for artillery were very scarce indeed, he proposed to have twelve guns horsed but pulled by bullocks on the march, with the teams marching alongside ready to replace the latter when rapid action was needed.[31]

In India there were two types of bullock required, the specially bred, strong, large siege train animals (see Plate 43), standing from 50 to 60 inches high behind the hump and 43 to 46 inches long from hump to tail, and smaller draught and pack animals, 48 to 50 inches high and 38 to 44 inches along the back. Plate 43 shows eight of the first class, the two wheelers in harness, the others in yokes. The Plate also shows the elephants of a siege train.

Although bullocks do well on grazing, they require to graze for 6 hours a day, often with large forces almost impossible. An ox eats four-fifths of its own pack load of 200 lb in six weeks[32] and carrying grain to feed in lieu of grazing meant a serious increase in transport, for the big siege train bullocks needed 7 lb of grain and 25 lb of dry fodder daily in war time and the other type 6 lb of grain and 20 lb of fodder in draught and 5 lb and 14 lb in pack.

During the Indian Mutiny, and as late as the Afghan War of 1878 to 1881, bullocks were used for both Horse and Field Artillery at times. Grain-crushing machines were carried for them, otherwise the grain was soaked.

The Siege Batteries were commonly known as 'Buffalo Batteries' and from this slang name came the once well-known marching song 'The Buffalo Battery', originally referring to 6/11 R.A., commanded by Major (later Major General) F. A. Tillard, in Afghanistan in 1879.

The Indian Service bullock yoke, sealed by British Ordnance in 1885,[33] consisted of two bars of pedouk wood, going across the necks of a pair of bullocks, one, the yoke from which the animal pulled, on top and the other below the neck. They were joined by detachable iron bars on each side of each bullock's neck and are shown in Plate 43 with the Indian drivers. This yoke weighed 41 lb.

The pack-saddle used in India at this time consisted of a saddle with a slit in the centre, a pad, surcingle or belly band, a crupper, a satchel or saddle bag, head and leading ropes. Major Burn, from whose book this description is taken, disapproved of bullocks for pack work.

In 1940 Indian Ordnance issued bullock saddles for use in Burma by the Chindits. The bullocks fell off in condition so quickly that it proved impossible to get the saddles to fit, so a blanket and groundsheet were used as a pad with two parachutes slung over to take the load. This worked well.

This is still roughly the method used in South Africa today, the parachutes being replaced by grain bags, and the Basuto bring full loads down from the mountains with rawhide girths tied over the blanket pad. Pack oxen loaded in this manner were tried in 1879 in the Zulu War, but competent drivers were not available and the pack oxen were not satisfactory. In the yoke the South African ox has always been a great success and in the South African War of 1899, in the early stages, the Republican forces took the few heavy guns they put into the field anywhere and everywhere. We copied their example and the so-called 'cow guns', mostly Royal Navy ordnance on field carriages, were drawn by matched spans of sixteen oxen with another span in reserve. The author or authors of the War Office Manual on *Animal Management* wrote as follows: 'the manner in which oxen drew heavy loads over rough ground across rivers and drifts, up steep long hills, on roads impracticable for English draught horses, was marvellous'.

The South African yoke is a plain bar of wood, rounded, with holes on each side of the ox's neck for a stout piece of wood. These fasten under the dewlap with a piece of twisted rawhide and the centre of the yoke, as in the Indian type, between the two oxen, is fastened to a long chain running back to the wagon. The British Army used the South African ox wagon, the lighter type taking 3,000 lb, until about 1870 and then the larger pattern, introduced about that time. In warfare with African tribes it was usual to form these waggons into a circular or square formation at night or when fighting was expected. The name laager, given to this practice, has survived and is still in use with mechanized transport. The South African ox varied in height from about 13 hands for the small compact native breeds to about 15 hands for the big rangy Afrikander oxen bred by the white farmers. During the South African War of 1899–1902 the transport spans when grazing was bad were fed about 14 lb of dry fodder and sometimes 4 to 6 lb of grain, usually crushed maize. But they do not work well without grazing. They are plucky enough up to a point, but if they lose heart they sulk and lie down. The Indian jhool or blanket was used in South Africa for transport oxen with great success.

In Southern Europe in some countries oxen pull from the horns with a pad on the forehead carrying a bar. It is on record that during the Peninsular War the Portuguese oxen stood 16 hands and pulled from the horns.[34] Single oxen in Southern Europe work with shafts attached to the end of the yoke, and although it is presumably only in Spain and Portugal in the early years of last century that ox transport was utilized by our Army, many soldiers must have seen the Italian methods of yoking during the last war. Various methods are in use, including one similar to the South African plan and there is a curious rig in the Trentino where the oxen pull from the neck and brake by means of a rope attachment fastened to the end of the pole, which is made extra long and curved upwards at the end.

THE BUFFALO

Mention has been made of the misuse of the name in Army slang under Bullocks. The buffalo was described in the 1850's as being 'seldom or ever employed, being too slow and impatient of heat'.[35] Buffalo were, however, used in the Crimea and Lord Wolseley in the *Soldier's Pocket Book* gives the daily ration as 20 lb hay, 15 lb of oats and 12 lb of barley.[36]

THE YAK

Yaks and donkeys were the sole means of transport during the campaign in Tibet in 1903–4. As a pack animal the yak is driven in droves at 1½ miles an hour and receives a little grain to eke out the grazing. He is long-haired and closely resembles the buffalo. Plate 52 shows the yak in single draught in an ekka. The pack-saddle with breast harness added and the shafts can be plainly seen.[37]

REINDEER

In North Russia in 1918 the British Army employed both Reindeer and Dogs with success. The reindeer were hired from the Lapps and Plate 54 shows the harness and sleighs used. In the winter months over 600 sleighs and about 2,000 reindeer were employed, all the drivers being the owner-Lapps. Though semi-wild, these animals work well and were invaluable for supplying inaccessible outposts. They can do considerable distances with a light load of 200 lb at an estimated speed of from 8 to 10 miles an hour, but in 1918 loads of up to 600 lb were in use and the locally made boat-shaped sledge stood up well to the weight. One man drove three sleds, the leaders of the two rear ones being tied to the sled in front. Three reindeer make a team with one behind acting as a brake. Reindeer can only operate where there are mossbeds on which they graze, digging pits in the snow with the fore-feet and using the browtines as a hoe. Obviously they could not be used in the same localities as the dog teams.

The sled will roll to 45 degrees without capsizing and a guiding pole is used. The harness consists of a leather saddle with a collar round the deer's neck. The trace is of rawhide, plaited square. There is a swingle-tree of bent wood, with a looped thong fastened in the middle. This thong passes through a hole under the forefoot of the sled and the loop is slipped over the bit on the stem-head so that the deer can always be cast loose from the sled at a moment's notice. The reindeer can carry a pack of 50 lb.[38]

WAR DOGS

'It is not unreasonable to say that the war dog is probably more firmly established today as a part of the armed forces than ever before . . . There will always be scope for the talents of trained dogs, no matter where the Army is called upon to operate. Nothing that man has invented, or is likely to invent in the foreseeable future, can replace those qualities which have made the dog such an outstanding member of the animal kingdom and the devoted servant of man.' Brigadier J. Clabby, Royal Army Veterinary Corps, written in 1963.[39]

This quotation, which will not improbably come as a surprise to many who have not studied the history of the dog in modern war, embodies the conclusions of a scientific officer of the British Army of the very highest standard. The paragraph is taken from the chapter on War Dogs in his *History of the Royal Army Veterinary Corps*. In it Brigadier Clabby has treated his subject in the fullest detail and it is not too much to say that all dog-lovers should read and re-read this masterly presentation of an aspect of the training of dogs, of their wonderful attributes and of the equally remarkable and amazing understanding of the volunteers of many races who have learnt to understand the wonderful mind of a dog and so to make the fullest possible use of him as an outstanding helpmeet to the soldier on active service.

It is not proposed in this chapter to do more than summarize the main points of Brigadier Clabby's description and perhaps to persuade those who are interested to read his book for themselves.

There is, however, one aspect of the use of dogs in war which does not come within the scope of his work and that will be dealt with first in some detail. In 1918, during the campaign in North Russia against what were then called the Bolshevist Forces, the British Army made use of teams of dogs from Canada harnessed to sleds – see Plate 53 showing teams.[40] In 1941 and 1943 dogs were again sent from Canada to the United Kingdom, but were only utilized for training purposes.[41]

Dog Transport by means of sleds is a subject which is familiar to many people from books and films and has been the means of opening up vast tracts in the North of the American continent. The Canadians and not least the Royal Canadian Police are the great exponents of the system. A team may consist of from four to seven dogs with an average load of some 100 lb per dog, which may be doubled on a good snow-surface. An average day's march would be from 25 to 30 miles; with four dogs and a light load of 40 lb up to 50 miles a day has been covered. If a fresh trail has to be made 16 miles a day with a heavy load would be good travelling.[42] The breeds of dogs brought over with their highly trained Canadian drivers were Siwash, Husky and Malmoot; many experts prefer the last two. All dogs should be closely bred to the wolf – hence the note in the section on Reindeer of the impossibility of working the two species of transport animal in any kind of proximity to each other. A dog should weigh about 100 lb, a bitch about 90 lb, and any dog weighing under 75 lb is considered useless for transport purposes.

If used as pack animals in summer they should be fitted with two belly bands, a breast and a tail strap and can carry a 50 lb pack, though half the weight of the dog should be a maximum load. The Army ration in Russia was 5 lb of fresh fish a day, supplemented by corn meal and seal oil. The sled used was the light type Shackelton pattern, long and narrow and capable of taking from 800 to 1,000 lb of load.[40]

The harness may consist of either a carefully fitted collar or breast harness (see under Harness for horses, and mules) with a 5-foot long trace and a ring on the trace for a snap fastening in front of the belly band. The latter and the back strap must be well clear of the point of the shoulder. The traces are sewn onto the back strap. The rope from the front of the sled to the swingle-tree is 7 feet 6 inches long. These notes are taken mostly from E. M. Bruce's article in the *Legion of Frontiersmen's Pocket Book*, who states that the sled is steered by a 'Gee-pole', 7 feet long, fastened on the right-hand side.

The Royal Army Service Corps Training, published in 1922, states that these dog teams were 'most useful'.

The War Dog proper, as distinct from the transport type, had been used intermittently for centuries in various combatant or protective roles. During the First World War two types were originated and developed in 1916 in response to an urgent demand, the messenger and secondly the guard dog.[39]

Although the various Dogs' Homes produced many suitable dogs it would appear that dogs loaned by private owners were a more profitable source of supply, not only in the First but also during the Second World War.[43] Once more the war effort of the country had benefited vastly from the voluntary efforts of a large section of the community, in this case the very numerous dog lovers, owners and breeders. This loan scheme not only saved the country a considerable sum of money but also obtained quicker results than any requisitioning would have achieved. It was, of course, dependent entirely on the goodwill of the public and as Brigadier Clabby stated, 'probably required more tact from the Veterinary and Remounts Directorate than any other task, except the scheme for the repatriation of dog pets for service personnel'. In all some 6,000 dogs were offered and some 55 per cent successfully trained and issued at home and overseas. In 1941 a centralized system of control was established and two War Dogs Training Schools set up, one for the Army and one for the Royal Air Force. In 1954, when the official report was published, the Training Scheme was fully in working.

At first guard dogs were wanted as watch dogs on military and R.A.F. stations and to act as sentries; then other activities were called for. They fall into six basic types for training purposes – guard, messenger, casualty detection (Red Cross), tracker, infantry patrol and mine detection (R.E.) dogs.[44] Modifications in the speciality training asked for are: guard dogs may be used as sentries, either for patrolling, either loose or on a lead, always with a handler, or as static sentries on a running wire not over 100 yards in length. The most usual method is that of patrolling with the dog in charge of his handler. These men, born, or so it seems, with an aptitude for this delicate and difficult job of both understanding and training a dog, are the keynote of the whole system. Their value as soldiers can surely not be overestimated. They may be of any race and are presumably the finest exponents of a craft which has fascinated and employed men since dogs were first domesticated. Unfortunately it is unlikely that the Bushmen of Southern Africa, whose dogs are of such exceptional use to them in guarding and tracking, could be brought to work on a training scheme for Army purposes! A variation of the guard dog is the security dog, who is trained neither to bite nor to maul but only to corner, pursue or detain the man he is after.

The messenger dog was at first employed in one way only, his work being to be led by a stranger to an outpost and to make his way back, usually with incredible quickness, to his handler at wherever the base might be. In the Second World War each dog had two handlers and would shuttle between the two. This very great improvement depends on the ability of the two men who work with a dog taking the greatest care that they each have an absolutely equal share of the dog's affection, so that he will work as accurately for each of them.[45] Messenger dogs can, if wanted, carry a pack of one-third of the weight of the dog himself. It will be noted that this is less than the weight considered correct for Canadian sled dogs, the reason being that the messenger dog is not normally using a trail or track and is in a hurry. The speed of some of these dogs is remarkable. In the First World War a dog made his way 'through barbed wire and a number of batteries in 22 minutes as compared with 70 minutes taken by a man'.

Casualty detection dogs were not used to any extent in the Second World War. A dog for this work should range and find casualties up to 75 yards in front of and on both sides of his handler. During the blitz some dogs were used in London to search bomb-devastated buildings for casualties in places unreachable by the searchers. This type of dog is also used by the Swiss in mountain rescue work.

The tracker dog has been most used in Malaya, Kenya and Cyprus. Their value in tracking with the utmost possible despatch single terrorists, to name only one objective, moving by night in most difficult country, can hardly be over-rated, as can readily be ascertained from a number of extraordinary accounts given in Brigadier Clabby's book. Normally a tracker dog was worked by his handler on an eighteen-foot line and the practice of using visual trackers (in Malaya these were Ibans who were regularly recruited for the work), to work with the dogs, had the most satisfactory results. These tracker dogs require the longest training of all, sometimes as much as two years. On them and on the skill of their handlers to understand them has depended and still depends the lives of very many soldiers working on the desperately dangerous work of hunting down and locating terrorists, enemy patrols and outposts. This is the work of the so-called infantry-patrol dogs who have been found capable of discovering the presence of an enemy at any distance from ten yards to five hundred. They were first worked off the lead in Malaya and proved quite invaluable to forces of the British Commonwealth in Korea.

The mine-detector dogs used by the Royal Engineers are possibly in some ways the most remarkable of all and surely inspired to no small degree the quotation which forms the heading of this section. They were first used in 1944 in N.W. Europe after the successful invasion by the Allied forces. Four platoons were sent, of which one took part in the Rhine crossings. Each consisted of an officer and 21 other ranks Royal Engineers, a sergeant of the Royal Veterinary Corps and 29 mine dogs. The dogs were most successful and in some respects more so than the electronic mine detector as they can detect non-metallic mines, are not affected by the presence of other metal, including railway lines, and work faster than men can when using the electronic detector. In November 1951, this type of dog was again used, this time in Korea. A further development of the high degree of skill developed by these detector dogs was in Palestine in 1946 when ten dogs were tested with great success as what were termed Arms-recovery dogs. The mechanical detectors used by the Sappers had failed to show the whereabouts of the many caches of arms buried, sometimes to a considerable depth, by the terrorists. Though it was thought almost incredible that the dogs could locate such caches, they succeeded beyond all doubt. Enough has been said, it is hoped, to persuade those interested in dogs to pursue the subject further, as already explained.

The types of dogs used are listed by Brigadier Clabby as follows:

World War I: Airedales were used for both guard and messenger work and small Collies for messenger purposes.

World War II: the Airedale was replaced by the Alsatian, unequalled for guard work and excellent for messenger, tracker and infantry patrol purposes. Although to a lesser extent a success as a casualty detection worker, the Alsatian nearly fulfils all needs.

The Labrador of the black type, which has proved better than the yellow variety, has produced a higher percentage of trackers than any other breed. Labradors are also good at casualty detection and cross well with terrier types for the purpose of breeding good mine detectors.

The Boxer was very popular in the Middle East as a guard dog, but the short coat tends to make the breed not so generally useful.

The Dobermann Pinscher has not been very satisfactory, but it is probable that the best specimens have not been available. His thin coat is also against him in some climates, and the Bull Terrier was a failure, partly for the same reason, but more because of a most wilful nature, as all those who know the breed will understand.

Neither the St Bernard nor the Bloodhound have been sufficiently tested to warrant any valid conclusions being arrived at as to their aptitude as war dogs.[46]

There remains to be discussed the mongrel, so dear to the heart of so many dog lovers. If the age, temper and conformation of a dog are as required by the experts and if the size is also right, the breed is immaterial. Naturally a dog must be active and inquisitive of ground scent. Those interested may note that 'many a first-class mine-detector dog would encounter great difficulty in trying to trace its ancestry'.

Mention has already been made of the qualities required in a handler of dogs. They have come from many races, as well as from men in the ranks, in some instances farm hands, stalkers, gamekeepers and poachers of our own country, and include Gurkhas, Chinese, Malays and Cypriots. In fact any willing man who has faith in his own capacity for handling dogs and will volunteer to serve is and presumably always will be welcome.

REFERENCES

1　For Remounts and Other Animals used by the British Army, see pp. 171–190, Clabby's *History of the Royal Army Veterinary Corps, 1919 to 1961* and *Army Veterinary and Remount Services, 1839 to 1945*.
2　Reitz, *Commando*, p. 231.
3　Parrino, *Introduction to Pack Transport*, p. 71 *passim*.
4　Burn, *Notes on Transport and Camel Corps*. Chapter on Mules. *Animal Management*, p. 270.
5　Sessions, *Two Years with Remount Commissions*, pp. 290, 291.
6　Preston, *The Desert Mounted Corps*, pp. 326, 327.
7　Graham, *History of Indian Mountain Artillery, passim*.
8　Preston as 6.
9　Summerhays, *Horses and Ponies*.
10　*Animal Management*, pp. 274, 275. Pocock, *The Frontiersman's Pocket Book*, section on Donkeys.
11　As 10.
12　As 6.
13　As 6.
14　Notes supplied by Major A. E. Matthews, Royal Ulster Rifles. He quotes the *History* of his Regiment, p. 142.
15　*Army Veterinary Services*, p. 425.
16　Marriott, *Source History of the South African Veterinary and Remount Corps, 1936 to 1946*.
17　Burn, *Notes on Transport and Camel Corps*, p. 106.
18　*Animal Management*, p. 276 et seq.
19　Burn, *Notes on Transport and Camel Corps, passim*.
20　Marling, *Rifleman and Hussar*, pub. Murray 1931, p. 131, and illustration on p. 132.

21 See Plate 70.
22 Lady Butler, oil painting 'Egyptian Camel Corps, Ceremonial Parade' in the United Service Club. Painted in 1886.
23 Aldershot Lectures, 1891.
24 *Animal Management*, pp. 292, 293.
25 *Manual of Horsemastership*, H.M.S.O., 1937, p. 64 *et seq.*
26 *Animal Management*, p. 295.
27 Fortescue, *History of the Royal Army Service Corps*, p. 62.
28 JAHR. Vol. XVIII, p. 244, for South Africa 1835, illustrated. There used to be a colour print showing a farmer riding an ox at full speed at a stiff fence, it is thought in Northamptonshire.
29 *Africana Notes and News*, published by the Africana Museum, Johannesburg, Volume VIII, p. 23, 'The Senior South African Regular Regiment'.
30 JAHR, Volume III, p. 266.
31 Whinyates *Corunna to Sevastopol*, published Allen 1884, p. 283.
32 As 30.
33 List of Changes in Warlike Material, No. 5002, May 1885. W.O. Library.
34 Cassels, *Peninsula Portrait*, published O.U.P. 1963, p. 14.
35 *Aide-Memoire to the Military Sciences*, Volume I, p. 199.
36 Wolseley's *Soldier's Pocket Book*, p. 52.
37 A.S.C. Training, Part III, 1911, Transport, p. 53. Fleming P., *Bayonets to Lhasa*, p. 7.
38 Pocock; *The Frontiersman's Pocket Book*, pp. 193–195. R.A.S.C. Training, Part III, 1922. Parrino, *Introduction to Pack Transport*, p. 74 for the pack capacity.
39 Clabby, *History of the R.A.V.C.*, 1949 to 1961, p. 192.
40 R.A.S.C. Training, 1922, Part III.
41 *Army Veterinary and Remount Services 1939 to 1945*, pp. 21 and 87.
42 Pocock, *Pocket Book of the Legion of Frontiersmen*.
43 Clabby, p. 174.
44 Clabby, p. 179.
45 Clabby, p. 180.
46 Clabby, p. 178.

CHAPTER FOUR

Riding Saddles of the Regular British Army until 1890

BEFORE the advent of mechanization the mobility of any army depended to a very great degree on the use of horses and mules and, as regards the fighting capacity of the cavalry, for so many years the masters of the battlefield, on the horse. Although it is possible for a man to ride and fight mounted without a saddle and even without a bridle – the Numidian horse archers of the days of the Roman Empire did both – it is not possible to develop the shock action of cavalry to the fullest extent unless the men have the secure seat on their mounts which only a saddle with supports for the feet of the rider can give. The introduction of a pad, on which the man sat, which was securely fastened on the horse by a band of some soft material going under the belly and two more going one round the chest and one under the tail, gave a fairly secure seat, and the addition of loops of leather, wood or metal hung from the pad by thongs into which the feet fitted, allowed the horseman to use his weapons, lance, sword, battle axe or mace as freely as if he was on the ground. (See Figure 3 on page 114 for the next paragraph.)

The strap under the horse is the girth, those going front and back are the breastplate and the crupper, the loop for the feet are the stirrups and they hang from the saddle by the stirrup-leathers or simply leathers. Long before the period with which this book deals, in the fourth century A.D., the saddle and in the sixth century the stirrup, were in use, and even before this the pad composing the saddle had been very much improved by the addition of a tree or framework made of some rigid material from which the girths, stirrups and other items of equipment were suspended. The pad by itself was still in use as it is today. A saddle tree consists of four parts, the two arches, the front one going over the withers and the back one over the horse's back behind the rider and the two sideboards, flat pieces of wood curved to fit the back below the spine and joining the arches together. (See Plate 11 and line drawing.) Plate 17b (R40) among others shows the tree in a simple form with the arches kept low. The extensions of the sideboards front and back, the burs and the fans, are for the purpose of carrying various articles of equipment. In Plate 17b both trees show a refinement added to the older type of tree. The front arches, instead of ending at the bottom of the sideboards are carried down below them for a few inches, forming what are called the points. (See page 154.) These add to the stability of the saddle and prevent lateral movement. The difficulty with the earlier forms of tree was to keep the weight of the rider off the horse's spine, where the skin is on the bone and rubs through very easily. This was achieved by stretching leather, with sometimes webbing below, tightly from arch to arch and sideboard to sideboard. If the pad, which was retained under the tree, was divided into two parts, one being fastened to each sideboard, a current of air should be free to pass along the spine and prevent any rubbing; always provided that the saddle is properly fitted to the horse.

Before the seat was stretched over the tree the weight of the rider came directly on the horse's spine.

An obvious and natural outcome of the development of the saddle was the reaction of the rider that he now had an admirable way of taking some of his belongings with him fastened to it. Possibly the least harmful way of doing this, from the point of view of the horse, was to put a man's meat ration in strips under the pad, as is said to have been the practice of some of the tribes on the frontiers of the Roman Empire! So serious was the question of overloading the saddle horse considered in those days, that the Romans were forbidden by law to carry 'cloak bags', which would have been some form of saddle bag, weighing more than 35 lb. The saddle and bridle were not to exceed 56 lb in weight.[1] Quite a considerable amount of space in this chapter will be devoted to the unending problem of how the cavalryman was to dispose of his equipment, other than that carried on his person, on his horse, what alterations should be made to the saddle for this purpose and how the weight was to be reduced. The greater the weight on the horse the less the mobility and, as will appear, there are very definite limits, not always realized by those responsible for the saddlery and equipment of the mounted fighting man, which cannot be exceeded without impairing his mobility and in a short time making a casualty of his horse.

The pad saddle does not need a great deal of explanation. As will appear it was improved until it had many of the characteristics of the saddle with a tree; in fact it is often difficult when examining old prints to be sure which type is being shown. Today the pad, known as a pilch, is in limited use for exercising and for children to learn to ride on. For short periods it gives a very strong seat.

There are two types of the saddle proper, that is to say made with a tree, known to the man and woman in the street, at any rate if they are among those who watch television. The first is the cowboy or Western American stock saddle, which will be described in the section of this chapter on Canada and is illustrated in Plate 93. It is a modern adaptation of the saddle used by the men-at-arms of the Middle Ages who wore armour, which in different forms was responsible for the high arches, front and back, in the military saddles of last century. These can be seen today in use by the Household Cavalry and the King's Troop R.H.A. Plate 34. The second type is the flat-topped saddle known as the hunting saddle, used in slightly modified forms for polo, racing, steeplechasing and show jumping, as well as by anyone who rides for pleasure. This is an English invention and though not strictly a military saddle has not only exercised a great influence on the development of the latter, but has been very often used by officers of all ranks and services in uniform both in peace time and in the field. It was also the official saddle of various grades of staff officers in the German Army before 1914.

The drawing shows the simplest form of this saddle and the various parts of a saddle, the burs and fans (see *ante*) excepted. In the course of this account we shall come to the Colonial, Staff, Semi-Military, or Yeomanry military saddle in use from about 1875 to the present day, when it is used by mounted officers and by mounted men of the Constabulary and Police. This saddle is simply an adaptation of the hunting saddle, and was once called by that name. Plate 17b shows the tree which will serve to explain the drawing. Plate 19 shows the saddle. See Plate 84 for this saddle as used by staff officers. The whole of the tree of this saddle, made during the last quarter of the nineteenth century, is of beech wood. Today it would be made of metal. The bars, to which the stirrup leathers are fastened under the skirt, are in the normal position for the cavalry or hunting seat, well forward of the centre of the seat of the saddle. For riding with a straight leg they would be more suitably placed an inch or slightly more further back; for the forward seat of today they should be an inch further forward or even more.

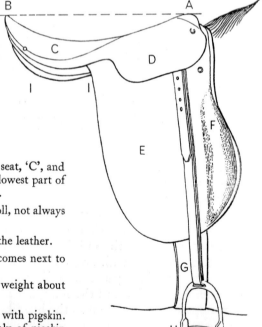

FIGURE 3   Hunting saddle.

'A' is the head, front arch, peak or pommel.

'B' is the cantle, or croup.
  The distance 'A' to 'B' gives the length of the seat, 'C', and a line dropped from the centre of 'AB' to the lowest part of 'C' gives the dip or depth of the seat, 4 inches.

'D' is the skirt and 'E' the flap with 'F' the knee roll, not always included.

'G' is the girth and 'H' the stirrup hanging from the leather.

'I, I' are the edges of the stuffed pannel, which comes next to the horse.

'A to B' should be from 17 to 18 inches and the weight about 10 lb.

A 'best' saddle has the seat, skirts and flap covered with pigskin. A 2nd-grade saddle has the seat and skirts only of pigskin and the flap of oxhide.

Although the hunting saddle has, as already stated, been frequently used by officers on active service, it is not suitable for carrying more than a macintosh on the pommel and, if Dees have been added behind the flap, a feed of corn in a nosebag or anything light. It has been said that a hunting saddle would not last twelve months on a campaign, which is probably not far from the truth.

It is extraordinary how long good quality saddles do last with ordinary work, and this is even more so in the case of the military saddle. Unless the front arch is broken, or cracked by a fall or by very careless handling, the life of an Army saddle is far longer than that laid down by regulation. From 8 to 14 years has been the period for which a saddle has been supposed to last, but the saddle of the middle years of last century, which had wood arches reinforced with strips of iron, lasted much longer than this and, after steel arches came in in 1890, with anything approaching careful handling a saddle could still be in use 30 years after it was made. In recent years a saddle was cast if it needed more than 25 per cent of repairs. The introduction of a new Universal Pattern of saddle did not mean that those of the last pattern were necessarily withdrawn. So a regiment might have two types of saddle in use, often differing considerably, and the older pattern saddles would only be cast when no longer fit for service. During a campaign, when both horse and saddle might be lost, a trooper would be thankful to lay his hand on any serviceable saddle which came to hand. There have been many occasions when saddles were scarcer than mounts and a mounted man is of no use without a saddle. It was therefore of vital importance that there should always be available in store sufficient saddles to make good losses and that the Regimental saddlers should always be with their units with sufficient tools and material for repairs. On their work, not less than on that of the farriers, who kept the horses shod, depended to a very great extent the efficiency of mounted men. A troop horse with a sore back caused by an insufficiently stuffed saddle was just as serious a loss to the fighting strength of an army as a man wounded by enemy action.

The foregoing pages should serve to introduce the subject of Army saddlery. Before going on to the details of the saddles used it will be as well to see how the Army was supplied and who was responsible for the quality of the equipment.

At the start of the Regular Army the Colonels of Regiments were responsible for all equipment and clothing and this included saddlery. For many years there were no patterns laid down for their guidance and in consequence there was little uniformity. It is on record[2] that Charles I in 1628 required saddlers to submit to the Council of War saddles made on a pattern designed by Lord Wimbledon. The only mounted troops in England at this time were the King's Bodyguard of the Gentlemen Pensioners and the Troops of Horse of the Militia and the London Trained Bands. Presumably this was an isolated example not followed up as were the Regulations for the inspection and provision of firearms, weapons and armour. During the Civil Wars, which began in 1642, whatever saddles were available would have been pressed into service; in the case of the Parliamentary forces paid for and for the Royalist army paid for if there were funds to be had.

From the time of the Restoration until 1690 there was no control of the purchasing by Colonels; at that date it was laid down[3] that the Colonel of a Regiment was to select two or three captains who were to check the quality of the raw material used by the tradesmen supplying the equipment etc., and to sign the contracts entered into with them, which had formerly been signed by the Colonel only. In 1703 a fresh check was instituted[4] by the creation of the office of Controller of Army Accounts. In 1707, when a Board of General Officers was appointed, we have the first specific mention of saddles. The Board lasted for 150 years; it was composed of General Officers, themselves Colonels of Regiments, who were to supervise the provision of clothing and equipment. It was laid down that saddlery worn out or lost in action was to be replaced by the Colonel, and if lost by negligence by the Captain of the Troop. There was no scale laid down for the provision or inspection of saddlery. The Colonel provided saddlery and equipment, which was repaired regimentally and kept in service as long as possible. As the members of the Board changed every year they would not necessarily acquire any knowledge of contractors and their methods. As General Forbes puts it,[5] 'they would know little or nothing of the tricks of the trade, or how to detect shoddy clothing, belts or saddles'. However, there was some sort of check; the Controller of Army Accounts was responsible for the regimental accounts, the muster rolls and for the issues of arms from Ordnance being booked up against regiments. The Board of General Officers held their meetings in an office which still stands in Whitehall.

As in 1729 it was thought impossible to 'fix a period of time for providing saddles', the General Officer appointed by the Board to review a Regiment was to be responsible for the condition of the saddles and by a Warrant of 1736 they were to last eight years,[6] a comparatively short life for an article which had to be strongly made to be of any use at all. According to Grose,[7] in this year Government supplied saddles and materials, presumably for repairs and alterations. In 1788 the Board of General Officers reported that some regiments of heavy cavalry had Light Dragoon saddles of an old pattern very high in front, some with burs and no fans. The Commanding Officer bought whatever suited him, dealing, as had always been the case, directly with the makers.[8] In 1796 a fixed pattern for heavy cavalry was decided on and in 1805 for Hussars; the latter became the pattern for all Light Cavalry. The choice was no longer left in the hands of the Colonels of regiments and the manufacturers now had to conform to definite patterns. The Colonels continued to buy saddlery on a money allowance up to 1855, when the Ordnance took over the whole of the supply of saddlery and equipment. The Household Cavalry continued to buy their own until 1880, in some cases having the saddles made up regimentally. The Board of Ordnance had no easy task. Not only were newer methods of construction coming in, with trial and error as the best or in some cases the only way of fixing on new patterns, but the commitments of the Army in various parts of the world were constantly increasing throughout the nineteenth century. Saddles had to be capable of being used by all sorts and kinds of horses and ponies, in most cases all narrower and smaller than the English remount, and replacements in countries a long way away without any chance of buying locally called for a large stock of reserves being kept in hand. If given anything approaching reasonable notice, the big firms who handled the Army contracts could be relied on and from 1890 onwards their work was so sound and the sealed patterns held by Ordnance so satisfactory that any old Army saddle when cast from the service was usually sure of a purchaser. This was no mean tribute to the quality of the workmanship. Before this date the trade in the United Kingdom were supplying Militia, Volunteers and Police all over the Empire, always with the most satisfactory results. The individual saddler, whether serving or a civilian, has always been and still is a craftsman, who takes that pride in his work which we are told is now disappearing in so many trades to the great detriment of our industry.

Officers' saddles were made by most of the well-known firms, as well as by the manufacturers who handled the Army contracts. Each regiment usually went for all their officers' saddles and horse equipment to the same man. Thus Messrs Champion & Wilton make for the Royal Horse Guards and most fortunately still have their equipment book dating from 1895; the late Major Wilton was an authority on the whole subject. The firm incorporates the once well-known firm of Whippy and Stegall, who used to make for the 13th Hussars. In 1813 the 7th Hussars went to Peter Laurie; he claimed to have a special method for fastening holsters securely on the front of the saddle. Another well-known firm was Souter, who made for the 1st Life Guards. It is not proposed to continue the list; enough has been said to show what was usually the case, that a man liked to have his regulation saddlery made by the same firm who made his hunting and polo saddles and had probably made his father's also.

REGULATION CAVALRY SADDLES
OF THE SEVENTEENTH CENTURY

Although the wearing of armour, especially full suits, was going out when the century came in, half armour (see Plate 2) was still worn on active service and very occasionally complete armour. The Great Saddle, as it was called and the Great Horse for whom it was designed, were still in use in small numbers by Royalty and senior General Officers for state occasions and for the manège; Van Dyck's paintings show them. The saddle weighed up to 60 lb, from 10 to 20 lb more than the cowboy saddle, and was described by William Cavendish, Duke of Newcastle, the foremost exponent of training and riding horses in manège work of his day in this country. His book (see in Bibliography), published in French in 1658, went through many editions in an English translation and was for years the best known work of reference on a subject which is again so much to the fore today. Newcastle wrote as follows: 'the saddle has an ample stuffed seat, with the pommel rising well in front of the fork (of the rider, understood), a high well-padded cantle extending round the sides to support the thighs like the body of a well-padded library chair.

117

It is so well made that a man must sit upon it with a good grace whether he will or no'. In the French edition of his book he adds *voici la plus excellente selle qui puisse être*. The cantle was a great help to a man fighting in armour, which had a very serious unbalancing effect.

During the Civil War Colonel Sir Arthur Hazelrig, M.P., commanded a regiment of Horse, raised in London, who wore full armour and were known as 'the Lobsters' and also as 'that impenetrable regiment'. They would presumably have ridden in the Great Saddle and as late as 1661, when Charles II reorganized the Militia, it was enacted that Troops of Horse were to have 'a Great Saddle or pad' (for a pad see *post*) with bars and a strap for affixing the holsters'.[9] This last detail would have applied to the pad. One reason for this permission to use the Great Saddle would have been that there were probably a considerable number of the saddles used by Hazelrig's Cuirassiers still in existence, for they must have been well nigh indestructible. The wooden tree, strengthened with iron, would ensure that. This is the last we hear of Newcastle's favourite pattern; the French called it the Royal saddle. Since the Wars of Religion the French Horse had a very good name and their influence, as well as that of the Dutch and Swedish services, is noticeable in the many books written on military subjects during the century. Newcastle also mentions a saddle of cloth, stuffed with straw and with no leather, wood or iron work, presumably a pad, used by the boy who carried the cuirassier's spare arms, oats and 'the sack of carriage' which was part of his equipment and got him his forage. This attendant rode 'a nagge'.[10] For nearly a century cavalry, of all classes, carried only a cloak fastened behind the saddle and no other impedimenta.

Among the books dealing with horsemanship, cavalry, their equipment and their arms, there are a series written by Gervaise Markham, c.1568 to 1637, which give a useful account of the saddlery of his day, still used during the Civil Wars. Markham had soldiered as a young man as an officer, both on the continent and in Ireland, and his book is useful, as he liked to make use of extracts from any contemporary sources which appealed to him. What he called 'the Perfite Saddle' was the invention of a Frenchman, Seigneur Maxime, Écuyer to the Amiral and Duc de Joyeuse, and an illustration of it, copied by Markham, was published in 1593 in a book by Salamon de Broue, 'Le Cavalerice Francois'. Plates 1 and 2 show the saddle, which it will be convenient to refer to as Markham's pattern. Plate 2 shows a harquebusier, the heaviest type of cavalryman, except the Parliamentary regiment already mentioned, employed in the Civil War, with the saddle. Plate 1 shows the detail and is an almost exact copy of the original drawing. For how long this original pattern survived in this country is not clear; it was extensively copied and survived in one form or another well into the next century. Markham called the first adaptation 'the Morocco saddle'. The height was reduced and what were known as the pillows[11] cut smaller. With both pommel and cantle lower and the removal of the large ball from the former, the saddle has some resemblance to the types used in North Africa, but it is not clear if this was the reason for the name 'Morocco'. The seat was ribbed and padded and there was a considerable amount of support for the man's back, thighs and knees. So far no details of the tree or measurements of this forerunner of the Army saddle have come to light, but it would not appear to have been very heavy. There was considerably more room in the seat than in the Great Saddle, which would have made mounting and dismounting much easier. There were various other saddles in use, the Hackney saddle and 'the large plain Scotch saddle'; both were lighter and the Hackney had an iron tree.[12] Markham also listed the Scotch saddle and 'the French pad', with a seat stuffed with down and quilted pads, and most interesting of all to us today, 'the lightest and nimblest' – the hunting or racing saddle. (See line drawing on page 114.) As already mentioned it survives today, little altered except that the skirt is sometimes shaped differently, merges in the seat and disappears at times and then comes back.[13] Knee rolls, and thigh pads or blisters, as they are known in the trade, are added as fashion or fancy dictates, but the wooden tree, shaped to the horse, with the plain leather seat tightly stretched across it have not altered. In the Third Volume of Lawson's *History of the Uniforms of the British Army* there is a copy of a drawing by a French artist of the Gentlemen Pensioners, the King of England's Bodyguard in 1637, riding in a procession in London on 'the English saddle, low and close to the horse' as described by Sollysel in 1654 in his book *Le Parfait Marechal*. How much the hunting saddle was in use by the levies and volunteers of the two armies engaged in the Civil War it is impossible to say, but right up to the end of the nineteenth century the yeomen who served mounted in any of the auxiliary forces preferred their own hunting saddles to the Government issue. There does not seem to be any definite date assigned for the introduction of the hunting saddle, which was certainly in use by about 1600 and probably earlier. All that modern authorities[14] say is that it was certainly common by about this time. It was probably so well known that no one troubled to record anything about its first appearance. As far as the British Army is concerned, the more one reads about it the more apparent is it that to most men who wrote about it a saddle was a saddle, just as a musket was a musket and there was no need to describe either.

Besides the Markham type the other saddle much favoured was the pad or pad saddle, which was light, easy to make, sat satisfactorily close to the horse and could conveniently carry the few things thought necessary for the cavalryman of the time. This was the saddle preferred for cavalry by General George Monck, afterwards Duke of Albemarle, a professional soldier who had learnt his trade abroad. Written in 1646, his book *Observations upon Military and Political Affairs*, was not published until 1671. Monck's detail of 'the Furniture that belongeth to an Horseman's Horse' is as follows: 'he ought to have a very good horse, and good pad saddle made so that it may very well carry a case of pistols, three good girts, a pair of good stirrups and stirrup leathers, with a crupper and a fore-pattern; also a good bitt, reins and headstall, with a good leathern halter'. A Dragoon had a saddle with only two girths. The words fore-pattern are a misspelling for 'peitrell' or 'pattrell' or 'paytrelle', a piece of armour fastened on the breastplate to protect the breast of the horse. It was often richly ornamented and is shown in Plate 1.[15] He considered that cuirassiers were not likely to be found in most armies and so does not describe them or their equipment. As already noted it was the cuirassier who used the Great Saddle.

In Patshull Church, near Wolverhampton, is a monument to Sir Richard Astley which Brigadier Peter Young considers was made many years after the Civil War.[16] One panel of the monument shows Sir Richard with his Troop of Horse, riding with a pad saddle, presumably the pattern as generally used. The saddle has under it a plain square saddle cloth, the seat is short and the men ride with a long stirrup but not exaggeratedly long. The cantle and pommel are low and without thigh or knee rolls; the cantle stops well up the rider's thigh. No girths are visible, so there are unlikely to have been three and there is no peitrell. The pistols are placed in the holsters with the butt pointing forward. The holsters have no covers and are kept in place by a strap going round the horse's chest like a breastplate. There are cruppers to the saddles. This is a valuable contribution to what is known of the saddlery of the period, even if the work was done some time after 1660, when there would no longer be any embargo on putting monuments to Royalists in churches.

Monck had served in Holland and there are various pictures by contemporary Dutch artists (Aalbert Cuyp (1620–91) is a good example), which show the pad saddle as described by him with three girths, one well back under the belly, and the long 14-inch barrelled Horse pistols and low cantle. As will appear the influence of the Markham pattern continued on many types of Army saddle, the tendency being to less and less high or protruding 'furniture' giving the rider what was presumably considered as a safe and comfortable seat, without the shutting-in effect so characteristic of the period when armour was worn.

Plate 3 shows a General Officer's saddle and was given to the Duke of Monmouth by Charles II. The similarity of this example of an officer's saddle to Markham's favourite type is noticeable. The stirrups are set well forward, so that the rider could get away from the straight leg seat and have the legs comfortably bent.

Plates 4 and 5 and Figure 4 are taken from a saddle in the Scottish United Services Museum in the Castle, Edinburgh. Mr Thorburn, the Curator, describes the saddle as follows: 'the weight is 12 lb, the length over all is 1 foot 8 inches; the leather is of a nice rich, reddish hue, the padding is buff colour, and the metal work of brass. The tree is firmly fixed to the saddle with nothing between them, the pommel and cantle being reinforced with iron plates bent to shape, joined by pieces of wood reinforcing the leather.' These side bars are clearly shown in the drawing at Figure 4. 'The wood is riveted to the pommel and cantle and has Dees to take the flaps and stirrups. The Museum Assistant has restored the whole saddle and repaired the seat padding.' As Mr Thorburn also states, the saddle must have been used with a thick pad or blanket underneath it.

In Sir George Arthur's *History of the Household Cavalry* are two plates, copied from Colonel Clifford Walton's paintings, showing saddles of James II's reign, almost identical with the 'Edinburgh Castle' one, which may be dated with confidence as a seventeenth-century military type. The hook for a pistol holster can be

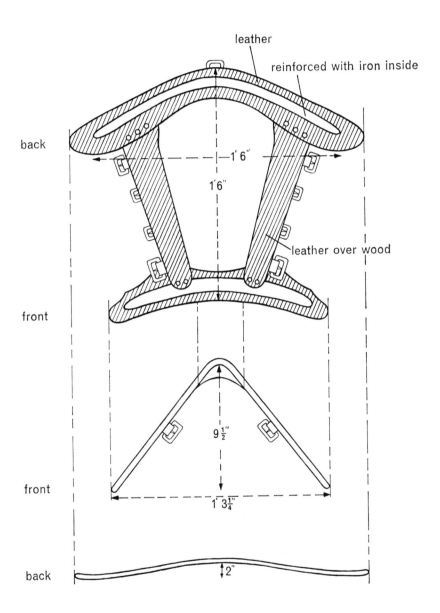

FIGURE 4   Seventeenth-century saddle, S.U.S.M. Edinburgh.

seen in Plate 5, and the two drawings of Walton's show the holsters in this position. It is very satisfactory to have the tree of this type of saddle so carefully described and it is a fair presumption that Markham's saddle had the same type of tree.

Plate 6 shows an Infantry officer's saddle of the end of the century, used at Killiecrankie and still in existence. The type varies little, the seat being very short and the tree of wood, with the holsters slung low without covers or 'holster caps'. Behind the cantle is a round valise with flat ends (for valises see under 'Furniture') taking the place of the rolled cloak shown in one of Walton's plates. Lawson quotes the Brecknock Militia Troop of Horse as having the men's cloaks strapped on behind the saddles in 1688.[17] From this time onwards more 'luggage' began to be carried by cavalrymen, as will appear in the next section. It is to be presumed that the type of tree described above went on into the next century. Plate 8, painted c.1715, shows little change from the seventeenth-century types.

REGULATION CAVALRY SADDLES OF THE EIGHTEENTH CENTURY

There are various moot points connected with the saddlery of the first half of the century. Little appears to be known about the tree and as the saddles were well covered for most of the period by the housings and, when the man was mounted, by the long skirts of his coat, pictorial evidence of what the saddle looked like is not easy to find. The pad saddle had presumably gone out of use; the burs on the front of the tree to take the holsters and the fans in rear to support anything fastened there did not come in for a long time and so it is difficult to find out what was carried on the saddle up to about 1750.

Major General Sir Frederick Smith, Army Veterinary Corps, whose research work at the end of the nineteenth century is so frequently referred to in this book, stated that up to the middle of the century the cavalry saddle was a remarkably low one. He quotes the illustrations in De Boxe's *Military History of Marlborough*, published in 1735, and Plate 8, as described below, also refers, as do the numerous paintings by David Morier. Morier takes us on from c.1740 to after the turn of the century. He was a Swiss artist, born in 1705, who emigrated to England and specialized in military subjects. As Lawson has pointed out, Morier very seldom shows troopers in marching order with their 'luggage' on the saddle, though the policy of making the cavalryman as independent as possible of any transport was coming in during Morier's period. The emphasis in the low, long-seated saddles with stirrups set forward is almost certainly derived from the hunting or jockey saddle, of which there are now a number of illustrations. The hunting saddle was and remained roomy, the jockey type differed only in cut from its successors of the next century and presumably the trees of the cavalry saddles followed the same lines as those of the civilian ones.

Major General Forbes, who wrote the *History of the Army Ordnance Services* in 1929, has this to say about the development of the tree: 'the saddle of the Middle

Ages consisted of two arches joined by a single bar in the centre and one on either side from which the stirrups were suspended. These bars later developed into the "trees".' It would have been clearer if he had used the modern term 'sideboards', though in many cases in the late fifteenth century the sideboards and arches are formed from one block of wood or in the case of one examined recently, of ivory. Forbes' account continues: 'by the eighteenth century the saddle had become more or less standardized, underneath was the pad in one piece and next the tree. Over this was a pad of leather or fur on which the rider sat, the various parts being held together by a surcingle.' This description would certainly apply to the saddles shown in Morier's pictures dealing with the fourth and fifth decades, but not to the saddles of the Marlburian era as shown in Plate 8; for Forbes goes on to say 'the saddle was extremely heavy and cumbersome and the rider's weight still rested directly on the horse's back'. Exactly what is meant by the expression 'extremely heavy and cumbersome' is not clear. Forbes might have been referring to the saddle shown in Plates 1 and 2, but without knowing the weights of the various saddles it is impossible to be more definite.

The 'Conversation Piece' (Plate 8), painted by Ross about 1715, and described as 'the battle of Ramillies' shows a scene during one of Marlborough's campaigns. Presumably the officer standing nearest the head of the white charger, held by a groom, is showing the horse off to the other officers. The saddle sits well down on the horse's back, has a long shallow seat of quilted leather with a low cantle not coming far down the sides on the flaps. The pommel is not very high and has a flange coming down the same distance as the sides of the cantle. The stirrup is set well forward, giving a 'hunting seat' with the knee moderately bent. The holsters are slung from the pommel with the butts of the pistols showing and the barrels are held in a slanting position by the same strap round the horse's chest as in the memorial to Sir Richard Astley. There is a crupper and one girth and a large rectangular saddle cloth. Lawson shows a plainer version as a trooper's saddle of the period. There seems to be no record of how the cavalryman had his possessions carried until about 1750. It is unlikely that 'the boy on a nagge' survived the Civil Wars as a servant to the cuirassier, so probably there was some form of transport hired to carry the many articles required to clean the horse, saddle and bridle, the man's accoutrements and the sickle or scythe for cutting grass or forage. Up to 1745 there is no evidence that anything except the cloak and holsters were carried on the saddle. There was also picketing gear to be carried, including some form of horse lines.

Plate 58, painted by Morier, shows as much of the saddle of the 1750 period as can be seen under the goatskin on which the man sat. An innovation was the water-deck, a painted piece of canvas, 4 feet 4 inches square, large enough to cover the saddle and bridle completely when on the ground. It usually had the title of the regiment painted on it and was carried on the saddle, in most cases over the holsters. Plate 58 also shows the short leather bucket, slung under the off holster to take the short musket carried by all cavalry. The butt fits into the bucket and the musket is slung from the pommel by a 'stay strap', going round the barrel just above the lowest ramrod pipe. The muzzle went under the man's arm, protruding behind him. The saddle has burs to take the holsters and a low cantle with the cloak rolled tightly and strapped on behind it. Fans to take the rear pack had not yet come in. There are both breastplate and crupper and a surcingle. The housing or saddle cloth showing behind the saddle will be discussed in a separate section. Stirrups are square.

We now come to the introduction of Light Dragoons into the British Army, the first unit having been formed in 1745. It had only a short existence and in 1756 a Light Troop was added to eleven regiments of Dragoons, followed by the raising of a regiment, the 15th Light Dragoons[18] in 1759. The whole idea was to reduce the weight on the horse as much as possible and the Warrant of the 14th April, 1756, lays down that the saddles were to be made 'with small cantles behind like the jockey saddles and to be 22 inches long in the seat, on the right side a holster for a pistol and on the left a churn to take a spade and felling axe or woodman's bill. There is to be a bucket to take the butt of the carbine, and a pipe to receive the end of the horse picket.' This was a short pole to tie the horse up to at night and was carried strapped alongside the carbine. In 1759 the saddle is described as being made of 'tanned leather, shaped after the old hunting stock', in other words a hunting saddle. The numerous illustrations showing racehorses saddled up do not differ as regards the shape of the cantles and the flaps from the hunting saddles of the period, except that they are smaller. Tanned leather is known today as 'Brown Crop' and is described as sole leather, the rawhide having been soaked in dilute tannic acid extracted from oak bark etc.[19] It is still used for both the seats and flaps of saddles. The cavalryman now sat on this leather seat, which was firmly fastened to the arches and sideboards of the tree so that his weight no longer bore directly on the horse's spine. There is a series of paintings by Morier at Wilton House near Salisbury which show all ranks of the 15th Light Dragoons. These were reproduced in JAHR.[20] An officer's saddle held by an orderly with a cover of brown leather going right over the seat shows the ordinary pommel and cantle of a hunting saddle. This type of saddle was in use with slight variations into the next century for Light Dragoons. The etchings by Cornet Cary, 16th Light Dragoons, in *Rules and Regulations for the Sword Exercise*, published in 1796, show little change. There was, however, a very definite idea during the last quarter of the century that we should follow the Continental armies and adopt some form of what was called a 'deep seating' type rising front and back in a somewhat similar way to the 'great saddle'. Plate 7 illustrates the tendency, though not to the exaggerated extent which characterized the Light Cavalry saddles of the next century.

The saddle shown is taken from Hinde's *Discipline of the Light Horse, 1778*, and *there is no evidence that it was ever adopted*. Hinde calls it 'a new saddle for the Cavalry' and quotes as follows: 'Mr Gibson's Account (Saddler in Great-Windmill Street, Piccadilly, London) of the new saddle for the Cavalry, which was invented by Sir William Erskine, Knight, late Lieut Colonel of Lieut General Elliott's

Regiment of Light Dragoons, and made by him, and showed to the King in July, 1775, which His Majesty approved of. This saddle was designed for either Heavy or Light Cavalry, it rises very high both before and behind, keeping the rider firm in his seat and answers every purpose of a peak saddle and is much cooler. On the near side is fixed the holster case for one pistol, and on the off side the case for four horse-shoes and nails, which has a cover with a strap and buckle to secure them. It is like a holster case with the pipe cut off. The forage pillion is contrived with an iron bow behind, covered with leather, to prevent the baggage etc. bearing against the rider's back; there are also slips of wood upon it through which the baggage straps pass. It carries the following articles viz. a pair of leather Necessary Bags containing four shirts, four pairs of stockings, two pairs of shoes, two pairs of gaiters, three shoe brushes and black ball. A clothes brush, powder bag and puff (for the man's hair). A horse picker, turnscrew and gun worm (for taking off the lock of the firearms and cleaning them), curry comb and brush. A mane-comb and sponge and watering cap (later known as a forage cap). A white wallet containing a waistcoat and pair of breeches. A sack containing three pecks of oats, 30 lb of hay, twisted or spun (into a sort of rope), a set of forage cords (which later were worn on the man's shoulder and became the French Decoration "la Fourragére"), a camp kettle, four tent pins in a bag and a nosebag (for the horse to eat out of). All the above articles are fixed upon the forage pillion very completely. A blanket also is folded and slid upon the saddle, over which the "sircingle" is put. The weight of everything above mentioned is 141 lb or 10 stone 1 lb. The weight of a Light Dragoon with carbine and pistols, sword, belts, cartridge box, boots and spurs, helmet, haversack and canteen, saddle, bridle, picket post etc., allowing 6 lb weight for ammunition bread (about the weight of an ammunition loaf), 2 lb of water, 3 lb for meat, 2 lb for ammunition, the whole weight 175 lb, or 12 stone 7 lb. Total weight of every article that the horse had to carry, including the Dragoon, 316 lb or 22 stone 8 lb Mr Gibson's account finished.'

This detailed estimate is of importance, as it shows the ever-increasing tendency to overload the horse. Everyone can judge for themselves how much of the above was necessary and how much more or less a hiker of today would be willing to carry.

A man is supposed to be able to carry 33 per cent of his own weight, a horse 25 per cent. The average weight of a horse is about 1,000 lb.[21]

Hinde gives the weight of the saddle of his day complete with bridle, arms, the housings and all equipment, but without any baggage, food, or feed, as 56 lb. He adds that the saddle had burs and a cantle.

Note that Gibson intends the carbine to be carried muzzle down in a pipe-shaped bucket, with a stay strap from the small of the butt. This practice came in soon after and lasted for many years.

Forbes[22] has this to say about the Light Dragoon saddle. 'Though lighter it was similar in construction to and must have been assimilated with the ordinary saddle. It bore no resemblance to the modern racing saddle.'

To return to the Heavy Cavalry saddle and its load: the weights given on page 125 should help to form a rough estimate of the latter.

Although, as already stated, Morier does not show packed saddles as used by British Cavalry, he does have a drawing of a Hanoverian Trooper of Horse in 1751 in marching order. He has as a rear pack a folded cloak and on the off side a water bottle, haversack, a nose bag behind the man's leg and below the holster a picket pole fastened to his carbine. No case for spare horse shoes is visible, but they will have been carried. In 1759 it was stated in evidence at a Court Martial[23] that this pole and 'everything that encumbered the men' was thrown away before the order to charge was given. Compare this with the French order to their infantry in the 1850's to throw off their knapsacks before attacking – 'Sac a Terre'.

Rogers quotes from an Order Book of the King's Dragoon Guards at this period that each squadron had two waggons allotted to it to carry the tents or the blankets and also a forage cart and a farrier's cart.[24]

The load carried by the Scots Greys in 1793 differed little from that shown by Morier forty years earlier. They had a scythe, a mallet, tent pins, a hatchet, a water bucket and a kettle. Probably some of these articles would have been left with the transport before action.[25] At this date the water deck was carried 'neatly folded on the valise'.

Forbes gives the details of the construction of what he calls 'the ordinary saddle', the word Cavalry being understood from the text, as follows: 'the framework was of wood and consisted of very substantial front and rear arches joined by two side bars, the whole being nailed and glued together and covered with canvas. Underneath was a panel in one piece made of basil (tanned sheepskin not resistant to water) lined with linen or serge. Above was a quilted leather pad of similar shape with holes through which passed the pommel and cantle. It is described in the Clothing Warrants as 'saddle with pannel and pad in one'. The assumption being that it was one complete unit, and the parts not detachable. There was no sealed pattern and each regiment used whatever seemed best to the Colonel, some units having Light Dragoon saddles.

In a recent publication by Stanley J. Olsen on the Development of the U.S. Army Saddle,[26] he gives the following details of a saddle of 1770 'of British design' as used by American Officers. 'The saddle most widely used was manufactured by the enemy, Great Britain. One was quilted cloth-covered, with leg rolls below the pommel, used primarily by officers and therefore few in numbers.' The illustration, reproduced on the next page, shows a well-padded cantle and the flap continued behind it to take a cloak.

The year 1791 saw the beginnings of an entirely new departure in the patterns to be issued to both Heavy and Light Cavalry. As this move resulted in the establishment of sealed types it marks the close of an epoch.

The Department of the Ordnance was now solely responsible for the patterns of all saddlery and harness and although Colonels could and often did continue to use old types which they preferred to new ones, this was only possible, to a limited

Pontoons of the
Royal Engineers on the March

Harry Payne

PLATE 35   Pontoon train of the Royal Engineers, 1890.

M

a. Officer

b. Sapper

c. Driver

d. Driver

PLATE 36   The Royal Engineers in 1929 showing types of horses and saddlery.

PLATE 37   The Royal Engineers Balloon Section in 1890.

PLATE 38   Mountain Battery, Royal Artillery, in Abyssinia in 1868.

a) Mule collar harness

b) Breast harness, South African type

PLATE 39   Commissariat and Transport Department, 1885.

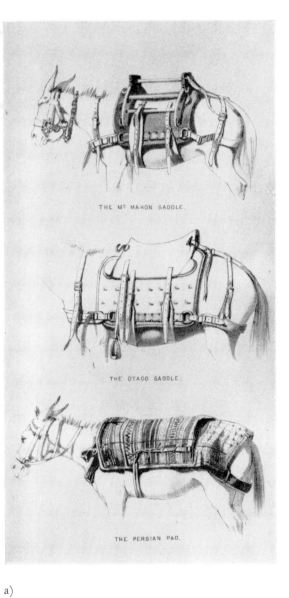

THE Mc MAHON SADDLE.

THE OTAGO SADDLE.

THE PERSIAN PAD.

a)

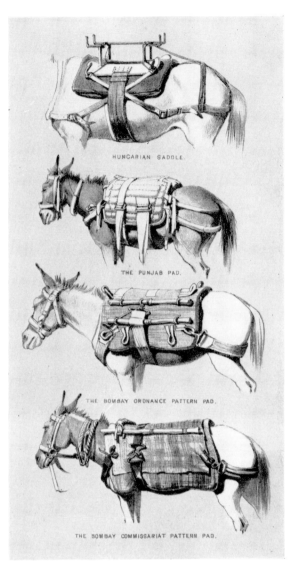

HUNGARIAN SADDLE.

THE PUNJAB PAD.

THE BOMBAY ORDNANCE PATTERN PAD.

THE BOMBAY COMMISSARIAT PATTERN PAD.

b)

PLATE 40   Pack equipment used in Abyssinia in 1868.

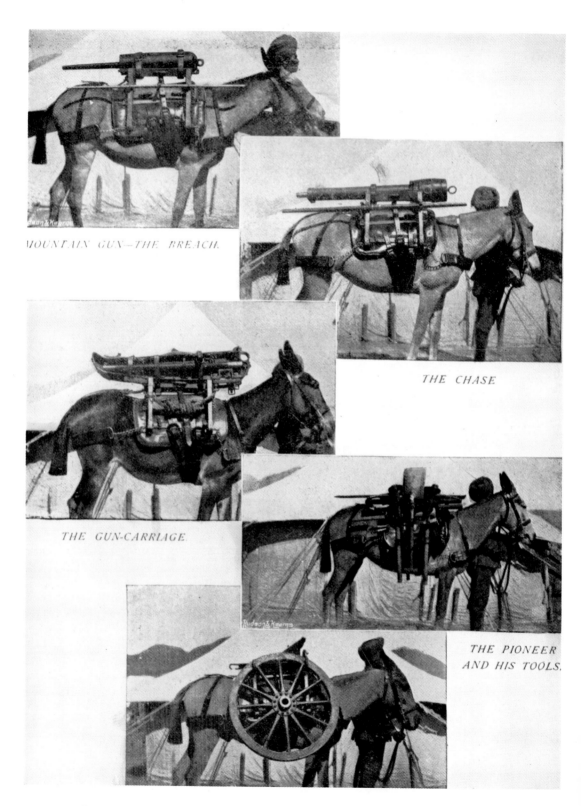

MOUNTAIN GUN—THE BREACH.

THE CHASE

THE GUN-CARRIAGE

THE PIONEER
AND HIS TOOLS.

PLATE 41   Royal Artillery, Indian Mountain Battery in 1898.

PLATE 42 Royal Artillery Elephant Battery in Abyssinia in 1868.

PLATE 43 Royal Garrison Artillery Siege Train, India, *c* 1898, elephant and bullock draught.

PLATE 44(a)   Ammunition mule, pack, 1896.

PLATE 44(b)   Machine gun, Infantry, in draught, *c*.1902.

PLATE 45   Universal Pattern pack-saddle, British Service, Mark V, 1904.

PLATE 46   Universal Pattern Italian Army pack-saddle, the 'Basto', 1943.

a)

b)

PLATE 47   Universal Pattern Indian Army pack-saddle 1932 in draft and in pack.

PLATE 48 Pack-horses of the Canadian Army on Home Service in 1943.

PLATE 49 Camel pack-saddles fitted with cacolets 1917, Near East.

PLATE 50   Locally made official pattern camel saddle, Egypt, 1917.

PLATE 51   Donkey with primitive pad, 1916, El Arish.

PLATE 52   Yak transport, Tibetan campaign of 1903.

PLATE 53   Dog sleigh transport in North Russia, 1918.

PLATE 54   Reindeer sleigh transport in North Russia, 1918.

PLATE 55   Two trackers and patrol dogs and their handlers, c.1960, in Malaya.

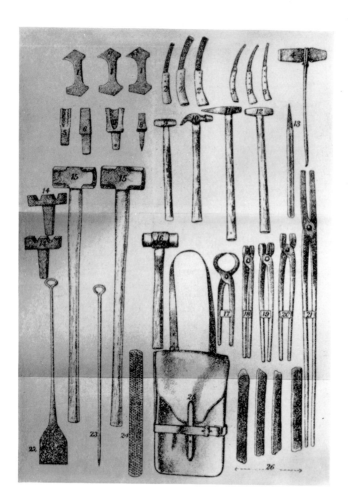

PLATE 57   The Remount depot at Melton Mowbray in 1963.

The Drum Horses of the Household Cavalry

Alexander the Great
Trumpet Major E. G. Madden, L.G.

Hannibal
Musician H. Gray, R.H.G.

degree, as for instance when a regiment was in India. The life of a saddle was laid down and was no longer left to be decided by the General Officer inspecting a unit, and though regiments were at times expected to wear out an older pattern, which would result in there being two types in use at the same time, there was as a general rule no glaring example of worn-out saddlery being in use.

In the case of Heavy Cavalry the change came in 1796. In the case of certain regiments of Light Cavalry it came in 1805 and in 1812 the whole of the Light units were re-equipped according to Ordnance standards. The Light Cavalry will be dealt with in the next section.

The introduction of new types of saddlery is directly traceable to the great interest taken, as has always been and still is the case, in the Army by the Royal Family. In 1780 Frederick, Duke of York,[27] in after years Commander-in-Chief of

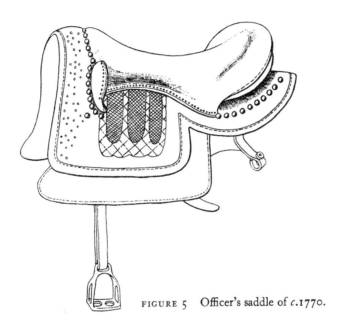

FIGURE 5   Officer's saddle of c.1770.

the British Army, was sent to Germany to get the best possible education in everything pertaining to soldiering, which he intended to make his career. In those days the Prussian Army under the most famous soldier of the time, Frederick the Great, was considered the best worth studying; the old King was most kind to the young visitor and showed him everything, including the cavalry especially. Of them the Duke wrote: 'The cavalry is infinitely superior to anything I ever saw', and his appreciation naturally extended to their equipment. He returned to England in 1787 and went out to Prussia again in 1791. While he was there, his elder brother, then Prince of Wales and later George IV, wrote to him asking him to arrange for two complete sets of uniform, equipment and saddlery of the Prussian cavalry to be

N   127

sent to England. The regiments selected were the Cuirassiers or Life Guards, very heavy cavalry and the Ziethen Hussars, light cavalry formed on the model of the Hungarian Hussars of the Austrian Army. In September the uniforms and equipment duly arrived in England.[28]

In 1796 a new pattern saddle was adopted by Ordnance and issued to all heavy cavalry. It is to all intents and purposes the same as the Prussian cuirassier saddle, which is described and illustrated in a book published in 1912 at Berlin by Paul Pietsch.[29] The main difference is in the cantle, which is of rolled leather in the Prussian and brass rimmed in the British model. See Plates 9 and 10, Officer's model. On the adoption of the British U.P. Heavy Cavalry type in 1796 a senior German Officer was sent over to procure patterns with a view to possibly introducing the saddle into their service.[30] The brass edging to the cantle is a help in preventing rubbing the leather, either by the straps of the rear pack or when putting the saddle on the ground upside down in order to dry out the padding. It also saves the leather if the saddle is knocked over when standing up on the front arch.

In June 1796 the Board of General Officers recommended the introduction of a brown leather saddle with black straps, the panel and pad to be in one and the panel to be removable. The breastplate was to be the same as used by Light Dragoons; the crupper to be divided in two and the girth to be 4 inches wide and divided into three at the buckling place for a distance of at least 8 or 9 inches down the girth. The stirrups were square sided in contradistinction to the round sided 'Hussar' type. The breastplate consisted of a single strap running from well below the pommel like a modern one. (The references are W.O. 3/29 and W.O. 30/13 A.) The saddle changed very little until after the Crimea, and was substantially the same as used by all services except those who had the Light Cavalry pattern, not excluding the drivers. It obviously stood up well to the hard work it had to do and was at least as successful as the Prussian model from which it was copied. The most important difference between this pattern and many of the models which followed it, lay in the shape of the front arch, which was continued for some way below the side-boards in two points. This had always been a feature of the English hunting saddle and it is surprising that it was not used in all military saddles. Commenting on the importance of these points the Board of Cavalry Officers, who sat in 1855 to consider the issue of a true Universal Pattern, minuted as follows: 'the wooden tree must assimilate to the bearing of the old Heavy Dragoon saddle, extending the extremities of the front crutch below its junction with the sideboards . . . This ensures the steadiness of the saddle and checks that tendency to roll which has proved so conducive to injury to the withers.' In other words if a trooper did not sit absolutely upright he stood a very fair chance of giving his horse a sore back. Yet the Austrian and later the United States armies never had points to their saddle trees.[31] Although officers of Heavy Cavalry had their 1796 pattern saddles made with fans the troopers had none for a long time and so the rear pack in their case rested perforce directly on the horse's back. As packs both front and rear were steadily growing heavier this must have been a distinct drawback, though the saddle seems to have stood up to the extra weight extremely well, especially in the Peninsula. The men were heavy, so was the load and so was the saddle, for the great point of heavy cavalry was the weight and size of the horses and experienced observers noted again and again the tremendous effect of a charge delivered by them. The close of the period from 1630 to 1800 is also the end of mounting British Cavalry on saddles chosen by an individual, made according to his ideas and the capabilities of whatever tradesmen he chose to employ and gradually becoming standardized to the extent that there were only a very limited number of types which would pass the eye of the General Officer who inspected the regiments. The system had worked well enough in an era when war was conducted on well-tried and liked methods. Armies fought, not seldom confining themselves to siege work, bloody enough from the foot soldier's point of view but not putting any undue strain on the cavalryman's equipment, throughout the warmer months of the year and broke off operations when winter came on. This meant that there was plenty of time to renew and repair saddlery and that there was not likely to be any pressing need for large stores of replacements. Relatively speaking armies were small and the amount of equipment required put no undue strain on the economy of the countries to which they belonged. With the start of the French Revolutionary Wars, the whole scene changed. Standardization came in and with it enough evidence to enable us to know far more about equipment than had been possible when dealing with the period covered by this section.

BRITISH ARMY SADDLES OF THE NINETEENTH CENTURY

So far there have only been two classes of saddles to be worked on, those in use by General Officers and those used by Cavalry. There does not seem to have been any great distinction between officers' saddles and those in use by senior and staff officers. In the century now under review we have to deal with saddles used by Staff Officers, by officers of Cavalry — not always of the same pattern as was used by other ranks, in other words troopers — by Royal Artillery officers, mounted gunners and by drivers, including those of the Royal Engineers and the corps which became the Royal Army Service Corps. There are also peculiarities, such as saddles of Indian and Colonial make and types, including two types of saddles made in the United States. Until after the close of the century drivers of all corps had their own type or types of saddle, always with low cantles and if they had fans these were made very short, barely coming clear of the cantle. The reason for this was that the driver's 'luggage', or most of it, was carried on the off horse, sometimes in the form of a folded blanket, but more often on a 'luggage saddle', made with a miniature seat not large enough to take a man. In time this was replaced by a riding saddle, without stirrups.

We have seen the century come in with both Heavy and Light Cavalry using a more or less roomy saddle of conventional English civilian type as regards the tree and small variations in the shape of slightly higher pommels and cantles. In a few

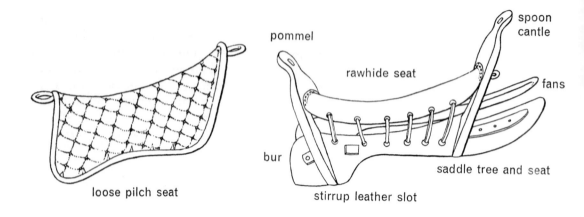

loose pilch seat

pommel

spoon cantle

rawhide seat

fans

bur

saddle tree and seat

stirrup leather slot

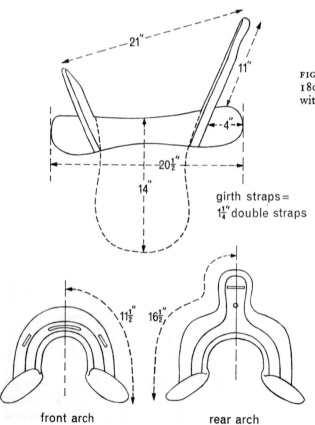

front arch

rear arch

girth straps =
1¼" double straps

FIGURES 6 and 7   The Hussar saddle of 1805, the loose seat or pilch and the tree without the flaps. Plate 11 refers.

cases saddles were used with what was called a demi-peak or pique, a pronounced rise to the front arch. A full peak came up like that of the 'Great Saddle'.

As already explained, the Royal family had been instrumental in procuring from Prussia a set of saddlery belonging to a Prussian Hussar Regiment, the Ziethen Hussars, called after the most celebrated commander of Light Cavalry in the army of Frederick the Great. Hussars had been introduced into the Prussian Army in 1721, copied from the Hungarian National Irregular Light Cavalry, first regimented in the Austrian Army in 1734.[32] They had existed in their homeland since about the fifteenth century and when they became part of the Austrian forces presumably brought their saddles with them. At any rate the Hungarian saddle became in due course the cavalry saddle of all Austrian mounted troops and was used for light cavalry in the German Army up to the introduction of a universal type in c.1890. It was used not only in our service, but in the French and in 1812 in the American as well.

This Central European saddle is very much of an Eastern type and there may be a possibility that it owes its origin to the Mongol horsemen who flooded into Hungary in the thirteenth century. The materials used are such as would be easily procurable in any country where there was sufficient wood, preferably beech, available to make the tree, which would be well within the capacity of any rough carpenter to fashion. The other materials used were ox-hide, or pigskin if it was to be had, the whole framework being glued and pegged together and fastened with strips of rawhide. See in Plate 11.

The line drawings copied from Forbes *History of the Army Ordnance Services* show the construction. The right-hand sketch in Figure 6 shows the 'high mounting' peak and cantle, later called a 'spoon', the rawhide seat pegged or nailed on to them which took the weight of the man, well above the horse's spine; the rawhide thongs holding the sides of the seat to the sideboards and fastened with pegs glued into holes cut for them; the slot for the stirrup leather; the bur in front and the long fans behind. The girth attachments are not shown. As adopted by Regular armies iron plates were sometimes added to the arches and can be seen on the fans. Flaps were fastened to the rawhide lacing between seat and tree. The left-hand sketch shows the loose soft leather cover, quilted on one side, on which the Hussar sat in our service. It could be worn either side up and was looped over the arches back and front. Beechwood was always used for the tree, as it was usually for all saddles. In the Austrian service the loose seat and the saddle flaps were made in one piece and in some drawings of the Hussar saddle, as it was commonly called, this appears to have been done in our service also. The tree has both burs and fans and no points and as originally adopted in our service was worn with a Witney blanket thickly folded instead of panels. These were used by some regiments as well as the blankets. The seat is a short one, only 16½ inches long and for some time the stirrups were not worn long, a normal hunting seat being used. Later on the very straight leg was adopted. In 1813 a Light Dragoon rode just over 20 stone.[33]

Plate 11 shows full details of one of these saddles, which is still in existence, with all measurements, the weight being 9½ lb completely stripped. From 1805 it was issued to all the Light Dragoon Regiments that were converted to Hussars and from 1812 to all Light Cavalry. A sheepskin and shabraque were worn with it and in 1816 the peak was slightly cut down, but the spoon cantle remained as in the original pattern. The saddle continued in use till after the Crimea and during that campaign a numnah was issued instead of the blanket. One regiment, the 11th Hussars, kept their 'Hungarian' saddles, this being the original name until 1866.[34] Although General Sir R. H. Vivian (1775–1842), who commanded a Hussar Brigade at Waterloo, considered that the wooden trees of the Hussar saddle caused sore backs,[35] there is no doubt the pattern was well liked and was freely used by Staff Officers, including the Duke of Wellington, who had a plain blue shabraque over his in 1813, and by General Robert Crauford and one of his staff. The future General Sir Harry Smith described Crauford as 'barely to be discovered, so entrenched was he behind his cloak strapped on the pique',[36] which gives an idea of how the high pommel looked to an observer with a sense of humour. The future Colonel Valentine Baker, 10th Hussars, writing as a junior officer just before the introduction of the new Universal Pattern in 1857, has this to say about the Hussar type:[37] 'the saddle could be much lightened if not made to take to pieces, as at present. I could never understand why it should be made so. Our ordinary hunting saddles never get out of order, and are easily cleaned, and why a dragoon's should be such a complication of movable straps and buckles, pilches (the loose seat), woofs (or wolf, the rawhide seat), etc. all made to take to pieces and put together, like a Chinese puzzle, has ever been beyond my comprehension.' He is presumably referring, among other things, to the triangular surcingle which held the shabraque in place, as well as the ordinary one which went over the sheepskin. There was no waterdeck issued. The sheepskin took up room and made the seat smaller, and another point objected to by some officers was the blanket, which in the 'fifties was folded in 16 thicknesses.[38] It was claimed that this made saddling up in an emergency a very slow process, but experience has shown that on service, with horses getting steadily thinner, a blanket which is large enough to be folded to any required thickness is most valuable in keeping the saddle well off the back of a thin horse. The numnah came from India and had been used by the Prussians for a long time.[39] It is a thick woollen pad.

The question of being able to saddle up quickly, especially at night, was a most important one and exercised the minds of commanding officers to such an extent, as well it might, when sometimes it took two men to lift a packed saddle on to a horse, that the troop horses were often kept saddled up all night when a unit was on the outpost line[40] and often by day for very long periods. In 1835 an inspecting officer of French cavalry decided to see what could be done about turning out quickly and their 4th Hussars were selected to make the experiment. No doubt the men were specially coached, for they unbridled, unsaddled and undressed in 40 seconds and dressed and saddled up again in 1 minute 8 seconds. Colonel Valentine Baker, from whose writings the account comes,[41] comments: 'Their equipment including their dress weighed 50 lb – less than half that of the British'. There can, however, be little doubt that experienced troops, provided the saddles are not too heavily loaded, can run in their horses if they are grazing close at hand, saddle up and move off in a very short time – less than 10 minutes. Always granted that the horses are thankful to get a bite of grass and are used to short off-saddles.

However much the seat being raised well off the horse is disliked by many horsemen, there is no doubt that the shape of the old Hussar saddle gave an excellent means of allowing a current of air to move along the spine between the panels and under the blanket, if it was folded with only two thicknesses above the sideboards. That this was fully recognized is shown by the issue of pattern after pattern, up to the end of the employment of mounted men as part of the forces, embodying the same high arches, with the addition of some form of points to the front arches as used in the Heavy cavalry patterns.

A minor point arising from the introduction of the spoon cantle is that even when the shabraque and sheepskin are worn it protrudes through them and so may be of use in fixing the date of an illustration. For these and the valise see the section on 'Furniture'.

The Hungarian pattern saddle was used by officers and mounted gunners of the Royal Horse Artillery from the first and is shown in Macdonald's *Dress of the Royal Artillery*, on an officer's charger in 1793 and a gunner's of the Rocket Troop in 1815. Plate 23a shows an officer with the same saddlery in 1821. During the period of the Napoleonic Wars the driver's saddle of the Royal Artillery and Royal Waggon Train were the same and were cut low in the peak and the cantle, the latter having a brass edging, like the saddle of the Heavy Cavalry. There were no fans. See Plate 23b. Saddler-Sergeant William Wisely, 1st Royal Dragoons[42] disliked the way the bars of the Heavy Cavalry saddle of 1796 were shaped and stated that in the Peninsula he had seen more than half of the horses of a regiment being led because of sore backs. He also wrote that the Royal Irish Constabulary, formed in 1819, had the same driver's saddle.

Drivers' saddles changed very little until after the end of the century and were of very much the same pattern for all Corps using harness.

Plate 82 shows an officer's Heavy Cavalry saddle at the beginning of the century, made like a trooper's with a square-ended valise as a rear pack. The officer is believed to have commanded the Bodyguard of the Governor General of India, and Hamilton Smith[43] has a plate showing a trooper of the Bodyguard with the same saddle.

Plates 9 and 10 show two views of an officer's saddle of the Greys used at Waterloo. The saddle is in the Scottish United Services Museum at the Castle, Edinburgh, and is one of the very very few examples of saddles of this period still existing. The wooden tree, reinforced with iron under the front arch, with the points coming down below the sideboards, can be seen in the close-up and the other photograph shows the only divergence from the trooper's pattern, the long fans continued behind the cantle in prolongation of the sideboards. These are longer,

133

narrower and more curved than in the Hussar pattern. They are also shown in a drawing of 1803 of Captain Quest, Riding Master to the Riding House Department of the Board of Ordnance.

The 'Waterloo saddle' belonged to Cornet James Gape, who was gazetted to the Greys in 1813 at the age of sixteen. During the charge of the Heavy Brigade against French Infantry, soon after 14.00 hours on the 18th June, 1815, Gape had his saddle pierced by two bullets fired at about 20 yards, one through the rolled cloak on the pommel and one through the back of the seat of the saddle. His mare had three slight wounds and he himself was untouched. The photographs show plainly where the bullets went. He must have been standing up in his stirrups. The above description was furnished by Mr W. A. Thorburn, Curator of the Scottish United Services Museum; he adds that the bullet which hit the pommel bent the metal straps running down the arch. The brass edging to the cantle is clearly shown and the crupper is still attached. The saddle is heavy, weighing 12 lb stripped.

This brings us to the end of the French Wars. The next changes following on the slight alteration to the Light Cavalry saddle already noted, were to those of the Heavies. All saddles had been made of brown leather since 1809 and the Heavy cavalry by a Warrant of March 1834[44] were to have 'a saddle with leather edged panels and pad, brass cantles and a pair of bearing flaps'. Presumably the latter were fans, as an oil painting of a Sergeant of the Greys of 1832[44] shows short fans as does Plate 62, a painting of the Sergeant Major of the 7th Dragoon Guards in 1838 by J. Dalby. It is not clear why the Sergeant of the Greys had this type of saddle before the issue of the Warrant in 1834 unless, as so often happened, the Warrant only confirmed and regularized the issue of articles already in use. The Dress Regulations for Officers of 1834 describe the saddle as follows: 'a high mounting saddle with fans behind, oval side stirrups (known as Hussar pattern), holsters with a brown leather flounce and cloak cover and a black sheepskin', called a shabraque.[44]

In 1840 a new saddle was authorized for heavy cavalry and a saddle blanket was introduced to be worn under it. There is a note that 'the Board of Officers had never contemplated the use of a blanket in the Heavy Cavalry in the manner mentioned. Lieut Colonel the Hon. George Cathcart[45] was to explain the manner of folding the blanket'. Presumably this was the introduction of the practice of placing the blanket folded double over the horse and much thicker up the two sides to give the required thickness under the panels or sideboards of the saddle as the case might be. This has already been noted in the description of the Light Cavalry saddle. Cathcart, killed at Inkerman, was a fine horseman with very sound ideas on the whole range of training in equitation as practised in his day.

In 1840 a saddle, 'constructed on Lukin's patent', was suggested by a Board of Cavalry Officers and two per troop issued to all regiments for trial. It was approved in July, but apparently no general issue was made. It was a common practice to send out a new pattern for trial, and for no more to be heard of it. In 1845 there was to be an alteration in the saddle which was to be introduced gradually.[44] Illustrations show Heavies with a spoon cantle and this is presumably the saddle mentioned by Nolan[46] when he wrote in 1853 of 'the great improvement made in the Hungarian saddle given to our Heavy Dragoons, for here the sideboards are cut like the tree of our English hunting saddle, the seat lowered and the man brought nearer the horse. It is used with a large blanket with twelve folds (see above) or with pads stuffed with horse hair.' He thought the Hussar saddle raised the man too high off the horse, which he disliked. He used the terms 'high mounting', 'Hungarian' and 'Hussar' indiscriminately. Plates 64 and 65 show the Hussar saddle of his day, which does not look as if it differed at all from the one shown in Plate 11. As already stated the Royal Artillery mounted men had the Hussar saddle during this period. In 1840 the drivers' saddles had low rounded cantles with a brass edging, weighing 4 stone 9 lb. complete with head collar, nosebag and chain. The R.H.A. mounted gunner's saddle, complete, weighed only 2 stone 12 lb.

From 1850 to the end of the century we have the evidence of Major J. Horton, a ranker whose original enlistment was in the 4th Dragoon Guards, and who was for many years Secretary to most of the Commissions appointed by the Ordnance to report on and consider the various types of saddlery, experimental and adopted, on issue to the Army. In 1909 he embodied his opinions in a long article, which appeared in the Cavalry Journal and is frequently quoted in this book. Sometimes his figures are at variance with the official ones, but this is easily checked and detracts little from the value of Horton's work. His work covers much of the same field as that of Major General Sir Frederick Smith, K.C.M.G. (1857–1929), who wrote the *History of the Royal Army Veterinary Corps*, in which he rendered such distinguished service, as late as 1927. There will be many references to his work.

Dealing with the pre-Crimea saddle of the Heavy Cavalry Horton wrote: 'It was similar to the Old Pattern Transport and Royal Artillery Driver's saddle. It did not go to all regiments. The tree was as a hunting saddle, but much heavier, with wood arches and plates to the gullet, bars and cantle. It had long points but no burs or fans. The seat was of cowhide on stretched web or serge, padded with flock like a hunting saddle. Some seats were very short. The panels were heavily stuffed with flock and in the Crimea a blanket was worn. Cruppers were used and the girths, stirrups and leathers, as well as the breastplate, were as issued with the wood arch (Hussar) saddle.'

Plates 64 and 65, already noted, show the Hussar saddle and Horton has this to say about it in addition to the description already given. He calls it the Wood Arch, Pilch Seat Saddle and the name Pilch Seat was generally used to differentiate the pattern from the one that followed it. This loose seat was very much liked by many who used it. Horton notes that the panels, which succeeded the folded blanket in 1855, were stuffed with horsehair and lined with white serge. The girth was of web and was permanently fixed to the bar on the off side. The single buckle to the stirrup was worn near the iron with the spare end in a roll, said to be intended to stop a sword cut aimed at depriving a man of his stirrup.

135

Plate 25 shows the wheelers and the hind quarters of the next pair of the team of a field gun of the Crimean and Indian Mutiny period. The harness is brown, it was changed from black in 1853, and there are no blinkers as there were before. This type lasted till the sixties. The drivers' saddles and the smaller pad saddles on the off horses can be clearly seen; a more correct name is 'luggage saddles', as they carried the driver's valise. With this pattern of harness they were carried by all the off horses and weighed 10 lb 4 oz. These saddles, both riding and luggage, were known after 1861 as the Old Pattern and weighed 16 lb 13 oz. The numnah weighed 5 lb 6 oz. The riding saddles were not on the same principle as the cavalry patterns and were quite different to the type that followed them. The riding saddle is a strong, heavy type and the fans, as was always the case with drivers' saddles, barely projected behind the cantle.

The Land Transport Corps of 1855 and its successor the Military Train, 1856–69, had the same saddles and Horton notes that they were similar to the Heavy Cavalry saddle in use by some regiments pre-Crimea, and had the same hunting saddle tree.

Plate 23 therefore covers the saddles used by Heavy Cavalry as well as Royal Artillery and Military Train drivers. The officers' saddles of this pattern are not noted; they rode 15 stone and other ranks of the Military Train about 18 stone.

Plates 12, 13a and 13b show photographs of two officers' saddles used at Balaclava in the Crimea on the 25th October, 1854. The latter two photographs are of the saddle of Cornet Richard George Glyn, 1st Royal Dragoons, who took part in the Heavy Cavalry charge, and the other belonged to the future Lord Tredegar, who, as Captain Godfrey Morgan, 17th Lancers, rode in the Charge of the Light Brigade. The saddle of the Heavies has fans and burs, a high peak, a brass edging to the cantle and knee rolls. It weighs today 10 lb without panels.

Lord Tredegar's saddle is a typical Hungarian or Hussar saddle, made with fixed seat instead of the loose pilch and has the high peak and spoon cantle, fans and burs – the latter with the open pistol holsters of the period. It weighs 19 lb 9 oz and is remarkable in that it has been preserved complete with the Hussar stirrups, breastplate, girths, bridle, holsters and panels.

The regiments which took part in the Indian Mutiny appear to have used the same patterns as those in use in the Crimea, although in 1855, two years before the Mutiny, a complete change in cavalry saddlery was already contemplated. The next section deals with this change.

Not the least important of the many changes introduced into the Army as a result of the Crimean War was the abolition of the centuries-old Board of Ordnance, which had hitherto had a separate existence from the rest of the Army, with the exception of the two so-called Ordnance Corps, the Royal Artillery and the Royal Engineers. The successor of the Board was the Army Ordnance Department, which took over the duties of the older Department and was in the same way responsible among other measures for the selection, testing, manufacture and issue of all saddlery and harness. Although as a general rule all the harness, in most cases the drivers' saddles and many other minor articles provided by Ordnance had been in use throughout the Service, there were many minor exceptions and the Cavalry especially liked to differ from the rest of the mounted branches and even Regiment from Regiment in various details of their saddlery.

The tendency from the Crimea onwards was always in the direction of more uniformity and the discarding of any but Universal Patterns. Although the progress made was very marked, it was not until the early years of the following century that one pattern of riding saddle was a regular issue to all types of mounted men, with the exception of the officers, who have always had slight differences in their saddlery from that in use by other ranks.

As a preliminary step to the introduction of a Universal Pattern a Board of Officers was assembled while the Army was still in Russia to consider and report on all Horse Equipment used by their arm and on what changes could be considered desirable. Previously there had not been a great deal of exchange of ideas between officers who had service in India, where there were an almost continuous succession of small campaigns, and those who had only served in Great Britain, who had had no chance of seeing active service since Waterloo. A considerable number of young officers who held constructive ideas on cavalry generally were seconded for service with the Army of the East, as the Crimean Field Force was called. Of these the best known was Captain Lewis E. Nolan (born c.1820, the exact date of birth seems not to be known), best remembered today by his dramatic death at the start of the charge of the Light Brigade on 25th October, 1854. Thirty years after he was killed he was described by Lieut Colonel James Keith Fraser, Inspector General of Cavalry and formerly commanding the 1st Life Guards, as 'one of the best Cavalry soldiers that ever lived'.[47] His career was a remarkable one; he was commissioned in a Hungarian Cavalry Regiment, in those days considered the best light cavalry in Europe, and saw active service with them. In 1839 he was commissioned to British Infantry, exchanged to the 15th Hussars, served in India and was sent to Russia on official duty before the Crimea. Nolan was a man who had thought deeply about his profession and in 1853 he published a book, *Cavalry, Its History and Tactics*, T. Bosworth, London, which was for many years a classic of its kind. The importance of the book to anyone working on the history of British Army Saddlery lies in the criticisms of saddles, with which Nolan was well acquainted both in peace and war. He had seen active service while in India and so had an all-round knowledge of Eastern as well as European types. The book is the first of a considerable number which deal exhaustively with the question of the weight to be carried by the horse, a point, the most important of all connected with the remount, which was never really satisfactorily settled, as the pull between what was considered necessary for the man was always in conflict with the amount a horse should carry, if he was to be used to the fullest advantage in war. Nolan took his ideas to the point of designing a saddle, which was manufactured in small quantities and issued to the Mounted Staff Corps, an *ad hoc* body of Military Police hurriedly raised and sent to the army before Sevastopol. It was not adopted by the British Army, though it was by a large part of the Indian Cavalry (see under the section on India). Nolan's saddle had, however, so much influence on the Universal Pattern adopted in 1856, that the latter was commonly, though incorrectly, known by his name.

In April 1855, while the Crimean War was still in full swing, a Board of Cavalry Officers was assembled at the Adjutant General's Office at the Horse Guards to 'consider and report upon the best form and construction of Saddle for uniform adoption throughout the Cavalry, and also upon other articles of Cavalry Equipment and appurtenances referred to in the Proceedings of a previous Board of Officers assembled in the Crimea, which Proceedings are laid before the present Board'.[48] As will appear in due course the saddlery evolved from the proceedings of this Board was adopted with only minor exceptions by the whole Army. The President of the Board was General Henry Wyndham, who had served with the 10th Hussars in the Peninsula and at Waterloo. The members were Colonel F. Griffiths, Commandant of the Cavalry Depot at Maidstone, formerly of the 12th Lancers, Colonel J. F. S. Clarke, Assistant Quartermaster General, the Scots Greys, Colonel J. Lawrenson, 17th Lancers, who had served in the Crimea, and was replaced by Colonel W. Campbell, who had commanded the 2nd Dragoon Guards. The Board opted for a wooden tree with points, as used in the Heavy Cavalry saddle (see *ante*), to be made in three sizes and desired that an instructor in tree-making should be established at the Cavalry Depot, Maidstone. Sergeant Bird, 12th Lancers, the master tree-maker at Maidstone, was recommended to be instructor. The Board fully recognized the importance of the effect of the points on preventing rolling and also the difficulty of deciding whether the new saddle was to have panels or be used with a folded blanket. They preferred panels, but intended that the saddle could be used with either method. Some regiments had used blankets under the panels in the Crimea, when the troop horses got so emaciated from want of anything to eat that the front and rear crutches came right down onto the unfortunate animals' spines.[49] The influence of the 'Indian school' of officers is very apparent in the minutes of the Board's proceedings. Cavalry in India had for some time been using the numnah, a thick felt pad cut so as to go completely under the saddle and obviate the use of panels. Later on, as will appear, strips of numnah replaced the panels altogether. The numnah probably made its first appearance in Europe in Russia, as the name for it in the Prussian service was 'Woylach', a Russian word. The Board recommended that the numnah should be cut to fit from the shoulder to the hips and be worn with a blue saddle cloth over it. It was to be kept on the horse at night when standing out. The weight of the saddle was to be 12 lb with 3 lb added for the panels. A saddle of this weight without stirrups, etc. was on the light side when compared with most military saddles in use in Europe and the U.S.A. during the nineteenth century, but weights carried were not at their highest at this time, except in France, where the Cuirassiers were said to have carried the greatest load on the horse, of any cavalry.[50]

The Board liked the loose leather seat of the original Hussar saddle and so did many practical men, for either the flat or the padded side could be used as desired and the seat readily cleaned or dried. The rest of the Board's recommendations were reasonable and well thought out, but do not greatly concern us, as most of them were adopted.

The illustration of the saddle as proposed shows the usual 'High Mounting' or 'Hungarian' type with the spoon cantle, a comfortably long seat and stirrups set forward so that a man could ride shorter if he was allowed.

As a first effort at a Universal Pattern the proposed saddle was distinctly in advance of former patterns, and like the one eventually adopted, owed a considerable amount to Nolan's ideas.

As already mentioned, three years after Nolan's death, Colonel Valentine Baker published his book on British Cavalry. He was then a man of thirty – he died in 1887 with a European reputation as a cavalry general – and his book took on the problems dealt with by Nolan. Baker liked the blanket and wished to use it with the panels. He had seen service in two small wars in South Africa and soldiered in India with the 12th Lancers before going on to the Crimea. He wished to substitute a waterproof for the cavalry cloak, a monkey jacket for the smart and unpractical stable jacket and to have saddle bags for all ranks. These were to be carried in light carts with the sheepskins, worn over the saddle by Light Cavalry. These details may seem immaterial today, but they show what Baker, like Nolan before him, and a very large number of officers of later generations were trying to do – to cut down the weight carried by the horse without impairing the efficiency of the cavalryman. Baker's ideal was to reduce the load on the Light Cavalry troop horse to about 13 stone in marching order, if the new saddle could be lightened and to just over 15 stone if it was to remain as issued. The formula on which the modern school based their calculations was explained in 1891 in a lecture at Aldershot by the future Major General Sir Frederick Smith, K.C.M.G., Director of Veterinary Services, who by his writings and lectures and in other ways, did more for the welfare and efficiency of the British Army Remount than any other individual. His figures, copied by many authorities and it is believed originally derived from Continental sources, were as follows: 'A cavalry horse should not carry more than one-fifth of his mean weight of 1,000 lb or a total of 14 stone 3 lb; 15 stone should be the maximum. The formula is to divide the known weight of a horse by the figure 5·67 (one-fifth to one-sixth of his weight).'[50] In this connection Major General Rosenberg, Inspector General of Prussian Cavalry, stated that 'cavalry carrying more than 15 stone 10 lb are fit for nothing'. The question revolved round the practice, considered necessary, of making the troop saddle pound for pound as heavy as the load of kit it had to carry in order to obtain sufficient strength to stand up to the stresses inevitable on active service.

During the nineteenth century both ourselves and the Continental nations made their cavalry mounts carry from 19 to 20 stone.

Before going into the details of the new saddle it should be noted that the question of saddles as used in the Indian Mutiny of 1857–8 will be treated in the section on India.

The new saddle was not however a 'Universal Issue'. General and Staff Officers, Personal Staff Officers, Officers of the Civil Departments, Mounted Officers of the Foot Guards and all the Infantry Regiments used a hunting saddle. A Field Marshal had a 'gilt cantle on a plain saddle'.

General Officers of Hussars and officers of all Cavalry Regiments, except those of the Household Cavalry, used the new saddle described in the Dress Regulations for 1857 as: 'Hussar saddle of brown hogskin, with a brass head and cantle, Hussar stirrup leathers and irons and blue girths'.

The Universal Pattern Wood Arch Saddle of 1856 to 1872, shown below, was not used by the Household Cavalry.

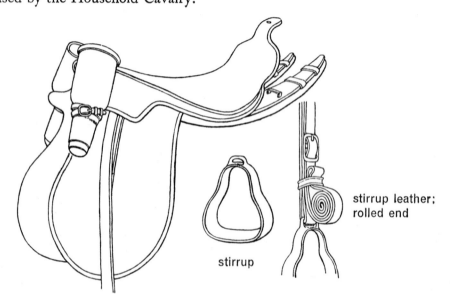

stirrup leather; rolled end

stirrup

FIGURE 8   The Universal Pattern saddle of 1856 to 1872, Wood Arch. With Panels, showing the stirrup leather rolled.

This tracing is taken from an article in the *Carriage Builders and Harness Makers Art Journal* of July 1859, entitled 'Saddlery, the 10th (or Prince of Wales Own) Hussars'. Signed C.J.M. and the description that follows is partly from this source and partly from Horton.

The saddle shown is an officer's with panels. The seat is of solid leather blocked and riveted, about $16\frac{3}{4}$ inches in length, but when the shabraque and sheepskin, each having a thick leather seat where it went over the saddle, were strapped down by the surcingle, the space left in which the trooper had to sit was only 16 inches. The Board of 1855 had wished to abolish both shabraque and sheepskin, weighing seven or six pounds, and it would have been a badly needed change. Numnahs, as recommended, were used instead of blankets and the two panels for the new pattern weighed from five to six pounds and were very heavily stuffed with horsehair, Horton thought altogether too thickly.

The beech wood tree had a high upright front arch, and a high spoon cantle not quite so upright as in the old Hussar saddle. The tree had points coming down from the front arch and the sideboards were continued to form burs and very adequate fans. The front arch had an iron gullet plate and three crown plates and would stand a strain of 4 cwt. The cantle had an iron plate and two fan plates. The sideboards were 24 inches long with slots for the stirrup leathers. In the first issues the girth was fixed to the sideboards, later iron staples to take the girth straps were added. The tree was made in three sizes and was a great improvement on that of former patterns. The R.H.A. officer's charger shown in Plate 26 shows the saddle as worn on parade.

Both crupper and breastplate were used with this saddle and for ranks armed with the carbine there was a small 10 inch leather tube with an iron-bound mouth, hung from the off side of the front arch, hanging a little below and in front of the wallet, with a strap going from the small of the butt to a ring on the arch. This muzzle bucket and stay strap had been in use since the last quarter of the preceding century and Plate 58 shows an earlier form.

The saddle was supposed to last 12 years and the weight was 15 lb 8 oz including the panels.

Although some men regretted the loose seat, there is no doubt that the U.P. Wood Arch Saddle was a great success. Though its official life ended in 1872 it was still in use by some British Cavalry Regiments as late as 1885 and a number, probably belonging to Yeomanry Regiments and so not having had much work, were issued during the period of great scarcity of saddlery during the South African War of 1899 to 1902.

In 1861 a further step was taken towards extending the issue of the U.P. Wood Arch Saddle, which had hitherto only been used by Cavalry of the Line. The other mounted services decided to adopt the pattern, but did not want the drivers to have the high spoon cantle and long fans. These were unnecessary, for as already explained, the bulk of the kit was carried on the off or lead horse. By 1864 the new drivers' saddles were ready, made with a low cantle and short fans; see Plate 27b for the saddle, shown separately. The photograph of the near wheeler also shows the saddle with a cover, and the photograph of the off horse shows the harness saddle. After the complete issue of the U.P. the harness saddle was only carried by the off wheeler, the other off horses having riding saddles without stirrups. The mounted Gunner rode eighteen stone. The change-over in all the mounted services was slow, as the Old Pattern saddles had to be worn until condemned.

The Household Cavalry were now the only troops not using the Universal Pattern.

In 1868 various moves were made in the direction of lightening the saddle. Colonel Valentine Baker designed a saddle 2 lb 2 oz lighter than the U.P. Twelve saddles of Baker's pattern were issued on trial to three regiments for twelve months, but no further action was taken. In the same year Captain Fenn proposed a new saddle with iron arches and straps going under the seat to support it. A patent was taken out and twelve were sent to R.H.A., to a Field Battery and to the Military Train, nine went to Heavy and Light Cavalry Regiments. Some units reported favourably on Fenn's pattern, but the reception given Baker's type was of a varied nature. At this time the stock of U.P. Wood Arch saddles was 3,892, enough to last for about $5\frac{1}{2}$ years. Reports from India were contradictory; some regiments liked straps going under the seat, others preferred webbing. The tendency of the seat to sag under prolonged work and let the rider down too close to the spine was very marked. The ideas as to the necessity for the spoon cantle were as varied. There was a definite opinion that the spoon was unnecessary on a driver's saddle, which did not carry the full pack; but, although some officers held that the long fans gave sufficient support to the rear pack, others disagreed and wished to retain the spoon. It was said to be a great help in mounting, but dangerous if a horse fell, also the sword sling was said to catch in it in the event of a fall.

The Wood Arch type was a good wearing saddle; some made in 1863 were still in good order in 1887 and those made by Middlemore were especially well reported on. After twelve years service it was noted that the gullet plates and arches were apt to break when used for jumping in the riding school! Which was perhaps not so very surprising.[51]

In 1872 the change came and a new Universal Pattern, the Flat Iron Arch saddle, was introduced. The cantle was round without a spoon, the points were smaller, and the side bars thinner and the arch stood a strain of $2\frac{1}{2}$ cwt only. The horsehair panels had heavy welts and facings like thick cord, otherwise the saddle was the same as the Wood Arch pattern.

This was the first of what may with justice be called the three trial-and-error patterns, evolved while Ordnance was groping for the right answer to as many of the problems as possible. The Flat Iron Arch was a complete failure and always let the pack down on the horse's spine. It was not nearly strong enough for the work it had to do.

Nor were the Ordnance officials the only people concerned about the unsatisfactory position of the Army saddle. In 1873 the London Saddlers' Company, acting for the rest of the trade, was offering premiums to any firm or individual, who would bring forward any new ideas. At this time all Army saddlery was made by contract. As a result two Commissions were appointed, in 1873 and 1874, with a membership of three officers appointed by the Horse Guards and two civilian saddlers by the Company. The terms laid down were that the saddle was to be as light as possible and to be strong enough to carry a total weight of 16 stone 10 lb in marching order, to be made in three sizes and to be capable of being altered to fit different sized horses. The high spoon was ruled out. It seems unfortunate that the pattern of the Flat Iron Arch had already been decided on and that manufacture was in progress. Nothing came of the work of the two commissions and from this time onward one Committee after another was appointed by Ordnance, with eventual results which will be described in due course.[52]

Major Horton was Secretary to the Committees and two officers who played a prominent part were Lieut General Sawyer, c.b. and General Sir Frederick FitzWygram, Inspector General of Cavalry. FitzWygram was President of many of the Committees and his name was very well known indeed, not only in the Army, but also among a very large number of hunting people and horse-owners, who read his books on horses, especially one entitled *Horses and Stables*, published in 1869. He was notable as having as a junior Cavalry Officer graduated as a Veterinary Surgeon, although he never practised.

In 1878 Ordnance ordered the issue of the U.P. Angle Iron Arch Saddle, the angle irons being considered stronger than the flat irons of the last issue. The arches stood a strain of 4 cwt and the front arch was tested to one of 1,129 lb. The girth straps were set further forward, the length of the seat was 17½ inches and the low cantle was retained.

Fortunately for those concerned with the problem, a number of these saddles were used in 1879 during the Zulu War by the King's Dragoon Guards and the 17th Lancers, the two Regular Regiments engaged, and in his Report, the Principal Veterinary Officer with the H.Q. Column, Veterinary Surgeon F. Duck (later Colonel Sir Francis) stated that the Wood Arch pattern with the high cantle was better than the round iron cantle, which made the men sit too far back. Both Regiments concerned reported that the arches of the 1878 U.P. opened out and that the saddle was very unsatisfactory. They also complained that the saddle flap was too short and caught on the top of the knee boot.

Duck had no complaints about the R.A. drivers' saddles, shown in Plates 27b and 28a, as used by the R.H.A. and other Mounted Services.[53]

Two years later, in 1881, an Ordnance Committee sat at Aldershot and issued a number of Steel Arch saddles for trial to the 4th Dragoon Guards. Lieut Colonel T. B. Shaw-Hellier, commanding the Regiment, reported most favourably on these saddles in 1882 and considered that they rectified all the faults of the Iron Angle Arch pattern. The material used was 'Siemens angle steel'. The Committee went into the question of numnahs and of numnah panels to be used instead of stuffed panels. These two innovations were adopted in time and it appears that the Committee's ideas were well in advance of any recommendations being brought forward in 1881.

To the great advantage of the Ordnance Committees, in 1882 the short sharp campaign in Egypt, which terminated in our crushing victory at Tel-el-Kebir on the 13th September, made it possible to evaluate the old Wood Arch saddle as compared with the new Angle Iron Arch type and to obtain from the commanding officers of Artillery, Cavalry and Engineers full reports on all articles of Horse Equipment. The fact that these reports were written within a very short time of the events with which they dealt, could not fail to add considerably to their value as evidence. There were only 1,500 Angle Iron Arch saddles manufactured, so not all units were issued with them. The 19th Hussars had the Wood Arch and the Flat Iron Arch issues and reported that the wooden arches held well. The iron arches opened out with the heat and the men were ordered to ride short and rise at the trot which stopped a certain amount of expansion from heat. Lieut Colonel Kendal Coghill, commanding, was in favour of the numnah.[54]

Generally speaking the wood arch was preferred to the newer iron arch patterns, but there were exceptions. Thus Major and Lieut Colonel L. F. Perry, R.A., commanding a Field Battery, reported well on the Angle Iron Arch saddles, but complained that the seats were too liable to sag. Lieut Colonel C. E. Nairne, R.A., was dissatisfied with the wood arches, which did not stand up well to the work. Though the new pattern Angle Iron arches did not break, he objected to the cantle as altogether unsuitable. He added 'there is no doubt that the correct remedies are steel arches, with the seat supported by webbing and sewn on to the arches'. The Engineers had little trouble with either type of saddle, though they found the iron arches liable to open in the heat. They were of the opinion that it should be possible to vary the size of the seats to suit the riders, as 'the saddle that fitted a boy trumpeter was altogether unsuitable for a fat Quarter Master Sergeant'. This last statement was made by Major and Brevet Lieut Colonel R. J. Bond, O.C. A Troop, R.E., and in the comments on Bond's report by the Commander Royal Engineers, Lieut Colonel H. Helsham Jones, R.E., the latter adds: 'It is argued that in civil life all sorts of shapes of men ride in saddles of the same form. The reply is obvious; they are under no obligation to sit in a particular way, and in fact do not do so. Soldiers, on the contrary, are required to have a uniform seat, and, unless their saddles are fitted individually to them, such uniformity can only be attained, if at all, by muscular exertion.'

Whatever is thought of the main argument, there is no doubt that the remarks on civilians riding as they like are most apposite.

General FitzWygram's Committee, which was convened in 1884, was fortunate in having so much fresh material on the effect of active service on horse equipment before it. It is a fair conclusion to draw from the opinions expressed on the steel arch, that the Committee would be most anxious to introduce it as soon as possible. The position with which they had to deal was as follows: in 1883 instead of a reserve of 5,000 Angle Iron Arch saddles, there were only 63 in hand. There were also 1,421 obsolete Flat Iron saddles in store. By July 1884 no less than 600 of these had to be issued. The Committee decided on the manufacture of 3,600 Angle Iron Arch saddles of almost the same pattern as the previous one, but with shorter fans and a removable seat which was fastened to the beech wood tree by straps. The weight was 10 lb 12 oz, that of the tree being 7 lb 4 oz (see Plate No. 16), and with a 10 stone 7 lb man in marching order the horse carried 19 stone 7 oz. The round cantle with no spoon was retained. Panels were used until 1888 when a saddle blanket was introduced.

The saddle was considered as experimental and not sealed till 1885. From the first the Committee had decided that the arch was to be reinforced with a steel plate as soon as possible and this vital change will be noted when the next pattern is described. The U.P. 1884 went to all Mounted Services, except the Household Cavalry, and the drivers' saddles and luggage transport saddles had the same tree. Army Service Corps and Regimental Transport had the Old Pattern Wood Arch in Plate 28a, and Plate 70 shows Mounted Infantry with the U.P. 1884.[55]

Contemporary with Universal Pattern 1884 was a brass runner, replacing the leather runner. Both were designed to take the loose end of the stirrup leather. This brass pattern had been in use by the Household Cavalry since about 1859 with a small mirror on it and this addition was adopted for all officers later on. At first the buckle of the stirrup leather had been run up close to the tree and later to the bar on the tree, as is done with hunting and polo saddles. The buckle was brought down to just above the stirrup iron about 1830 by most cavalry, but the Household Cavalry kept the buckle on the bar at first. The practice of rolling or folding the loose end of the leather had been adopted for some time and in 1884 became general. In the 'thirties most of the Light Cavalry had rolls or folds, but the Heavies kept the buckle high up on the bar. The Ackermann series of Military Prints show practically all regiments with the folds or fold between 1840 and 1850, and most of them continued the practice up to about 1885. Some regiments wore the loose ends of the leather between the two folds with the runner just above the stirrup. The point is of little importance and was connected, no doubt, with the idea of protecting the stirrup leather from a sword cut. The runner is shown in Plate 18, at the bottom, called 'stirrup slide, Regimental pattern', and in Plate 20, with the loose end of the leather inside, as described.[56] See also Figure 8.

The man who exposed the weaknesses of U.P. 1884 was Veterinary Major F. Smith. Both in his lectures at Aldershot to officers and in his once well-known book *Saddles and Sore Backs*, published in 1891, he showed the faults of the saddle in diagrams illustrating the text. Perhaps the most unfortunate flaw was the tendency of the front arch to open out if the saddle was dropped on the ground, as can easily happen in saddling a packed saddle, especially at night. The low cantle allowed men to sit right back on the edge, for the seat was of the same length as when the trooper rode with a straight leg. Riding with the leg bent required more room in the seat and this the new saddle did not provide. The man tried to get more room by sitting further back, thereby bringing the rear arch down on the horse's spine. Smith liked a shallow seat with a dip in the centre of from 4 to $4\frac{1}{2}$ inches. He disliked any attempt to reduce the stuffing in the panels in order to bring the man nearer the horse, as is done in the hunting saddle, and wrote as follows: 'we cannot compare the military saddle with a hunting saddle unless we are prepared to throw away 8 stone of the weight carried'. The slit in the sideboard, through which the stirrup leather passed, was another mistake, as if the buckle was pulled by accident under the sideboard a bad sore back must result. The gist of the book was included in *Animal Management*, issued by the Veterinary Department for the General Staff in 1908 and republished in 1914.

Smith's book was the standard work of his day on sore backs and the school of officers who grew up with it were apt to know a great deal of it by heart. Before going on in strict sequence to the steel arch saddles of the 'nineties, it will be convenient to consider in detail a very different type of saddle of purely civilian origin, as far as is known, which grew in favour from the 'seventies until in the 'nineties it was issued in thousands.

The Cape Fan or Colonial Saddle

The Cape Fan is the trade name for the tree. Other names are 'Colonial', used at the Cape of Good Hope from about 1870; 'Staff Officers Pattern', a limited issue in use from about 1878; 'Semi-Military' – to distinguish it from the various Universal Patterns; in the early 'nineties 'Infantry Officers Pattern'; then 'Staff' as well as 'Officers Pattern' and for a short time 'Yeomanry Pattern'. Plates 17, 18, and 19 refer. Plate 17b shows the tree, very like the wooden reinforced tree of a hunting saddle. It is made of beech with steel straps and a hinged spring latch, as in a hunting saddle, to take the stirrup leather. Plate 14 shows the future Field Marshal Lord Methuen holding his pony during the Bechuanaland Expedition of 1884. He is using the Staff Pattern, ordered to be used 'by all British Officers' serving with Irregulars. The raised front arch, the roomy seat and the long fans are characteristic of the type.[57] The skirt and seat are cut in one and the short rifle-bucket – it was its debut in the British Army – hangs from Dees under the cantle and there are no panels, both numnah and blanket being used. This is presumably as laid down in Dress Regulations 17th May 1883: 'A saddle has been approved as optional for all officers using hunting saddles. It is to have a seat and flaps as a hunting saddle but with fans as a cavalry saddle. The panels are to be lined with soft leather and stuffed with curled horse hair. Regulation wallets and a brown leather waterproof pocket on the off side may be worn but no surcingle.' Plate 14 shows small variations from the above.

An early note on this saddle is in Hurst's *Volunteer Regiments of Natal and East Griqualand* (Durban, 1945), where it was said to be in use in the 1870's. In the Progress Report by the Principal Veterinary Officer with the H.Q. Column in the Zulu War is the following notice, 'the best saddle is the Staff Officers U.P.; it is comparatively light and has no facilities for carrying weight. The Irregulars had the hunting saddle (a name used at the Cape at this time for the Cape Fan) without blankets or numnahs, very unsatisfactory. They had many sore backs.'[53]

The date of approval by Ordnance of this troopers' pattern was the 27th November, 1884, under the name of 'Saddlery for Special Service in South Africa'. Some 2,000 sets were made, in far too great a hurry, in England for the Irregulars of Warren's Bechuanaland Expedition and in Warren's Confidential Report there is a sketch of the saddle by Lieut Colonel Carrington, 24th Foot, the trade name being given as 'hunting saddle'. The sketch shows the Colonial type as in the Plates listed above, especially Plate 19.[58]

There were complaints about some of these saddles, but from this time onwards there was no further dissatisfaction and the 'Colonial' saddle was manufactured in thousands all over the British Empire. With the exception of the early Staff pattern all these saddles had panels and many of these were detachable, being secured to the tree by a strap or screw fitted above the point on each side. The weight was about 18 lb complete.

Plate 17a (R40), shows the Staff Pattern as issued by Ordnance and the Plate showing officers' saddles with lambskins etc., shows the same saddle as used by Mounted Officers of Infantry.

The illustration R40 shows the officers' saddle as used from 1912 onward (see *post*). The detachable panels are shown in Plate 15b as issued to the Household Cavalry in 1884.

REFERENCES

1   Aldershot Lectures No. XXXII. June, 1891. Vet. Surgeon Major F. Smith *Saddles and Saddlery*.
2   Calendar of State Papers; Domestic, Charles I, 1628 to 1629.
3   Forbes, *History of the Army Ordnance Services*, Volume I, p. 134.
4   Forbes, pp. 136, 137, 138.
5   Forbes, p. 139.
6   JAHR, Volume XII, p. 187. Forbes, p. 140.
7   As 1, quoting Grose *Military Antiquities*, pub. 1801.
8   JAHR, Volume XIV, p. 17.
9   Lawson, *History of British Army Uniforms*, Volume I, p. 183.
10 As 1, quoting Cruso, *Military Instructions for the Cavalry, 1632.*
11 *Shakespeare's England*, Volume II, p. 419.
12 West, John, *Village Recorder*, published Macmillan, 1962. Worcestershire Village Probate Records *passim*.
13 Aldershot Lectures as 1; Sherwell J. W., see Bibliography.
14 As 1.
15 JAHR, Volume III, p. 51.
16 JAHR, Volume XXXVIII, p. 12.
17 Lawson, Volume I, p. 186.
18 In 1965 the 15th/19th The King's Royal Hussars.
19 Handbook for Military Artificers 1915, p. 135.
20 JAHR, Volume XIX, p. 65.
21 As 1, quoting Bloch, *Modern Weapons, 1900.*
22 Forbes, Volume I, p. 236.
23 Lawson, Volume II, p. 167.
24 Rogers, p. 129.
25 JAHR, Volume XVI, pp. 44, 45.
26 Olsen in the *Military Collector & Historian*, Spring 1955, p. 4. Figure 1, published in the U.S.A.
27 Burne, *The Noble Duke of York*, pp. 23–25.
28 Board of Officers WO 30/13 A; JAHR, Volume XXV, pp. 116, 117.
29 As 28 and P. Pietsch, *Die Formations und Uniforms-Geschichte der Preussischen Heere*, Volume II, pp. 246, 247 and Figure 76, number 5.

30 Tyndale, *Military Equitation*, 1797.
31 Carter, *Horses, Saddles and Bridles*.
32 Knotel-Sieg, *Handbuch der Uniformkunde*, p. 277, but the Hussars had been in existence from 1700.
33 JAHR, Volume XVI, p. 170. See in the section on 'The Cavalry Seat'.
34 Cavalry Journal, 1909, pp. 359 to 370, Major Horton's 'Evolution of a Cavalry Saddle'.
35 Vivian, *Lord Vivian*, p. 261.
36 Brett-James, *Wellington at War*, p. 264, quoting Stocqueler *Wellington*, Volume I, p. 211. For Crauford, see *Autobiography of Sir H. Smith*, Volume I, p. 17. See also a painting by Denis Dighton, No. 16709 in the Royal Library, Windsor.
37 Baker, *Remarks on British Cavalry*, p. 57.
38 Parry, *The Death or Glory Boys*, p. 230.
39 As 34; see also Parry, p. 230.
40 Tomkinson, *Diary of a Cavalry Officer*, p. 24, written of 1810.
41 United Services Journal, 1864, Part III, p. 342. *The Dragoon, His Horse and Training*, unsigned but from the context undoubtedly written by Colonel Valentine Baker.
42 United Services Journal, 1831, Part I, p. 396.
43 Hamilton Smith, Lieut Col. C., *Costume of the Army of the British Empire*, 1815.
44 JAHR, Volume XVI, pp. 195 to 198.
45 For Cathcart, see Plate 95.
46 Nolan, Captain L. E., *Cavalry, Its History and Tactics*.
47 Aldershot Lectures as 1.
48 Papers Relating to a Uniform Horse Equipment for the Cavalry, September 1855, Illustration. War Office Library.
49 Whinyates, *From Corunna to Sevastopol*, p. 222.
50 Aldershot Lectures as 1, p. 25 *et seq*. Surgeon Major F. Smith, *Weight Carried by the Troop Horse*.
51 Reports on Miscellaneous Subjects Unconnected with Ordnance, Volume IX, 1868, pp. 3, 4, 5; 1869 Oct. to 1870 Oct. Minutes of Evidence given on Commissions (in the same series). Volume XVIII, 1863 and 1887.
52 Sherwell, *Introduction to the London Saddlers Exhibition Catalogue*.
53 Minutes of Evidence on Ordnance Commissions on Saddlery, Progress Report 27th May, 1880, and Appendix B., Evidence of Veterinary Officers Serving with the Zululand Field Force. W.O. Library.
54 Reports on the Service Saddle, Replies to 54/7712/General Order No. 39818, Horse Guards 7/XI/ 1882. War Office Library.
55 Committees on Army Matters 1806 to 1900, bound volume in the War Office Library, Papers 1884, No. 282. FitzWygram Report, Papers 1886, No. 310. See also in 34, but the dates there do not agree, though the differences are slight.
56 From very full notes sent by the Marquess of Cambridge.
57 Regulations for the Bechuanaland Field Force, published Cape Town, 1884.
58 Confidential Report on the Proceedings of the Bechuanaland Field Force, p. 193.
    Minutes of Evidence of Ordnance Commissions of Enquiry on Saddlery, 1886.
    Miscellaneous Subjects (Reference (51)), Volume XVIII, 1887, query No. 3066. List of Changes No. 4672 of 1884.
    All in War Office Library.

CHAPTER FIVE

Riding Saddles continued, including those of all Commonwealth Armies to the present day and side saddles

UNIVERSAL PATTERN 1890 STEEL ARCH

THIS new and revolutionary saddle, Steel Arch Universal Pattern Mark I, was sealed by Ordnance on the 30th January, 1891[1] and was on issue to some units shortly afterwards. It had a high spoon, except for Drivers, who had a low cantle, a high pommel and for other ranks the seat was blocked, the leather being wetted, secured to the tree and dried *in situ*. Instead of being sewn as in the officers' pattern, the seat was all in one piece. Mark I had a slit cut parallel to the horse's spine in the centre of the seat, but this was found to pinch the men and was sewn up and discontinued in Mark II, issued in 1893. Mark III appeared in 1898. The most important innovation was the substitution of the straight up and down girth straps by a 'V'-shaped arrangement of straps with the wide points of the 'V' on the sideboards. Plate 17b shows the tree, called 'Military Steel Arch', made in four sizes. The smallest, which weighed $13\frac{1}{2}$ lb was for M.I. cobs. The new method of attaching the girths is shown in a line drawing on page 154 with a full description. The stirrup was no longer attached by putting the leather through a hole cut in the sideboard (Plate 11f), a prolific cause of sore backs. Instead, a square link and brass roller on the sideboard was provided to take the leather, so that henceforth the buckle on the leather could no longer work up behind the sideboard. The stirrup was set slightly more forward than in older patterns, though not quite as far as in the Colonial pattern. With Mark I stuffed panels were issued, but all other marks used a numnah $28\frac{1}{2}$ by $29\frac{1}{2}$ inches next the horse with a blanket above replacing the panels. This saddle blanket was brown, weighed 4 lb 6 oz and was folded in four with the front turned back to bring six folds under the front arch. By 1899 numnah panels shaped to the sideboards and to the points, with pockets fitting over the fans, were on issue (see *post*). The fans were of normal length, except for drivers, who had short ones as their rear pack was still carried on the off horse.

The steel arch was very strong and stood a strain of 6 cwt. Indeed the saddle will stand an immense amount of knocking about and a number of the 1890 U.P. were still in use on farms in the Dominions up to a short time ago and probably are still today, in 1965.

Although the Household Cavalry received the new U.P. in 1895, there was no general issue until 1898.

All the U.P. 1884 were converted by replacing the angle iron arch with a steel one and altering the girth attachments. These conversions were listed as U.P. 1884 Star and were issued at the same time as U.P. 1890.

As a unit normally retained any U.P. 1884 Star on issue after a partial issue of the U.P. 1890 until the older type wore out, it is not always easy to decide from a photograph or drawing the date when it was done. This is especially the case with illustrations purporting to show types of troops engaged in the South African War (see *post*) by taking their saddlery into account. Issues of drivers' saddles during this war also confuse the issue.

The Handbook for Military Artificers for 1899 gives four patterns of drivers' saddles in use.

The Old Pattern. In this the sideboards do not extend beyond the arches; the cantle is edged with brass and the panels, stuffed with hair, are nailed and seamed in. (Plate 27b.) The pattern was obsolete, but the A.S.C. and Regimental Transport still had some not yet worn out.

The Iron Arch Pattern. The fans do not protrude beyond the low cantle and the bars are short.

The Angle Iron Arch Saddle Mark II Star issued to all units for drivers.

The Steel Arch Pattern. This is U.P. 1890 with the same front arch as the general issue and a hind arch of steel, similar to the angle-iron U.P. 1884. In other words the cantle is low as in U.P. 1884.[2]

Although, as will be apparent, U.P. 1890 Steel Arch underwent two more phases, which resulted in an even better type being evolved, it does represent the start of the modern type of cavalry saddle. During the time that the last three models had been issued, tried out and found wanting, committee after committee had wrestled with the two problems of strength and weight. Strength, great strength, they had attained and as little weight as was consistent with the heavy loads still considered necessary for the troop horse to carry. Generations of cavalry officers had fulminated against the overloading of their horses. Now the new steel arch saddle was to be tried out in a war of mounted men, who either had to reduce the weight on their horses or fail to carry out the tasks allotted to them.

Plate 17a (R39) shows the Troop saddle without panels and R41 the officers pattern with panels, often made detachable, as in the Colonial Pattern. The white metal on the pommel and cantle show clearly. Plate 18 shows, *above* an officer's saddle with sheepskin in review order; *centre left*, the 21st Hussars saddle with leopard skin — they became Lancers in 1897; *right*, another Hussar saddle — they differed slightly from the pattern used by the rest of the Cavalry of the Line; and *below, centre*, a saddle with wallets only. On the left a stirrup with lance bucket and special slide and on the right two throat plumes. These will be discussed in another chapter. Plate 17a, R40, is the Staff Pattern of the Colonial saddle, also used by mounted officers of infantry.

Plate 71 shows the Troop saddle as used by Mounted Infantry. The sergeant has the normal Hussar stirrups with the brass slide close to the stirrup iron; the blanket, folded between the sideboards and numnah, and kept well up in the arch by a strap from the numnah. He has the regulation breastplate – cruppers were no longer on issue – and his rifle is carried in the short butt bucket in use from 1884 until after the First World War with the Long Magazine Lee Enfield rifle.[3]

The South African War of 1899 to 1902

When war broke out in October 1899, no one in authority, except a handful of officers to whom no attention was paid, envisaged anything different from the constant succession of small wars waged in the last twenty years. Least of all did it occur to the various departments concerned that hostilities would last for three years and that we should employ very large numbers of mounted troops, all raised in a hurry and all wanting saddles at a moment's notice.

There were 16,000 sets of saddlery on issue, with a reserve of only 500 sets and in the first few weeks after the declaration of war in one area alone 30,000 sets were urgently wanted. This was in Natal, where fewer mounted men were employed than in any of the other sectors.[4] By the end of hostilities 76,100 sets had been obtained all over the world. The quality naturally varied a great deal, for although the big houses in Great Britain, which had been supplying the Colonial markets for years, turned out admirable work, this was not the case with many suppliers. Among other purchases were a number of American Cavalry saddles, excellent in the hands of those who thoroughly understood them, but not suitable for issue to men who had never even envisaged this type of saddle. For a description of this most interesting saddle see Appendix A to this chapter and Plate 21.

The wastage of saddles was appalling – long marches on insufficient food and water broke the troop horses down in very large numbers and a horse foundered and left out on the flanks of an advance on a wide front meant a saddle lost, for the enemy, or the nearest African, would never leave a saddle lying. In one trek of 175 miles in bitter cold with hardly any grazing, one Regular regiment lost 70 sets of saddlery, perforce abandoned.[5]

War broke out in October 1899 and in January 1901 the weight carried by Regular cavalry was at last somewhat reduced by leaving certain articles at the base.

In Messrs Champion and Wilton's Equipment Book, a valuable source of reference, is a cutting from *The Times* of 7th March, 1901, giving an extract from a letter by an officer serving in the field, during one of the most arduous series of marches undertaken with the object of heading off the Republican guerilla leader, Christian de Wet, who had invaded the Cape Colony. The marching was very severe. Obviously this letter was written before the equipment was cut down. The late Major Wilton kept the cutting, as an example of what the troop horse was actually carrying on active service.

South Africa. Weighed in the Field when after de Wet. From *The Times* of the 7th March, 1901. Name of the Regiment not given.

Saddle, wallets carbine bucket, etc.	31 lb	6 oz
Bridle	7 lb	
Shoes and nails	2 lb	
Lance	4 lb	8 oz
Carbine	8 lb	
Sword	3 lb	14 oz
Ammunition for carbine, 150 rounds	9 lb	6 oz
Bandolier, mess tin and waterbottle (full)	7 lb	4 oz
Knife, etc. and towel		8 oz
2 days' groceries and 1 day's meat	3 lb	4 oz
1 day's corn (horse feed)	10 lb	
Great coat, forage nets, saddle blanket and numnah	27 lb	
Emergency ration	1 lb	
	115 lb	2 oz
Average weight of man	166 lb	
TOTAL	281 lb	2 oz

or 20 stone 1 lb

The average weight carried by 'the enemy' would be about 16 stone and many of their men would have had two ponies apiece.

The point of view of the rank and file of the regular Regiments of Mounted Infantry, men who fought right through the long war, is surely not to be lightly put aside. In his *Soldiers Diary, South Africa, 1899 to 1901*, Corporal, later Sergeant, Murray Cosby Jackson, 2nd Hants, whose Section of M.I. served in the 7th Battalion Mounted Infantry, wrote as follows: 'If it had been insisted on, every man of ours could have been as mobile as the Boers in a week. It is only a matter of custom whether you sleep warm in a big coat or a 5- or 6-lb blanket. That was when there were white frosts and for long periods we had nothing but the sweaty saddle blanket and we got used to it in a few days. We hardly ever carried anything on the saddle after the first month or two.' Jackson is writing of the High Veldt, 5,000 feet above sea level, in the winter, when running water is frozen up to midday. He illustrated his own book and shows only the rolled cloak on the front arch and a nosebag on the Dees behind the leg. The M.I. had the smallest size U.P. 1890. He shows the saddle blanket on the horse at night.[6]

In an earlier chapter there is a note on what is considered to be the correct load for a horse to carry, and the table on this page shows in detail what the troop horse actually carried on active service in 1900. Jackson's opinion of what should be carried on the saddle is the result of three years hard trekking and in the account of the operations in the Near East in the First World War, we shall read the hard facts, as told by a senior officer, of what was carried successfully seventeen years after the South African War. Circumstances alter cases and the experienced old hand who chances to read this book will draw his conclusions from his own experiences!

152

It is, however, safe to say that Continental military opinion caused too much weight to be piled on the average troop horse. If we followed their lead, as we did for many years, it may fairly be said that, except for the French in Algeria, we had very different countries from the average European area in which to operate. The Americans kept as much weight off their troop saddles as possible; their recent experience was in North American Indian warfare only.

Opinions on the two main types of saddle used in South Africa, the U.P. and the Colonial, differed. As a general rule most people liked the Colonial type, which could be made to fit any horse, should be used with a blanket and needed re-stuffing. These were the opinions of three Regular officers, who had no bias against the U.P. but liked the lightness of the other type. On the other hand Major General Sir F. Smith, from the wealth of his experience both before and during the war, held very different views as regards the 1890 Steel Arch U.P. He thought it 'quite unfit for war conditions' and that, as well as the saddle blanket and numnah, there should have been panels stuffed with horsehair fitted, as was done with older U.P. saddles. His comment on the Colonial saddle was that it was 'all right but not suitable for heavy weights'.

As regards the Colonial saddle it seems only fair to say that the panels do require a great deal of restuffing, if the saddle is used hard and continuously, and though they are easily removed and the stuffing worked over, this is not a fair job to ask a trooper to do when trekking hard and saddlers usually have their work cut out repairing. Though it is ill work disagreeing with the written opinions of an expert like Smith, it must in fairness be said that the balance of service opinion was against him.

The British Army ended the long war with a well-founded belief that the steel arch had come to stay and that the Colonial saddle was eminently suitable for staff and all other mounted officers and, for some time, for all ranks of Yeomanry as well. It is still, in 1965, used by Mounted Constabulary.

So much saddlery and harness had been collected by Ordnance and was in use that a very large part had to be burnt, as there was no market for it.

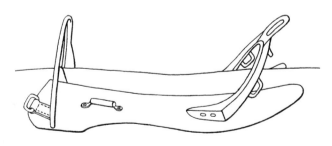

U.P. 1902 Steel Arch. See Plate 20

From the Handbook for
Military Artificers 1915.

FIGURE 9a   Universal Pattern of 1902, showing the tree
without points.

153

Figure 9a shows the new pattern Universal Saddle Tree adopted after the South African War. Plates 32a and 20 show the saddle used as an R.A.S.C. driver's and by Cavalry with the deep bucket to take the Short Magazine Lee Enfield rifle. This pattern really was in 'universal' use, for it superseded all other types of riding saddle throughout the Army, with the exception of the officers' patterns. The most important change is shown in the drawing of the tree, where it will be seen that there are no longer any points to the front arch.

The absence of these points from the new tree – they were cut off in the case of the older patterns, needs explaining. As will be remembered, it was these points that had always given stability to the civilian hunting saddle and their adoption for the cavalry saddle had been warmly recommended and introduced with success. In the 'pointless' tree the altered shape of the front points of the side bars adapted each size of saddle – there were three – to a wider fitting. There was also a numnah panel (see under) strapped to the tree and coming down to a long point. The introduction of a new fitting between girth and tree has already been mentioned under U.P. 1890. A description has been held back until this page, as the vital importance of the triangular or 'V' girth attachment was the steadying effect it had on the saddle, which made the retention of the points unnecessary. No numnah was used except the panels, the blanket was worn folded in six, and the increase in stability was shown by the issue of only 10 per cent of breastplates and 5 per cent of cruppers.

FIGURE 10 Tree of the U.P. 1890 to show the points no longer in use after 1902.

The 'V' attachment which came in with the saddle is described in the Handbook as follows: 'the upper ends of the attachment straps being set wide apart prevent the saddle being tilted to one side. The attachment should not be worn as a true 'V' with the front and rear straps of equal length.

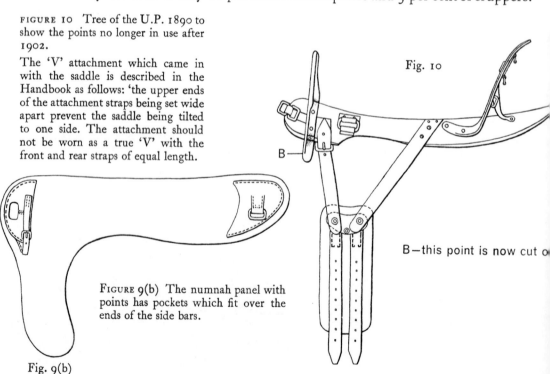

Fig. 10

B—

B—this point is now cut o

FIGURE 9(b) The numnah panel with points has pockets which fit over the ends of the side bars.

Fig. 9(b)

The 'V' attachment which came in with the saddle is described in the Handbook as follows: 'the upper ends of the attachment straps being set wide apart prevent the saddle being tilted to one side. The attachment should not be worn as a true "V" with the front and rear straps of equal length; such a set would drag the middle forward and depress the hinder part of the saddle. It would be equivalent to fixing the girth to the centre of the saddle. The front upper strap is the true girth strap, the rear one being the steadying strap.' The new saddle, from which there are no very great variations in the U.P. of today, weighed complete 44 lb 12 oz about 3 lb less than the 1890 pattern, the weight on the horse being given by Forbes as 252 lb or 18 stone. Officers kept to the Colonial pattern saddle. Otherwise U.P. 1902 went to all mounted men, drivers included.

At the start of the First World War in 1914 there were still five kinds of saddles in use: Officers', Universal, Drivers', Luggage and Pack Saddles. The latter are dealt with in a separate chapter.

Officers' saddles: Mark III had a high brass cantle and solid seat and 'V' girth attachment. It was issued to Royal Artillery, Royal Engineers, and Army Service Corps. When worn out it was to be replaced by Mark IV. This was the latest pattern for all officers and had hitherto been known as the 'Staff' pattern. The tree is similar to that used on a hunting saddle, but with fans and the points of the front arch broad in the bearings. Side bars are 23½ inches, large, and 23 inches, small size. The seat and skirts are of hogskin. There are no knee rolls and the seat measures from arch to cantle about 17¾ inches. Tall and heavy officers can be fitted with a 19-inch seat. The wallets can be set well forward on the burs. Plate 17a, R41, shows Mark III, and R40 is the same as Mark IV, but has knee rolls. These officers' saddles are usually made with removable panels and are beautiful examples of the saddler's craft.

The Universal saddle 1902 has already been described.

Pending the issue of U.P. 1902 as O.P. saddles wore out, Drivers had angle iron and steel arch 1890 patterns, with the points cut off and the side bars shortened. Luggage saddles used on lead horses, on mule harness and on infantry machine gun harness had iron arches and were worn with numnah panels. Royal Horse Artillery had pads, luggage, and panels, luggage pad.

In 1912 a saddle was approved to supersede Pattern 1902, the Steel Arch Universal and Drivers' saddles. It was made to suit horses and cobs and gave one size for all Service purposes other than officers. The seat is a little longer and the hind arch lower than pattern 1902, otherwise the saddle has the same outward appearance; the front arch is held by clips and the hind arch by sockets. Struts were added to support the arch, to strengthen the lower angles forming the feet and to prevent the arch working backwards out of the sockets. The arches were all jointed to allow of their fitting themselves automatically to the backs of different sized animals. The seat is supported by double webbing from front arch to rear to stiffen it, especially in wet weather when the leather is liable to stretch and become unshapely. The flaps are buttoned on to steel studs in the side bars instead of being screwed to the side bars. The side bars, sockets, arches and steel studs are special to this saddle.

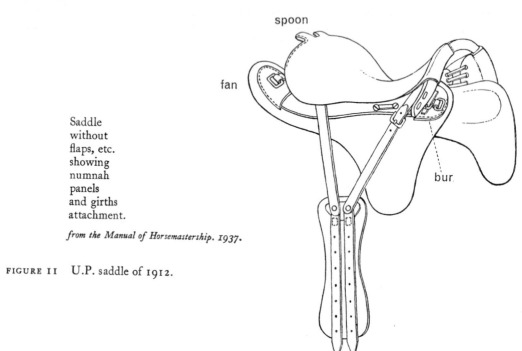

spoon

fan

bur.

Saddle without flaps, etc. showing numnah panels and girths attachment.

from the Manual of Horsemastership. 1937.

FIGURE 11   U.P. saddle of 1912.

These jointed front and rear arches were brought to the notice of officers of the British Army by General Keith Fraser, C.M.G., Inspector General of Cavalry, who obtained one in Austria *c.*1887, where it had been invented by a 'small saddler'. Both Sir Evelyn Wood and Veterinary Major Smith took a great interest in the saddle and Sir Evelyn, a former officer of the 17th Lancers, agreed with Smith that 'as far as the side bars and arches and this new attachment it is the acme of a soldier's saddle'.[7] This hinged type of arch was also adopted for the G.S. Pack Saddle in due course. Plates 36b and c and 34 show the saddle in use. The first two show packed saddles as used by the Royal Engineers in 1929 and the other by the Kings' Troop R.H.A. in 1961. Officers have the Colonial Pattern, as already described, Marks IV, IV Star and V.

This brings the description of Army riding saddles up to the present day. We now return to the First World War, and the load actually carried by the steel saddles, firstly in France and Belgium, where the cavalry fought mainly as infantry, and secondly in the Near East, where in Palestine cavalry once again had the chance of coming to their full status as hard-hitting, hard and far-riding spearheads of an army engaged in mobile warfare.

This account of cavalry on the Western Front is taken from Captain P. F. Stewart's *History of the XIIth Royal Lancers*, all compiled from letters and documents in the possession of the historian. The kit carried was as follows:[8] 'The officer: Macintosh and sou'wester rolled up in a macintosh sheet behind me. Two blankets under the saddle, one being for the charger. Two pairs of wire nippers, one on the belt and one on the saddle and in a saddle bag, on the off side, emergency food and maps. On the near side of the saddle, the sword, with watering bucket and picketing pin attached to the scabbard. In the wallets on the front of the saddle were washing and shaving kit, spare socks and handkerchiefs. On the man were various necessities, smoking material, steel helmet and field dressing, and on the belt revolver, ammunition, field glasses and an enormous pocket knife; in a haversack, plate, cup, warm waistcoat and probably food for one meal.' The list ends as follows: 'There is nothing I can dispense with. I have carried them all the way and find I can still run a few yards with full load on'.

Other Ranks: On the horse, in addition to the man and his equipment, which included 140 rounds, belt, frog, bayonet, gas mask and steel helmet, lance, sword, rifle and bayonet, he carried a ninety-round bandolier round his neck, two blankets under the saddle, wallets with a spare pair of boots, iron rations, two Mills bombs and, up to 1915, a corn sack. On the near side of the saddle was the sword, a shoe case with two horse shoes, surcingle and pad, picketing peg, hay net and one day's corn ration. On the off side went the rifle bucket and rifle, mess tin and canvas water bucket. The cloak, replaced later by the coat, warm, British, went behind the saddle. The comment was: 'In the circumstances mounting was no joke' and the author adds 'the cavalry soldier still went into action encumbered and restricted'. When going into the trenches further heavy articles were carried.

This was trench warfare and the weight on the horse must have been very great, but as there was little likelihood of long marches having to be undertaken with this burden up, the problem was not as acute as it might appear.

We now turn to the operations of the Desert Mounted Corps in Palestine and Syria in 1917, 1918. Originally composed of three, later four Cavalry Divisions, the personnel comprised Australians, New Zealanders, British Yeomanry, Territorial Horse Artillery, Indian Cavalry, and for the last operations, French Cavalry. So the saddles were probably given as thorough a trial by different types of men, Regulars and Irregulars, and horses, as was possible. To quote Lieut Colonel Preston, R.A., the historian of the Corps, who served right through the operations: 'the standard of horsemastership reached a high level and at the end of each series of operations, there was hardly a sore back in the force'. In contrast to this at the end of the campaign which resulted in the capture of Damascus, nearly every horse in the French Cavalry Regiment attached to the Corps had a sore back.[9]

Although the greatest care had been taken to cut down the load on the horse as much as possible, the average weight carried was over 21 stone, all day and every day for seventeen days hard marching during one phase, and there was no repetition of the saddlery difficulties, which had been so prominent in the South African War of eighteen years earlier.

Each man had a pair of officers' wallets holding three days' rations, including the iron ration, with a few articles of clothing. On each saddle were two nosebags, carrying 19 lb of grain – two days forage on the marching scale – and the man's weapons, rifle and sword and ammunition.[10]

It was twenty-seven years since the publication of Major-General Sir F. Smith's *Manual of Saddles and Sore Backs*, now long out of print and the author was still serving, on the Home Front. If ever a man saw his work bear fruit it must have been the late Director of Veterinary Services.

Although a load of 21 stone had been carried successfully by the Desert Mounted Corps it was not considered that the question had been solved. As already stated it is too much for a horse to carry on a long campaign, and horseflesh was not cheap in the years after 1918, that is to say of the type required for remounts. The standard load of the post-war period was fixed as near as possible at 18 stone, including rifle, sword, two bandoliers, wallets and great coat with two blankets under the saddle. In 1934 it was decided to cut this to 16 stone and to provide transport to carry the great coat and wallets and one day's feed instead of two. The wheel had swung back to the South African War when 'the Boer', as the Afrikaner on commando was popularly known, used a light saddle and rode the lighter weight without any transport to help out.

By the time of the Second World War the Cavalry saddle hardly counted at all; from the manufacturing point of view its place was taken by the Pack Saddle.

This concludes the review of the Saddlery of Cavalry of the Line. A separate section follows describing the saddlery special to the three regiments of Household Cavalry.

The Household Cavalry[11]

According to Lieut Colonel W. Tyndale of the 1st Life Guards, who wrote on Military Equitation in 1797 (see in Bibliography), his Regiment and so possibly the other Regiments of the Brigade used the Heavy Cavalry saddle introduced in 1796 with the panels nailed in. Two illustrations in the book show this saddle. This saddle was replaced by another pattern in 1840 and it was presumably about that time that, as Major Horton notes, the Household Cavalry adopted the same type as was used by the Royal Artillery and Transport Corps, which they kept until after the Crimea. This old Pattern R.A. saddle had a tree like a hunting saddle with wood arches plated over the gullet, long points, burs and a cantle with a brass edging. It weighed 16 lb 13 oz and had fans. It would seem to have been suitable for 'cuirassiers', with whom the Brigade was classed, who in 1871 rode 21 stone 13 lb, slightly less than the Prussian cuirassiers, and two stone heavier than the British Heavies. Since the three regiments continued to buy their own saddles until 1895, it is convenient to deal with them in a separate section.

Obviously they required a saddle with a strong tree – their old nickname of 'the

Lumpers' expresses the size of the troopers – and the U.P. saddles of the nineteenth century were not always remarkable for the strength of the trees. The steel arch U.P. of 1890 finally solved the problem, but until its appearance the Household Cavalry saddles were either designed or approved by their own officers and might differ from one unit to another.

The Dress Regulations of 1857 give the following details of officers' saddles:

1st Life Guards: High mounting saddle with brass cantle, shoe cases, square-set stirrups and a white cover for dress.

2nd Life Guards: Fans, brass cantle and fittings for shoe cases, and oval stirrups.

Royal Horse Guards: Brown high mounting saddle, fans, princes metal cantle, brass nails with regimental cyphers and square stirrups.

In the *Carriage Builders and Harness Makers Art Journal* of 1859 is a full description of an officer's saddle of the 2nd Life Guards with notes on those of the troopers; the only difference being that the officers had pistol holsters and other ranks had wallets.

The drawing below is taken from the illustration in the article.

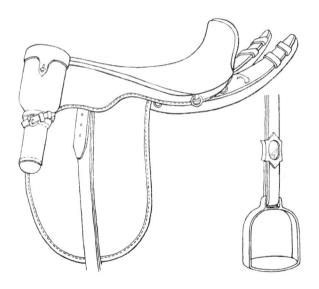

FIGURE 12   Household Cavalry saddle of 1860.

The text of the article reads as follows: 'the saddle is about 17 inches long from head to cantle with corresponding flaps. The cantle is very high and plated with brass. The tree is continued beyond the cantle in two long pieces, inclining up-wards and called fans, with staples and dees or rings behind the cantle to take the valise straps. The panel of the saddle is continued under the fans, to protect the horse's back from abrasion. There is a staple in the front, over the gullet, and a loose dee on the head to fasten the cloak strap to. There are two dees on each side under the bellies, for horse-shoe cases; and a stout loose ring directly under the bellies upon the point of skirt, on each side. ("Bellies" are the under line of the seat from B, through I, to the back of E: see Figure 3 on page 114.) The holsters are made of strong brown leather, blocked to shape and bound at top; they are made with covers, and are fastened to the forepart of the saddle by straps – the straps being 3 feet 6 inches long. The girths are six inches wide, and have two strong buckles at each end. The crupper, like the bridle and breastplate is made of patent leather; the body part 1 foot 6 inches long split up 7 inches, by a piece taken out behind the boss, leaving two straps, five-eighths of an inch wide, one fastened to the dock, and the other to buckle into the other side of the dock. The body has a three-inch circular boss upon it, and the leather is cut gradually narrower from that width to one inch where the strap commences, which is 18 feet 8 inches long and 1 inch wide. The stirrup leathers have handsome brass slides upon them with oval mirrors of steel; these are placed just above the eyes of the stirrups (these are square, hunting shape). For all ordinary purposes the whole of the seat of the saddle, the valise, cloak, and holsters are covered with a black Ukraine lamb-skin (black bearskin in the 1st Life Guards; author); this is kept in place by a brown leather surcingle, $2\frac{1}{4}$ inches wide, and 5 feet 8 inches long with a strap 1 foot 8 inches long and 1 inch wide.' The shabraque is then described (see in the section on horse furniture) and the troopers' girths are noted as having three buckles instead of two and on all occasions they had white sheepskin covers to their saddles.

In 1872 the 2nd Life Guards made up their own saddlery and in 1878 all the Household Cavalry ceased to buy their own saddlery.

In 1882–4 the List of Changes in Ordnance Material gives a very full description of the saddlery to be issued to the three regiments. Plates 15a and b refer. The tree was made of beech, covered with glued canvas and partly with hog skin. Steel plates support the gullet, cantle and fans. The seat was made of English crop butt (sole leather tanned but not curried, i.e. made flexible by stretching and dressing with oil and dubbin; the butt being the prime part of the hide); the flaps of brown crop. The seat was secured to the tree by copper rivets and the flaps by screws.

Two girth straps are fixed on each bar of the saddle tree. See the illustration, which shows the girth straps plainly. The seat measured 19 inches from gullet to cantle. The stirrups were set $1\frac{1}{2}$ inches further forward than in the U.P. 1884 Line Cavalry saddle. Horton has this to say of this saddle: 'the Household Cavalry had a tree of the same type as a hunting saddle and the Old Pattern Transport saddle; the cantle was brass bound and the seat was 1 inch longer than the old pattern. This was disliked.' See the illustration of the stuffed and removable panels, which are identical with those used with the Colonial Pattern saddles. The backs were made of basil (sheep skins tanned, but not curried), with buff leather facings. They were lined with white serge and stuffed with white flock. There were leather pockets fitting over the fans and points of the tree and a chape and buckle at the top of the front for fastening to a strap on the saddle. (Plate 15b.) Later many of the Colonial saddles had a socket on the tree into which a long screw with a Dee head screwed.

The Household Cavalry saddle weighed 19 lb 1 oz complete with numnah, sheepskin, and wallets. The stirrups were hunting pattern and the brass slides were worn close to the stirrups. (Plate 15a and b.)

The report on the Service Saddle, as used in Egypt by the 2nd Life Guards, presumably deals with this saddle, though it had only very recently been 'approved' by Ordnance. Colonel Ewart, commanding, stated 'I have the honour to report that I consider the present sealed pattern saddle issued to the Household Cavalry answers very well, but I would, in future, reduce the weight of the saddle with a view to its utility on active service'. He wished that 90 per cent of the breastplates and all the cruppers should be withdrawn, disliked the use of a small blanket under the numnah and wished the extra stone imposed on the horse by the valise should be done away with. Colonel Ewart approved of the deep carbine bucket (Plate 89) and would have liked to fasten the picket peg to it. He preferred that one shoe case instead of two should be carried.[12]

Plate 20 shows an even deeper bucket, used with the Short Magazine Lee Enfield rifle.

There is a note in the Introduction to the catalogue of the London Saddlers Company Exhibition of 1892 that for six months the Royal Horse Guards had a saddle introduced by Colonel Brocklebank.[13]

The following note, sent by the Marquis of Cambridge, goes fully into the question of the saddles in use by officers of the 1st Life Guards from 1895: 'from 1895 the saddle used by officers in full dress with the shabraque was a padded hunting saddle without burs or fans. The cantle was brass bound and a white cover was used over it when the gold-laced bridoon reins were used. In Drill or Service Order a saddle on the lines of Colonial saddles was used. This was designed by the C.O., Sir Simon Macdonald Lockhart, ex-Inspector General of Cavalry. It had the seat raised some inches above the horse's spine and gave the rider the feeling of not being part of the horse. The stirrup leathers were placed too far forward and it was known regimentally as the Keith Fraser saddle. No other Regular regiment used the white cover over the shabraque.'

In 1895 the Household Cavalry received the U.P. 1890 saddle and from then onwards conformed to the rest of the Cavalry, with the exception that part of the saddlery is black.

Two more illustrations deal with the Household Cavalry; one is the frontispiece, which shows Queen Victoria inspecting the 2nd Life Guards at Windsor in 1839 with the Duke of Wellington in attendance. This is believed to be the only painting by Landseer showing troops. The colour plate of the drum horses of the Life Guards and Royal Horse Guards shows the equipment in detail. The third or 'foot' rein fastening onto the stirrups on the inside is clearly shown. Special stirrups with a metal loop on the iron to take this rein are on issue. With this rein the drummer guides his horse, the bit and bridoon reins lying on the neck.

The Yeomanry

As every formation of Yeomanry, whatever the strength might be, was to all intents and purposes a law unto itself as to what uniform and equipment was to be used, it is not easy to say what saddlery any one unit had. By the end of the nineteenth century U.P. saddles were drawn from Ordnance, the type varying with the state of the saddles in store. The annual camp, not always held, and the few days' drill in the year did not lead to undue wear and tear, so saddlery would last a Yeomanry unit considerably longer than a Regular one.

There is extant a list of 24 units in existence in 1850 who made returns of saddlery in use.[14] Certainly up to about 1890, and in some cases later, many men rode on their hunting saddles, called 'plain saddles', irrespective of the type selected by their unit.

In 1850 the Derbyshire and West Somerset units had these saddles, presumably used by all ranks. In many cases the officers had different saddles to the men.

Three units, Ayrshire, Cambridgeshire and Cheshire, had Heavy Dragoon patterns, as had the Long Melford Lancers of Suffolk. The Ayrshire men had the old pattern, probably that of 1796.

The light cavalry patterns were popular and were called 'Hussar', 'Light Dragoon', or 'Cossack' saddles. As one regiment, the 1st West Yorkshire, had 'the old Light Dragoon saddle', the three names presumably refer to the post 1816 loose pilch seat Hussar pattern, as used by Regular Light Cavalry to 1855. The Staffordshire unit had black saddles for the officers and brown for the men.

The North Devon had saddles as for the 14th Light Dragoons, but with panels instead of blankets, and an illustration[15] shows the Royal 1st Devon in 1840 with an officer using an Hussar saddle with a lambskin and no shabraque. After 1855 the U.P. wood arch saddle was used when available. Thus the Gloucestershire Hussars were issued with 200 in 1881[16] and in 1885 the Berkshire Regiment had round cantle saddles, possibly an experimental issue of the 1884 pattern, which had been on trial for some time.[17]

Faced with the problem of providing some 10,000 sets of saddlery for the Imperial Yeomanry companies raised in 1899 for the South African War, the civilian Committee, which was responsible for all equipment and uniforms, but not arms, had to take whatever was available. There was an attempt to get saddles made by the firms who supplied civilian types, but this proved impossible; for one thing the price would have been prohibitive, and the result was that any types available were got together and issued. These varied from the U.P. wood arch saddle to the Colonial type, and included R.A. drivers' saddles, known as 'Artillery' saddles and liked. By 1901 many of the units had the Colonial saddle, which stood up well to the rough work and, as by this time as little as possible was carried on the saddle, they proved amply strong enough. With a big surplus of these saddles on hand they were issued to the Imperial Yeomanry in Great Britain in 1902, the manufacturers making a slightly lighter pattern for other ranks than the officers' pattern. By 1916 the Yeomanry, no longer 'Imperial', but part of the Territorial Force, were receiving the U.P. steel arch saddle.

Sidesaddles, as used for Military Purposes

The Frontispiece of this book shows the main reason for describing the sidesaddles used by Royalty when inspecting troops. It is impossible, when dealing with the saddlery of the British Army, to exclude those used by so many Royal ladies, whose names are perpetuated in the Honorary titles of so many regiments. The other reason is that one of our most celebrated Women's Volunteer formations, known colloquially as the 'Fannys'[18] rode sidesaddle in the early days of their existence. (Plate 22.)

From the date when this book starts up to about the middle of the eighteenth century the normal saddle in use had a flat padded seat with one pommel or crutch just on the off side of the peak. The right leg was hooked over this and the left leg hung down unsupported except by the stirrup.[19] There is a picture by Van Dyck in the Royal Collection[20] showing Charles the First's Queen, Henrietta Maria, holding a horse with this type of saddle. As far back as the sixteenth century Catherine de Medici had been using a saddle with a second pommel on the near side, giving room for the right leg to be wedged between it and the off or original pommel. This seems to have been in more or less general use in this country by about 1770.[20] It is not easy to determine how firm a seat this type of saddle normally gave. Accounts vary between a very insecure seat needing a specially well-broken horse and a seat which allowed some women to ride to hounds on more or less equal

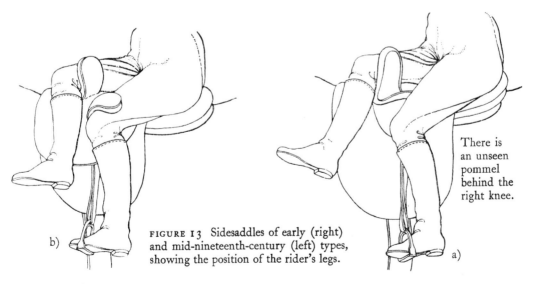

There is an unseen pommel behind the right knee.

b)

FIGURE 13 Sidesaddles of early (right) and mid-nineteenth-century (left) types, showing the position of the rider's legs.

a)

terms with men. Generally speaking the lack of support for the left leg militated against a firm seat, except in extreme cases.

In 1830 came the greatest improvement of all, the invention of the third pommel, or leaping head, curving downwards below the second pommel on the near side and allowing the left leg to be supported by the stirrup and by the grip of the thigh against the new pommel. This modern type was in general use by 1860.

Why it took so long for the double pommels of mediaeval days and the third or leaping head of the early nineteenth century to be generally adopted is not clear, except that we are by nature a conservative people.

The honour of having introduced the third pommel in 1830 has been claimed by three men, two Frenchmen, Jules Charles Perrier[21] and Monsieur Baucher, and an Englishman, Mr Fitzharding Oldacre.[22] The latter is said to have evolved the idea in order to enable a man to ride a match for a wager on a sidesaddle. Although the original pommel on the off had now no practical use, it was retained by some saddlers up to the end of the century, getting smaller and smaller until it was only a sort of token.

This survival of the off pommel makes it impossible to say with certainty whether a drawing or painting shows a woman on an old-fashioned saddle with two pommels or a more modern type with three. Only from the date, if given, can we be certain. Thus the frontispiece by Landseer, which shows Queen Victoria inspecting the 2nd Life Guards with the Duke of Wellington in attendance, was painted in 1839, so we can be sure that Her Majesty is using the two pommel old-fashioned type. Apropos of the Duke of Wellington, it is known that he objected to the Queen riding when inspecting troops and wished her to be driven. There is little doubt that the fact of the old-fashioned saddle giving only a modicum of grip (see Figure 13a on the last page) must have weighed on the Duke, who probably was well aware that in the event of any contretemps taking place his Royal Mistress might have a nasty fall.

Not until the accession of Queen Victoria does there appear to be any very satisfactory evidence as to the saddlery in use. Except that Queen Anne before her accession rode hard to hounds there seems to be nothing known about her. If she rode sidesaddle – she may well have ridden astride as did various princesses at a later date – she would presumably have had a single pommel, as shown in various paintings at the time of her reign and just before.[23]

The Hanoverians reigned while the saddle with two pommels was coming into fashion, and when Queen Victoria took to the leaping head seems not to be known.

As far back as the early sixteenth century[24] the ladies of the Spanish Court had ridden on the off side and this came into fashion with our Royal Family in the nineteenth century, only they rode on either side, sometimes on saddles on which the pommels could be changed over and sometimes on a saddle made for use on the off side only. This last pattern was known as the Princess of Wales'[25] presumably because she introduced it. It was first made in Paris[26] and, according to Messrs Champion and Wilton, was in use up to 1957.

About 1902 Mayhew introduced and patented a saddle with very wide pommels, which became very popular and is still in use today.[27] (Figure 14.) Her gracious Majesty Queen Elizabeth II today rides sidesaddle on parade.

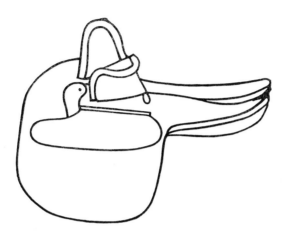

FIGURE 14   Modern sidesaddle.

Indian Cavalry

Because nearly all the Indian Cavalry Regiments were organized on the Silladar system, which meant that each unit furnished itself completely with everything except firearms and ammunition, it is not easy to determine exactly what types of saddlery were in use. The exceptions were the three Madras Regiments, who were equipped in the same way as British Cavalry.[28] In later days there were various factories making saddlery in India, so that supplies were not dependent on conditions in Great Britain.[29]

In pre-Mutiny days the Irregular cavalryman on joining brought his own horse, arms and equipment, and there is a record of the cost of his outfit to a sowar of the 1st Punjab Cavalry in 1849 including 'sound horse gear'.[30]

The Scinde Horse (14th Prince of Wales Own Cavalry) were raised in 1839 and, up to the time when the Silladar units adopted the U.P. British Cavalry saddle in c.1862, had native saddles with stirrups, stirrup leathers, bridles and bits made in Great Britain and usually of Universal Pattern. The head stall and crupper were made of cotton rope covered with green cloth, the standing martingale was of blue dyed cotton plaited rope and all ranks had a square plain green shabraque of cloth completely covering the saddle.[31] In 1852 in the Punjab Frontier Force the Commanding Officer provided his regiment with arms as well as horses, equipments and clothing.[30]

Probyn's Horse, later the 11th King Edward's Own Lancers, were raised in 1857 during the Indian Mutiny. In their Regimental History[32] there is a very full description of their saddlery recorded by one of their officers, Captain L. B. Jones. He wrote as follows: Lucknow 20/VIII, 1859. 'The khatee or Sikh saddle is in use in this Regiment.

I have never found it after hard work detrimental to the horse's back or produce sore backs, provided the sowar does not place an extra pad or blanket under the

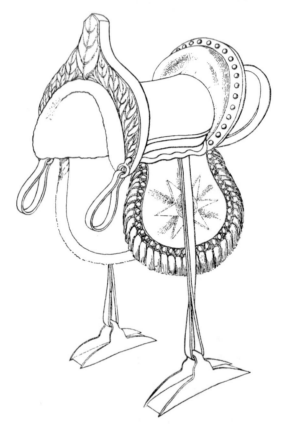

FIGURE 15 The 'Khatee' or Sikh saddle of the mid-nineteenth century as used by Indian Silladar Cavalry Regiments.

permanent padding or Koorjeen. This rubs the withers. I consider Nolan's saddle well adapted to Irregular Regiments with a few modifications; at present it is too much the shape of the old Hussar saddle (Plate 11) and does not give the rider a free seat. I consider the pad or charjawah unsuitable; it galls and has too much material in it.'

There was no fixed rule and in contrast to the above Hodson's Horse, the 4th Duke of Cambridge's Own Lancers, were issued in 1858 with English saddles, and at first upwards of a thousand men in the three regiments had no saddles.[33]

166

Presumably these saddles (the pattern is not stated) were liked; for according to the official handbook, *The Army of Great Britain*,[28] the nineteen Regiments of Bengal Cavalry, all Silladar, adopted 'Nolan's Saddle with a bit and single rein' for other ranks and for officers a saddle similar to that of the Regular Cavalry. The Sind Horse adopted the U.P. saddle, according to the account already quoted,[31] not long before 1868. The officers of the Bengal Cavalry would have used the Wood Arch U.P. of 1855–61 and this saddle was often known colloquially as Nolan's saddle, but the latter differed slightly from the U.P.

Nolan described his saddle as follows in his book *Cavalry, Its History and Tactics*, published by Bosworth, London, in 1853. 'The tree is constructed to combine the advantages of a hunting saddle with the simplicity of the Hungarian troop saddle. (Nolan had served in the Austrian cavalry.) The sideboards are cut away under the man's leg; they then spread out under his seat and are feathered and brought well off the horse's back in rear. The hind fork is broad at the base where it joins the sideboards and is bevelled off to add length to the seat. The front fork is constructed with a peak and with points to give the tree a firm hold on the horse's back and prevent it from turning round, as well as bringing the man's bridle hand low. Both forks are strengthened with iron plates. The holes cut for the stirrup leathers (see Plate 11f) have a whole back, to prevent the stirrup leathers from bulging or embedding themselves in the panel and pressing on the horse's back. Over the tree a seat of blocked leather is stretched, like that of a hunting saddle and fastened with screws to the forks.' At the time when Nolan wrote the Light Cavalry U.P. saddle had a loose pilch seat; the blocked seat, though shown by Hamilton Smith as used by the Governor General's Bodyguard in 1812 – they had the U.P. Heavy Cavalry saddle with brass cantle – would be comparatively unknown in India. No British heavy cavalry went there until 1893, the 6th Dragoon Guards, Carabiniers, being equipped as Light Cavalry when they served in India in 1856. The paintings of Indian Cavalry by Major Lovett, Gloucestershire Regiment,[34] which were published in 1911, show a variety of saddles. He shows a sowar of the Jodhpur Sardar Rissala, Imperial Service Troops, using a saddle with a low square cantle with a wide short spoon; the bridle has a single curb and one rein. This is unlike any British cavalry U.P. and could well be Nolan's saddle. The sowar of the 18th Bengal Lancers in the photograph of 1898 (see Plate 89) also has a single curb and rein, but the details of his saddle are hidden by the front and rear packs.

Other types shown by Major Lovett are as follows:

19th Lancers 'Fane's Horse', a shallow seated saddle with a low rounded cantle; this man also has only one rein.

31st Lancers 'Duke of Connaught's Own', a saddle with the high spoon of the U.P. of 1890.

32nd Lancers, the saddle has fans and cantle as the U.P. of 1884.

The Central India Horse had the U.P. saddle with blanket[35] before 1914, when the U.P. 1912 was issued to all Indian cavalry,[36] the saddlery was all manufactured in India.[29] As far back as November 1803, Colonel Wellesley had strongly recommended that the Indian Government should order Cavalry saddles from England.[37]

During the campaigns of 1902 and 1903 in Somaliland, the Mounted Infantry had the 'Indian Army Iron Arch Saddle' as well as the Colonial type.[38]

SADDLERY IN THE DOMINIONS

As a general rule the Mounted Forces of all the Dominions adopted the U.P. Cavalry or Driver's saddle, as used by the British Forces. Sometimes the type was still in use after the issue of a newer one and this makes it difficult to be certain when exactly a new pattern was adopted. There was also in the pre-South African War period a tendency to allow men to use their own civilian saddles. It was some time before firms capable of filling large orders for saddlery came into being; when they did they tended to manufacture the so-called Colonial type. With few exceptions the troops were either volunteers or militia, sometimes a distinction without much difference, and the wear and tear on saddlery was like that obtaining in the Yeomanry. The main exceptions were in Canada.

Australia

The earliest example of a description of the saddlery used by an Australian unit is dated 1863, when the Victorian Local Forces used a 'hunting saddle' with plain stirrups and white girths. The bit had the Royal Cypher and the bridle a blue brow band and rosettes.[39]

Photographs taken in the 'nineties of various corps often show a mixture of U.P. and stock saddles. The stock saddle was the peculiar and individualistic production favoured by the magnificent horsemen of Australia and New Zealand. Here is Will Ogilvie's description: 'the tree is deep and curved; the saddle is quite short, set low at the pommel, raised somewhat at the back and with short flaps. Its distinctive features are the large knee pads and thigh pads.'

'The surcingle (not shown in the line drawing) is generally run over the seat of the saddle and brought through a slit in either flap, which keeps it steady. Some years ago (written c.1930) it was brought over the pommel and brought down just inside the knee pads. Cruppers are used on young horses.' Apropos of this Sidney, writing in 1878 in the *Book of the Horse*, said: 'A rolled blanket is sometimes used on the pommel for buckjumpers (there have always been plenty). The crupper was passed through under the seat and fastened to a stick, which stuck out on both sides and helped the rider's knees.'

Writing in 1892[40] Captain M. H. Hayes, formerly of the Buffs and once well known as a writer on everything connected with the horse, was very struck with the stock saddle, which he saw in use in Australia. He said, 'if Cavalry roughriders had an Australian buckjumping saddle, they could teach a man to ride any horse, for it was almost impossible to be thrown off. They could have the necessary rolls to take off and put on the U.P. saddle.' His idea was not, it seems, accepted, but it gives a good idea of the way this saddle impressed experts, for this both Ogilvie and Hayes were.

The South Australian Lancers in the 'nineties had either U.P. 1884 star or the 1890 Steel Arch with regulation bridle, breastplate and carbine bucket. The Queensland Field Artillery were equipped as the Royal Artillery with harness of Pattern 1865[41] (Plates 29 and 30). From 1896 the New South Wales Lancers had one squadron issued with the 1890 U.P. As well as this issue photographs show men of other squadrons riding with the stock saddle with either flange kneecaps or knee

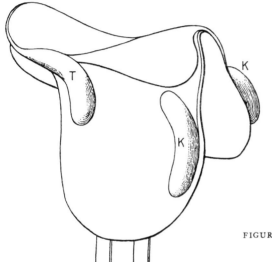

The line drawing is from Sidney's *Book of the Horse*, 1878. 'T' shows the thigh pad, and 'K' the knee pad.

Brookes & Sons, Walsall, catalogue for 1904 shows slightly smaller pads on both the stock saddle and the 'Park Saddle', which is similar to the drawing, but with less dip.

FIGURE 16   Australian Stock Saddle, *c.*1878.

rolls. A numnah cut very wide all round was used and all have square stirrups, regulation breastplates and carbine buckets with civilian bits – Portsmouth – and bridles. (Plate 91.)

The contingents that went out to South Africa in 1899 and 1900 usually took their civilian saddles, as regulation sets were in very short supply. The N.S.W. Lancers had one squadron with a mixture of U.P. and civilian saddles and the half squadron which had been in England had U.P., issued to them at the Cape. Another N.S.W. unit, the 1st Australian Horse, had civilian saddles supplied by a local contractor. They were not found satisfactory and as soon as U.P. saddles became available they were exchanged.

The Citizen Bushmen, also from New South Wales, took civilian saddles, presumably in most cases the men's own. In December 1899, there was only one saddler in camp and many of the men lined and stuffed their own saddles. They were no doubt used to doing this up-country, but it must be very seldom that one finds such competence in the ranks. This unit found that the South African ants got into the knee pads at night when the saddles were on the ground and this corps also changed to the U.P.

By March 1900, the position was better; a photograph of the Queensland Mounted Infantry, probably the 3rd Contingent, shows regulation saddlery with hay nets, white head ropes and the Portsmouth bit.

After the end of the South African War, indeed up to 1914, there were still not enough U.P. saddles available to fit out the numerous freshly raised Light Horse Regiments, so men had to use civilian saddles. From 1915 onward the whole of the Expeditionary Force was properly equipped with Regulation saddlery and this continued as long as the units retained their horses.[42]

Canada

The saddlery situation in the Armed Forces of Canada differs considerably from that obtaining in the other Dominions. As was the case with all part-time units, saddlery tended to last for a long time and it is not easy to determine when fresh types were first issued.

The first evidence so far obtainable refers to the Governor General's Body-guard, volunteers wearing Hussar uniform.[43] In 1864 they imported what they called Hungarian saddles from England, without a doubt the U.P. of 1861 with the wood arch. This saddle was well liked, for in 1866 when the Fenian risings took place there were not enough saddles to go round and hunting saddles had to be used with disastrous results to the horses' backs. There were so many sore backs that the U.P. saddles were pooled and issued to men going on patrol, etc.

We now go over to the celebrated North West Mounted Police, later the Royal Canadian Mounted Police. Their first saddle, imported in 1874, was the Driver's saddle of the British Army, U.P. 1861 (see Plate 27b). This saddle, often known incorrectly as 'the Artillery Saddle', was well liked in the Dominions. It weighed 11½ lb and though it was old fashioned by modern ideas it was a good, hard wearing saddle.

'The Mounties' were not satisfied and like all Western men in North America very much preferred the Western, Californian, or Cowboy type. This tendency was still very strong when the *Frontiersman's Pocket Book* was written for the League of Frontiersmen in 1909. The weight can run as high as 50 lb; 40 lb was not uncommon and the lightest were about 30 lb. This seems a great weight, but the saddle was designed for very rough work on the range, for serving as a hold fast for the lariat or lasso and for being used on work which required two or three ponies a day. After trying various makes the N.W.M.P. finally settled on the Californian model, as shown in Plate 93. It weighed 40 lb, was used with a blanket under it and issued until the force became the Royal Canadian Mounted Police, when the British U.P. was substituted. The cowboy saddle derived directly from the Mexican type, although the latter was shorter seated and was evolved from the Spanish knights and men-at-arms mediaeval model as imported by Cortes. The stirrup leather has been kept in its original place, set well back for a straight-legged seat.[44]

This was the saddle used by the Canadian Contingents which took part in the South African War. Although the Bodyguard, and, according to a photograph,[45] the Royal Canadian Dragoons and presumably the Royal Canadian Horse Artillery, had the U.P. saddle, it is most unlikely that there would have been a surplus of these. On the other hand, there would have been plenty of stock saddles available, if not enough in Canada there would certainly have been enough in the States and the men would be used to them. There is an account by a youthful member of Strathcona's Horse of having to carry his 40 lb saddle a long way into camp when his horse died in the veld.

It was not, however, to the Steel U.P. 1890 saddle that the Canadian Ordnance turned after the war. The Auditor General's Reports for the years 1903, 1904, 1905 and 1906 show purchases of 3,500 sets of Colonial saddles and bridles from two firms, Adams Bros, Toronto, and H. Lamontagne, Montreal, presumably manufacturers. The Dress Regulations for the Militia, 1907, describe this saddle, called incorrectly, 'universal', as follows: 'this is an English pattern saddle, which has been largely issued under the designation of "Colonial" for particular work.[46] The tree is similar to that used for a hunting saddle, but has the side bars extending behind the cantle.'[47]

In 1909 the U.P. 1890 was on issue, as well as the Colonial saddle. Next year the standing orders for the Bodyguard read as follows: 'Saddles, Hussar Pattern, with white metal head and cantle, regulation stirrups, blue girths, brown leather wallets'. This could be taken to mean that all ranks had the officers' Hussar pattern. (See Plate 17a, R41.)

In 1921 after the First World War the pattern had changed and the Dress Regulations for that year give Saddlery, Canadian, detachable panels (presumably the Colonial saddle) and Saddlery Universal Pattern 1902 and 1912.

The steel arch patterns were obviously ousting the Colonial type, for in 1948 there is a paragraph which reads: 'Saddlery required for recreational riding is listed as Colonial Type Officers' Saddle.'

At the same time Strathcona's Horse required Officers' Saddles Mark IV with the normal $17\frac{3}{4}$-inch seat and Princess Patricia's Canadian Light Infantry wanted Officers' Pattern, which would be the same.[48]

It is interesting to see how the Colonial saddle caught on with the Canadians, who had had ample opportunities during the South African War of comparing different types. The change from the heavy stock saddle was a radical one, for men who have used the latter usually take more kindly to the Steel Arch type than to the Colonial.

There is hardly a line of this account which does not owe a great deal to the unsparing help given by Mr Charles H. Stewart, Librarian of the Library of the Department of National Defence, Ottawa. Not only is he personally responsible for much of the detail, but he has also enlisted the help of others, including Mrs Sorly, Historical Record Office, Lieut Colonel R. H. Hodgson, R.C.E.M.E., Lieut Colonel D. V. Cook, and R.S.M. J. P. Reain, to all of whom the author is greatly indebted. Mr Stewart's name will appear again under Pack Saddles.

New Zealand

Little is known officially about the saddlery used by the Armed Forces in New Zealand until the period of the First World War. It has, however, been possible to form a reasonable estimate from contemporary illustrations.

The first Militia Act passed dates from 1845 and the one relating to Volunteers from 1858. In 1860, at the start of the fighting with the Maoris, there were only 40 mounted men, and during the fighting in 1865 most of the mounted troops belonged to the Armed Constabulary. Fortunately, a series of water colours of this campaign was painted by Major G. F. von Tempsky and is still in existence. Von Tempsky, who was killed in 1868 at the head of a corps of Forest Rangers, shows us in one painting the British Service Universal Pattern Wood Arch Saddle with wallets used by an officer.[49] These saddles had a very long life and we shall meet them again.

A photograph taken in 1875 shows an officer of the Canterbury Yeomanry Cavalry with a white sheepskin and a dark saddle cloth and what appears to be a cavalry saddle.[50] During the 'eighties there were a very large number of Volunteer mounted units raised and a Sergeant Major of one of these, the Canterbury Mounted Rifles, photographed in the 'nineties, has an Artillery Driver's type of saddle with Hussar stirrups and a brass runner on the stirrup leather. He is riding with the 1890 Reversible pattern bit with one rein and has a dark saddle cloth. On it are the initials of his unit.[51] (Plate 92.)

Photographs taken just before the outbreak of the South African War of 1899 show other ranks of the New Zealand Contingents with the old U.P. Wood Arch saddle with square stirrups.[51] It is understood that some of the Contingents had the 1890 U.P. Steel Arch Cavalry pattern.

The Official note on the First World War Mounted Contingents who went to the Near East states that some had the 'Colonial Fan Tree Pattern' (the Cape Fan so called), manufactured in New Zealand. They also had a number of the 1902 and 1912 British Army Patterns and officers had Marks IV, V, and Pattern 1915 Officers' Saddles, all of the improved Cape Fan Type. Locally purchased saddles were also issued, presumably the type listed in manufacturers' catalogues as the Australasian Stock Saddle. This is a short saddle built on a deep curved tree; see under 'Australia'.[52]

From 1920 onwards other ranks had the U.P. British Cavalry Saddle and the officers the patterns already mentioned.[52]

The author is very much indebted to Mrs Edith Tylden of Auckland, New Zealand for most of the material used in this account. This includes the picture by von Tempsky, photographs of stock saddles and all the contacts with official and private sources.

South Africa up to 1948

Includes the two British Colonies, the Cape of Good Hope and Natal, and the Transvaal Volunteers of 1903, all of which formed part of the Union Defence Force of South Africa from 1912 onwards. The Transvaal and Orange Free State Republics were independent until 1902 when, after the South African War of that date, they became British. There were no Volunteers, only Police, in the Orange Free State prior to 1912.[53]

The first issue of saddlery with which we have to deal was to the Cape Corps, later Cape Mounted, Rifles (Imperial) of 1827 to 1870, a Regular Local unit of the British Army. They received the Wood Arch Light Cavalry Pattern of 1816 with the loose pilch cover.[54]

The next units issued with U.P. types were the Frontier Armed and Mounted Police of the Cape Colony of 1855 to 1878 and their successors, the Cape Mounted Rifles (Colonial) to 1912. The dates of issue are not known, but the two units had U.P. Drivers' saddles, either 1861 or 1864 Patterns, probably from about 1870.

The C.M.R. exchanged theirs for the 'old iron arch' in 1881[55] presumably the U.P. Flat Iron Arch of 1870, and later Iron Arch Patterns as they became available. Officers had the same.

The Natal Police of 1874 to 1912 had the U.P. Drivers' saddle 'with solid seat' from 1874 to 1894. Then they changed to the Colonial Pattern.[56]

All Volunteer Artillery units and the C.M.R. Battery of 1874 had the U.P. Artillery harness of 1865 up to c.1899.

The Mounted Volunteers of the Cape and Natal from the early seventies[57] used, as a general rule, a saddle developed in the Cape Colony, called by the Trade 'the Cape Fan'; Plate 17b, R40, shows the tree which is like that of a hunting saddle, but with rather more dip and long fans behind. These were common enough on military saddles but not, it seems, on civilian types. The early types, see Plate 14, had no burs. This particular saddle was one of the type, presumably made in England, known as the Staff Saddle. It was very well reported on indeed during the Zulu War of 1879.[58] The Colonial-made issues would appear not to have been so well made. The cant name at this time for them was 'hunting saddles' and as most of the Volunteers used them without any blanket or numnah they got a very damning report.[58]

In 1884 when Warren's Expedition to the Transvaal-Bechuanaland Border was being formed, it was decided to issue the three Regiments of Colonial Mounted Riflemen recruited by the War Office with these saddles and an order was to be placed in South Africa with local firms for 2,000 sets. There were only small businesses at the Cape, quite unable to cope with an order of this magnitude, and as a result a rush order had to be placed with English firms. Middlemore[59] made 600 sets 'of superior quality' at £4 10s 0d a head at a 'peace price' valuation; Mason made 400, and Ross of London 1,000 sets of very inferior quality, made in such a hurry that 100 had no fans. They were Trade articles as supplied to the Cape, and the Saddlers' catalogues are full of them from about 1890 onwards.[60] It is fortunate that Colonel Carrington, 24th Foot, commanding one of the Mounted Rifle units, included in his Report[61] on the operations, a sketch showing the saddle. In the Regulations issued for the Expedition it is laid down 'that all officers are to have a Regulation Staff Pattern saddle'[62] (see Plate 14). Carrington's sketch shows a similar saddle and the difference would appear to be mainly in the workmanship, strength and finish of the Staff Pattern. On the whole the Cape Fan or Colonial saddle came well out of the trial and it was adopted, but not sealed by Ordnance until the 27th November, 1884, with special fittings under the heading of 'Saddlery for Special Service in South Africa'.[63] This then was the saddle which has been used ever since and is still issued for mounted officers and often used by Constabulary as well. The various plates show some of the many changes, all of minor importance, made since the first patterns were issued. Thousands were in use during the South African War of 1899 to 1902; it was manufactured in most if not all of the Dominions and still in use during the First World War, though not to the same extent. With panels the saddle weighs about 18 to 20 lb and although it was not designed to take the heavy packs possible with the steel arch U.P. type, it would hold ample for all practical purposes and stand up to a great deal of hard work. The other Imperial unit in South Africa, the Bechuanaland Border Police, 1885 to 1895, had U.P. Cavalry saddles, presumably Pattern 1884, judging by Carrington's note on them in a contemporary catalogue.[64]

The Union Defence Force of 1912 had the U.P. 1902 with the Colonial Pattern for officers, but both in South West and East Africa during the First World War practically all the *ad hoc* mounted units had the Colonial pattern.

REG. HOR

PLATE 58   The First Regiment of Horse (later 4th Dragoon Guards), 1751.

Q

RE.G. of DRAº

PLATE 59   The 11th Regiment of Dragoons (now 11th Hussars), 1750.

PLATE 60   The 12th Regiment of Dragoons (later 12th Lancers), 1750.

PLATE 61   An officer's charger of the 7th Dragoon Guards during the period of the Peninsular War.

PLATE 62   Serjeant Major, 7th Dragoon Guards, 1838.

PLATE 63   Major Charles Philip Ainslie, 4th Dragoons (later 4th Hussars) in 1813.

PLATE 64 Two non-commissioned officers of the 7th Hussars, c.1850.

PLATE 65 Two officers' chargers, 7th Hussars, c.1850.

PLATE 67 Officer, Royal Horse Guards, 1888.

PLATE 66 Officer, 2nd Life Guards, 1888.

PLATE 69   Two officers, 3rd Hussars, 1890.

PLATE 68   Officer of the 12th Lancers, 1888.

PLATE 70   Two privates of Mounted Infantry on Home Service, *c.*1890.

PLATE 71   Serjeant of a Mounted Infantry detachment on Home Service, 1896.

FIG. 1

FIG. 2

PLATE 73   Troop horses, Cavalry (above), and
Mounted Infantry (below), 1899.

FIG. 1

FIG. 2

PLATE 72   Officers' chargers, 1899.

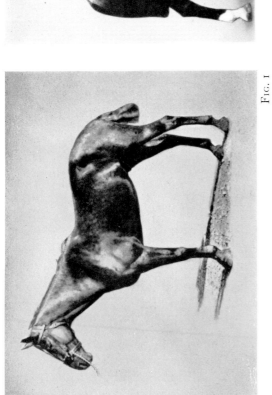

FIG. 1

FIG. 1

FIG. 2

FIG. 2

PLATE 75   Line Cavalry (above) and Household
Cavalry (below) horses, 1910.

PLATE 74   Royal Horse Artillery (above) and Army Service
Corps (below) team horses, 1899.

FIG. 7

FIG. 8

PLATE 77   Royal Engineers (above) and Army Service
Corps (below) team horses, 1910.

FIG. 3

FIG. 4

PLATE 76   Royal Horse Artillery (above) and Royal Field
Artillery (below) team horses, 1910.

FIG. 9

FIG. 10

PLATE 78   Mounted Infantry Troop horses, 1910.

PLATE 80   Royal Horse Artillery team horse, 1927.

PLATE 79   Cavalry Troop horse, 1927.

PLATE 81   Royal Field Artillery and Royal Engineers team horse, 1927.

Appendix A

THE McCLELLAN SADDLE, AMERICAN CAVALRY

On page 151 mention was made of the purchase and issue of American Cavalry saddles during the South African War of 1899 to 1902. Plate 21 shows this saddle, with a deep carbine boot, as used by U.S. Cavalry. As will be seen the saddle is of the simplest construction. The tree is of wood, beech or poplar, with a leather seat over a black rawhide cover and iron gullet and cantle plates. There are no points to the tree, worn over a blanket, and the girth, known as a cinch, is fastened to a ring which is hung from the tree by two straps, one from the pommel and one from the cantle. The cinch has a ring at each end and is secured to the cinch ring by a strap. The stirrups are of wood and the weight of the saddle, with double saddle bags, is 21 lb 3 oz, without the bags 17 lb 3 oz.

The saddle necessitates the trooper sitting very still and upright and probably does not give the same amount of grip as the British saddle. The great objection our troopers had to the saddle was the cinch fastenings, which were utterly strange to them and to which they had to accustom themselves in the field.

From the purely historical point of view this saddle is of great interest. The future General McClellan, U.S. Army, has fortunately left for posterity a copy of a letter written by him from Europe in 1856, in which he states that he had decided on a saddle 'adopted from the Prussian Hungarian Saddle'. This was first used by U.S. Cavalry in 1858, patented in 1865 and used with a few very slight variations as long as American Cavalry rode horses. This saddle is also known as the 'American saddle'. It has no connection of any sort with the Western Stock or Cowboy saddle, described in the section on Canada. So much has been said about the Hungarian saddle as used in Hungary, Austria, Prussia and Great Britain in this chapter that those interested should decide for themselves how much of the original type remains in the McClellan saddle. Plates 11 and 12 show respectively the details and the whole saddle of the British Cavalry Hungarian Pattern.[65]

In Colonel Denison's *Modern Cavalry*, Bosworth, London, 1868, is an account of some Confederate Officers whom he met. They preferred the McClellan to the British Hungarian model, as they thought the latter too heavy. They had certainly had considerable experience.

REFERENCES

1 List of Changes No. 6261, 1891. Handbook of Military Artificers, 1915.
2 Handbook of Military Artificers, 1915. Table of Drivers' Saddles on p. 87.
3 Confidential Report on the proceedings of the Bechuanaland Field Force, p. 193.
4 Forbes, *History of Army Ordnance Services*, Volume II, pp. 32, 56. See also *Times History of the War in South Africa*, pp. 452, 453.
5 Head, *Wear and Tear of Horses During the South African War*, under dates 20th May to 6th June.
6 Jackson, Murray Cosby, *A Soldier's Diary in South Africa*, pp. 205, 206.
7 *Saddles and Sore Backs*, p. 15, where Surgeon Major Smith states that the saddle had been brought over as described.
8 Stewart, *History of XIIth Royal Lancers*, pp. 281 to 283.
9 Preston, *The Desert Mounted Corps*, pp. 190 and 319 for the French Cavalry and *passim*.
10 Preston, pp. 12 and 13.
11 Arthur, *The Story of the Household Cavalry*. Two plates in Volume I show saddles in 1680.
12 Reports on the Service Saddle, Replies to 54/7712 General Order No. 39818, Horse Guards 7/XI/1882. War Office Library.
13 Aldershot Lectures No. XXXII, June 1891. Vet. Surgeon Major F. Smith, *Saddles and Saddlery*.
14 JAHR, Volume XVII, pp. 38 *et seq*. Extracts from Arthur Sleigh's *Royal Militia and Yeomanry Cavalry List*, 1850, edited by the Rev. Percy Sumner. Unfortunately many units had omitted to include saddlery in their reports.
15 JAHR, as above, p. 182.
16 Wyndham Quin, *The Yeomanry of Gloucestershire and Monmouth*, Cheltenham, 1898, p. 215.
17 Shown in a sketch by Caton Woodville in the *Illustrated London News* of 24th July, 1886, signed and dated 1885 – he was a sergeant in the Regiment.
18 In 1909 the First Aid Nursing Yeomanry, a Women's Volunteer Unit, was raised as a mounted corps, just before riding astride for women had become general. They therefore rode sidesaddle as is shown in Plate 22; See also Figure 14. The uniform worn was very smart, a scarlet peaked cap, a scarlet tunic braided white Hussar fashion, with collar and shoulder straps edged with white piping and a dark blue habit with three rows of white braid round the bottom. Officers wore a white pouch belt. In 1910 the F.A.N.Y. took to riding astride and wore khaki. Members served in various capacities on all fronts in the 1914–18 war, became the F.A.N.Y. Ambulance Car Corps officially in 1927, in 1933 the Women's Transport Service (F.A.N.Y.) and in 1939 part of the Motor Companies, Auxiliary Territorial Service. From JAHR, Volume XXIII, *Womens Work with the Army*, by E. J. Martin, p. 61.
19 See Figure 13a.
20 Lida Fleitmann Bloodgood, *The Saddle of Queens*. p. 21.
21 As 20, pp. 42, 43.
22 Sidney, *The Book of the Horse*. In the chapter on Women's riding, he calls them Amazons.
23 Especially those by Johannes van Wyck, *c.*1652 to 1700.
24 Prescott, *Spanish Tudor*, p. 1. I am indebted to Mrs A. M. H. Westland then of A.M.O.T. for this reference.
25 Sidney, illustration.
26 As 20, p. 62.
27 Bliss and Co., London and Banbury. *The London Catalogue*, 1904.
28 *Strength, Composition and Organisation of the Army of Great Britain*, 3rd Edition, H.M.S.O., 1865, p. 103, 'Organisation of Local Forces in India'.
29 The North West Tannery Ltd. Cawnpore and the Cawnpore Mills.
30 *Memoirs of General Sir Henry Daly*, Murray, 1905, p. 66.
31 *Record of the Expedition to Abyssinia*, Volume I.
32 Maxwell, *History of the XIth King Edward's Own Lancers*, p. 162, Appendix II.

33 As 30, pp. 194, 196.
34 MacMunn, *Armies of India*.
35 JAHR, Volume XXXI, p. 141.
36 Jackson, *India's Army*, p. 45.
37 Supplementary Despatches of the Duke of Wellington, 7/XI/1803.
   Other notes on Silladar Cavalry are taken from Forbes, *History of the Army Ordnance Services*, Volume II, p. 208.
38 War Office Handbook on Somaliland, H.M.S.O., 1907.
39 From notes dealing with the whole subject sent by Mr Robert Gray of South Australia.
40 Lectures given at Aldershot from 1888 to 1895.
41 Photographs, n.d. from *Under the Union Jack*, 1900.
42 From very full notes collected by Mr P. H. Bullock of New South Wales. Those on the Citizen Bushmen were sent by Major F. W. Weir, D.S.O., to Mr Gray. *The History of the New South Wales Lancers* has also been used and the author is indebted to Mr B. T. Hinchley for the photographs from *Under the Union Jack*.
   The article by Will Ogilvie appeared in *The Field*, c.1930. Ogilvie was born in Scotland in 1869, and is best known for his books of verse published in Australia. He was an authority on horses and saddlery and had a wide knowledge of conditions in Australia and in the Western States of the U.S.A.
43 Denison, *Modern Cavalry*.
44 Article by Will Ogilvie in *The Field*, c.1930. Trew, *Accoutrements of the Riding Horse*.
45 *Under the Union Jack*, n.d., but c.1900; the men are in full Home Service kit. Plate 94.
46 See under Saddlery.
47 See List of Changes 4672, 27th November, 1884.
48 Handbook for Military Artificers, 1915, pp. 79, 80.
49 Reproduction in a New Zealand paper of a picture entitled 'British Camp Surprised by Maoris, 24th Jan., 1865'. An officer and a trooper are shown; both have saddle cloths with rounded ends.
50 JAHR, Volume XXVI, p. 161.
51 Reproductions in *Under the Union Jack*, n.d., but certainly early in 1900. Presumably taken c.1899. One man has facings to his khaki jacket.
52 By courtesy of the Librarian of New Zealand Army H.Q.
53 Tylden, *The Armed Forces of South Africa*, illustrations, pp. 1 to 32.
54 Brabant, *Autobiography*.
55 M.S. Notes from the late Colonel B. C. Judd, formerly Adjutant of the Cape Mounted Rifles.
56 Notes from Major A. A. Wood, late Natal Mounted Police, and Captain G. F. Court, formerly Adjutant of the Corps. Captain Court's notes are to be found in Major Wood's book, *Natal, Past and Present*. They state that the Colonial saddles issued in 1894 were supplied by G. Smith & Sons, 151 Strand, London, made of oak tanned leather, and were 'the best in the world, British made'. They had the usual detachable panels, and cost £7 10s 0d apiece. Up to 1907 a saddle blanket was used, 6 by 5 feet, and a straight bar Pelham bit with two reins. Stirrups were Hussar pattern to 1902, then hunting pattern. Plate 98 shows the saddle. It was sent by Captain Court.
57 Colonel G. T. Hurst, *Volunteer Regiments of Natal and East Griqualand*, pub. Knox, Durban, 1945, especially p. 10.
58 Report of the Inspecting Veterinary Surgeon on the Zulu War; signed and dated 1880.
   Minutes of Evidence of Ordnance Commissions of Inquiry on Saddlery, several volumes in War Office Library. Progress Report 27th May, 1880, and Appendix B; by Veterinary Colonel Sir Francis Duck, R.A.V.C., enclosing reports of his subordinates. Many officers qualified to judge thought that Duck should have been awarded the Victoria Cross for his conduct at Inhlobane Mountain, Zululand, on the 28th March, 1879.
59 Report on Miscellaneous Subjects; *Ordnance*, Volume XVIII, 1887, query no. 3066.
60 Probably as early an instance of this as is likely to be met with is William Flashman (from Peats, Bond Street) Catalogue of the early 'eighties (no definite date given) Harness and Saddlery for Home and Foreign Service; address, 12 Lower Tulse Hill, Brixton, London, S.W.

61 Confidential Report of the Proceedings of the Bechuanaland Field Force by Major-General Warren, 1885, p. 193, Colonel Carrington's Report.

62 Regulations for Field Service, Bechuanaland, 9th December, 1884. Bound by Saul Solomon, St George's Street, Cape Town. Second Part, Regulations for Mounted Riflemen, p. 118, Dress and Equipment.

63 List of Changes, No. 4672, 27th November, 1884. War Office Library.

64 George Smith & Co. Catalogue of 1899. Letter of pre-1893 when Colonel Carrington gave up the command of the Bechuanaland Mtd. Police, referring to the saddle used by the unit.

65 Carter, *Horses, Saddles and Bridles*. Olsen in the *Military Collector and Historian*, spring 1955, and also James S. Hutchins, *Variations in the M.58 McClellan Saddle*, on p. 48 under the title 'Collector's Field Book'.

CHAPTER SIX

Pack-saddles, Harness,
Bits and Bridles

THE pack-saddle, whether used on horses, mules, donkeys, oxen, camels or elephants has always played a large and important role in the British Army, a role which persisted into the last World War, when pack-saddles were more used than riding saddles.

From the mid-eighteenth century they were known as bat-saddles, from the French, and from this are derived the words bat-horse, bat-man or as batt, baugh, baw, or bor. The latter was the usual pronunciation, but all these spellings were in use.

It is curious to find in the *Soldiers Pocket Book* of 1869 the future Field Marshal Lord Wolseley writing, 'there is a prejudice in favour of pack animals in the British Army which has come down to us from the Peninsular War. The worst transport and the most difficult to manage is that by pack animals.' He was an officer with a very pronounced modern outlook, given to generalizing, not always with very happy results, and one wonders if he would not have written in a different strain after his experiences with carriers in Ashantee in 1878. Actually the British soldier had great experience of packs since the time of the Civil Wars.

Pack-saddle transport has the great drawback that a much smaller aggregate load can be carried by this method than drawn by the same number of animals with wheeled transport. Roughly speaking a man carries about 50 lb and must be fed all the time and animals, which can often be grazed instead of having to carry their own feed can take weights ranging from about 200 lb for a pony or mule, up to 450 lb for a camel and as much as 1,800 lb for an elephant. A donkey takes about twice as much as a man. At the time that Wolseley wrote, two horses pulled 800 lb in a cart, four horses 21 cwt and six 3,300 lb in waggons. But wheels require roads, or at worst tracks which can be more or less levelled with pick and shovel. Horses, ponies, mules and donkeys can go nearly everywhere that a soldier carrying his arms and equipment does, and in mountain country and thick bush wheeled transport becomes impossible.

Professional packers, men of any race who spend their lives organizing and running pack trains, will make shift with any materials available to fasten almost any load of reasonable size on to the animal bred in their own country.

A couple of blankets, the man's bed in some cases, and two sacks joined together slung over the animal's back with a load in each of the two ends is the simplest form of 'saddle'. With a sack stuffed with grass or wool tied tightly on over the blanket the contraption becomes more efficient and easier on the animal.[1] There are many variations of this, the simplest and easiest sort of pack-saddle to make, and Plate 40 shows four types, as used in the East in 1868, and also three saddles proper, with trees, all of European manufacture. They will be described in detail further on. The important one is the centre saddle on the left of the Plate, which became the British Universal Pattern in due course and was originally evolved by miners and prospectors in New Zealand. They used it as a riding saddle as well, and it takes its name 'Otago' from the place of its origin.

As showing early types this Plate should include a drawing of what is perhaps the commonest of all, the sawbuck, so called from its close resemblance to the triangular bench or rest on which the carpenter places his work preparatory to sawing the wood. Instead of the circular pommel and cantle two pieces of wood are fastened together in the form of two double X's with the sideboards secured to the lower part or legs. This triangular shape, well packed with soft materials, makes a good form of pommel and cantle and the upper portion takes the lashings or straps for the load. Major Parrino (see in Bibliography), considers this makes an excellent tree for light loads and should not weigh much more than 7 lb. It is still widely used by civilians and is very simple to put together.[2]

Major Parrino also describes the 'Aparego', common in the South West areas of North America and in his opinion of Arabian origin. It has leather panels, ribbed with willow, a common wood used for pack-saddles in other countries and stuffed with hay. A strip of canvas also ribbed with sticks goes on top and a blanket underneath.

Most hired pack transport had some form of pad and there have been many men who preferred this type to the patterns with a tree. But the balance of military opinion has for many years preferred the tree, made roughly like a riding saddle with metal hooks on pommel and cantle also made of the same material. The armies of all the European powers, of the Dominions and of India all had very similar patterns, as do the forces of the United States, though they use stronger and heavier models, derived from their long experience with big, hefty pack animals. The average weight of the British patterns has varied little from about 40 lb to 50 lb.[3] Pack-saddles designed for the carriage of artillery will be dealt with in a separate section and those for camels, elephants and bullocks will be described under these headings.

Horses, Ponies and Mules

The fittings of the General Service horse and mule pattern have to vary with the nature of the load. Probably the commonest has always been the pannier, either a single one on each side or two or even three smaller ones. A drawing showing a seventeenth-century pack train in hilly country in Great Britain shows men, civilians, well mounted on a strong type of ride or drive horse, with a train of about twenty stout cobs, with large deep panniers and breastplates and presumably cruppers, tied one behind the other. In most cases the saddles have high arches rising from the pommels with bells on them. In some cases the loads are finished off on top of both panniers. Bells on pack mules were common in Spain and there is an account of the anxiety with which a cavalry regiment who were out of rations listened for the sound of the bells coming up from the rear![4]

It would have been from these saddles that the Army types were in due course evolved. The G.S. saddle of the mid-nineteenth century stood a great deal of knocking about. On one occasion a General Officer of great dash and impatience found a pack pony stuck in a narrow cleft between two rocks on a mountain foot-path. Though not stated, it is probable that the load was ammunition in very strong boxes. Without off-saddling the pony the infantry escort were ordered to turn him head over heels, the load cleared the obstacle and the pony proceeded down the pass with the saddle still in place.[5]

During the Civil Wars the pack-saddles were known as 'cantle pad saddles' and were more expensive than troop saddles, costing 17s apiece. A 'pad' normally had no tree, but presumably the 'cantle' was reinforced in some way to take the lashings. The term cantle referred to both front and rear arches at this date so the load could be lashed fore and aft.

We know more about the pack-saddles issued to Wellington's Army in Spain and Portugal from 1808 onwards.[6] They were called 'Devonshire crooks' or 'haucoms', the meaning of the last name being a mystery up to the time of writing. We do, however, know what a Devonshire crook was and presumably 'haucom' is simply an alternative title. The 'Devonshire crook' saddle, as used on the farms in the West for all classes of farm produce, tools etc., was made by bending strong poles of willow sapling, cut green and bent into the required shape for the two arches, and when dried out connected by sideboards like any other saddle. The arches, or pommels and cantles, were known as the crooks and were connected with longer sideboards for loads like sheaves of wheat and shorter ones for heavier material. A third type for carrying manure etc., was known as a 'dung-pot' and must have been some sort of pannier. The same type was in use on farms in central Spain.[6] This then was the prototype of the Army pack-saddle of the time, which, judging by its successor, would have weighed between 40 and 50 lb. The whole tree would certainly have been made of beechwood like the Army Saddles, both for Heavy and Light cavalry. Each infantry battalion had 13 mules with these pack-saddles and each cavalry regiment 14. In addition, each squadron of cavalry had mules, four in number, for the portable forges issued to each regiment. Each company of infantry had a mule for the camp kettles, the surgeon had one for his panniers, these being the crooked haucoms – the boarded haucoms took entrenching tools and the straight haucoms the paymaster's books – with a special set of baggage straps. Cavalry had two mules for the sergeant-armourer's panniers and two for the sergeant-saddler's.

The Portable Cavalry Forges were invented by Captain Scovell – later General Sir George (1774–1861), Deputy Assistant Quartermaster General on Head-quarters Staff, in 1810. He was in charge of the Corps of Staff Guides. In countries having passable tracks for wheeled vehicles, especially in Ireland, the farriers' forges and tools were carried on two-wheeled carts with two horses abreast, the off horse being in shafts; but the carts were too heavy for a pair and on the Portu-guese and Spanish tracks could not keep up with mounted men. A horse requires to be shod all round about every three weeks, more often if the roads are rocky, and though a horse will carry on for some time in grass country unshod or shod only in front this is never satisfactory. On active service if the farriers were to keep abreast of their work their forges had to be available immediately their unit halted for the night, which was never the case with the carts. This was the sort of problem that Wellington thoroughly understood. As soon as sets were available early in 1811 two were issued for trial at Headquarters, the pattern was slightly modified, and by April 1812, all regiments had them. Each mule carried a load of about 200 lb excluding the saddle. The specification for the fitting of the saddle taking the anvil, weighing 37 lb, was that it should be contained 'in a strong leather case with a back of wood larger than the anvil so as to lie easy on the side of the mule with things of equal weight to balance it on the other side, or the side of the saddle should be of wood'. Presumably this means that both sides should be fitted with 'boarded haucoms'. This arrangement was a great success and these portable forges were still in use in the present century fitted for packs. One mule carried iron and one coal, the other two had the tools and anvil.[6] The Arsenal at Lisbon made these forges and though it is not so stated it is presumed that the saddles were the G.S. pattern.

These were not the only pack-saddles used in the Peninsula; the Spanish so-called 'Albarda' of the treeless type was used in large numbers by the Commis-sariat mules hired in thousands in Spain with their own muleteers. This saddle, like all those used in Spain, weighed about 60 lb, was heavy and bulky, well stuffed and very satisfactory. There were various types of fittings, a pair of panniers of tri-angular or sugarloaf form, thrown over the saddle, points downwards and fastened together by a rope under the belly; and the Small Arms Ammunition carriers taking 1,000 rounds of ball cartridge, slung as high as possible up the mule's sides with lighter packages on top between them. Bales, portmanteaux or canteens were slung in the same way and as officers had to carry everything on packs, the con-tainers were made specially to fit the saddles. This is the earliest description of ammunition saddles so far met with. These saddles had covers, either woollen or tarpaulin, and the muleteer rode on the pommel of the leading mule with two or three mules each fastened to the pack of the mule in front. A sumpter mule had two or three small wicker panniers a side, 'and if the load is light your cook can ride too'.[7] If no containers were used each saddle had two large rectangular panniers to hold whatever was required.

In 1840 the G.S. pack-saddle weighed 45 lb and took 2,000 rounds of musket ball cartridge, 200 flints, in process of being replaced by percussion caps 50 to every 40 cartridges, and a tarpaulin, a total load of 265 lb, according to modern ideas a full load for a pony, or mule. Each battalion had two animals with a man detailed to lead them.

The line drawings below show the saddle of 1845, taken from the *Aide Mémoire to the Military Sciences*, Volume I, 1850. The details given above are taken from the *Artillerists Manual and British Soldier's Compendium*, 1840, by Captain F. A. Griffiths, Royal Artillery.

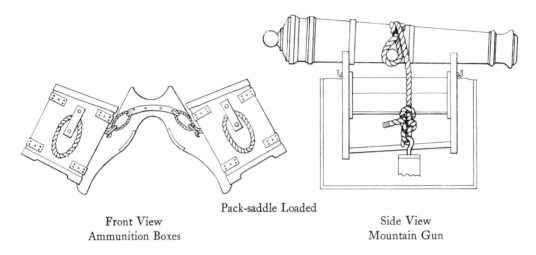

Pack-saddle Loaded

Front View   Side View
Ammunition Boxes   Mountain Gun

FIGURE 17   Pack-saddles, 3-pounder Mountain Gun, 1845, and Ammunition Boxes, 1845.

This G.S. pack-saddle will have been in use in the Crimea and there is evidence from W. Simpson's portfolio of drawings, done during the campaign, of the 'Devonshire crook' pattern being also in use. The common name for a pack-saddle was a 'cradle', sometimes the term 'ladder' was used, and most of Simpson's sketches show the connections between the arches formed by rungs very like either of the above implements. Some have arches made of poles as described in the detailed account of the Devonshire home-made saddles and some have solid arches cut out of planks. Another type probably used in the Crimea was 'the old Cape saddle' of which the Commissariat Transport Corps in New Zealand in 1865 had 800. Dep. Commissioner General J. W. Baily (1826–93) had them all converted to the Otago Pattern (see under), brought to his notice by Lieut H. Spiller, 3rd Waikato Regt., N.Z. Forces.[8] The Cape Saddle was described in 1850 as having wooden cross bars projecting over the top like the civilian types so common in North America.[9]

The next saddle to be considered is the Otago Pattern, evolved in New Zealand as stated above from a local pattern in use at Otago in the South Island, and used by the Commissariat Transport Corps there during the fighting against the Maoris in 1864. Among 600 pack horses using this saddle there were no sore backs and the saddle was sealed by Ordnance on 9.8.1868. Plate 40 taken from *The Record of the Expedition to Abyssinia in 1868* shows the detail. The weight was 43 lb, a fair average for this type, but it was made later by Ordnance weighing from 25 to 27 lb. The flat saddle into which the sideboards fit is long, with a shallow upper line and hooks on both arches. There are two girths set widely apart, and a large pad goes next to the animal held by the breeching and breastplate, which are continuous with supporting straps over the rump and wither. Just in front of the forward girth is an attachment for a stirrup. As a riding saddle it was not satisfactory but for pack it is closely allied to the G.S. Ordnance pattern which was evolved from it. Ordnance made the Otago in three sizes but even the smallest was too big for small mules.[10]

In 1865 each battalion of infantry was issued with four pack-saddles weighing 47 lb 3 oz apiece which took a load of 200 lb inclusive. Reserve ammunition was carried by the Royal Artillery in six horse waggons carrying 39 boxes of ammunition holding 440 rounds each. On each waggon were 'ladders' for the centre and lead horses, each taking four boxes of ammunition.[11] Presumably these were the pack-saddles described above. The next saddle to be introduced weighed 34 lb and the fitting or cradle a further 15 lb. This was on issue by 1869 and took 2 boxes of S.A.A. for the Snider rifle each of 560 rounds and a third one on top in an emergency. The weight of the load was slightly less than with the former pattern.

In 1868, as already stated, we had to force our way into Abyssinia and this campaign introduced the British Army to a range of pack-saddles, some purely experimental, some brought from India, and led to considerably more interest being taken in the whole of the pack problem. This was especially the case with the Royal Artillery, see later. Five thousand Otago saddles were sent out by Ordnance, all with stirrups, and were a success, though they were too long for most of the mules and needed the front and back of the pad cutting back. It was noted that they wanted careful fitting and stuffing and that the muleteers should be properly taught how to work with them.

Two other saddles were tried, the MacMahon and the Hungarian. The former weighed 56 lb plus another 10 lb with the waterproof sheet issued with it. It was a well-made saddle but too heavy. The Hungarian saddle weighed only 17 lb and had a light wood and iron framework with a folded horse-cloth underneath. It took two boxes of even weight, but was not suited for bundles or packages. The Otago was considered much the best all-purpose saddle. See Plate 40 for these saddles and for the pads described below.

Earlier in this chapter is a description of the two types of pack-saddle, the saddle proper with a tree and the pad with no tree. In Abyssinia four types of pad were in use, the Punjab, the Bombay Ordnance, the Bombay Commissariat and the Persian. Major Holland, Bombay Staff Corps, joint author of the official account of the campaign, was of the opinion that as a general rule, for pack purposes 'a pad is better than a saddle, being more easily repairable, better capable of being fitted to mules of any size, carried with greater facility to the post from which it is to be used, lighter in weight, simpler and far more economical in construction; it also affords protection to the mule at night, which the saddle does not. When saddles get out of order they are difficult to repair; the leather which covers them is liable to get damaged when in the hands of muleteers, who, tired with their long marches, content themselves with simply taking them off their animals and never give any attention to keeping them in good order.'[10]

Of the four pads the Persian type was the least satisfactory. It weighed 25 lb and those bought were made of very flimsy material and did not stand up well to hard work. The Bombay Commissariat pad weighed 40 lb, was simple and durable, but too heavy, especially when saturated with rain. The Bombay Ordnance type weighed 26 lb. It was too thin and unsuited for long marches.

The Punjab pad, weighing 34 lb and covered in leather with the two sides separated and connected by bands, was considered the best of the pad saddles. There was, however, no means of preventing the loads from slipping backwards and forwards in mountainous country.

A fifth type, the Egyptian, was to have been issued, but the whole consignment was rejected at the port of disembarkation as being hard, uncomfortable and unsuited to the work for which it was wanted.

The Ordnance pattern of the Otago saddle had emerged with credit from the very severe conditions imposed on pack transport in Abyssinia. In an improved form it was adopted by the Indian Army transport in 1882 in Egypt in the Tel-el-Kebir campaign and was then adopted in England.

In the Afghan War of 1878–80 the Bengal Commissariat pad was at first generally adopted and worked well when the muleteers took sufficient trouble to look after it.[12] The lighter Universal Pattern saddle derived from the Otago was on issue c.1872. It had a flat iron arch like the riding saddle of the same date. In 1882 this type was made in a larger size, but without the leather seat, and in 1885 two new U.P. saddles were sealed, known as Mark III, the large size weighing 53 lb complete and the small 45 lb 4 oz. The sideboards are of beech with high angle iron arches and horizontal hooks to take the lashings. These arches correspond to the pommel and cantle of the riding saddle. The larger size Mark III pack-saddle has two side bars, the smaller only one.[13]

Mark IV, introduced in 1890, has the arches of steel, again following the construction of the riding saddle.

The horizontal hooks, as shown in the drawing, are $17\frac{1}{2}$ inches apart and the saddles are fitted with breeching and breast collars, and a double girth with two web strips joined by a connecting piece through which the surcingle passes and cruppers. Although not usually necessary for riding saddles the latter are vital on a pack-saddle used with all sorts of animals, some with very straight shoulders, especially in a mountainous terrain, which is where packs are most used. There are two baggage ropes, each 13 feet 6 inches long, and the baggage straps on the saddle had a cross strap for securing ammunition boxes. If signalling apparatus was not

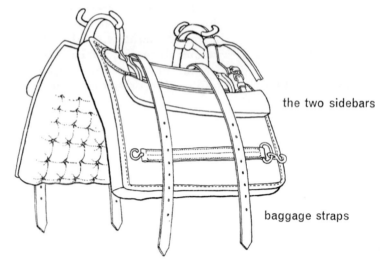

Showing the front of the
panels of leather, stuffed
and lined with white
duck, later tan dowlas.

the two sidebars

baggage straps

FIGURE 18   Pack-saddle, Universal Pattern, Mark III, Large G.S., 1884.

packed in boxes of a convenient size, it could be carried in the panniers with
wooden bottoms issued with the saddles.

The instructions for loading this saddle, evolved from the Otago G.S. pattern
with improvements added as the result of successful experiments made in India,
are as follows. The saddle was intended for use, not only for pack purposes, but also
as a substitute in mountainous terrain for the ambulance. Cacolets, iron-framed
adjustable chairs, to be used by casualties or sick men able to sit up and made to
fit on the G.S. saddle one on each side, had been in use during the Crimea and were
based on a pattern used by the Turks. Another type allowed of the men lying down.
The average load when used as a pack was 200 lb, including the saddle. The girths
were to be from 10 to 12 inches apart, the rear one being kept well away from the
animal's sheath. Both breeching and breastplate were to have a hand-breadth's play
and the load was to be secured by a web surcingle, known as a wantie (see in
Glossary), which went right over the load and under the animal's belly. It took two
men to load a mule and the load should not be lower than the side of the pack-
saddle. There should be a dismounted driver to every two or three animals and a
mounted non-commissioned officer in charge of every twenty animals. It is especially important with all types of saddles and packs to have the loads on each side of
the same weight.[14]

The difficulty with pack transport in any quantity is to be able to provide
drivers who either know or are willing to be taught their work. It makes no difference whether a man has to saddle up a riding horse or a pack animal, horse, pony,
mule or donkey. The principles are the same, except that the riding saddle will be
used at fast paces and the load either with or without the saddle can easily be taken

off at any halting place; with the pack-saddle the load must stay on the animal until the end of the day's march and the pace is always a slow one. Though disliked by civilians, as already stated, there is no doubt that the 1885 G.S. saddle and succeeding patterns were excellent for general use, with one serious exception. The difference in width through the body behind the withers, where the front arch of a saddle fits, between a stoutly built cob and a small donkey is very considerable and no amount of padding can ensure that a saddle which is too big will not be constantly slipping forward or back, tightening the breeching or the breastplate, as the case may be, and rubbing the animal. As will appear this difficulty was overcome, but not until after the South African War. The infantry soldier in charge of a good type of mule, carefully trained in saddling up and loading ammunition boxes and with his mule well used to the work, bears no comparison with an untrained driver in charge of animals whose loads are not standard and whose animal the G.S. saddle does not fit. The civilian who hires himself, his animal and gear, to which both are well accustomed, is usually satisfactory. He has a stake in the animal which the untrained man in charge of a Government animal has not. Taking fighting men from the ranks to help with transport can be very effective from the transport point of view, but hardly from the standpoint of the fighting machine. Yet it costs a great deal to keep transport in peace time on anything approaching a war-time basis and if this is not done the job of the Transport Staff becomes one of the greatest difficulty. Losses mount from negligence or ignorance on the part of the drivers and the strictures on our transport in the 'eighties and 'nineties so freely quoted reflect the inevitable result of improvisation, usually at the last possible moment.

An army moves on its belly as everyone knows, and, though it is not usually so stated, on the bellies of the transport animals, perhaps especially of the pack train, as in the Peninsula, in Abyssinia and on the North West Frontier of India. It was on this last front that so much work was done in perfecting saddles suitable for all classes of pack transport.

The South African War of 1899–1902 made no great demand on the supply of pack-saddles, for the terrain generally speaking is suitable for wheeled transport and, except for regimental ammunition mules and animals issued for machine guns, pack transport was hardly used.

In 1904 a new G.S. pack-saddle was issued, known as 'Tree, Adjustable, British Pattern' for Horse and Mule. It weighs just over 40 lb and superseded the various Marks of the former pattern, of which the latest was sealed in 1891.[15] Sealed as Mark v, this saddle was in use throughout both World Wars and is an outstanding success. The important point is the adjustable tree. The arches, front and back, are jointed to the sidebars so as to allow of their turning and so adjusting themselves to the backs of all sizes of animals down to the small donkeys available in Palestine. This principle was tried out by the Austrian Army in about 1890 and a specimen was brought to this country by General Keith Fraser.[16] It was a riding saddle, but though well thought of, the idea was not taken up. It certainly works well with loads of any kind.

187

The arches, hooks, loops and plates of the G.S. saddle are of steel and the side bars of sabicu wood, 20 inches long and $3\frac{3}{4}$ inches wide, curved and twisted to obtain a correct fitting. The sideboards are so set on the arches that when turned horizontally the distance from edge to edge is 6 inches across the front and $7\frac{1}{2}$ inches in rear. When turned so that the upper edges are as close to the arches as possible the distance from edge to edge is $7\frac{1}{4}$ inches in front and $8\frac{3}{8}$ inches in rear, this being the widest setting suitable for an equine with a broad back. It will be realized what a great improvement this was and how much it facilitated the business of fitting the saddle to most types of animals.

When carrying a Machine Gun each arch is fitted with a fixed horizontal loop made to engage in the standing staples of the Frame, Wood, Mark II, which carries the spare part box or the belt ammunition box on the saddle when the hanging bars (see line drawing) are attached. These are suitable for taking any load that requires lower bars. They are also used for cacolets. The panels of this saddle have a leather back with tan dowlas lining, stuffed with horsehair, which fit into leather pockets on the sideboards. The other fittings do not differ very much from those described for the earlier patterns. A waterproof cover, 6 feet by 6 feet, is issued with each saddle and a Universal Carrier made of narrow ash slats riveted on to leather straps, 33 inches long by 30 inches wide, which can be used to take loads such as petrol cans.

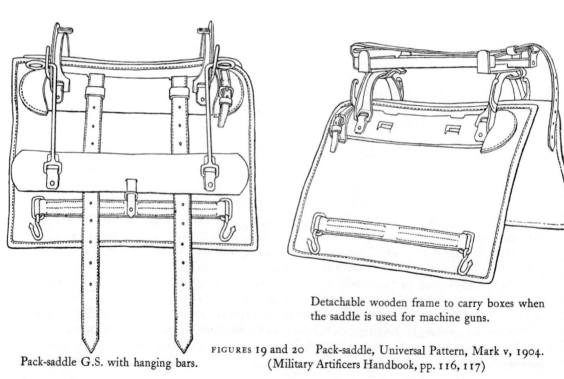

Detachable wooden frame to carry boxes when the saddle is used for machine guns.

Pack-saddle G.S. with hanging bars.

FIGURES 19 and 20   Pack-saddle, Universal Pattern, Mark v, 1904. (Military Artificers Handbook, pp. 116, 117)

Various types of pannier – called khajawahs and yakdans in India – are provided, for groceries, medical stores, general stores, artificer's tools, signalling equipment and engineer and pioneer equipment.

Cacolets have already been mentioned; they are iron-framed adjustable chairs weighing 56 lb a pair, and taking a man in a sitting or lying position on each side of the animal. (Plate 49.) There are not many forms of equipment, including such things as 6-feet sheets of corrugated iron, screw pickets, angle-iron pickets and telephone wire, which a pack-saddle will not take. They are not primarily intended for top loads, such as mountain artillery (see in the section on the pack batteries), although part of the load can sometimes be on top in order to reduce the bulk of the side loads.

The best pack load for a mule is 28 by 14 by 10 inches.

This was the saddle used in both World Wars. In the Second the Indian Army Pattern was also used with any local form of improvised saddlery available. 'This improvised material was a constant source of worry, loads were lost and full loads could not be carried. In Italy military pack-saddles were less easy to replace than the mules themselves, and a dead mule floating out to sea with its saddle was a tragedy mainly because of the serious loss of saddlery.'[17]

In the chapter on riding saddles will be found a note on a rather similar state of affairs in South Africa in 1900. It is never easy in war time to expand saddlery manufacture with sufficient rapidity to keep pace with the constant demands for replacements as well as for fresh consignments. In the Second World War the pack-saddle counted for much more than the riding saddle.

The prime authority for the Sicilian, Italian and Burma Campaigns is Brigadier Clabby's *History of the Royal Army Veterinary Corps, 1919–1961*, which has been used throughout this account. To it all those who wish for more information should apply.

In July 1943, the invasion of Sicily, held by the Germans, began. The only part of the forces which landed with pack-saddlery was the Canadian contingent, who had the British U.P. pattern. The bulk of the pack equipment had to be improvised and this was not easy, as the locally made Sicilian saddle was quite unsuitable for military loads. There were enough mules in the hands of the civilian population available, but the saddlery position was most unsatisfactory. Brigadier Clabby quotes the following report written on the spot by a young Veterinary Officer, which runs as follows: 'It is clear that improvisation is a complete myth. It is not practicable to take the equipment off a soldier and if this is not done it is found that the numerous blankets, ropes and pickhelves required for pack improvisation are not to hand in the field. At best, they are a very inferior substitute for real saddlery, which should always be available.' Nothing could be clearer; in this writer's experience, pack-saddles, without which infantry operating under the conditions prevailing in modern warfare cannot be efficient in mountainous country, must be provided and accompany the troops, even if enough animals can be requisitioned to fulfil the essential requirements. The same rule applies in thickly wooded, roadless areas.

Large quantities of Italian pack-saddles were captured in Sicily and were used to great advantage during the Italian campaign. See Plate 46, which shows the longitudinal ribbing of this saddle, known as the 'Basto'. Plate 45 shows the British Mark v U.P. saddle for comparison. Plate 48 shows this Mark v saddle being used on pack horses by Canadian troops engaged in a test in peace time in the Rocky Mountains.[18]

In July 1947 the Commonwealth Conference on Development, Design and Inspection of Clothing and General Stores submitted a paper by their Interservices Technical Committe, sitting in India, on the question of a design for a pack-saddle of Universal Pattern for possible use by the Allied Forces. Attached to it is a most interesting memorandum issued by the Master General of the Ordnance Branch, Army H.Q., New Delhi, on the whole subject. The conclusion arrived at was that the most generally adaptable pattern was that in use by the Indian Army. Originally designed for draught as well as pack, it has a connecting bar riveted to the centre of the front and rear arches. This bar allows a detachable Top Load Frame to be attached to the saddle, which made the latter available for all types of load. It was therefore recommended that the Indian type of pack-saddle should be adopted by both Great Britain and India, the only two countries which require pack-saddles for their post-war armies.

The fact that the stocks of saddlery left on hand after the war were sufficient not to require fresh issues does not affect the interest of this report. For the Indian Pattern Saddle in both pack and draught, see Plate 47a and b. The other saddle, not shown in the plates, used so very extensively during the Italian campaigns was the Phillips Pack Saddle used by the Forces of the United States. There are two types in use, the smaller Cavalry pattern, also used by most Infantry units, which weighs 43 lb exclusive of girths etc., with pads measuring 23 by 19 inches, and the larger type, used by Pack Artillery, by Infantry for heavy weapons and by all pack trains and known as the Cargo Pattern. This weighs 72 lb, the pads are 23 by 25 inches, and there are aluminium alloy side bars with steel arches. It must be remembered that in the U.S.A. very large and powerful types of mule are comparatively common and for these this heavy saddle is presumably ideal. The above details are reproduced by courtesy of the U.S. Government Printing Office and are taken from the War Department Field Manual of 1944.

Twenty years later the British Army is still using the Mark v Adjustable Tree Pack Saddle. Not only do the units of the Strategic Reserve use pack animals in regions like British Guiana, Aden and Cyprus, but as recently as October, 1963, the Service journal, *Soldier*, had an illustrated article dealing with 29 Company R.A.S.C. (Pack Transport) and their work at Hong Kong where, with 50 mules, 22,500 lb of sand, gravel and cement were transported daily up 5 miles of steep rocky hillside in order to build water tanks for coping with forest fires. Three trips a day were made with temperatures in the 'nineties. This Company, the only one of its kind in the British Army at the moment, enlisted mostly local Chinese as muleteers. The loads averaged 150 lb, and the editor's comment is – 'the mule still has its uses.'

PACK OR MOUNTAIN ARTILLERY *

Ordnance, even the lightest types, made a heavy load for a mule, averaging with the saddle not under 300 lb. Consequently, the mules issued to the Mountain, later called Pack, Batteries, had to be picked animals, not necessarily large, but always extremely well built.

The mountain guns used by the Royal Artillery in the French Revolutionary Wars were 3-pounders, the lightest weighing 270 lb with the very short length of 3 feet. The howitzer, with a calibre of four and two-fifths inches weighed 300 lb, and was used by the R.A. in Sicily in pack without wheels. In 1813 in the Pyrenees we had 4-pounder Spanish mountain guns, presumably with their pack saddle.

In 1826 the British Legion, raised for service under the Spanish Royalist Government, had the same howitzer as described above on a heavy, bulky Spanish saddle, but well made and approved of.

According to the *Aide Mémoire to the Military Sciences* (see in Bibliography) in 1845 the R.A. had a mountain howitzer weighing 280 lb, the carriage weighing 105 lb and two ammunition boxes 330 lb; the saddles for the gun and carriage weighed 41 lb each and those for the ammunition 45 lb (Figure 17). The Spanish saddles weighed respectively 86 and 70 lb.

In India light pieces mounted on their wheeled carriages were at times carried on elephants and also packed in the normal manner on mules, and in Abyssinia in 1868 Ordnance equipped two batteries (see Plate 38) for A/21st Bde R.A., with a steel 7-pounder R.M.L. gun weighing 150 lb with a barrel length of 2 feet 2·5 inches. This allowed of the gun being carried across the animal's back. Twenty-eight special saddles were made for the guns and carriages and each battery had also 28 of the Otago saddles of normal type (see *ante*) weighing 25 to 27 lb, as adopted in New Zealand in 1864, for ammunition. These batteries were issued with shafts and the mules could be harnessed tandem fashion and pull the guns on wheels. The leader mules were ridden, the Otago saddles having stirrups. The saddles used for the guns were fitted with iron cradles, as being preferred to wooden ones, to take the loads. These cradles weighed 14 lb, making a total load on the mules carrying the gun of about 200 lb. Hale's rockets, 6-pounders, were also packed on Otago saddles and worked by detachments from the Royal Navy, and the R.A. also had six 5½-inch mortars packed on elephants (see Plate 42, which shows the saddle and method of loading).

The 150 lb mountain gun used in Abyssinia was superseded by an identical piece weighing 200 lb with a barrel 3 feet 2 inches long. Two kinds of cradles were used, one taking the gun, muzzle to the rear, and one the carriage, breast to the front. Both cradles were of iron, the one taking the wheels having a special fitting and both had the same panels. The saddle used for entrenching tools had leather racks. Ten years later, in 1880, the once well-known 'screw gun' was introduced,

---

* For the equipment of a camel pack battery in 1884 in Egypt, see page 99

made in two pieces which screwed together, as shown in Plate 41, where a gun of an Indian Mountain Battery is seen on the mules. By this time (the photograph was taken in the late 1890s) the Imperial and Indian pack equipment for artillery had been assimilated. The gun weighed 400 lb and the loads averaged 300 to 320 lb. The saddle, illustrated below, had two leather panels lined with collar cloth and stuffed with horsehair and the cradles had wooden arches connected by two wooden sidebars with steel straps at the bottom and wooden sidebars underneath.

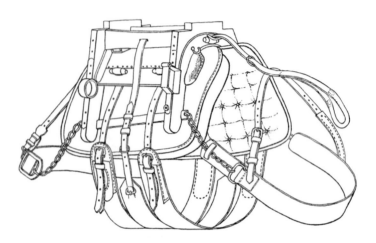

FIGURE 21   Royal Artillery pack-saddle for Ordnance, 1890.
(Military Artificers' Handbook, p. 113.)

The cradles differed slightly according to the loads to be carried. A mountain battery could come into action in one minute after halting with this screw gun and the ones that followed it.

The immediate successor was a 10-pounder B.L. gun introduced in 1902, the gun furnishing a load for five mules. The saddle shown above was converted to take the new equipment.

In 1911 a 2·75-inch B.L. screw gun was introduced, furnishing loads for 6 mules and in 1915 a 3·7-inch Quick Firing howitzer was the subject of experiments. It was issued about 1920 to British batteries, by this time termed 'Light', and by 1930 the Indian batteries had also been rearmed with the howitzer.

Thus far most of these details of the equipment of mountain artillery have been taken from the Handbook for Military Artificers, editions of 1899 and the tenth and last edition of 1915. Fortunately, Brigadier General Graham has taken the account on in his book *The History of the Indian Mountain Artillery*, published in 1957. Dealing with the period 1920 to 1935 he describes the new saddlery introduced by Lieut Colonel G. P. MacClellan, D.S.O., at about this time as follows:

192

'The method of transporting artillery loads in pack was, in the case of the heavier loads, to strap them on top of a saddle-tree which rested on two panniers stuffed with horsehair (otherwise known as panels, author) to fit the mule's back. (See Plate 41.) The saddle-trees differed in construction according to the nature of the loads, all of which were dissimilar and required different fittings to receive them – e.g. breech, muzzle, carriage and so on. Ammunition and certain stores and boxes were loaded on to saddles of a simpler pattern with two hooks on each side from which the boxes were slung. There had been no change in the general principle for 75 years, but steel frames had replaced the original wooden saddle trees.' This presumably refers to the Otago pattern of saddle of the 1860's (see Plates 38 and 40). 'The established principle was that each of the top-load mules (the three upper photographs in Plate 41 refer) had a duplicate; i.e. in a battery the existence of the "relief" line doubled the number of mules required for the gun and carriage and as the saddles were all different a "relief" mule could only be used for one particular load. This was uneconomical and particularly so in the case of the 3·7-inch howitzer, which required eight mules to carry it, as against six for the 2·75-inch gun. With the new type of pack-saddle, noted above, except in the case of the "Pivot" saddle (the carriage and trail were more complicated, author), alternative loads could be carried, thus reducing the number of "relief" mules by half (four instead of eight per gun). This system also reduced the number of drivers and fourteen mules and drivers were saved in the battery. In the case of ammunition boxes it was a simple matter to fit hooks to several other types of saddle trees. The Peace Establishment for a 3·7-inch howitzer battery was now 149 mules; War Establishment 120.' The 'other types' of saddle trees referred to were presumably the British and Indian Armies U.P. pack-saddles, the former the Mark v, Plate 45 and the latter Plate 47.

In 1961 the Support Artillery of the Royal Marine Commando Brigade was issued with the Italian 105 mm. pack howitzer, with the old-fashioned, presumably McClellan, saddle, modified to take the new gun.

This completes the section on the once so justly renowned Mountain Batteries, both British and Indian. The doubtless apocryphal story of the Horse Artillery officer of the old days, who is supposed to have said 'How we could gallop if it wasn't for these damned guns', had no counterpart among the Mountain Battery officers. They merely claimed that they could take their guns anywhere where a man could go, and did so. They and their men were not less renowned for their hawk-like vision, which could pick out the lone Afridi sniper on the distant hillside who was annoying the advance with his modern rifle. Whether they and their pack mules are a thing of the past must still be a moot point; in their day they were, among many other things, probably as competent users of a pack-saddle as were to be found anywhere.[19]

HARNESS FROM CIRCA 1798 TO 1935

Horses and Mules

A great deal of this chapter depends on the illustrations and especially on Plates 24, 29 and 32b. All three have the parts of the harness lettered and numbered and if once the two main principles of the purpose of harnessing an animal are understood it is not difficult to see the reason for the many other straps, shown in the three plates.

Double Harness Wheelers

However complicated a set of double harness for two animals placed immediately in front of a vehicle may look to those unacquainted with horses, they are far easier to understand than the very much simpler looking riding saddle. The essentials of a well-fitting saddle are hidden from the eye of the casual onlooker, but anyone can see almost at a glance the purpose of the important parts of harness.

The two horses or mules attached to a vehicle have to exert their power to move it forward and, to a limited extent in some cases, and fully in others, to stop or check the forward movement as required.

Collar and Breast-harness

The strength of the animal is in the neck, which is fitted with one of two devices, either a horse collar or breast-harness (see below); Plates 24 and 29 show the collar and Plate 32 the breast-harness. From these run the traces, ropes or chains fastened to the vehicle. By leaning forward against the collar or the wide breast strap the horse pulls on the traces and sets the vehicle in motion. More power is possible with the collar than with the breast-harness, but the collar requires skilled fitting for each animal wearing it and the breast-harness can be adapted to any sized horse or mule with very little trouble.

Traces

This then is the first main principle; to move the vehicle forward by means of the traces. They should be fitted so that in draught they are nearly parallel to the road. When the animal is standing at ease they should be at an angle of 15 degrees to the horizon.[20]

Breeching

In order to exert his strength to stop the vehicle the animal must push backwards against a wide belt fastened about a foot below the root of the tail and secured to the collar or breast-harness by a strap running the length of the body and connecting with the end of the pole. Plate 31a shows this plainly. Plate 35 shows the wheelers, as this pair are called, exerting their force backward, partially to stop the heavy pontoon waggon down hill. They are said to be 'sitting on the breeching', which is exactly what they are doing.

Leaders and Centre Pairs

Harness worn by the leader and centre pair of animals will be treated in the main section of this chapter; the changes were complicated and frequent.

Four-wheeled Vehicles

Practically all four-wheeled vehicles are fitted with brakes; some have only a skid or drag shoe, a short length of wood or metal fitted to go round a section of the wheel to prevent it turning, used on a hind wheel.

Two-wheeled Vehicles

There is no difficulty with four-wheeled vehicles as regards balance, but in the case of two-wheeled vehicles there are complications. As the gun, the ammunition waggon and the limber, used with both, are all two-wheeled and as they must be able to move at fast paces, their problems are of special importance. When the gun or ammunition waggon is hooked on behind the limber, to which the wheelers are harnessed, they keep it more or less balanced. But a two-wheeled cart with a pair of horses is always easily tipped forwards or backwards and must be fastened securely to the harness in one way or another.

Shafts

There are two ways of doing this. Either the cart is provided with one or two pairs of shafts or with a pole. Plate 25 shows the off wheeler in the shafts and the near, or driver's horse, with traces only. Shafts, made of wood, come forward to the animal's neck with the points adjusted to come above the line of draught. The off wheeler's breeching is buckled to rings fixed on each shaft, as is the off-side breeching strap of the near wheeler. Plate 30a, and the off-wheel horse in Plate 29 refer. The back-pull on the shafts gives very considerable stopping power. The above deals with Field guns; heavier guns had two pairs of shafts.

Pole Draught

In the early 1890's the shafts were replaced by a pole in all Field guns. Plate 31 shows pole draught with collars and the breeching connected with the end of the pole, thus giving the necessary stopping power. In order to prevent the pole from tipping up or down or working too much sideways it is supported by the pole-bar (Plate 31b), which is suspended from each horse's collar, and fastened round the pole.

Cape Cart Rig

In breast-harness the pole is supported by a strap going over the neck (Plate 32a and b). This method was introduced into England from South Africa c.1878, and known as the Cape Cart Rig.[21]

Curricles

In Regency times the smart turn-out in London was a pair in a two-wheeled carriage with the pole supported by a metal bar running between the small saddles used in civilian harness, with a support going down and round the pole. This was the so-called Curricle rig. In the Royal Artillery, if the off shaft of a limber was broken, a 6-foot handspike, a wooden lever carried on the gun, was lashed from saddle to saddle and to the shaft, now functioning as a pole. If the near shaft was broken it was replaced by the other one. The official name for this was 'Driving Curricle'.[22]

Single Draught

The description of shaft draught applies to all single animal vehicles, machine-gun carriages, for infantry, medical stores carts, etc. with breast-harness after c.1890.

The Fighting Limbers of the Machine Gun Corps, 1916–22, were horsed and harnessed with breast-harness and pole draught like the Royal Artillery.[23]

Drag Ropes

There existed two other types of harness used in the Service; man harness or drag ropes, used to move guns when horses were not available, as in the case of a very light piece in mountain or bush country, or where it was inadvisable to use horses because of enemy action or impossible because of the space available being too confined.

The Lasso

The other type was the Lasso issued to Artillery, Engineers and Cavalry for short periods and finally superseded by the breast-harness shown on riding horses in Plate 30c.

In 1825 Captain Francis Bond Head, Royal Engineers, who after retiring had seen the lasso used in South America, brought to the notice of Authority the possibility of using it in warfare, in order, among other things, to remove captured cannon during an engagement. The proposal aroused considerable interest, but was not taken up, though Head was knighted. During the Crimean War of 1854–5, Head was asked to demonstrate the method of using the lasso. This he did, and his suggestions were embodied in a pamphlet, which was printed at the R.E. Establishment at Chatham incorporated with Captain Siborne's 'The Lasso, with Instructions for its use and practice as adopted in the Royal Engineer Train', 1860. The original pamphlet was written by Sir John Burgoyne in 1857.[24] In Army Equipment 1865, Part II, Artillery, the following notes on the breast-harness, mentioned previously, explain the lasso as follows: 'The breast-harness is to enable riding horses to be used in an emergency to help draught horses; it has superseded the lassos which used to be provided in a small number to each battery, and which are still issued to cavalry. A lasso consists of a leather surcingle and a long rope trace; the surcingle can be girthed on a riding horse over the saddle, and the trace attached to it, when in use, at one side. It has been found that riding horses, however unaccustomed to draw, are always tractable when fastened to a lasso, and can be depended on for carrying off captured guns or assisting in any occasional draught work.' The weight was 11 lb 6 oz, and it was used by the R.E. only in Egypt in 1882. The Cavalry had the breast-harness and preferred it. Breast-harness was issued to Cavalry in a regular proportion up to the introduction of mechanization, and to Artillery, Engineers and Army Service Corps.

HARNESS, HISTORICAL

The preceding section dealt with the principles of draught and their solution by the Ordnance in the nineteenth century and after. This section deals with the historical side and includes the early period before 1798.

The references for this phase are not very satisfactory. Farm or cart harness of purely civilian type was in use and was as a general rule impressed with the horses and oxen (see under that heading), waggons, carts and drivers. The latter were under contract and retained their civilian status and clothing.

Up to about 1680 the teams had to pull directly from the trail of all guns, which was at first a very heavy balk of timber, later cut down to more reasonable dimensions. To this were attached the shafts, one pair only, and in front of the shaft horse were the team in pairs in the heavy gun and tandem, or singly in the case of the light pieces.

The limber, a two-wheeled cart with shafts to which the trail of the gun was hooked when in transit was introduced about 1680.[25] At first one wheeler was used, but later a pair.

What type of horse was used is uncertain, though it is obvious that up to the introduction of the limber the heaviest horse procurable would be in the shafts. In Henry VI's reign 'trotting geldings', pack horses, later known as Hackneys (not the Hackney of today), were required for artillery.[26]

The earliest mention of artillery harness known to the author is an order from Henry VII's officials to the Loriners of Walsall, Staffordshire, to make sets of harness.[27] Walsall is still the seat of the largest makers of the limited amount of saddlery and harness required today.[28] The Most Worshipful Company of Loriners, founded in 1245, made spurs and all-metal articles needed for saddlery, and were closely allied with the saddlery trade.

Farm harness has changed but little, if at all, up to the present day. The horses pulling plough or harrow and the leaders of all teams had traces and collars, as specified to be sent with each horse requisitioned by the King's Waggon Master General in 1643 during the first Civil War.[29] Presumably the shaft horse had the same harness as is described on page 198, a thill with a cart saddle. Thill or thiller is the old name for shafts and wheeler harness is still called 'thill or cart or breeching'. There are no traces, the pull is from the collar which has a short length of chain hooked to an iron fixture on the shaft. A second fixture takes a piece of chain running from the breeching, which is held in place by straps running down from the crupper. The cart saddle, not possible to ride on, has either a length of chain or a stout leather loop or tug holding up the shaft.[30] A variation is shown in a fifteenth-century print where there is a ring on the collar taking the end of the shaft. The breeching is as described, but the chain running to the shaft has the loose end fastened under the horse by a girth.[31] The principle is the same as described above.

197

'Farmer's Draught', as the type with the saddle was called by the various Transport Corps, was in use by the R.A.S.C. as long as they took over civilian vehicles for Service use. This type continued in use for artillery until *c.*1800; see *post*.

In 1637 Henry Hexham, Quartermaster to the Regiment of the Hon. Colonel Goring, brought out a book giving details of the Ordnance of the period. A 'cannon', the name of a siege gun weighing 90 cwt and taking a 48 lb shot, required no less than 'fifteen couple of lusty horses, besides the thiller horse or wheeler'. The heavy guns were mounted on 'block waggons or their own carriages'.[32] The traces of the 'couples of lusty horses' would be hooked on to those of the pair behind, and probably the pair next to the shaft-horse had long traces, on swingle-trees on the waggon or gun carriage as the case might be.

As the requisitioning order of 1643 does not mention shafts it is probable that the shaft harness was requisitioned with the vehicle and shaft-horse. In Burne and Young's *Great Civil War*[33] it is noted that at one time the Royalist cavalry had 'galloping guns' with the detachments riding the teams, the earliest known form of horse artillery. If the trail had been reduced to modern dimensions as in the case of the 3-pounder mountain gun of the first half of the nineteenth century with shafts fitted[34] the farm harness should have functioned satisfactorily.

Lawson, in his *History of the Uniforms of the British Army*[35] states that the Royal Artillery kettle-drum carriage of 1705 had a pole and breast-harness and the illustration shows no blinkers, which is surprising (see *post*). Breast-harness was common all over Central Europe at a very much earlier date.

Normally the civilian drivers walked by the wheeler and the leader or leaders, but there are prints showing them riding on the teams.

Although at times the Royal Artillery did move fast into action, notably at Minden, guns seldom moved out of a walk, or at least a trot. It follows that the harness used was quite adequate and sets could be bought easily if they could not be requisitioned.

In 1722 the Flag Gun, which flew a Royal Artillery Colour, was on a 6-pounder with four horses in single file and five years later the heaviest piece in the Train was the Flag Gun with a team of twelve. At this date the 12-pounders had 4 horses apiece and the drivers were civilians, who walked beside the teams. The harness was still the farm type.[36]

In 'Army Equipment', 1865, is a note on 'Harness of Last Century'. As long as the field artillery was organized by trains, and was not required to execute rapid movements, the harness was of a much simpler description than that which is now used. In Adye's M.S. (1766), harness is included among the artillery stores, and is entered thus:

Horse harness for each gun	Traces, prs. for each horse, I
	Thills, with cart saddles, I
	(see note at foot of page 199)
	Bit Halters
	Wantys

It would appear that all the articles required for the care and grooming of the horses were provided by some other department, or by the 'conductors', who then marched on foot, and were only temporarily employed. Bit halters and wanties are still used for horses led by hand. Thiller being an old word for shaft, the thills refer to the shaft-horse only.

Writing in 1850[37] Colonel Cater, Royal Artillery, puts the position as follows: 'It would appear that until the close of the American War in 1783 our armies were encumbered with heavy artillery, the weight of guns and carriages being out of all proportion to the means of moving them with facility'. He excepts various well-known examples of the employment of light guns in the field and goes on to say that the Battalion guns of a later date were horsed locally and driven by waggoners in smocks.

In 1788–9 experiments were carried on with curricle guns – see *ante* for details of the harness – by the Duke of Richmond, a most enterprising Master of the Ordnance. They were continued till 1793, in which year the Royal Horse Artillery was formed.

In 1798 at Woolwich the 8th Battalion Royal Artillery had three horses harnessed tandem to each gun, the drivers being contracted civilians in short white frocks with blue cuffs and collars and a waggon whip. It was presumably the end of the era of farm or cart harness.

The comment on the so-called 'experimental drill' made by the Garrison Adjutant, Captain Spearman, to General Lloyd, the Commandant, was 'that it was impossible the movements could be quicker performed', to which the General assented. So the harness must have functioned well.

This type was still in use in the campaigns of 1795, 1798 and 1799 in France and Flanders, but in 1793 when the Royal Regiment of Horse Artillery began its career, the era of harness as described in the first section of this chapter had begun.

The Nineteenth Century and After

The Royal Artillery had decided by the end of the Napoleonic Wars what they required in the way of harness for the various types of Field Ordnance. It was not so easy to formulate a correct theory as to how the horses should be harnessed with a view to making them fit for any work which they might have to do and yet put as little weight as need be on their backs. In the chapter on Remounts where the fighting for Palestine in the First World War is described, there is a quotation from a Senior Officer of the Royal Regiment dealing with the work of an artillery horse as compared with a cavalry troop horse. As stated the balance of hard work was heavily weighted on the side of the gun team, whose task was in every way more arduous.

According to Plates 23 and 34, the Horse Gunners ended just as they began, with the least possible weight on the off horses, a pad strapped on a surcingle.

NOTE: Hogg, see[26] notes a 'Lymoursadel' as on issue to Artillery in 1430. This may be the earliest mention of a cart saddle.

Although it is entirely irrelevant to the subjects on which this book is written it is interesting to note that there has also been practically no change in the men's jackets in over a hundred and fifty years!

In the List of Stores for a Troop of Horse Artillery in 1813 in Adye's *Pocket Gunner* there are included 'panels near side and off-side Drivers'. Presumably the off horses had 'pads or off saddles', which on the showing of the Brigades, today Batteries, of Field Artillery, would be the small 'luggage' saddle. (See Plate 24: 'D', the panel of 'A', the saddle.)

One painting of an R.H.A. team in the Peninsula [38] shows this very small pad on the off leader. Possibly Alken (Plate 23a) drew the R.H.A. in drill order. For in 1840, in Plate 24, the off horse's saddle pad is clearly shown in 'A' and 'k'. Probably this is what Alken was trying to show; in drill order the canteen 'd' and saddle-bag 'c' would not be worn.

It is very improbable there would be much change, if any, between Peninsula days and 1840 and Captain Griffiths' *Artillerists Manual* of that date, from which Plate 24 is taken, gives many further details. The leaders had rope traces, longer than those of the wheel pair, to allow a yard from nose to croup, so that there was no danger of their striking each other with their feet when extended at a gallop. The wheelers had chain traces just long enough to keep their quarters clear of the splinter bars (see Plate 25, which shows them on the limber with the traces taut) when the horses sat back in the breeching.

There were eight sets of lasso harness (see in previous section), the drivers' leggings and one leather wanty. All drivers always have a special legging on the right leg with an iron 20-inch side plate on the outside to prevent the leg being injured by the led horse or, when shafts were used, by the shaft, or by the pole. In teams of twelve horses, four abreast, with a heavy gun and double shafts in the limber, the drivers of the off pairs ride on the off horses and wear the leggings on the left leg.[39]

Up to 1853 all the horses in the teams wore blinkers, flat rectangles of leather curved slightly outwards, attached to the bridle so as to prevent the horse seeing in any direction except to the front. The idea was that he should not be frightened by anything in the vehicle he was drawing. Horses have considerably more sense than many people are wont to believe and a horse works better and more intelligently without these ugly attachments.

Plate 25, photographed from a model in the R.A. Institution Museum, shows no blinkers and so can be dated with certainty as post-December, 1853, when all harness was made of brown instead of black leather and blinkers were abolished.[40] Note that there is only one strap from breeching to crupper instead of two as in Plate 24. The pad saddle has been replaced by the luggage saddle, a shorter version of the riding saddle with no room for a man to sit. There is a numnah under the saddle. The narrow iron hames running right round the outside of the collar strapped together at the top, to which the traces are fastened, can be seen in both Plates 24 and 25. The front pairs have no breeching in either set, therefore if both wheelers are out of action their harness must be taken off (not so easy with a dead horse) and put on the leader or leaders who are to take their place. The swingle trees to which the wheeler's traces are hooked are shown in Plate 25. Though the driver's cloak is on his own saddle, his valise is on the led horse, strapped on the luggage saddle. In 1840 a driver averaged 11 stone 4 lb in marching order. His cloak added 6 lb. The wheeler he rode carried harness weighing 4 stone 9 lb, the luggage saddle on the off horse weighed 4 stone 5 lb and the valise etc. 1 stone 13 lb. The total weight on the near horse was 15 stone 13 lb and on the off horse 6 stone 4 lb. In comparison the mounted N.C.O. and gunner rode 18 stone 12 lb. The brass cantle on the driver's saddle, used from 1813, was continued.[41] Plate 36c, Driver in marching order, shows the legging.

The next series, Plates 26–28, show the harness introduced in about 1860. The battery was a Horse Artillery one and all details are clearly shown. The wheeler sets do not differ much from those in Plate 25, except in the luggage saddles, which appear to be smaller. Plate 26a, the officer's charger, shows the high wood arch post-Crimea saddle, sometimes called incorrectly Nolan's saddle. Plate 26b shows the shaft horse, the off wheeler. Plate 27b shows the driver's saddle and 27a the near wheeler with a cover to the saddle and the driver's cloak on the pommel. Plates 28a and b are the leaders with no breeching.

Plates 30a, b and c are from a Handbook[42] dated 1883, but have been copied from a book dated 1881. Plate 29, also dated 1883, has an important difference. This will be described later on. Except for this the set shown for R.H.A. is Universal Pattern 1865 as described in Army Equipment of that date. The 'Artillery' pages are signed by Major Muller, v.c., and give full details of the old pattern of c.1860 and of the new pattern of 1865, which was in process of issue, though the large stock of old pattern harness had still to be used until worn out. The chief difference between the two sets is that the old pattern has a luggage saddle on all the off horses and in the new pattern only the shaft horse has this saddle. The other two off horses have drivers' saddles without stirrups. A driver could therefore quickly replace a casualty to a riding horse by shifting the stirrups to the lead horse's saddle. The weight on the lead horse was slightly increased. Sheep skins to cover the valise came in with the old pattern. Both sets had wallets on all saddles. The weights remained the same; 140 lb for the lead and 152½ lb for the wheel sets. The mounted gunners rode about 18 stone in marching order.

The difference in the leader set shown in Plate 29, but not in 30b is that in 29a there is a narrow breeching strap. Whether this is a mistake on the part of the draughtsman or not, or whether the breeching was an experiment, one thing is clear – it was not proceeded with. A photograph of N/R.H.A., the Eagle Troop, showing a section on parade, in the author's collection, shows the normal 1865 U.P. with the date 1883. Nor do any of the numerous sketches and paintings of the 'eighties show any breeching on the leaders. The off wheeler in Plate 29 is correct according to the description in 1864 Army Equipment. On the first page of this description it is stated that the 'harness for artillery horses is the same as for other services'. As a matter of fact the Army Service Corps of the future had slightly different sets. There were, however, by 1884, but probably earlier (see Plate 39), entirely different sets of harness used 'for special service', when mules replaced horses for transport work. 'Special service' presumably meant in most cases active service and throughout the decade we were engaged in various 'Small Wars', as they were called in many quarters. Plate 39a shows 'six mules harnessed for pole draught', though the pole is not shown. This was known as 'farmer's draught' and the hames and general cut of the harness is civilian. Only the wheelers have breeching and the traces run normally from mule to mule, hooking on behind the collar. If the waggon has no fittings for the type of harness as shown and if there is a pole, the breechings must be altered, presumably by attachments running through to the collar (Plate 39). From 1877 to 1881 we were fighting somewhere in South Africa and using the normal South African mule waggon with a pole and also the local harness. This was sealed by Ordnance in 1884 as 'Harness, Mule, Breast, South African Service' and by 1902, when the South African War of 1899 ended, thousands of sets of this simple harness were in use by the A.S.C. On the pole is a swingle tree for the wheeler's traces and a ring forward for the breeching straps. Ox-harness or 'trek' chains run singly from the end of the pole, with swingle trees for the traces of the next two pairs of mules. The swingles are slung round the necks of the mules right up against the bridle as shown. The next or second pair of mules have swingles and no chain and the leader's traces are hooked on to the breast-harness of the pair behind. Blinkers, or winkers as they are sometimes called, are used on both sets. The extreme simplicity of the South African method will be readily apparent.

In 1875 the Royal Artillery had received Gatling Machine Guns as part of their equipment. They were treated like Field Guns, had a limber with shafts and harness, all as laid down and already described. When the Maxim came in about ten years later, it was issued gradually to Cavalry and Infantry and not to the Gunners. A variety of carriages, nearly all without limbers, were introduced, those issued to Cavalry being higher than the Infantry type.

The single harness, differing very little from wheeler shaft harness as used for horses, was found too big for animals under 15 hands, ponies or mules, and 'No. 4670, 1884, List of Changes mule breast harness, general service' was used for Infantry machine guns, but without the leader harness used for a tandem in water carts. The leader had breast-harness with two straps instead of a surcingle on the traces, the wheeler had an old pattern wood arch luggage saddle, tugs and belly-band and breeching all as the U.P. harness, but lighter. A slightly modified pattern for machine-guns was sealed in 1881.

Cavalry equipment varied. A photograph[43] understood to be of the Royal Dragoons dated 1889, shows a small carriage with a pair of horses in normal U.P. harness with a pair of shafts and a single leader with traces to the breast-harness, as already described as issued to all mounted branches. This method is known as 'driving pickaxe or unicorn' and was not common.

The normal equipment was a high carriage with a pair of horses, but one regiment, the 13th Hussars, in 1899 had a limber with the gun carriage behind and a pair of horses.

Plates 31a and b show an entirely new departure made in 1890 by the Royal Artillery. Collar harness with pole draught, as described, was worn by both wheelers and there were no shafts on any Field Gun limbers. The lead and centre pair were harnessed exactly like the wheelers with breeching, but no pole-bar (Plate 'b'). All horses had drivers' saddles without stirrups and wallets as in the Old Pattern sets. This meant that any horse in the team could take the place of any other, wheel, centre or lead. Another innovation was the introduction of rapid release attachments on the pole-strap, pole-bar hook and traces; this not only helped hooking in and unhooking the team, but made for extreme rapidity when casualties occurred. This was the U.P. used in the South African War of 1899–1902, and the following incident is taken from the Diary of a Corporal serving in the 7th Mounted Infantry.[44] A convoy with a very strong escort was being attacked and held up on the right flank of the advanced guard. The Boers extended along the whole right flank and then attacked the rearguard. The 7th M.I. were sent back to the rearguard and were galloping fast when a Royal Artillery gun came past them, also moving very fast and going to reinforce the rearguard. 'A pom pom[45] shell cut a poor old gun-horse's hoof right off above the coronet. He was an off-sider, and the driver blew his brains out, cut him out and they were under way again before we passed them, and we were galloping.' The driver used the quick release and his revolver, which all drivers carried since 1879.[46]

At the time this incident happened the Boers still had a considerable amount of artillery, but by August, 1900, nearly a year after the war started, they had lost practically all their guns. The British troops were engaged in never-ending long marches and the question of weight on the horses became of great importance. (See in the chapter on Saddlery.) The Commander-in-Chief, Field Marshal Lord Roberts, had served as a subaltern in a Battery of Bengal Horse Artillery. Every horse in the team was ridden and, as is usual, the officers used to practise riding in a team, so that they had a very practical knowledge of the drivers' work. In a General Order to the Royal Artillery of the above date they were instructed to hand in the saddles and breeching worn by the centre and lead off horses. Later on traces, crupper and collar[47] only were worn. This not only relieved the teams, but also gave the driver much less work. The following story from the pen of Major General Bannatyne-Allason, C.B., C.M.G., illustrates the sort of work a driver might have to do and the spirit of the Royal Regiment. The General wrote as follows:[48] 'It was, especially I think with gunners, a matter of honour that as few things as possible should be abandoned on the veldt. A driver of G Battery, R.H.A., lost both his horses, but he walked into bivouac at night carrying a double set of harness. He was not well, and died eventually. But there is no doubt, in my mind, that his splendid gunner spirit militated against his recovery.' This would have taken place before the harness was reduced on the off horses.

Up to 1890 the Army Service Corps had the G.S. Pattern, 'in existence for a very large number of years with many modifications'. For one thing the G.S. Waggon had brakes, so the wheelers had no breeching. In 1890 Harness A.S.C. was issued,[49] the near set weighing 76 lb and the off set 69 lb. This was considerably lighter than the old pattern as was the R.A. 1890 pattern. The A.S.C. sets had the neck collar and breast collar interchangeable. The off wheeler retained the luggage saddle, from 1885 fitted with shaft tugs. In pair horse and four-in-hand driving from the box seat of the waggon a back pad was used. It could be used as a roller for keeping on clothing at night. Either pole or shaft draught was in use. The stirrups were square, those of the R.A. being the round Hussar pattern.

In 1902 breast-harness replaced collars for Royal Artillery, all horses had riding saddles, the off without stirrups as before. The crupper and loin strap were abolished. In 1904 came further changes, all drivers' saddles were replaced by the U.P. saddle, issued with panels.[50]

Both the 1902 and the 1904 issues were conversions and the latter is shown in Plate 32a, the pole-bar is as before, but the chains running to the pole have been replaced by straps. The R.H.A. reverted to pads for the off horses. In 1911 the latest U.P. harness replaced all others. Plate 32b shows the breast collar, neck strap and neck-piece pole-bar. It is taken from *Manual of Horsemastership, 1937*, where there is a full description. This states – 'the outstanding feature of this harness is the fact that the old method of supporting the traces and breeching from attachments is entirely dispensed with, and thus the crupper with its hip straps and the flank straps disappear, and the one description of saddle can be used for both harness and saddlery'. Plates 34a and b show the whole harness and Plate 36c the wheel driver mounted. The near wheel set weighs $55\frac{3}{4}$ lb, the off wheel $52\frac{1}{2}$, the near lead $49\frac{1}{2}$ and the off lead $46\frac{1}{4}$ lb.

As already mentioned the R.A.S.C. drive both pairs and four-in-hand from the waggon box and similarly the Royal Engineers drove their Light Spring Waggon R.E. from the box. The Field Company had a Tool Cart, unique in their Corps. It was a limbered vehicle drawn by four horses. Each of the two-wheeled elements contained the tools of one section of a Field Company. If necessary the Cart could be split in two, a pole pulled out on the rear element and the leaders, who had breeching on their harness, put to it. The wheelers took on the limber.[51]

This historical review began with farm harness and in the 1937 Manual quoted above there are directions for altering the modern set to this, the oldest type of all. A luggage saddle was to be used, just as ordered in 1766 and still with a wooden tree. The paragraph ends as follows – 'the back band and tugs are removed and replaced by short back-bands and belly bands of harness, "Farmer's Draught"'.

The 1937 harness was of the simplest, with the riding saddle in universal use. The R.H.A. had reverted to a pad on the off horses as in 1821 (Plate 23a), but the R.F.A. still kept to a saddle, though no longer a luggage pattern. Plates 34a and b of the King's Troop of today should be a reminder to those who watch them of the days when the horse in his harness took the guns into action whatever were the conditions and however heavy was the enemy fire. Lieut Colonel Alfred Burne, Royal Artillery, has a description in one of his books[52] of one of the early actions of the First World War. He writes of the limbers 'thundering down a hill to the rescue of their guns', before a retirement; which is exactly what horsed guns sounded like when at speed.

THE BRIDLE

Both under the saddle and in harness the horse and mule are controlled by the bridle, shown in a very simple form in Figure 22. The bit (the term is used in two senses) is made of metal and passes through the mouth. It is fastened over the top of the head behind the ears by the cheeks of the bridlehead and kept in place by the brow band, passing round the front of the head below the ears, and the throat lash which goes round the throat high up. Secured to the bit are the reins, which run back on each side of the neck to the rider's hands as he sits in the saddle or right back to the vehicle to which the animal is harnessed. In the British Service only three sorts of bits have been used: the curb as shown in Figure 22 used by itself until late in the eighteenth century; the snaffle, used with the curb from then onwards until 1902; and the modern Universal Pattern Reversible or elbow bit, which combines the actions of the two others. The snaffle is shown in Figure 22; it is

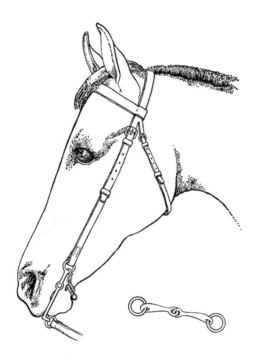

FIGURE 22   Civilian bridle with single curb bit. Inset, plain snaffle or bridoon bit.

205

jointed in the middle and is also made solid. Worn with the curb it was known as a bradoon or bridoon and the whole bridle as a 'double bridle'. The curb is known also as 'the bit' which is confusing. 'Bit and bridoon' is another name for a double bridle. The action of the snaffle is on the corners of the mouth and it is comparatively easy on the animal. The curb acts through the pressure of the curb chain on the chin groove, as in the drawing. The mouth piece may be a straight bar, but in the Service it is usually raised in the centre so that the tongue can lie in the port, or raised portion. The curb can be very severe.

This very rough and generalized description should serve as an introduction to the edict promulgated in 1627 by Charles I that the snaffle was forbidden to be used except 'in times of disport'. All riders were at other times to use curb bits only. The King, who was no mean horseman, had been taught in the severest form of the school which favoured the *manège*. His meaning is clear enough; for racing, and presumably hunting and hawking, the snaffle was permissible, but if the horsemen of England were to fit themselves to use the sword – the lance was temporarily in abeyance – they must accustom their horses to the utmost degree of control. At this date practically all horsemen carried the sword for self defence, for the pistol was still unreliable.

Plate 103 refers from now onwards. It was specially drawn by Harry Payne for the *Cavalry Journal* and shows practically all forms of bridle used in the Service from 1660 onwards. The bridle of that date differs from that shown in Figure 22 and Plate 2 only in having a noseband. The curb bit of 1668, shown by itself, has thistles as bosses where the bridle joins it. These ornamental bosses tended to grow larger and had monograms or coats of arms engraved on them.

The bridle of 1780 is a double one with two bits, both curb and snaffle or bridoon, each bit has separate cheek pieces, the brow band is decorated and there is a separate halter, of white leather, for securing the horse either in a stable or to a horse line stretched and fastened so as to take a number of troop horses. The strap for tying the horse up can be seen round the neck. Alternately, the bridle itself can be used as a halter, the curb bit being taken off complete and the bridoon unbuckled, leaving the rest of the bridle as a so-called head-collar.

The Light Cavalry and R.H.A. bridle of 1812 is of this type, the head-collar strap being looped round the neck and the long end twisted up. The triangular piece hanging down behind the strap is the jowl or throat piece, purely ornamental and in this case ending in a tassel. The bridle has the newly introduced cross face pieces and is decorated with leather rosettes and bosses. The Hussar officer's bridle of 1825 is very similar, but more ornate and is almost covered with cowrie shells sewn on to the leather, a fashion copied from the Prussian Hussars. The ornament on the jowl piece is in the form of a medallion, instead of the more usual plume as shown in Plates 18, 65 and 69.

Noticeable in the bridle of the Light Dragoons, Hussars and R.H.A. of 1847 is the curved metal bar joining the bottom of the cheeks of the curb bit.

The Universal Pattern of 1860 shows the head collar chain used for tying the horse up. Owing to the practice common among swordsmen, either on foot or mounted, of slashing through an opponent's reins in order to make him unable to manage his horse, some regiments used these chains over one of the reins on active service. This bridle has a link and bar fastening the bridoon to the bridle and the whole effect is severely plain and workmanlike.

The officer's bridle of the Royal Horse Guards of 1870 is best described in detail from an article in the *Carriage Builders and Harness Makers Art Journal* of approximately the same date. 'The bridle is made of black patent leather, mounted with brass D-wire buckles, and ornamented with brass bosses, rosettes and scales on the head-piece, studded with steel; the scales are in the form of half Maltese crosses, studded with steel, the centre one being double.' These head-piece scales are intended to stop an opponent slashing the head-piece of the bridle through with a sword cut to make the bit drop out of the horse's mouth. They are still worn by the Household Cavalry and are the last vestige of the horse armour of the past. The description continues: 'the head-piece should be cut two inches wide, thirty inches long and split up eight inches at each end, by a piece being cut out of the centre, so as to leave two straps, three-quarters of an inch wide, at each side; one to take the cheek of the bridle and the other for the throat band. The front is covered with white in the case of the Life Guards, and is twelve inches long between the loops, and cut one inch and a quarter wide. The throat band is twenty-one or twenty-two inches long, exclusive of the buckles and three-quarters of an inch wide. The cheeks are about eight inches from buckle to buckle, with billots about seven inches, three inches and a half being turned up to the buckles after passing through the eyes of the bit; the whole to be cut for three-quarter buckles. The nose-band should be about twenty-three to twenty-four inches long, and one inch and a quarter wide. The bit is a "pad-bit" and mounted with handsome brass bosses, bearing the Royal crest in the centre – viz. a lion on a crown, surrounded by motto – to correspond with the rosettes. A strong black leather head-collar (similar to a stable-collar) is used with the bridle, one inch and three-eighths wide, to the middle square of which a strong steel chain (with rings and tee-piece) is attached by a swivel spring hook; this chain is passed round the off side of the neck to a leather loop, on the near side of the saddle attached to the holster strap. The bridoon rings have tee-pieces and links to attach them to cheek squares of the head-collar, which is provided with loops to slip one end of the tees into. The reins to be cut seven-eighths to three-quarters of an inch wide, and eight feet long; they should be provided with a sliding loop and stop; the billots about six inches. The bridoon reins about seven feet six inches long, as the above. For dress purposes there is a head and rein for bridoon, covered with oak pattern lace.' See colour plate, drum horses of the Household Cavalry.

The U.P. bridle of 1885 shows little change and the bridle entitled 'Present Date' and still in use is even simpler. It came in in 1902 with a white head rope which had replaced the chain in 1891. The U.P. bit shown separately and marked '1924' is the reversible elbow pattern which can be used with the bars or cheeks

T   207

turned either way. It is made in three sizes, usually with a smooth mouth piece, though it can be issued with the mouth piece 'twisted on one side'. There is a port to the mouth piece and it is called the 'Portmouth bit'. This type of bit, which combines the snaffle or bridoon and the curb, has been widely used by civilians, especially for polo for many years. Made with a jointed mouth piece and called a Pelham, it is a most unsatisfactory one. With a solid mouth piece, with or without a port, it was very widely used by Colonial mounted units and was usually known as a Portsmouth, although sometimes as a straight mouthed Pelham. Plate 91 shows a Portsmouth with the very simple form of bridle shown in Plate 19 and used from *c.*1900 onwards. Plate 19 has the U.P. Reversible bit. An obvious advantage of the single mouth piece is the facility it gives for watering a horse with the bit in place, in an emergency.[53]

REFERENCES

1 Alderson, *Pink and Scarlet*, pp. 200 to 203, where the need for a saddle with a tree is discounted and Pocock, *The Frontiersman's Pocket Book*, pp. 162 to 167.

2 Alderson, p. 200, Pocock, p. 161.

3 Burn, *Notes on Transport and Camel Corps*, p. 48.

4 Ward, *Wellington's Headquarters*, p. 97 and footnote. From this authority came also the details of the Cavalry Forge evolved during the Peninsular Campaign and noted on the next page.

5 Maguire, *Strategy and Tactics in Mountain Ranges*, pp. 126, 127. The officer was General Sir William Eyre and the occasion the Eighth Kaffir War in South Africa of 1851.

6 Ward, *sup. cit.*, pp. 200, 201. The saddles were also known as 'cradles'. There was an explanation of the term 'Devonshire Crooks' in *Country Life* (26/IX/1961) by Hoole Jackson. In Cassell's *Peninsula Portrait*, O.U.P. 1963, on p. 115 is a note on the same pattern being used by Spanish farmers in 1812.

7 *Aide Mémoire to the Military Sciences*, 1st Ed., Volume II, p. 423; *The Mule for Burden*, by Colonel R. Alderson, R.E.

8 *Report on the Otago Saddle*, 1865 by Deputy Commissary General J. W. Baily.

9 Lucas, *Camp Life and Sport in South Africa*, p. 60.

10 *Record of the Expedition to Abyssinia*, 1870. Volume I, p. 61.

11 Army Equipment, 1865, Part II. Military Train, p. 47, under the heading of 'First Reserve'.

12 Burn, *sup. cit.*, p. 39.

13 Military Artificers Handbook, 1915, p. 115.

14 Burn, *sup cit.*, p. 37.

15 *Manual of Horsemastership*, p. 57, Section 25. List of Changes, November 1904, number 12,462.

16 *Manual of Saddles and Sore Backs*, p. 15.

17 Notes supplied by Brigadier Clabby, referring to the Campaign in Italy.

18 Correspondence with Lieut Colonel Westmorland, late of the Canadian Forces, who has had great experience in pack transport and was responsible for Plate 48, which shows the Mark V U.P. saddle being used by Number I Pack Train in 1943 during training in the Rocky Mountains.
Plates 38, 40, 41, 44a, 45, 46, 47, and 48 show Pack Saddles.

19 The early accounts of mountain gun equipment are to be found in Volume II of *Aide Mémoire to the Military Sciences*, published in 1852, pp. 409, 413 and the illustrations in Volume I, Plate 23 'Carriages', Volume II, Plate LV on p. 35 for the Spanish equipment.

    Major Parrino, *Introduction to Pack Transport and Pack Artillery*, has useful notes on early British practice and on the whole subject. The author is greatly indebted to Mr C. H. Stewart, Chief Librarian, National Defence H.Q. Library, Ottawa, Canada, for intensive help with the whole question of pack-saddles.

    The Record of the Expedition to Abyssinia, Volume I, p. 61, and numbers of the *Illustrated London News* of 1868 give full details of the 7-pounder batteries used in that campaign.

    The article by Major General Sir Stanley von Donop, 'Artillery Equipments Used During the last 25 Years', in Volume L, No. 12, 1924, *Journal of the Royal Artillery Institute*, p. 479, refers generally. As do the Military Artificers Handbook, editions of 1899 and 1915. Brigadier General C. A. L. Graham's, *The History of the Indian Mountain Artillery*, has been quoted in the text.

20 Artillerists Handbook of Reference, p. 234.

21 Philipson & Nimschivitch, p. 51 *et seq.*

22 Manual of Artillery Exercises, p. 187.

23 Hutchinson, *Machine Guns*, p. 256.

24 JAHR, Volume XXXV, p. 44 *et seq.*

25 Hogg, p. 40.

26 Hogg, p. 99.

27 From Dr R. J. Hetherington of Birmingham. Sent by Mr B. T. Hinchley.

28 The catalogues of some of the firms working today are most useful. Plates 17, 18 and 19 are taken from them.

29 *Charles the First's Waggon Master General*, Oxfordshire Record Society, 1961, p. 16.

30 List of Changes, 1885, 1886, p. 61, illustrations of animal in ordinary shafts, a contractor's drawing of civilian harness, no traces. Still used on farm carts in the South of England and presumably everywhere. Notes from Mr R. Scurfield and various ex-carters. A tug can be a short length of chain or rope or a short strap connecting two longer pieces. A shaft tug is the thick round band on each side of the saddle taking the shafts. Sometimes lined with iron. The word 'shaft' is usually omitted, causing confusion. Plates 24 and 29.

31 Gilbey, *Horses, Past and Present*, p. 16.

32 *Aide Mémoire*, Volume II, pp. 512, 513. *Ordnance, British*, by Colonel Cater, R.A.

33 Page 86.

34 *Aide Mémoire*, Volume I, 'Carriage', Plate 24.

35 Volume I, p. 164. Ill.

36 JAHR, Volume II, p. 113.

37 As 32, but p. 515.

38 By Lady Butler, entitled *Halt on a Forced March*. The harness and saddles are very carefully drawn in.

39 Manual of Artillery Exercises, *Field*, 1875, p. 181. Four Horses Abreast.

40 Jocelyn, pp. 12, 22. Harness of black leather, gun teams blinkers. 1853 Dec. Brown leather harness. No blinkers. Blinkers retained in India for some time.

41 Griffiths, p. 157.

42 Field Artillery Service Handbook 1883, and Manual of Artillery Exercises, 1881.

43 Longstaff and Atteridge, *Book of the Machine Gun*, p. 14, illustrations.

44 Jackson, *A Soldier's Diary in South Africa*, p. 118.

45 The 1-pounder automatic Vickers Maxim used by the Artillery on both sides.

46 From about 1840 to 1860, both dates are problematical, drivers had swords on the saddle in the R.H.A. Plates 27b and 28a. Before and after these dates drivers were unarmed. The killing of the drivers of N/5 R.A. at Isandhlwana on 22.1.1879 during the Zulu War led to their being issued with revolvers.

47 Childers, *In the Ranks of the C.I.V.* Childers was a driver in the Honourable Artillery Company's Battery, forming part of the City Imperial Volunteers, a London volunteer unit raised for the South African War.

48 *Journal of the Royal Artillery Institution*, Volume L, No. 12, p. 475.

49 Army Service Corps Training, Part III. Transport 1911.

50 Military Artificers Handbook, 1915, p. 87.

51 From a series of notes dated 20th June, 1962, sent to the author by Brigadier J. H. S. Lacey, O.B.E., Secretary of the R.E. Institution.

52 Burne, *The Noble Duke of York*, p. 125.

53 This section is based on: *Manual of Horsemastership*, pp. 45–50. Aldershot Lectures 1891, Section VI, by Veterinary Surgeon Major F. Smith, 'Bits and Bitting', and many notes from the late Mr L. E. Buckell.

CHAPTER SEVEN

The Cavalry Seat, 'Furniture' used with Saddlery; The Horse's Tail and Coat; and Farriery

THERE is an old saying, 'the science of riding is balance, grip and stirrups'. Whether in 1965 people will admit that riding is a science is beside the point, at any rate there is no doubt of the correctness of the adage.

Balance can be taken for granted, without it no one can 'ride' anything from a bicycle to an elephant and balance can only be learnt, usually the hard way. Grip is a question of muscle and training and once the cavalry recruit had passed out of the riding school and been accepted by his squadron leader as a trained man his grip could be taken for granted and the riding muscles in his thighs would be well developed. In the course of this chapter will be found a description of a period when he was not supposed to grip! It was not a satisfactory effort on the part of those who were responsible for the equitation of the British Army! Whether a man rode by balance and grip, as he should, or by balance alone, he still had to rely to a great extent on the stirrups and it was their position on the saddle and their use that was the subject of so much argument and, it should be added, false reasoning for over a century.

The arguments of today over the pros and cons of the Forward Seat as used in racing and show jumping do not concern us; they go back at least to 1891, when an expert wrote dismissing the method as impossible for cavalry.[1]

There have always been two schools, each with its own advocates, the one favouring the long stirrup and the straight leg and the other the short stirrup with the leg bent. There are many variations of each method and neither can claim complete success.

A man who has to ride long distances day after day, especially, as cavalry usually had to do, at a walk, likes to have a long stirrup with his leg more or less straight. This may and very often does entail using a saddle with a short seat, measured from the top of the front arch or pommel to the top of the rear arch or cantle. The straighter the leg the shorter the saddle can be and in most cases the more the rider prefers what was once called a 'high mounting' saddle with a deep dip. The dip is the length of the perpendicular dropped from the line between pommel to cantle to the lowest part of the seat. The deeper the dip the greater the amount of support given by the front and rear arches. Plate 1 refers for the medium bent leg seat in Plate 2.

The fully armoured horseman of the Middle Ages is the prototype; his successor today is the Western cowhand of North America, who from Mexico to Canada rides in the familiar stock saddle with a horn on the pommel to take the Lariat or Lasso (see Plate 93). Intermediate between the two is the modern soldier using a saddle like the Universal Pattern of today, which has a considerable amount of dip and is well raised off the horse like the two older types. The polo player, hunting man or jockey dislikes being raised above the horse and so uses a saddle as flat as possible, which would not allow of any weight except that of the rider being carried on it. In order to carry the weights considered necessary for cavalry there must be a clearer and more open space along the horse's spine than is the case with the civilian saddle. Hence officers on the Staff, who need not carry much on their saddles, have always tended to use hunting saddles.

The school of cavalry officers who favoured a shorter stirrup liked to teach their men to sit in what may be called a normal position, as shown by the mounted figures on the Parthenon Frieze. They sat further back and the short stirrup gave them more power to use their weapons. When British cavalry, riding with the long stirrup, met the Sikh irregular horsemen in the eighteen-forties of last century, they found that their adversaries using short stirrups had a considerable advantage in a mêlée.

In Great Britain the change-over, which began in 1780 when men started riding fast to hounds over fences, led to many men taking their stirrups up from the old Cavalry seat and this did not necessitate any change of saddle, for the flat-seated close-fitting type used for hunting, racing and hacking can be used with varying lengths of stirrup. Mention has been made of Staff officers using this saddle and so did many Rough Riders in Cavalry regiments when breaking officers' chargers or tackling a queer-tempered remount. The Australians and New Zealanders, magnificent horsemen, like a slightly deeper seat to their saddles. Figure 16 in the chapter on 'Saddles' shows the Australian pattern. As a rough guide to the difference between the two seats, the straight leg and the bent knee fashion, it is convenient to accept the practice of the early part of last century, when men pulled up their leathers two holes or $2\frac{1}{2}$ inches from one seat to the other.[2]

The length of the seat of the saddle varied from $16\frac{3}{4}$ inches with the Hussar type to 20 inches in the Universal Pattern of today. The extra space provided makes a great difference to the way a man sits and allows, as is correct, of his not sitting too far back, provided he leaves a little space between himself and the cantle.

The rough-and-ready and perfectly correct method of buckling a stirrup leather to the proper length for the ordinary hunting seat was to put the tips of the fingers of the left hand on the stirrup bar on the saddle, raising the stirrup itself with the right hand and putting the bottom of the iron in the left armpit touching the side.

The illustration from Grose's *Antiquities*, Plate 2, shows an armoured cavalryman of 1640 with a well-built-in saddle, as the expression went, and the leg bent in a natural position. The Duke of Newcastle, who wrote his once well-known book on *The Manner of Feeding, Dressing and Training of Horses for the Great Saddle and*

Fitting them for the Service of the Field in Time of War in 1667, was a very able exponent of manège work and of the Haute École system. He liked to ride with a straight leg with the heel well in and turned down lower than the toe. Probably the illustration mentioned above gives a picture of the seat generally adopted during the Civil War and in the succeeding period well into the eighteenth century. The drawings of saddles of the late seventeenth century, with one exception, do not show very short-seated saddles with a long stirrup and nor does Plate 8, of officers and a charger of Marlborough's day. The exception is the infantry officer's saddle of 1689 which looks as if the rider must have used a very long stirrup (Plates 4, 5 and 6).

There is not a great deal of evidence forthcoming before the publication in 1761 of a little book on *Military Equitation* by Henry, Earl of Pembroke. He commanded the Royals from 1764 to 1794 and his portrait, now at Windsor Castle, shows a natural seat with the knee very slightly bent and no exaggeration at all in the whole pose. He is riding with what was known as a double bridle with two bits and his bradoon, or snaffle rein, is hardly held looser than the bit or curb rein, in contradistinction to the established practice of riding almost entirely on the curb. He looks like the best type of cavalryman, entirely at ease and yet very smart. The above notes are intended as a prelude to his reference to 'the wretched system of horsemanship at present prevailing in the army', and to 'the common method of putting a man on a rough trotting horse, to which he is obliged to stick with all his might of arms and legs'. Probably a very fair description of the methods of a certain type of instructor is intended; such men were common long after the time of the writer. This Colonel of one of the best Regiments in the Army, the Royal Dragoons, originally raised for the defence of Tangier, then goes on to say that 'most of the officers, when on horseback, are a disgrace to themselves and the animals they ride'. Doubtless he is not referring to his own Regiment. An Army Order of 1742 prohibited men from riding too long, which Pembroke is certainly not doing; and from 1750, when Light Dragoons were first introduced into the Army, a different school of horsemanship came into being and held its own until after the Napoleonic Wars. The Light Dragoon saddle had a seat measuring 22 inches and the trooper was instructed to have his stirrups of such a length that when he stood up in them there should be four inches of clearance between his fork and the saddle. This was practically what became later on known as the hunting seat, though the stirrup was shorter than that commonly in use by civilians. Up to 1780, when riding fast to hounds came into vogue, civilians had taken fences at a slow pace; they then began to ride fast at them, as did the Light Dragoons in due course.

Apparently some of the Heavy Cavalry Regiments followed Pembroke's method and pulled their stirrups up, for in 1773 the 1st Dragoon Guards, the K.D.G.s, were reported on as riding too short. In 1796 a Fencible Regiment is reported on as riding too long in contradistinction to Pembroke's old regiment, the 1st Royal Dragoons, who were 'keeping to the King's order as regards length of stirrups'.[3] In 1797 Lieut Colonel W. Tyndale, 1st Life Guards, published a book on Cavalry Equitation[4] in which he states that the Riding Masters of the Cavalry were teaching a seat which 'poked the man's chin up in the air, squeezes his arms and elbows close to his sides, like a fowl trussed for the spit; pulls his legs down straight from the hips, so that they hang over the saddle like a pair of tongs, throwing the man on his fork'. An illustration shows a trooper in this position and another one shows what the author considers the correct seat with the knee very slightly bent and the man sitting as described and shown in the portrait of Lord Pembroke. The 'tongs' or 'scissors' seat will be met with again.

In 1805 a civilian riding master, John Adams, published a book called *The Analysis of Horsemanship* and described the hunting seat as 'riding in the stirrups . . . the first thing to be considered is their length. They must not be too short though they should be somewhat shorter than those recommended for road or military riding.'

It is evident that there were two schools of thought in the Army, the one favoured by a proportion of commanding officers serving in Great Britain, who liked the trooper to ride as long as possible, and the other, adopted by officers in the field, who obviously felt that this seat gave a man insufficient control in combat. Thus in 1803 at the battle of Laswaree in India, Colonel Thomas Pakenham, who was commanding a cavalry brigade and was about to go into action against both infantry and guns, ordered the brigade to go threes about and take up their stirrups two holes. They then went about again and made a most successful charge. In other words Pakenham put into practice exactly what Adams suggested two years later.[5] It would be of interest to know if Adams knew the story of what happened at Laswaree. Colonel Tyndale, previously mentioned, was of the opinion that the seat he recommended with the knee slightly bent and the man sitting squarely in his saddle, 'sitting plump' is the expression used, 'so far from spoiling the hunting seat will give it more force'. He also states that the Light Dragoons mounted quicker and with less motions than the Heavy Cavalry.

Contemporary illustrations of the period of the Peninsular War from 1808 to 1814 show Hussar Regiments riding with moderately short stirrups on active service and there is an account of an officer of Hussars who, when wounded at Waterloo, took up his stirrups two holes to the hunting seat before riding to the rear to get his wound dressed. Obviously he wanted a stronger seat. It is not out of place to note that in 1930, over a hundred years later, stirrups two inches shorter than used out hunting were advised for riding in a Point-to-Point.

The account of the 16th Light Dragoons at Llerena in Spain on the 11th April, 1812, charging French cavalry, describes them as coming down hill at a trot, jumping a small stone wall in line and then riding home.[6] They were presumably not riding with the very long stirrup and the 'tongs' seat.

Colonel Tyndale was not in favour of training a remount in the manner practised in the manège; he considered that the troop horse should merely be 'prepared for the squadron', as he puts it. He expected the men to sleep on their horses, 'when fatigued', and states it was an undenied fact that they did. He accordingly wished them to be able to support their backs on the rear pack which suggests that the men of his own regiment, the 1st Life Guards, did in fact sit well and squarely in their saddles. While no one of experience will query that it is comparatively easy to go to sleep on a night march without one's horse quitting the ranks, it seems surprising that it was considered a regular thing for men to sleep in their saddles in peace time, though the author does not specify the occasions when they did so.[4]

In those days practically all Army officers would have ridden and a very large majority would have hunted. A proportion, especially in the Cavalry, would have had a certain amount of instruction in the manège as practised by the Haute École system, now in 1964 revived in Great Britain. It had never died out altogether on the Continent and the very upright seat with the long stirrup leather was the natural result of Continental influence. But the average horseman of any age is usually no formalist and men who ride constantly on different sized and gaited horses and ponies get into the habit of taking their leathers up or letting them down according to circumstances. This is especially the case with men who have habitually to ride long distances. The Duke of Wellington, a workmanlike and indefatigable horseman and one who was accustomed to cover very long distances at a fast pace, is an example of a man who, though originally educated at the military school at Angers in France, noted for its fine manège, never practised high-school horsemanship. He sat very upright, using an Hussar saddle, which had a very short seat, riding with a long stirrup, as would be natural, but never with the exaggerated seat of the manège. He always rode horses of hunter type, good walkers, but without any 'parade' action.[7]

On the other hand men like the Marquis of Anglesey and Lord Combermere, both very distinguished cavalry generals, rode perfectly broken horses trained in Haute École methods with very long stirrups. Sometimes these were 3 inches longer than those used out hunting and only the toe touched the stirrup iron. These were the two schools of thought and though, as was natural during the long French Wars, the simpler and less exaggerated style of riding was in general use in the field, the pendulum was almost bound to swing away from commonsense methods once the general peace which came in after Waterloo took men's minds, or some of them, away from the practical side of things.

The Duke of York, for so many years Commander-in-Chief, favoured a seat with a slightly bent knee, not at all exaggerated. His views were put forward in a publication by Major J. G. Peters, a Cavalry officer on the Unattached List who was Superintendent to the Riding Establishment of the British Cavalry in London. Peters' book, 'Respectfully Dedicated' to the Duke, was called *A Treatise on Equitation* and dated 1817. The illustration shows a seat without stirrups with the leg very straight, so that a line passing from the rider's nose to the wrist (of the left hand holding the reins) and running behind the knee would cut the sole of the foot. With stirrups the knee was to be slightly bent, the line should run from the nose at its base, pass across the middle of the forearm of the left hand and fall in front of the heel. The difference, if any, between Lieut Colonel Tyndale, Major Peters and the commanding officers of cavalry in the field was very slight, but once a war, especially a long one, is over the military mind is all too prone to revert to the ways of peace. So in 1819 an official publication appeared, under the direction of the Adjutant-General, which put the whole question of Military Equitation on a firm if unsatisfactory basis. The seat differs little from that laid down by Major Peters, who was responsible for the plates at the end of the book, but the following points are stressed – the man is never to grip with the knee, he may use the calves of his leg as a support to the aids, i.e. when turning the troop horse, the inside of the thighs should be turned to the sides of the horse and placed flat on the saddle, the heels should be down and the toes raised. The seat must be preserved by balance chiefly and not by the pressure of the knees, the knee should be a little bent and the upper edge of the bottom bar of the stirrup should be a finger's breadth below the inner ankle bone.

The most surprising detail of these official instructions is that it is laid down that with Hussar saddles the stirrups should be one inch longer than with Heavy Cavalry. That is to say that the Light Cavalryman, whose aim it was to cross any country and any obstacles, was to ride in an even more constrained position than the Heavy Dragoon, whose place was in line of battle or on the march. Any of the numerous prints published between the issue of this Drill Book and the eighteen sixties will show the above seat. Comments on it will be found later on in this chapter. Both emanate from serving officers with experience in the field in other parts of the world. In parenthesis it may be of interest to note that the trooper in 1819 was taught to mount on either side with both carbine and sword slung on his person, a sensible precaution when a man may have to mount in a hurry on the off side horse of a group of 'threes', later 'fours', placed with his near side as often happened very close to the next horse; this would have been when a unit was acting dismounted.

Unpractical as this seat may seem today, it was easily surpassed by the most rigid form of the so-called 'German', more properly 'Prussian', variation. Although Frederick the Great of Prussia (1712–86) had seen to it that his cavalry, justly renowned all over Europe, had ridden with a more natural seat, those responsible for training the Prussian cavalry during the Napoleonic wars adopted the extravagantly long stirrup characteristic of the school who believed in training the troop horse in the Dressage or Haute École system of the riding school. The Prince Regent, afterwards George IV, had always been impressed with Prussian ideas and not long after the end of the wars brought over a Prussian Riding Master and employed him in training a small body of British cavalrymen in the use of this Continental seat. The stirrups were let down until the leg was as straight as it could possibly be and the men rode on their forks and not on their buttocks with the result that so many of them were ruptured that the drills were discontinued. Sidney recorded this in his *Book of the Horse*, and states that his 'informant was the late R. B. Davis, the animal painter, who frequently witnessed this barbarous performance in the fields where Belgrave House now stands'. There were variations of this 'fork seat', as it was called; other names being 'the scissors' and more exactly 'the balance without clinging' method. The toe only could be in the stirrup with the heel well down and the leg in another version could be straight and stuck out well forward. This last extraordinary mode was called the 'tongs across a wall' seat. In these unofficial versions the man sat on his fork.

However impressive the Dressage system may be to watch, its value as a training for troop horses is not as great as it was once thought to be. One of the foremost exponents of the present day civilian 'forward seat', Captain V. S. Littauer, an ex-officer of Czarist Hussars, has recorded in his book *More About the Forward Seat* how impressed he was when, after he had passed out of a Cavalry riding school and learnt the methods of the Haute École, he saw Cossacks obtaining admirable results riding with a snaffle and no curb bit with their stirrups holed up short!

Very much the same seat, which gives the man armed with a sabre great power when delivering a cut when he does so standing up in his stirrups as already noted, was in use all over the East. As the historian of an Indian Silladar Cavalry Regiment, Probyn's Horse, wrote of the men when the regiment was raised, 'no man had the Cavalry seat, all were undeniable horsemen'. The truth of the whole matter is simply that men who have ridden well all their lives will be in fact 'undeniable horsemen', like those sowars of 1857, whatever seat they use.

In countries where very long distances have to be covered, day after day, the pace used is generally a canter, comfortable for both horse and rider. So some variation of the 'fork' seat is adopted, the man rides light and in other words has learnt to take as little out of his mount as possible; guides his pony by pressure of the reins on the neck and however strange he may look to eyes accustomed to other ways, does what he has to do in workmanlike fashion. A generation brought up on 'Western' film-shows need not be told that the cowboy rides with a straight leg, just as cavalry did at the start of last century and for fifty years afterwards. Cavalry in time rode otherwise and using lance and sabre in the ranks as they did, eventually had the leg more bent, and worked mainly at a trot, except when actually charging.

There was obviously a certain amount of doubt in our Service as to the correctness of the long stirrup and in 1819 stirrups were ordered to be lengthened. In 1832 they were to be shortened and in Spooner's 'Upright Series' of uniforms by Mansion & Eschauzier, 1833 to 1840, nearly all the officers are shown riding shorter though some of the men still have the long stirrup. Not until after the Crimean War was the long stirrup finally abandoned and men were no longer taught to ride on their fork. It was known to many officers as 'the Old German Seat', presumably from the fact, already mentioned, of the Prince Regent having imported a German Instructor for a short time. Colonel Valentine Baker (1827–87) has this to say of it: 'from long habit we have been taught to regard this as the military seat. It is certainly neither a graceful nor a comfortable one.'[8]

Another most unfortunate outcome of the mania for copying Continental military ideas was the Prince Regent's great liking for the tight clothing so popular

217

with the European armies, the French excepted. By the time he had succeeded to the throne as George IV, the Prince had put the cavalry into overalls strapped tight over Wellington boots, jackets without a crease fitting like gloves, and head-dresses so high that they could not be worn in a strong wind. It is hard to think of a cavalryman so strapped up that he could not mount on rough ground without help or use his weapons properly because of unwieldy headgear.

There follow two contemporary accounts of cavalry in the field, both in and out of action. The first was written by Captain Lucas of the Cape Mounted Riflemen on the Eastern Frontier of the Cape Colony in 1850. They were a Regular Regiment engaged in duties connected with keeping order on a turbulent border.[9] Lucas is describing the Brigadier commanding. 'The Major-General sat his horse like a pair of scissors with his toes well turned out, the instruction being to avoid clinging with the knees. In consequence men rode entirely by balance, and if a stirrup gave way or rough ground had to be crossed they were quite dependent on it. If a man with a seat of this kind was put upon a plain saddle he was quite helpless in time of difficulty. An officer who had served in the ranks of a Cavalry Regiment in England and had been a sergeant before he was commissioned, acknowledged that he had no seat on a plain saddle. The present military seat (written in 1878) which is in fact the hunting position with the knees tight to the saddle flaps and the legs taking their natural place, the feet not thrust quite so far into the stirrups as in hunting, but far enough to afford a good hold, differing again from the old seat where the point of the toe was only just allowed to touch it, is now all that can be desired, and at the same time neat and soldierly. Our Riding Master, who had a long experience in South Africa, though he was particular enough in the riding-school, did not for instance insist on our bumping the saddle, as it is termed, at the trot but allowed us to rise in the stirrups on the march as he said it was too fatiguing for men and horses in a hot climate.'

Rising in the stirrups at the trot was the civilian method, universally used as being both easy on the horse and comfortable for the rider. At about the time when Lucas states that at least one Riding Master was allowing the practice, Captain Nolan,[10] described as 'one of the best cavalry officers we ever had', stated that rising at the trot took less out of a man (he could have added 'and a horse') in fifty miles than bumping the saddle would in ten. He had served in the Austrian Cavalry, where the men were taught to rise. The procedure is perhaps simpler to learn than to describe; at each step of the horse the rider presses on the stirrups and straightens the thighs just enough to raise the body clear of the saddle when the horse is at the highest point of his stride. As the horse comes down before starting the next step the rider's body comes back into the saddle in time with the movement.

The soldier was taught to sit down in the saddle and remain in that position without moving at all. An old description says he must not cling with the knee but lean very slightly back from the perpendicular and preserve his balance. This was with the long stirrup. The writer adds 'the Dragoon bumps away on his sheepskin as best he can'.

The idea seems to have been that a body of troops looked much smarter sitting down to the trot and that if they rose the effect of each man bobbing up and down in time to his own horse's movements would not look well at all.

Unfortunately, as well as tiring the horse, the cavalry method was also very liable to cause a sore back. It was high time that the civilian method was introduced officially, although it was not until about 1878 that Sir John Watson, v.c., at that time commanding the 6th Duke of Connaught's Lancers, introduced rising in Indian Cavalry. It was taken up in the British Service not long after, bumping the saddle being retained for ceremonial occasions only.[11]

It must be added that men trained in the old method liked it well enough. There is on record an account of the Commanding Officer of a Cavalry Regiment in 1891 who still adhered to the practice of bumping the saddle. He was seen trotting and not rising in the saddle with his trumpeter coming on behind him rising in his stirrups as he was entitled to, the occasion not being a ceremonial parade.[1]

Rising at the trot was at one time known as 'posting' because it was used by postboys to lessen the fatigue of their long hours at this pace. Later it became known as the 'English trot' in contradistinction to the 'French trot', for in France they did not rise in their saddles for some considerable time.

Though not used officially there is a phase of the trot to which all men sit down. This is the very slow pace known as a 'hound's jog' and rising is not necessary. It is a pace of about 6 miles an hour, or rather less.

The illustration of Major General Sir George Cathcart (1794–1854) and his staff on active service in South Africa in 1852 (Plate 95), shows the two styles of riding as described by Lucas. Sir George, who had commanded a Cavalry Regiment, the King's Dragoon Guards, and was an accomplished horseman, is riding with the hunting seat and rising at the trot. In the letter which he sent home to Lady Cathcart with the painting he describes how his charger was trotting and keeping all the other horses at a gallop. The other officers in the group are using the long stirrup as laid down in the Regulations and the artist, Captain T. W. Goodrich, C.M.R., has put himself in at the extreme right rear of the party.[12]

The escort in the background are also using the long stirrup. They are men of the 12th Royal Lancers and are wearing the tightly strapped down overalls already mentioned. Shortly after the picture was painted two squadrons of the Regiment were in action against superior numbers of Basuto horsemen on the 20th December, 1852, at the Berea Mountain. The Basuto, described by Cathcart as 'equal to Cossacks', were well mounted and carried battle-axes as well as assegais. The Lancers had captured cattle from the Basuto and had got broken up into small parties driving them. The Basuto counter-attacked, drove in the rearguard and forced two of the small parties away to a flank. In some instances the troopers' horses fell – the going was very bad – and would not stand to be remounted with the enemy close behind. If a comrade did not come back to hold the horse of a dismounted man, the latter was invariably killed, as he could not mount in his tight overalls without help. Several men were killed in this way.[13] To such a pitch had training and uniform of Light Cavalry – Lancers were not yet classed as Medium Cavalry – brought our men.

After the Crimea (1854–5) the cavalry seat became modified and pictures show men riding with a seat indistinguishable from the hunting seat of the day. In a book published in 1878 are a series of drawings showing the correct hunting seat. It hardly differs at all from the position described further on as the Regulation military seat of 1875.

In spite of this the cavalry continued to be dressed in an unsuitable fashion for any sort of dismounted work and both Sir Henry Havelock in his book *The Three Main Military Questions of the Day*, published about 1870, and an officer of an Hussar Regiment, writing of the Afghan War of 1878, stated that the men were so hampered by their leg gear, overalls and tight riding boots, that they were kept in their saddles as much as possible.[14]

This reluctance to dismount continued to be a noticeable feature for the next thirteen years at least, when the author of *Saddles and Sore Backs*, Veterinary Surgeon Major F. Smith, wrote about the practice as being in the highest degree unsatisfactory. He said that there was a great dislike of dismounting the men in order to rest the horses, 'which were generally looked upon as machines'. He was at the time a Professor in the Army Veterinary School at Aldershot and his lectures, which were printed, are a most valuable contribution to our knowledge of the conditions of his day. He wrote: 'We have a singular notion in cavalry that it is a dishonour for a man to walk or be seen off his horse. The sooner we get rid of such ideas the better for horses' legs and backs. I see no reason why it should not be a recognized thing in our service for men to lead their horses for a part of the way in order to afford the animal the needful rest he requires.' How or when the idea that it was wrong for a cavalryman to dismount became prevalent it would not now be easy to determine. It may go back to the days of armour or of half armour, when a man had a tremendous weight to hoist into a narrow saddle. It may have been encouraged by the necessity for vedettes remaining mounted on account of their being better able to see. Probably also the height of the rear pack with the carbine butt hanging beyond it made a tired man unwilling to go to the trouble of dismounting and mounting again.

It is perhaps a fair question whether the reluctance of the average hunting man, wearing smart, tightly cut breeches and boots, to dismount except to change horses may not have influenced the officers. It is a very different thing for a man out for a day's hunting to echo the boast of Mr Jorrocks' once well-known huntsman James Pigg, 'Ar niver gets off',[15] than for the same man to keep his troopers sitting on their weary horses when halted. In time, with the advent of looser and more sensible kit, the practice died down and the Regular Cavalryman got off and on his horse as readily as the irregular, whose tradition in most countries had been for years to spare his horse as much as possible. Tradition is one of the most valuable assets an army can have, but unluckily bad ones are clung to just as determinedly as good ones, perhaps as firmly by those in high places as by the officers and men of the regiments themselves. No doubt the practice of dismounting the men whenever possible instead of keeping them in their saddles varied from one regiment to another, but there is also certainly no doubt that a competent authority thought that the subject should be publicly ventilated. Hence the paragraph in the official manual on *Saddles and Sore Backs*. In his book on the *Desert Mounted Corps* in the Near East in 1916–17, Colonel Preston noted that a Composite Regiment of French Cavalry attached to the Corps practically never dismounted their men during operations. He added that they had a very high percentage of sore backs. Earlier in this chapter an officer of Household Cavalry is quoted as stating that our men were accustomed to sleep on their horses. This was also done by the French during the same period; in fact a French author has recorded that many of their cavalry slept in the saddle the night before Waterloo.

The chapter on Equitation in the Manual of Artillery Exercises of 1875 gives the following details (on page 118) of the military seat as taught at the time: 'The body balanced in the middle of the saddle; head erect and square to the front; shoulders well thrown back; chest advanced; small of the back slightly bent forward; upper part of the arms hanging down straight from the shoulder; elbows bent and lightly closed to the hips; little fingers on a level with the elbows; wrist rounded, throwing the knuckles to the front and thumbs pointing inwards across the body; each hand holding a rein. . . . The thigh well stretched down from the hip; the flat of the thigh to the saddle; knees a little bent, legs hanging straight down from the knee and near the horse's sides; heels well stretched down, the toes raised from the insteps and as near the horse's side as the heels. A plummet line from the front point of the shoulder should fall an inch behind the heel. This is the position halted or at the walk; at a trot the body must be inclined a little back, the whole figure pliant and accompanying the movements of the horse. The position with stirrups is the same as without, the heels well stretched down and lower than the toes. The foot kept in its place by the play of the ankle and instep, the stirrup being under the ball of the foot.' Drivers rode a hole shorter than gunners.

There is not a great deal of difference in the instructions given in Cavalry Drill, 1898; it says 'the man must be taught to turn the flat part of the thigh from the hip towards the horse's side and not to merely bend the foot inwards from ankle or knee. Riding with saddle and stirrups the knee should be a little more bent and a plummet line from the point of the knee should drop directly on the ball of the foot. A man with a thick thigh requires slightly shorter stirrups.' The illustration of a sowar of the 18th Bengal Lancers, c.1898, refers. (Plate 89.)

From the 'seventies a new type of mounted man had been evolved–the Mounted Infantryman, the direct descendant of the Dragoon of the seventeenth century. Raised from Infantry Regiments and at first trained *ad hoc* in whatever country his services were required, he might or might not have come under a Cavalry N.C.O. In Great Britain and India the training in equitation would be on cavalry lines but wherever the work was done the M.I. became sufficiently efficient to cross any kind of country in which they had to operate. The illustration of Sergeant Seymour of the 2nd Battalion the Gordon Highlanders, the old 92nd (Plate 71), shows a man trained in Great Britain. If the toe is a little further forward than the regulations laid down, there is no doubt that he looks well on his cob.

There is a note in a technical publication *The Military Artificers Handbook* of 1915 which reads: 'short stirrups place the weight of the rider too far back in the saddle, causing the weight to press unduly on the horse, forcing the saddle forward and allowing it to tilt readily, causing galls'. Seven years earlier the issue of the 1908 thrusting sword had given the cavalryman a weapon with which he could outreach an enemy lancer by $1\frac{1}{2}$ inches when standing up in his stirrups and leaning forward. Presumably John Adams would have said that the men were 'riding in the stirrups' as he had advised in 1805. The stirrups were taken up two holes.

Finally we come to the *Manual of Horsemastership*, the official handbook published in 1937, which embodies the lessons of the past and takes us on to what is practically the end of mounted troops, except for some isolated instances. The instructions for fitting stirrups are as follows: 'first allow the man to sit loosely in the saddle and let his legs hang freely down, then let him squeeze the saddle lightly with his knees and raise his toes, and then adjust the stirrups so that the bars are in line with the toes of his boots. The stirrups are intended to be an aid and convenience to the rider; if they are too long, he will lose his seat by leaning forward in his endeavour to retain them; if they are too short the seat becomes cramped and the rider is prevented from using the lower part of the leg correctly.

'To secure the maximum benefit of "grip", the instructor should place the pupil's leg in the saddle with his knees at the height best suited to his build and in placing the leg should draw back the large muscle at the back of the leg to the rear, so placing the flat portion of the thigh against the saddle, from which position the maximum power is gained. . . . The leg from the knee downwards should hang slightly behind the perpendicular. The inside portion automatically comes in contact with the flap of the saddle and this contact can be developed into grip, care being taken that only the inside portion of the calf is allowed to be used for this purpose.

'Care should be taken to fit the stirrups to the length suitable to the build of the rider. A man with a short thick leg requires his stirrups shorter in proportion than does a man of equal height with a flat thigh and a thin leg. In riding at attention the feet should normally be pressed home in the stirrups; in ceremonial the stirrups should be on the ball of the foot (except at the gallop); at all other times it should be left to the discretion of the rider. A good position depends on balance, a firm seat and a complete suppleness of the whole body.'

Although not included in the Manual, the following notes on tent pegging and tilting at the ring (known colloquially as 'peg and ring') given by an old hand may round off the above description of the modern cavalry seat. The stirrups were taken up two holes and the body brought forward until the eye could see the point of the toe in the stirrup. For practice with the lance it was usual to keep the ball of the foot on the bar of the stirrup and not push the foot right home. This was because in the

PLATE 82   Charger, senior British officer, India, *c.*1806.

U

PLATE 83   9th Lancers during the siege of Delhi in 1857.
From a contemporary water colour by Captain Roger Upton.

MUMMOO·PAINTER

PLATE 84   Officer's charger, probably stud-bred, *c*.1871.

PLATE 85(a) Turcoman horses in action.

PLATE 85(b)   Turcoman horses saddled up.

PLATE 86
Infantry officer's
Arab charger, 1894.

PLATE 87   A six-year-old Gulf Arab stallion, 1931.

PLATE 88   Bikanir Camel Corps in 1898.

PLATE 89   Sowar, 18th Bengal Lancers, 1897.

PLATE 91   A 'Waler'; Australian troop horse, *c.*1898.

PLATE 90   An Indian country-bred troop-horse of 1899 on service in South Africa.

PLATE 93   The California stock-saddle used from 1878 to 1919 by the Canadian Forces.

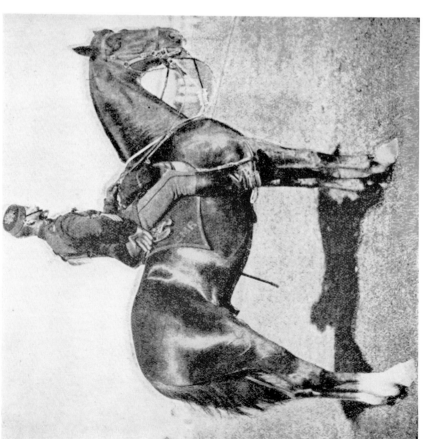

PLATE 92   A New Zealand troop horse of 1897.

PLATE 94   Troop horse, Canadian Regular Forces, *c*.1899.

PLATE 95   HQ Staff, South Africa, with escort of 12th Lancers on active service, 1852.

PLATE 96
Basuto pony, 1900.

PLATE 97
Two country-bred
South African
ponies, 1899.

PLATE 98   Argentine Troop Horse; South Africa, 1902.

PLATE 99   China Pony issued in North China, 1937.

PLATE 100   Percheron stallion bred in the U.S.A.

PLATE 101   Royal Artillery remounts from the U.S.A., 1916.

PLATE 102   Egyptian Cavalry horses, Syrian Arabs, 1896.

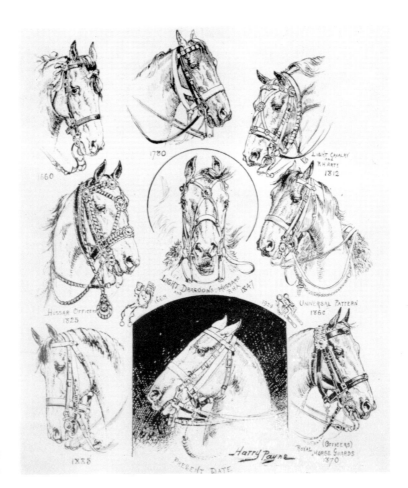

PLATE 103
British Army bits and bridles
from 1660 to 1960.

George R. I.

by J. Lambert Weston.
Folkestone.

PLATE 104   His Majesty King George V as Colonel-in-Chief, Scots Guards.

PLATE 105   General Officer's Shabraque of the period 1825–55.

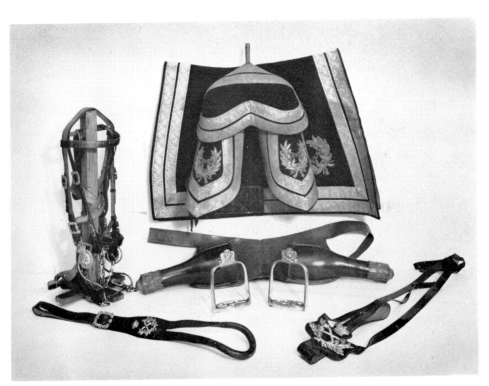

PLATE 106   Field Marshal's Horse Furniture, 1855–80.

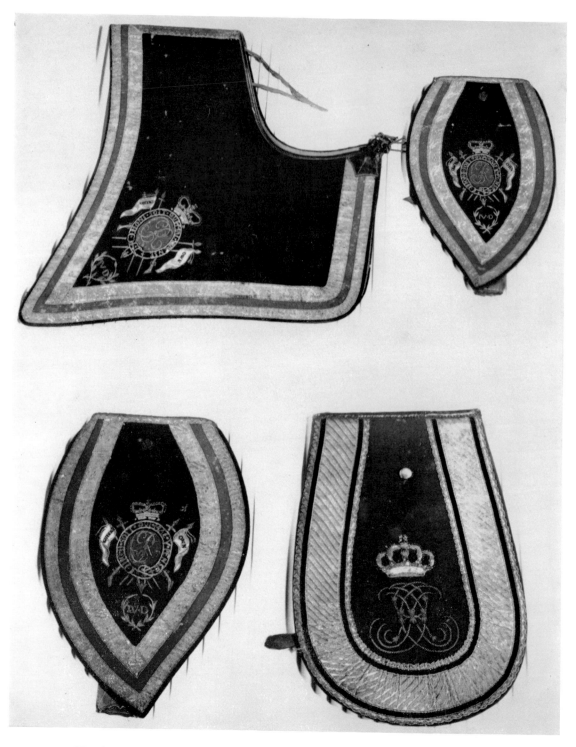

PLATE 107   Housing and holster covers of an officer of the 4th Queen's Own Dragoons (later Hussars).
1788 and 1795.

event of any mischance when taking the peg the foot would more easily come clear of the stirrup.[16] The lance was not only carried by the Lancer Regiments; in the 'nineties of the last century the front rank of all British Line Cavalry except Hussars carried it up to the early stages of the South African War. It was also normal practice for men not carrying the lance to practise with it.

The 'Cavalry Seat' had at last become perfectly natural and allowed the trooper to make use of his weapons and to save his horse and himself from undue fatigue in a way which was impossible as long as those responsible for teaching equitation clung to methods which had suited men in full armour well enough, but should have gone out with its disappearance.

'FURNITURE' – HOUSINGS, HOLSTER CAPS OR FLOUNCES, SHABRAQUES, SHEEP OR OTHER SKINS AND TRAPPINGS GENERALLY

Most of this section has been written from copious notes supplied by the late Mr L. E. Buckell, recognized as a leading authority on uniforms of the British Army. Fundamentally, except for the coverings which protected the pistols, carried for many years on the front of the saddle, from wet and damp, 'furniture' or 'trappings', whichever name is used, played very little useful part in the equipment of the horse soldier. They did, however, add very considerably to the attractiveness of his appearance, a very important consideration in the opinion of high authority and of many officers and men of all ranks in the past.

The blanket, horse-cloth, pad or numnah which protected the horse's back from abrasion by the saddle itself, when worn for long periods or when the animal was falling off in condition, have been described under 'Saddles'. Except the horse-cloth, which was sometimes ornamented, they were kept severely plain, as they had to be frequently scrubbed or at any rate washed. It is true that 'furniture' did serve some purpose in keeping the horse warm over the loins, a real consideration in cold weather and also prevented various articles of equipment from rubbing his skin, but most trappings were purely ornamental and added considerably to the weight carried – in 1815 the shabraque weighed some seven pounds.

The ornamentation varied from embroidery, gold or silver lace laid on in considerable quantities, regimental devices, crests, titles and battle honours, to coloured stripes in various patterns. The shape of the shabraque came in time to vary according to the type of cavalry or the arm of the service. The housings consisted of rectangles of cloth either covering the horse's back behind the saddle, and fastened to it by straps, or continued in some cases under or in others over the saddle to join on to the coverings of the holsters. If joined over the saddle, as was first done by Light Dragoons in 1759, the housing became in fact a shabraque.

Plates 3, 6, 8 (really a horse-cloth), 58–61, 106 and 107 show housings and 63 shows one embroidered both behind and before the saddle. Although the housing was generally speaking replaced by the shabraque in 1812 it was still worn in certain cases into the present century: Plate 104.

The holster cap or flounce came in very early (Plate 58). It was made of goat-skin or any skin with thick fur, such as bearskin, and was continued when wallets began to replace holsters in c.1840. It appears in many of the Plates. The pair were joined together and the caps might have a central piece shaped to cover both.

The shabraque or shabrack (both spellings were used) went right over the saddle, covering the horse from behind the saddle and going over the holsters. Officers' shabraques were lined with moleskin and sometimes had leather between the moleskin and the cloth of the upper layer, in which case there were three layers of material. Other ranks had their shabraques lined with heavy leather or rawhide. In the case of saddles with a spoon cantle a hole was cut in the shabraque for the spoon to go through: see Plate 65.

Up to 1805 the skin covering the holsters normally did not extend over the seat of the saddle, though Plate 58 shows one that does. In 1805 the newly formed Hussar Regiments were issued with sheepskins covering the shabraque from above the holsters to behind the cantle; officers of these units had leopard skins or cheetah skins instead of sheepskins. These skins could all be worn with or without the shabraque and though they further reduced the space available in the seat of the saddle, they did provide a satisfactory surface for getting a more secure seat when riding with a very long stirrup than the slippery leather of the saddle itself. Plate 61 shows the sheepskin with a housing, Plates 66 to 69 as worn with the shabraque and Plate 18 as worn by itself. The surcingle, sometimes reinforced by special straps, kept the shabraque and sheepskin in position.

In 1812 all cavalry were given shabraques and sheep- or lambskins, either black or white. One or the other or both were worn in different orders of dress.

A description of the shabraque and lambskin used by the 2nd Life Guards in 1860 follows. It is taken from the *Carriage Builders and Harness Makers Art Journal* and goes into detail: 'The whole of the seat of the saddle, the valise, cloak and holsters are covered with a black Ukraine lamb-skin; this is kept in place by a brown holder surcingle, $2\frac{1}{4}$ inches wide and 5 feet 8 inches long with a strap 1 foot 8 inches long and 1 inch wide. For state purposes a shabraque is used, made of fine blue cloth, cut to regimental pattern, to cover the saddle holsters etc. – coming down behind to a point over the flanks of the horse – bordered all round with very wide scarlet cloth, upon which rich old pattern double gold lace, $2\frac{1}{2}$ inches wide, is sewn; the Royal crest, star of the Garter and two scrolls with 'Peninsula' and 'Waterloo' on them are richly embroidered on each of the four corners; this is lined with serge and stiffened with black leather at the wearing parts. In this regiment there is very little difference between the style of the appointments of the troopers and the officers; the differences are that the troopers have holster-wallets instead of pistol-holsters. They wear upon all occasions white sheepskin covers for their saddles.' See Plate 66 for an officer of a slightly later period, and also the colour plate of the drum horses of the Household Cavalry.

The shabraque of the 10th Hussars of the same period, *c.*1860, is described as 'of fine blue cloth, made to fit the seat of the saddle with a hole to let the cantle (technically the spoon) through. It is ornamented with two rows of gold lace all round, with "V.R." and an Imperial crown embroidered in gold on the front corners. The hind corners, or points, have the Prince of Wales feathers with motto surmounted by an Imperial crown; under that a scroll, with "The Prince of Wales Own" upon it and "10" in the centre; below that, at the extreme point, the letter "H" – the whole handsomely embroidered in gold and silver. The shabraque is lined with strong fustian enamelled cloth and leather at the wearing parts and made up with straps, loops and strings, where required. With this a cheetah skin is used, cut to regulation shape to cover the cloak (rolled) and valise, edged all round with cloth and gold fringe; these together are used for review and dress purposes. The surcingle buckles over the whole. For marching order an entire cheetah skin is used – the head, paws and tail being stuffed soft (Plate 18); the head has a false tongue and glass eyes and is tied on the crupper, a hole being cut in the shoulder of the skin to let the cantle through and two holes over the holsters, the fore legs hanging on both sides. The hind legs hang on each side in front and are tied to the breastplate straps. The tail hangs loosely on the near side of the neck, the whole also secured by the surcingle. On all occasions the troopers use a shabraque, with woollen embroidery and lace with a black lamb-skin seat kept in place by the surcingle.'

The above should give a good idea of the amount of costly ingenuity which went to make up the trappings of our cavalry during most of the nineteenth century. In Great Britain officers wore shabraques until 1897. They were discontinued by Heavy Cavalry from 1847 to 1857.

Heavy Cavalry were supposed to have square corners to the shabraque, but note Plates 66 and 67 for variations; Lancers rounded ones, Plate 68; Light Dragoons the same and Hussars pointed, Plates 65 and 69.

An Hussar officer of the 1840's detailed for duty on a travelling escort to the Sovereign, proceeding by road from Windsor to London might have his 'furniture' and also his heavily laced jacket, pelisse and sabretache so ruined by a sudden rain storm – he would not be able to stop and put on his cloak – that he would have to replace them at very considerable cost.[17]

Later the sheepskin was worn in two parts, over the pommel and cantle, joined by leather over the seat of the saddle; see Plate 26a. Plates 26b and 28b show the R.H.A. driver with the sheepskin rolled round the valise on the off horse.

The valise, a round or square case of leather or cloth, usually with the initials and number of the unit on the ends, was always worn behind the saddle, either directly on the horse's spine, on a small pillion or pad or on the fans of the saddle strapped to a 'D' on the cantle and to the fans. It was 27 inches long with a diameter of $6\frac{1}{2}$ inches in 1857 with the centre hollowed out between the fans to keep it off the horse's back. It held various articles of spare clothing and cleaning materials and was discarded for officers in the 1870's and for other ranks in 1894.

Plate 6 shows a valise on an officer's saddle in the late eighteenth century, but Morier, who painted from c.1743 to 1760, shows no valises on the saddles, the rear packs being always rolled cloaks, often with waterdecks and other articles on top. Major General Sir F. Smith in the Journal of the Aldershot Military Society of July 1891, gives the date of the introduction of the valise as c.1750, just as high front and rear packs were coming in. In 1793 the Greys had valises (see under 'Saddles') and in 1802 they had saddlebags, though this may be a misnomer for valises.[18] According to the Regimental History of the 6th Inniskilling Dragoons they 'replaced saddlebags with red valises in 1815' and from 1812 some Heavy Cavalry had red valises with square ends and the number in Roman numerals with initials on the ends. The saddlebags were double, one hung on each side of the saddle behind the flap.[19]

Hussars always had blue circular valises with the number and initials, usually 'L.D.' instead of 'H' and these replaced a 'square leather baggage case' formerly carried by Light Dragoons.[20] By the early 1830's all cavalry had the round ended valise with Arabic numerals and initials. The valise had the shabraque under and the sheepskin over it. Plate 82 shows the square-ended valise and Plate 62 the round-ended type. Plates 65 to 69 show shabraques and sheepskins and Plates 18 and 69 sheep-, lamb-, leopard- and cheetah-skins. In 1813, in the Peninsula, the 7th Hussars had saddlebags and valises.[21]

The cloak with its cape was carried as a rear pack if the valise was not worn. If a rear pack was carried the cloak and cape rolled to the length of a sword blade and hilt went over the wallet as a front pack. For some time a leather guard was issued to keep the cloth from being rubbed by the reins. Wallets, shown in Plate 18, replaced holsters for other ranks in 1840.

One understands why it was that Colonel Valentine Baker wrote in 1858[22] as follows: 'why a dragoon's saddle should be a complication of movable straps and buckles, pilches, woofs, etc. all made to take to pieces and put together, like a Chinese puzzle, has ever been beyond my comprehension'.

ON TAILS AND CLIPPING

Where there are horses there are flies and other stinging insects and although nature has provided the horse with a long tail reaching down to the ground if left to grow, man has only too often shortened it. By thus depriving the troop horse of an almost perfect fly whisk the soldier has for many years protected his uniform and appointments from the dirt and mud thrown over them when the tail is put to its normal use. In the opinion of a very large number of those interested in horses a well set on tail, either shortened just below the hocks or 'banged' by squaring it off so that it hangs about six inches above the points of the hocks in the modern fashion, enhances the whole appearance of the animal and perhaps more especially of a formed line of troop horses. The Plates show great variety; Plate 64 shows tails squared just about level with the hock, Plate 71 cut much shorter and Plate 34b, taken in 1961, a much longer trim.

Another objection to the long tail was that in harness, especially when a pair or a team was driven from the vehicle, the wheelers might get their tails over the reins, which can be both dangerous and at the best difficult. Plate 2 shows the tail left as provided by nature and Plate 8 a sensible way of dealing with a full tail by tying it up, a method practised by the Household Cavalry as late as 1797, when in wet weather this was done 'in the approved fashion'. To return to Plate 8, painted during Marlborough's campaigns of the early part of the eighteenth century: the trooper of a Dragoon Regiment riding back view close to the tree in the middle of the picture has his horse's tail 'docked' and this is shown in Plates 58 to 60 and in Plate 62. This practice of 'docking' consisted in cutting off the dock or tail bone at the third joint, leaving what was known as a bob tail. With the remaining hair cut short and the ears cropped, supposedly to make them less liable to be slashed by an opponent's sword, the troop horse was disgustingly disfigured. Lord Cadogan, Quartermaster General to the Duke of Marlborough, is said to have started the two-inch long stump called after him 'the Cadogan tail'. Not until 1764 did the British Army leave the ears alone and the tails long, except in the case of Light Dragoons. They had tails not docked so short with a switch left, called nag tails. In 1794 the tail was left long to halfway between the hoof and fetlock, and in 1799 by an Army Order the Household Cavalry had long tails and the rest nag tails. Not only were tails cut off at varying lengths, but it was also a common practice to nick the tail in order to make the horse carry it higher. In order to effect this the muscles underneath the dock were cut through. In the civilian world a thoroughbred horse had one cut, a hunter two cuts and a hackney three cuts under the tail. From this originated the expression 'cock tailed' frequently used to describe our troop horses during the Napoleonic wars, to distinguish them from the French cavalry whose horses had the tails left long. Wellington is quoted as saying 'a cock-tailed horse is a good mark for a dragoon', for at some considerable distance a sideways view of the horses of a cavalry post or a line of vedettes would tell to which nation's army they belonged. This was more especially the case in the Peninsula after 1812 when our Light Dragoons adopted the same shaped shako as was worn by the French.

On one occasion when British infantry had inflicted severe losses on French cavalry during a withdrawal, the French cut off the long tails of their dead troop horses in order to make the local Spaniards think that it was the British who had experienced such sharp casualties. Plates 23a and b show docked and cocked tails and Plate 24 the same in 1840 just before the fashion went out in the Army. Plate 61 shows an officer's charger of c.1815 with his tail merely cut short and Plate 63 another charger with a nicked tail. Plate 62, dated 1838, shows a tail nicked and docked with most of the hair cut short. After 1840 docking and nicking was abandoned, except in the case of polo ponies, although these would officially have only been ridden in the field. Tails were cut short, except in India, where they were always left long and Plate 70 shows a very short tail in 1890. By 1899 all remounts were to have long tails but Plates 76–8 show both Artillery and Mounted Infantry in 1909 to 1912 with tails cut off close and docked.

Plate 82 is deceptive; it shows a charger imported from England and painted in India with a docked and nicked tail.

Very strong representations were put forward by Veterinary officers in 1891 condemning docking and this was practically the end of the practice.

CLIPPING

The thick coat which a horse grows in winter and which keeps him warm becomes a great drawback when hard and especially fast work is required of him during the winter months. As campaigning in winter was very much the exception among European armies up to about the end of the eighteenth century, cavalry were not troubled by their troop horses' extra growth of hair. The men had harder work grooming, especially in the spring, when the horse began to shed the long hair of his winter coat.

Once cavalry and artillery were expected to march and fight in the winter the problem arose of how to deal with the horse's coat, which in winter became a hindrance and caused undue fatigue. It has been stated that the idea of clipping the horse originated with officers who had served in the Crimea. It was easy enough for officers to have their hunters, often used as chargers as well, clipped, just as it was for all remounts who were serving under conditions which allowed them to be stabled and rugged if desired, but on active service it is normally impossible to stable and very difficult to carry rugs for troop horses. As already stated it was found possible to carry rugs for remounts during the final stages of the South African War of 1899 to 1902. Horses imported from Europe to South Africa grew their winter coats during the South African summer, which was a further difficulty.

It has been considered that troop horses should, if possible, be clipped, either all over or, in the case of those used mainly for slow draught, as high as the line of the traces only, the upper portion being left long. The idea of leaving a patch on the back to take the saddle unclipped is not satisfactory in the case of remounts and has not been generally used.

In 1895 Major General H. Thompson, A.V.C., reported that 'we have gone a little way by clipping the bellies and the inside of the legs from the knees and hocks upwards'. This he considered satisfactory but in Northern India the legs were left unclipped, the body being clipped and rugs issued. The officer commanding the Cavalry Depot at Canterbury had all the remounts clipped in September and blanketed on the 28th December. The saddle blanket may have been used as a rug though this was not thought to give good results, as if it got dirty it could not well be folded and put under the saddle as it was meant to be. This officer reported that during the winter of 1894–5 there were no cases of pneumonia or colds among the horses, which were stabled.

In 1908 it was considered that a troop horse should be clipped at the beginning of winter, say about November, and again about the New Year.

During the first three years of the War of 1914–18 all horses in the Field units serving in Army Areas were clipped throughout the winter. It was finally decided that they should be clipped up to the 15th November and not afterwards. During the last World War animals were clipped once only between the 15th September and the 1st November and not again until the winter was over.

The great saving of time and work to those in charge of horses if they can be clipped is too obvious to need stressing.[23]

Notes on Shoeing Horses

There is an old saying 'No foot, no horse', which is merely a trite way of saying that a horse depends for his usefulness more on his feet than any other part of his body. The hard horn of the foot, which comes in contact with the ground, grows fast enough to serve when the horse is running loose and will stand a great amount of work under the saddle or in harness in countries where the soil is soft or sandy and the roads are dirt tracks. But the horn does not grow fast enough to stand up to hard work on hard or rocky ground and even less on metalled roads, so for a very long time horses have been shod with a semi-circular band of iron nailed through the lower part of the horn. The mule is shod in the same way and bullocks have small plates, one on each claw.

A shoe is supposed to last a month, by which time the horn has grown down so much that the outside sheath of the horny material in the centre of the foot, the frog, no longer presses on the ground and so can no longer take some of the concussion, and the shape of the foot has altered. This is because the shoe is nailed on at the toe and not at the heel. The fewer nails used the better, usually five are driven through the shoe into the horn, and the correct placing and driving of the nails, indeed the whole process of shoeing, is a complicated matter calling for the services of a highly skilled man.

Under the general direction of the Veterinary officers this work is done in the Army by farriers and shoeing smiths, ranking from Warrant Officers through the grades of Quartermaster Sergeant Farriers, to Sergeants, Corporal Farrier and Shoeing Smith. These 'tradesmen' are in constant demand, for a horse can lose a shoe on the march and in the field at any moment from a variety of causes. Plate 56 shows the tools used.

The life of a shoe naturally depends on the type of work required of the horse and in wet weather on a macadamized road good hind shoes may be worn through by between 100 and 150 miles of travelling. The average for road work varies from 200 to 250 miles, according to the pattern of the shoes used.

The British Army pattern horse shoe is made in 10 sizes weighing from 8 oz to 45 oz per shoe. A Universal Pattern shoe was first introduced in 1853 and weighed from 12 to 15 oz; six nails were used on the fore feet and seven behind and there was a single clip on the front gripping the horn.

The modern shoe, already mentioned, is machine made, with three to five nail holes on each side of the toe. There are clips, single on the fore and on wheelers' hind shoes; and double clips for riding and lead hind shoes. Specially made frost nails or calkins are fitted in conditions calling for their use.

This very cursory description should make it clear that one of the most serious problems of warfare in the days of horses and mules was not only to supply sufficient horse shoes and nails to the mounted branches, but to supplement the shoes, either two or four carried on the man's saddle, and those that the farriers could take with their unit either in forge carts or on packs. Shoes can be fitted cold or heated in a forge and shaped when hot. In all cases the weights involved were a serious consideration and though horse shoes might be captured from a retreating enemy, or either shoes or suitable iron requisitioned in the country where operations were taking place, the main dependence was on supplies carried with the force itself.

Those interested in the details of shoeing will find the whole operation described in the War Office publication *Animal Management*, republished in 1914.

The following table gives the names and uses of the tools shown in the Plate.

Tools, Farriers and Shoeing Smiths. Horse, Field and Mountain Batteries. Plate 8 in *Handbook for Military Artificers*, 1899.

1. Buffers, farriers	Used for cutting off clenched nails, etc. when removing horse shoes
2. Knives, drawing, farriers	For paring and taking down horses' hoofs
3. Knives, searching, farriers	For paring and searching for broken nails, corns, etc.
4. Chisels, farriers, handled	For cutting iron generally
5. Cutter, anvil, nail	For cutting shoe nails from the bar, after forging
6. Cutter, anvil, flat, smiths	For cutting iron generally
7. Cutter, anvil, half round	For cutting off the heels of horse shoes
8. Stake, farriers	For pointing and straightening horse nails
9. Hammers, farriers, pointing	For pointing horse nails
10. Hammers, farriers, shoeing	For driving horse nails, wringing off clenches, etc.
11. Stamps, farriers	For stamping holes in horse shoes
12. Fullers, farriers	For fullering hand-made shoes
13. Pritchells, farriers	For clearing holes in shoes after stamping and back pritchelling
14. Cresses (set of two)	Forming
15. Hammers, farriers, sledge	For striking purposes in turning horse shoes
16. Hammers, turning	For hand use in turning horse shoes
17. Pincers, farriers	For pulling off shoes and pulling out nails
18. Tongs, smiths, turning, small	For holding small shoes while turning
19. Ditto, turning, medium	For holding shoes while turning and clipping
20. Ditto, turning, large	For holding moulds and large shoes while turning
21. Ditto, fire	For holding shoes, etc. while taking heats
22. Slice, farriers	For putting coal on the fire, etc.
23. Poker, smiths	For stirring up the fire
24. Rasp, farriers	For taking down and levelling horses' hoofs before shoeing
25. Tool bag	
26. Stones, rag	For sharpening drawing knives, etc.

REFERENCES

1   Manual of Saddles and Sore Backs, p. 10, 11.
2   Rogers, *Mounted Troops of the British Army*, pp. 181, 193. At the end of the nineteenth century the hunting seat with stirrups of medium length and the man sitting well back was known as 'the squire's seat'.
3   Burne, *The Noble Duke of York*, p. 239.
4   Tyndale, *Cavalry Equitation*.
5   Grant, *British Battles on Land and Sea*. Pakenham was killed and his black thoroughbred charger kept his place at the head of the Brigade.
6   Tomkinson, *Diary of a Cavalry Officer*, p. 150. This officer notes 'the quickness of the advance on the enemy, with the spirit of the men in leaping the wall and the charge immediately afterwards, was one of the finest things I ever saw'. He had great experience.
7   Brett-James, *Wellington at War*, on p. 272, quoting William Maginn's *Military Sketch Book* for the saddle, and on p. 264 quoting Stocqueler's *Life of Wellington*, Volume II, published London, 1852, 1853. See also the frontispiece to Brett-James book by Heaphy, and No. 16709 Royal Library, Windsor, in the painting by Denis Dighton of the Duke of Wellington in *c.*1812.
8   Baker, *The British Cavalry*, p. 50. Written while this brilliant officer was still junior, but a standard work.
9   Lucas, *Camp Life and Sport in South Africa*, pp. 69, 70. He was quoting from a Riding Master who had trained at the Cavalry Depot at Maidstone. Lucas served in the Cape Mounted Riflemen during the Kaffir War of 1850–1.
10 Aldershot Lectures, 1891. Major General J. Keith Fraser quoting Captain Nolan.
11 Jackson, *India's Army*, p. 66.
12 Cathcart, *Correspondence*, p. 353.
13 Cunynghame, *My Command in South Africa*, pp. 87, 88, 89. Wood, *Winnowed Memories*, p. 10.
14 Bethell ('Pousse Cailloux'), *His Majesty's Shirt Sleeves*, in the chapter 'The Silver Hand of Alexander'.
15 Surtees, *Handley Cross*, 1854.
16 Notes given by ex-Saddler-Sergeant A. W. Croft of the 3rd Dragoon Guards, Carabiniers, now of Lambourn, Berks.
17 Fortescue, Volume XI, p. 33, FN 3.
18 JAHR, Volume III, p. 243. In 1802 the Greys had saddle bags and no valises.
19 Jackson, *The Inniskilling Dragoons*, p. 137. Pomeroy, *The 5th Dragoon Guards*, Volume II, p. 36.
20 From the Long MS in the R.U.S.I. Library.
21 JAHR, Volume XLII, p. 8.
22 *The British Cavalry*, London, 1858, p. 57.
23 Sources: *Animal Management*. Aldershot Lectures, 1895. Army Veterinary and Remount Services, 1939–45. Fawcett, *Riding and Horsemanship*, published Black, 1948, p. 162, for the introduction of clipping after the Crimea. *History of the Army Veterinary Services in the Great War*. Royal Army Service Corps Training, 1922.

CHAPTER EIGHT

Artists and Photographers
and notes on the Illustrations

THERE can have been very few artists who drew and painted horses who have not at one time or another included fighting men and the horses they rode among their subjects. In the case of a number of well-known portrait painters, they have often called in the services of an expert in the portrayal of animals to paint the charger on which their subjects liked to be posed. It is to a considerable extent from such pictures, and also from statues, that it is possible to obtain many valuable details of what the war horses of the past and their equipment looked like. There have also always been a large number of battle scenes painted and from these, especially when dismounted or killed and wounded horses are shown, it is possible to see in detail what the equipment of all ranks of the mounted branches really was when in the field.

Plate 8 is a good example; it shows not only an officer's saddlery, but in the distance the farm harness in use by the artillery train.

The charger or troop horse at rest presented no difficulties. He was used to holding himself properly for long periods on parade or when held dismounted; in fact, a horse used to drill, which he usually picks up quickly, gets in the way of standing smartly, head up and limbs well under him. Nor do the movements of a horse at the walk present serious problems to the artist. The ordinary walk in four-time and the unofficial 'pace' or slow amble with the two legs on the same side moving together are most correctly shown by the average artist. The amble was often a favourite with senior officers, Napoleon being a good example, so, as had been done from the days of armour, chargers were frequently schooled to this very comfortable gait. The trot was far less easy to convey on paper and the canter, often in reality a slow gallop, and the gallop proper completely eluded the artist until motion photography was introduced at the end of last century. The human eye does not follow the movements of a horse's legs at fast paces with accuracy and the well-known French painter of war pictures, Meissonier, is known to have broken down one horse by having him galloped round and round in a ploughed field whilst the artist tried in vain to catch the movement of the limbs correctly. Meissonier was probably one of the first men to work from motion pictures.

Fortunately the public, who in the last century were keenly interested in military pictures, knew as little or less as to how a horse moved and as long as the artist conveyed some idea of the dash and speed of cavalry and artillery teams moving fast no one minded much if accuracy had been achieved or not.

Plates 2, 22, 23, and 34 show the walk; Plate 63 the amble and Plate 59 a slow gallop, or rather an interpretation of it, as is Plate 85a of a fast gallop with some horses being pulled up suddenly. In this last plate they certainly look to be moving fast!

By the middle of the eighteenth century uniforms had become so specialized and so spectacular that more and more artists began to find it worth their while to produce work showing how army uniforms differed, not only according to the unit in which the wearer was serving, but also to the rank he held. A typical example was the Swiss painter, Morier, specimens of whose work are shown in Plates 58, 59 and 60, dated about 1750. He had many imitators and although it is not intended to give more than a few well-known names in this account, some emphasis will be put on the work of serving soldiers, who obviously had exceptional opportunities of knowing their subject. Prominent at the commencement of the nineteenth century was Lieut Colonel Hamilton Smith, who served in various areas during the French and Napoleonic Wars which ended in 1815. He paid very considerable attention to cavalry and in his portfolio of colour plates, *Costumes of the Army of the British Empire*, published in 1815, he showed remounts and their riders in every sort of order from full dress to watering. He worked at a time when a large number of commercial artists were not only producing colour plates to the order of the big publishing firms, but were employed by them to re-draw the work of officers of all arms of the Service, who worked in the field, especially during the numerous Indian campaigns. Even men like H. Alken, whose work was of a pronouncedly sporting nature, found it worth while to deal with military subjects. Plate 23a is by Alken and 23b by Hamilton Smith. A few of the well-known names of the first half of the century were Daubrawa and Eschauzier, the Dightons, Drahonet, Hayes, Heath, Harris, Martens and later on Norie.

Very full particulars will be found in Ralph Nevill's *British Military Prints*,[1] and Colonel C. de W. Crookshank's military battle prints.[2]

Reproductions of many of these and other artists' work are frequently re-published in various forms today.

Both the Peninsular and Waterloo campaigns were well covered, often by serving officers, and the last named, though only lasting such a very short time, gave rise to a spate of illustrations which continued for many years. At least one French artist dealt very efficiently with the British Army during the time of the occupation of Paris.

The example of officers serving in India was copied during the fighting in South Africa and Plate 95 was, as is known from contemporary evidence, painted in the field in 1852 by Captain Goodrich, at that time serving in the Cape Mounted Riflemen, a unit of the Regular Army. Working in the earlier campaigns as an accredited war artist was Thomas Baines, who was accustomed during the Kaffir

War of 1847 to accompany the skirmish line, rifle in hand. Both Baines and Goodrich drew horses in motion in the traditional style as did the many artists who worked on the Crimea in 1854 and 1855.

The siege of Sevastopol saw the first photographer working with a small covered waggon and producing remarkable pictures. He was Roger Fenton and, though horses were not his speciality, he foreshadowed what was to come; Plates 26–8 show the work of the camera in *c.*1861. No better example of the detail of harness could be expected from the camera of the day. Obviously whoever commissioned the photographer knew what he was doing and he has left us a wonderful picture of the R.H.A. remount of his day.

Plate 83 takes us back to the artist, in this case Captain Upton of the 9th Royal Lancers; it was drawn during the Indian Mutiny in 1857. Two notable officer-artists who worked during the various campaigns of this long war were Lieut Colonel H. Hope Crealock[3] and Captain Atkinson.[4] Crealock took a special interest in the mounted branches and among other interesting subjects drew a battery of Bengal Horse Artillery on the march, showing every horse in the team ridden, as was the custom in the Honourable East India Company's service.

A serving officer, Lieut Colonel Marshman of the 28th Gloucestershire Regiment, was drawing in the 'seventies and showed many aspects of service life. Notable are illustrations he did for an edition of the poems of Adam Lindsay Gordon, which show the 1st Royal Dragoons with all details of saddlery most carefully drawn. Very closely associated with the British Army was Lady Butler, wife of Lieut General Sir William Butler, who began exhibiting as Miss Elizabeth Thompson and went on painting throughout the Victorian era. Her first great success was with a picture entitled 'Missed'! It shows a sowar of Indian cavalry pulling up at tent pegging after missing the peg. The sketches for the painting are today in the National Army Museum at Sandhurst. Her work as regards detail of equipment is meticulously correct and she obviously enjoyed painting gun teams of the Royal Artillery. One of her best known paintings, 'Scotland for Ever', shows the Scots Greys charging French infantry at Waterloo. In order to get the effect of what the French saw Lady Butler sat on a camp stool in the Long Valley at Aldershot and was charged by the Greys, who opened out and swept past on both sides of her. The resulting impression of the furious rush of a cavalry charge is most realistic. In 1886 Lady Butler was making studies for a painting of the Egyptian Camel Corps moving at speed. This was well before the introduction of any form of ciné camera and she made over a hundred sketches of camels' legs in motion before producing a most effective impression of intense effort on the part of both riders and mounts.[5]

The same artist also showed men returning from the charge of the Light Brigade at Balaclava on their tired horses. She had many contemporaries, of whom one, Major Seccombe, a Gunner, is also a valuable guide to detail, as is Captain W. W. Lloyd, 24th Foot, the South Wales Borderers, who showed exactly what was worn in the Kaffir War of 1877 and the Zulu War of 1879.

There were three men painting military scenes during the last two decades of the century, Harry and Arthur Payne, the former serving in the West Kent Yeomanry, who painted troop horses as they saw them and, best known of all in his day, Richard Simkin. He worked for most of his life at Aldershot and today his books of colour plates are of great importance. Plates 66 to 69 show some of his officers' chargers and Plate 103 by Harry Payne a range of Army bridles. These men, like other artists, may have been rather apt to show only one type of remount and there were naturally many horses in the ranks who fell below the standard which each man liked to draw.

That is where the camera came in, as many of the plates show, though the types in Plates 75 and 79–81 were carefully selected to show precisely the best types of remount required.

To return to the subject of the correct portrayal of horses in movement; it was not till about 1890 that experiments carried out in England, France, Germany and the U.S.A. had succeeded in bringing photographs showing horses trotting, cantering, galloping and jumping within the reach of anyone who wanted to draw them. In 1895 and the following year the cinematograph was publicly exhibited and more and more artists drew horses in motion as they actually moved. By 1899, when the South African War stimulated public interest in war pictures to an enormous extent, the new technique was well established and a flood of drawings of horses in action appeared in the illustrated papers. For some considerable time these had been in the habit of retaining the services of competent men, who were employed in rendering, in a form suitable for reproduction, sketches and in some cases photographs sent from the many and various small wars being fought all over the British Empire to the headquarters of the papers. Many of these men afterwards became well known and some famous in other lines of art. One such man, who worked on the staff of the *Illustrated London News*, was Russell Flint, afterwards very well known indeed. In a life of him (*More than Shadows, Russell Flint* by F. N. Palmer, published by Studio in 1943) there is a passage, written of the period 1903 to 1907, which gives a description of the procedure as outlined above. It deals with his appointment to the staff of the *Illustrated London News* 'as showing more than anything else how rapidly he was rising in his profession, for of all the black and white artist-journalists none were so famous and exclusive as the specialists in war. Melton Prior, Frederic Villiers and Caton Woodville are three names by which anyone of that era can be carried back to the early years of the century. They were possibly the most widely known artists in the Britain of their day. The world has changed, their trade has gone, the camera has replaced them, but their names were comparable with Fougasse, Low and even Alvan-Liddell.' Those were the great days of the war artist and, though there is little doubt that in the main the writer is correct, there were still good men who drew scenes of the 1914–18 war with great success. One and all owed much of their appeal to the great attraction felt by so many people to drawings of the remount, the horse and to a lesser extent the mule, shown both in and out of action. Other well-known names were René

Bull, Stanley Wood, Matania and W. B. Wollen and to a lesser extent a serving officer of Indian Cavalry, Douglas Giles, who was exhibiting from 1887 onwards. Also once well known was Lord Baden Powell, who could draw horses in action as well as he could ride them. He was, of course, also a cavalry officer.

C. J. Payne, whose work is signed 'Snaffles', once a Horse Artilleryman, and Captain Lionel Edwards are still with us and the last named is still at work. An illustration in this book by him shows the Remount Depot as it still is. Both men's work was very much in evidence from the beginning of the century, and though the camera can do wonderful work there must be few who would not prefer sketches and paintings by these men and by Munnings, who also handled military subjects.

How much longer these gifted men will find any military subjects to handle it is impossible to say. There remain with us the Household Cavalry, the King's Troop Royal Horse Artillery and mounted senior officers and sometimes representatives of other units who have contrived to mount a few of all ranks for special ceremonial occasions. There are also, to the satisfaction of many people, the mounted men of the Metropolitan Police, and as already noted, the Remount Depot in the Midlands.

There are still on active service the pack mules which serve in some of the countries 'policed' by the British Army and recent photographs have shown Pack Transport of the R.A.S.C. before the name was changed, in action, though not in warfare.

There are probably a number of people who either collect, keep or take an interest in the drawings and paintings of the chargers and remounts of bygone days. To them the following story of the difficulties which the artists of the past encountered may not come amiss. A certain well-known artist of the late seventies and eighties of last century was, as were so many others, in difficulties when drawing horses jumping. In order to try and get the position of the hind legs correctly he used to get two friends, who were in fact subalterns who rode a great deal, to go on all fours and jump chairs laid on their sides. A comment by one of the actors on a published drawing was 'that's your style, hind legs well under him'. Such were the shifts and expedients of the past.

REFERENCES: Artists and Photographers

1   Nevill, *British Military Prints*.
2   Crookshank, *Prints of British Military Operations*.
3   Crealock, Lieut Colonel H. Hope, Portfolio published by J. Hogarth, 5, Haymarket, London, 1861.
4   Atkinson, Captain F. (Bengal Engineers), *The Campaign in India, 1857–8*. Bay & Son, London, 1859.
5   The painting by Lady Butler, 'Egyptian Camel Corps, Ceremonial Parade', mentioned in the text belongs to the United Service Club and was reproduced in E. W. Sheppard's *Red Coat*, Batchworth Press, 1952.
    The note on the preliminary sketches is from Marling's *Rifleman and Hussar*, p. 162.

MORE READILY AVAILABLE TODAY ARE:

Carman, W. Y., *British Military Uniforms*, 1957 and *Indian Army Uniforms, Cavalry*, 1961, both published by Leonard Hill (Books, Ltd), London.

Rogers, Colonel H. C. B., *Mounted Troops of the British Army*, 1959, Seeley Service.

Swift Picture Book, *British Military Uniforms*, Longmans Press.

THE ILLUSTRATIONS

These have been selected from a very large number examined. As far as possible the object aimed at was to try and include as many desirable features as possible in each plate. Thus a drawing or photograph showing clearly a type of saddle and a class of horse described in the text has been included rather than one showing for instance the horse but not the saddle.

It is in many cases unavoidable for the reader not to have to turn back to plates already examined. As it is the number of plates has increased until it is now hoped that not many references in the text cannot be found somewhere among the plates.

As an ex-Saddler sergeant of the Carabiniers who has helped in many ways said, 'Give me photographs, I don't trust artists', but unfortunately this has not always been possible and a most important drawing had to be left out because the artist had not bothered to put in a vital part of the harness! However, the artists who worked before photography was discovered, as a general rule seem to have taken immense pains to show things as they were, except that many of them were prone to adopt a sort of sealed pattern of their own where horses were concerned.

In some cases the original illustrations, because of their age, did not lend themselves to good reproduction. It was decided, however, to include them with the others because they still had something of value to show.

ILLUSTRATIONS IN COLOUR

The frontispiece   This painting by Landseer, apparently the only one he ever did of a subject of this sort, shows Queen Victoria, accompanied by the Duke of Wellington, inspecting the 2nd Life Guards at Windsor in 1839. It was reproduced in the *Journal of the Society for Army Historical Research* in Volume xxxviii. The off-side pommel of the sidesaddle can be plainly seen. At this date the third or lower near-side pommel had only just been invented and was not in use except in very few cases. The colour blocks were kindly loaned by Messrs Leggatt Bros, of St James's Street, London.

The colour plate   The Drum horses of the Household Cavalry, reproduced by kind permission of the Officer Commanding Household Cavalry and Mr B. Godfrey Argent who took the photograph, shows the Trumpet Major of the Life Guards and the Kettle Drummer of the Royal Horse Guards in detail. Their horses are as near as we can get today to the Great Horses of the days of armour.

The round-ended shabraque of the Life Guards and the pointed one of the Royal Horse Guards with the Battle Honours, the drum banners and the bits, bridles and foot reins can be studied in detail.

The bit or curb rein is taken over the neck either within the drummer's reach or for use as a bearing rein, the bridoon or snaffle rein is left loose over the neck and the extra third or foot rein running to the stirrups can be clearly seen. Usually the stirrup iron has a small dee on the outside, cast as part of the stirrup to take this rein, with which the drummer controls the horse.

BLACK AND WHITE PLATES

Plate 1 This plate has been selected from Grose's *Military Antiquities*, Volume 1, published in 1801, facing page 106. The saddle is presumably the one described by Gervase Markham in 1607 in his book *Le Cavalerie* as 'the Perfite Saddle'. Markham took the illustration from Salamon de la Broue's book of 1593 *Le Cavalerie Francois*. Markham refers to it again in his *Soldiers Accidence* of 1625. The piece of armour above the spanner (for winding up the lock of the wheel lock pistol also shown) is a 'Pattrell' or defence for the horse's neck. The pistol was carried in a deep holster in front of the saddle, often with the barrel end held steady by passing it through a loop on the breastplate.

Plate 2 Is from Grose also. It is number 5 of 'the Exercise of the Horse' and shows a harquebusier, described by Markham in the *Soldiers Accidence* as having besides his arms 'Gorgets, Curats, Culasses, Pouldrons, Vambraces and a Light Headpiece, wide sighted and the Beevor to let down on bars of iron. He carries a sword and a Harquebus (or long heavy pistol) of 3 feet 2 inches.' The horse carried nearly as much weight as that of a cuirassier and it is not certain if the Harque-busiers normally wore as much armour as is shown here. The saddle is probably a variation of the one described by Markham as 'a Morocco saddle'.

Plate 3 Seventeenth century General Officer's saddle; presented by King Charles I to the Duke of Monmouth. The photograph is reproduced by courtesy of His Grace the Duke of Buccleuch, and Messrs Constable & Co., publishers of Sir George Arthur's book on the Household Cavalry.

This saddle is of the same type as those shown in Plates 1, 4, 5, 6 and 8 and the photograph shows also the single curb bit and the holsters.

Plates 4 and 5, and Figure 4 Show the front view and the side view, and a line drawing of a saddle now in the Scottish United Services Museum at the Castle, Edinburgh. They are reproduced by courtesy of the Curator, who has been at great pains to investigate and record the details of the tree of this example of a seventeenth-century military saddle as also shown in Plates 6 and 7. The pommel and cantle have metal reinforcements and the sideboards are of wood with dees for the flaps and other attachments.

In Sir George Arthur's book, noted under Plate 3, are two drawings reproduced from Walton showing almost identical saddles to this one, dated late on in the century. The pistols hung straight down in front and a rolled cloak is shown behind the cantle of one of them.

Plate 6 The so-called Killiecrankie infantry officer's saddle of 1689, also of the same type. This illustration is reproduced by permission of Captain R. W. F. Cuninghame, of Caprington Castle, Kilmarnock and was published in JAHR, Volume xvii. The pistol holsters have open tops and there is a valise on the cantle.

Plate 7 An experimental saddle for Light Dragoons shown by Captain R. Hinde in his book *The Discipline of the Light Horse*, published in 1778. There is a pillion arrangement to take a rear pack.

Plate 8 One of four paintings by James Ross showing scenes from Marlborough's campaigns. It was possibly painted in 1715. The officer without any cuirass is presumably showing his saddled charger, of Barb or Arab type, to some friends. The saddle appears to vary little from those in the preceding plates. Crown copyright: reproduced by permission of the Ministry of Public Buildings and Works.

Plates 9 and 10 These two plates, reproduced by courtesy of the Scottish United Services Museum at Edinburgh, show an officer of Heavy Cavalry's saddle of the official pattern introduced in 1796. Presumably the saddles shown in Plates 61 and 63 are the same.

Mr W. A. Thorburn, Curator of the Museum, describes the saddle as follows: 'This saddle was used by Cornet James Gape of the Greys at Waterloo. He got a bullet through his rolled cloak fired at 20 yards from a French musket during the charge of the Union Brigade. The bullet chewed up the leather of the front top of the flap, burrowed into the wood and bent the metal. The position of the hole bears out the direction. Another bullet went through the rear part of the seat. Gape himself was unhurt – he was aged 18. His mare received three slight wounds, one was a ball through the ear.' It is of interest to see that behind the cantle, which has a brass edge, the tree is continued in fans which carry the rear pack. The same pattern is shown in Plate 62 in 1838 as used by other ranks.

Plate 11 Six prints, and line drawings of Figures 6 and 7 showing measurements drawn by Mr John Mollo who also had the photographs taken. This 'Hussar Saddle' of 1805 onwards is the property of Sir Cliff Tibbetts, J.P., by whose permission it is reproduced, of the firm of Jabez Cliff & Co. Ltd, old-established saddlers and harness makers of Walsall, Staffs. It was on exhibition in 1961 at the Rural Industries Bureau in London. The loose seat (see in the text) is missing. (a) shows the off side; (b) the view from the near side front; (c) the underneath; (d) the front view; (e) the view from behind; (f) the girth straps attached to the tree on the off side and the hole for the stirrup leather with the flap folded back. Note the fans in rear and the burs in front. This is the only example of a trooper's saddle of this extensively used pattern which has so far been discovered in England or Scotland. The author is much indebted to Mr F. J. Chandler, Saddler of Marlborough, for help in tracing this saddle and many other items.

Plate 12 Saddlery used in the charge of the Light Brigade at Balaclava on 25th October, 1854, by Captain Godfrey Charles Morgan, 17th Lancers, later Lord Tredegar. Reproduced by courtesy of the National Army Museum. This is the

Hussar pattern shown in Plate 11 as slightly altered in 1816 and used with a plain leather seat integral with the rest of the saddle. The pistol holsters are set on the burs at a convenient angle for avoiding the knee of the rider. Revolvers were carried by many officers at this date and it looks as if these holsters would take one.

Plate 13a and b Heavy Cavalry Officer's Saddle used by Cornet Richard George Glyn, 1st Royal Dragoons, in the charge of the Heavy Brigade at Balaclava. The photograph is reproduced by courtesy of Sir Richard Glyn, Bart, and the Dorset Military Museum, and the Curator kindly furnished the following measurements.

Top of cantle to top of pommel   1 foot   9¼ inches
End of fan to point of bur   1 foot   10¼ inches
Flap 1 foot ¾ inches wide; 1 foot 2 inches long. Knee rolls

Plate 14 Staff saddle as used in the seventies and eighties of last century, which was slightly altered and became Plate 17a, 'R40'. The Confidential Report on Warren's Bechuanaland Expedition, 1884, states that all British Officers had this saddle. The future Field Marshal, Lord Methuen, was one of them.

There are no panels shown. Otherwise there are only minor differences from the later pattern. The photograph was copied from one in *Black and White Budget* published in 1900.

Plate 15a and *b* Household Cavalry Troop Saddle 1885, 1886. See List of Changes 4703 and in the text. The saddle has fans but no burs. b. Detachable panel for the above.

Plate 16 Removable Iron Angle Arch Troop Saddle U.P. List of Changes 1885, 1886, No. 5017. Plate 70 shows this saddle with the Namaqua Rifle Bucket as used by Mounted Infantry, Camel Corps and Mounted Rifles (Yeomanry) from 1881 to *c.*1891. The Mounted Rifles had it from 1860. It was introduced by Sir Francis Galton, who had used it in S.W. Africa.

Plate 17a and b The first shows the Universal Patterns including Staff (R40) of 1890, and b shows the trees. See in text. The first steel arch saddle.

Plate 18 Shows the U.P. Officer's saddle with equipment, sheepskin and Hussar's leopard skin. See in text. Except in Hussar Regiments all cavalry officers had lance buckets.

Plate 19 Staff, Yeomanry and Colonial pattern saddle, with the butt rifle bucket introduced for M.I. in 1884. This is the Trooper's pattern, but differs very little from the Officer's pattern saddle as still in use.

Plate 20 The 1902 Universal pattern. Shown with the deep rifle bucket introduced *c.*1904 to take the Short Magazine Lee Enfield rifle.

Note. *Plate 89* shows the carbine bucket of 1884 taking the Martini-Henry and *Plate 98* the one of 1892 taking the Martini-Enfield.

Plate 21 This is the Universal Pattern United States Cavalry Saddle, the McClellan, on issue with only minor changes from 1858 to 1942. It was used by British Cavalry during the South African War of 1899–1902. With it is the 'long carbine boot' or as we should say 'bucket'.

Plate 22 The First Aid Nursing Yeomanry, see in text, in the full dress worn with the sidesaddle (Figure 14), in 1909. The photograph is reproduced by courtesy of the *Evening Standard*, and shows a section taking part in the Lord Mayor's Show of 1958.

Plate 23a and b These show respectively (a) an officer and a lead pair of Royal Horse Artillery of the Peninsular period, and (b) an officer and a covered waggon with a team of four horses of the Royal Waggon Train of the same period. The R.H.A. are from a drawing by H. Alken and are from a book published by I. and J. Fuller, Rathbone Place, London in 1821. (b) The Royal Waggon Train is from a series of colour plates drawn and etched by Colonel C. Hamilton Smith and published in 1815 in *Costume of the Army of the British Empire*, by courtesy of Lieut Colonel Penna, o.b.e., formerly Curator, R.A.S.C. Museum. The R.H.A. officer is leading his charger and the Hussar saddle (Plate 11) shows plainly. The harness worn by the lead pair should be compared with Plate 34. The wheeler harness, near side, is shown in the Royal Waggon Train Plate and would be the same for all Ordnance Corps, including the R.A. The end of the near-side shaft of the off wheeler is just visible. Note, blinkers are worn.

Plate 24 Shows harness of an off leader and an off wheeler of the Royal Artillery in 1840 with a full description. It is taken from Captain Griffiths' *Artillerists Manual*, 2nd Edition, 1840, between pages 136 and 137. Note, blinkers are worn.

Plate 25 Wheelers and part of the off centre pair in a field-gun of the Crimean period. In 1853 blinkers were given up and in 1850 brown leather harness replaced black. This plate is from a photograph of a model in the Museum of the Royal Artillery Institute and is published by kind permission of the Curator who had the exhibit photographed.

Plates 26a and b, 27a and 28a and b are from the Collection of the Marquess of Cambridge, g.c.v.o., by whose courtesy they are reproduced.

The date is *c.*1861 and the full equipment of a battery of R.H.A. is shown, a most valuable and comparatively rare example, due, no doubt, to the keenness of an unknown gunner officer to have a complete record of his unit.

26a Officer's charger with the 1855-6-wood arch saddle only just adopted by the R.A.

26b The off wheeler, the shaft-horse; the tugs for the shafts can be seen below the luggage saddle with the valise and sheepskin on top.

27a Near wheeler, with a cover to the driver's saddle (see 27b). Note sword on saddle carried by drivers from *c.*1840 to the sixties.

27b Drivers' saddle pattern 1861. From Turner's *North West Mounted Police*, published Ottawa, 1950, Volume II, p. 449; by permission of the Queen's Printer, Ottawa. The Mounties had this saddle in 1874.

28a The near leader. The sword and the rolled cloak on the front of the saddle are distinct but it is not easy to see if the saddle has a cover or not.

28b The off leader with luggage saddle and a bearing rein.

Plates 29 and 30a, b and c From the Brackenbury Series *Artillery in the Field*, 1883. Official Text Books. Reproduced by permission of the R.A. Institution.

29 Near leader and off wheeler, shaft horse. With a full explanation below. Note the driver has no sword and the luggage saddle is of a different pattern.

30a R.H.A. shaft horse with luggage saddle. Service marching order.
b Near leader in service marching order.
c Mounted N.C.O. on gunner's horse, service marching order.

Plate 31a and b From a photograph taken at the R.M.A., Woolwich, in 1892, reproduced in *The British Army* by a Lieut Colonel (Lieut General Sir J. M. Grierson).
a The wheelers, off-side view.
b The wheelers, front view. The shafts have been replaced by a pole, which is held in place by the cross bar in front of the horses. There are no luggage saddles, the off horses having drivers' saddles without stirrups. All have breeching as wheelers. Rapid release attachments on traces, pole strap and pole-bar hook.

Plates 32a, b and 33 These plates show the U.P. harness as used in the First World War. a From the R.A.S.C. Training Manual of 1911, shows the near wheeler with U.P. Breast Harness and U.P. Steel Arch saddle.
b From the 1937 *Manual of Horsemastership*, reproduced by permission of the Controller of Her Majesty's Stationery Office, shows the detail of the breast-collar, etc. and Plate 33, from a photograph in Captain Sidney Galtrey's *The Horse and the War*, opposite page 64 (reproduced by courtesy of *Country Life*), shows a gun team of 'Yanks' (see in text), the First Prize winners at a Divisional Horse Show held in France. The team had been in action a week before. According to the *Artificers Handbook*, 1915, the R.H.A. should have pads and the R.F.A. saddles on the off horses. Actually both types appear to have had pads. There are rapid release attachments on the traces, neck piece and pole-bar.

Plate 34a and b The King's Troop, R.H.A., in 1961. The only horsed artillery left, just as the Household Cavalry are the only corps still mounted. Photographs by courtesy of Lieut Commander K. B. Hook, R.N. (retd).

Plate 35 This painting by Harry Payne, a Sergeant in the West Kent Yeomanry, shows a pontoon train of the Royal Engineers in 1890 with harness of the 1883 type. See Plate 30b for the leaders. This plate is reproduced from Major Percy Groves's *On Service*, with illustrations by Harry and Arthur Payne, published 1891 by Raphael Tuck, by whose permission it is reproduced.

Plates 36 and 37 These plates are reproduced by courtesy of Brigadier J. H. S. Lacey, C.B.E., B.A., Secretary of the Institution of Royal Engineers, who furnished copious notes with them.

Plate 36a, b, c and d

a Officer's charger, Field Company R.E. Marching Order. The officer is Lieut J. Marsh who started the R.E. Drag in 1928.

b Sapper Mounted in Marching Order. Wallets over front arch of U.P. steel arch saddle 1912. Waterproof sheet folded on top of wallets. Greatcoat on front arch if wallets not worn. Nosebag near side of cantle. Rifle bucket off side, if no bucket rifle slung over right shoulder. Tool bucket near side. Mess tin and water bucket (folded) also on rifle bucket. Bed blanket folded over saddle blanket. Surcingle pad on surcingle under belly (worn when off-saddled with surcingle holding blanket over horse). Grooming gear near side over waterproof sheet.

c and d Drivers and N.C.O.s of all units other than Field Squadrons. Greatcoat rolled on front arch. Waterproof sheet on greatcoat or on top of blanket on led horse. Nosebag near side cantle. Both haynets on off or led horse or one haynet rolled near side rear arch. Mess tin and water bucket near side on rear 'D'. N.C.O.'s rifle bucket off side, driver's rifle in vehicle. Bed blanket over saddle blanket or on off horse with waterproof sheet and surcingle round it. Surcingle pad under belly or on led horse on near-side hip and loin strap.

Plates are taken from *Engineer Training*, Volume 1, Drill, p. 283, Plates, published 1929, and are reproduced by permission of the Controller, Her Majesty's Stationery Office.

The photograph, dated *c.*1890, Plate 37, shows the same 1883 pattern harness. The inflated balloon is being topped up from a tube waggon, of which there were three in each Section, which comprised a waggon for the balloon and basket, etc. and a winch waggon with the cable for the balloon and telephone line and equipment. This Balloon Section R.E., became in 1912 the Air Battalion R.E. and, in Brigadier Lacey's words, 'from the Sappers' pioneer work in military aviation, balloons, man-carrying kites, airships and powered aeroplanes have sprung today's Fleet Air Arm and the Royal Air Force.'

Plate 38 Abyssinian Campaign 1868. Mountain Battery A/21 Royal Artillery with mules carrying the steel 7-pounders across the pack-saddle. From the *Illustrated London News*. There were four mules to a gun.

Plate 39a From List of Changes in Warlike Material, 1885. War Office Library. Mule collar harness, English Trade Pattern as used for special service by the Commissariat and Transport Department which became the Army Service Corps in 1888. This type is adapted for pole draught.

Plate 39b As (a), the South African type, still in use in that country, also for pole draught but with breast-harness. Adopted in 1884.

Plate 40a and b There are four types of Indian Army pad pack-saddles shown, two from Bombay, one from the Punjab and one borrowed from Persia, also a French and a Hungarian pack-saddle. In the centre of (a) is the Otago pack-saddle as adapted by the Commissariat Staff Corps in New Zealand from a local pattern. This saddle is the forerunner of the saddles in Plate 38 and of the A.S.C. patterns. From the Record of the Expedition to Abyssinia, 1868, Volume II. War Office, 1870.

Plate 41 An Indian Mountain Battery in 1898 showing the 7-pounder screw gun in two pieces for pack transport by mules, five to a gun. From the *Navy and Army Illustrated*, as also Plates 43, 44a, 71, 88, 89 and 102, reproduced by permission of George Newnes Ltd.

Plate 42 From the *Illustrated London News*. A Royal Mortar $5\frac{1}{2}$-inch being loaded on an elephant by the Royal Artillery in Abyssinia in 1868.

Plate 43 Royal Garrison Artillery Siege Train, India, 1898. A 40-pounder Rifled Muzzle Loading gun drawn by two elephants and a team of eight oxen with ammunition waggon. From the *Navy and Army Illustrated*.

Plate 44a Ammunition Mule, Pack, of an Infantry Battalion on Home Service in 1896.
b Mark III Maxim Machine Gun Infantry Carriage, shaft draught, a single mule. Infantry Battalion on Home Service *c.*1902. The undress cap is the so-called Brodrick. From *The Book of the Machine Gun*, by Major F. V. Longstaff and Captain A. H. Atteridge. By courtesy of Major C. C. Longstaff.

Plate 45 U.P. Pack-saddle, Mark v, British Service. From R.A.S.C. Training 1911.

Plate 46 As 45, showing the Italian U.P. pack-saddle, known as 'the Basto'. Used by British troops in Italy during the Second World War.

Plate 47 Indian Army pack-saddle 1932. (a) in draft with A.T. (Animal Transport) Carts, and (b) in pack with Infantry. Poona. By permission of Mrs A. M. H. Westland.

Plate 48 British Army U.P. pack-saddle, Mark v. Pack-horses of the Canadian Army being loaded in an experimental exercise in Mountain Warfare Training in the Rockies in 1943. Photograph from the collection of Lieut Colonel Westmorland, who was in command of the Pack Troop, taken by the Department of National Defence Canada (War Records Collection No. 3526), by whose permission it is reproduced.

Plate 49 This and the two following plates are from the Collection of Captain B. T. Hinchley, who served with the Camel Transport Corps in Egypt and Jordan in 1917. Nearest the camera: Camel Cacolet for lying-down wounded. Behind: Cacolet for sitting wounded.

Plate 50 Typical Egyptian Camel with saddle nets, loading ropes and girths. The saddle was of local manufacture.

Plate 51 Donkey and boy at El Arish in 1916. To show the most primitive type of pad with breeching.

Plate 52   The Tibetan Campaign of 1903. Ekkas drawn by Yaks. From Fleming's *Bayonets to Lhasa*, published by Rupert Hart-Davis, 1961.

Plate 53   Dog Sleigh Transport in North Russia in 1918. From R.A.S.C. Training, Part III, 1922.

Plate 54   Reindeer Sleigh Transport in North Russia in 1918. From R.A.S.C. Training, Part III, 1922.

Plate 55   A Crown Copyright Army Public Relations photograph reproduced by permission of the Controller of Her Majesty's Stationery Office. It shows a patrol in Malaya *c.*1960 with two tracker and patrol dogs and their handlers.

Plate 56   Farriers' Tools. Plate VIII of *Handbook for Military Artificers, 1899.*

Plate 57   'The Remount Depot at Melton Mowbray in 1963' by the well-known military and sporting painter, Lionel Edwards, by whose kind permission it is reproduced. This drawing marks what must be nearly the end of the story of remounts as set forth in this book. The setting is in High Leicestershire in the heart of the best fox-hunting country in this island. The artist has shown us specially selected troopers and also girls, employed to save manpower. Most of them are riding one and leading one remount round a ring with an officer in the middle. All are in shirt sleeves and the type of horse is the hunter. The saddlery is what may well prove to be the last Universal Pattern.

Plate 58   Painting by D. Morier (1705–70) who came to England *c.*1743, showing a Trooper of the 1st Regiment of Horse, later the 4th Dragoon Guards, in 1751. The troop horse is one of the black type of weight carriers considered the correct mount for Heavy Horse.

This painting, and Plates 59 and 60, are reproduced by gracious permission of Her Majesty The Queen.

Plates 59 and 60   David Morier's impression of the lighter type of troop horse as bought for Dragoons, respectively the 11th and 12th Regiments in 1750. Became the 11th Hussars and 12th Lancers, respectively.

Plate 61   Painting of the English School in the early nineteenth century showing an officer's chestnut charger of the 7th Dragoon Guards. The shabraque and holsters are green edged gold and the black lambskin is edged red. The fighting in the background shows the uniforms of the late Peninsular period and the charger is very like a bay hunter in a painting by William Webb, *c.*1825 to 1845, ridden by 'The Master of Hounds'. In other words the charger would make an ideal heavy-weight hunter. Reproduced by kind permission of Baronne O. de Juniac.

Plate 62   Another hunter type, this time the trooper of a Senior N.C.O., Serjeant Major of the 7th Dragoon Guards in 1838, painted by J. Dalby. Shows the Heavies' 'high mounting' saddle with fans and oval-sided stirrups. Reproduced by kind permission of Colonel B. M. Knox, M.C., T.D., of Kersland, Monkton, Ayrshire.

Plate 63 Painting by Reinagle of Major Charles Philip Ainslie of the 4th Dragoons in 1813. Later the 4th Hussars. This painting shows a light-weight charger of hunter type, obviously well bred. Reproduced by kind permission of Sir George Schuster, K.C.S.I., K.C.M.G., C.B.E., M.C.

Plates 64 and 65 By R. R. Scanlan, showing Sergeant Major Haynes and Troop Sergeant Major Borthwick of the 7th Hussars in 1850 and two officers' chargers. The latter are either thoroughbred or very nearly so. The two troop horses are a very good type of medium weight general-purpose saddle-horses. From the Badminton Collection by kind permission of His Grace the Duke of Beaufort.

Plate 66 This plate and the following three, reproduced by kind permission of George Newnes Ltd, are by R. Simkin, the well-known military artist who turned out a very large number of colour plates in the eighties and nineties of last century. He lived at Aldershot for many years and had therefore every opportunity of drawing from actual models. This plate shows the 2nd Life Guards in 1888; the officer's black horse is a fine type of parade charger.

Plate 67 Officer of the Royal Horse Guards, 1888. A weight carrier, like Plate 66, also showing a great deal of breeding.

Plate 68 An officer of the 12th Lancers, classed as Medium Cavalry at this date, in 1888.

Plate 69 Two officers of the 3rd Hussars in c.1890. A light-weight hunter type.

Plate 70 Two privates of a Line Regiment c.1890, trained as Mounted Infantry and forming part of the M.I. Detachment of their Regiment. They are mounted on troop horses of Light Cavalry type. The painting is by Frank Dadd.

The rifle bucket shown is the Namaqua pattern, in use by the Regular Army from c.1881 to c.1890 for M.I. riding ponies or camels.

Plate 71 Serjeant Seymour, 2nd Gordons, in an M.I. unit in 1896. From the *Navy and Army Illustrated* of 29th May, 1896. He is riding the correct type of M.I. cob with the U.P. steel arch saddle of 1890 and the short butt bucket for the rifle introduced in South Africa in 1884.

Plates 72–4 Six types of remounts in 1899 specially selected by Lieut Colonel (later Lieut General Sir Edwin) A. H. Alderson for illustrations to his book *Pink and Scarlet*, and reproduced by permission of the Trustees of his Estate. Plate VIII in the book, Figures 1 and 2 are medium- and light-weight chargers, both were hunted and were winners of Point-to-Point races; Plate IX, Figures 1 and 2 show a Cavalry Troop Horse; a Mounted Infantry Cob; and in Plate X, Figure 1 is an R.H.A. lead horse and Figure 2 an A.S.C. team horse. General Alderson, formerly Royal West Kent Regiment, had seen active service and hunted hounds before he wrote the book. He was well qualified to select representative types of remounts for the period immediately before the South African War.

Plates 75–8 Eight types of remount from the booklet issued in 1909–10 by The

Board of Agriculture and Fisheries, entitled *Types of Horse Suitable for Army Remounts*, H.M.S.O., 1912 revised from June 1909. Lent by Brigadier J. Clabby, O.B.E., Director of Army and Veterinary Remount Services to whom the author is indebted for assistance in many sections of this book.

Figure 1 Cavalry of the Line, 9th Lancers. Deep, short-legged, short-backed, good-barrelled horse of the hunter stamp, with substance and quality, true action and not brushing. Light active well-bred horses, that move truly and well in their paces, well ribbed up, with plenty of bone and short backs are the Cavalry type. At four years 15·1½ to 15·2½ hands; over four years, 15·2 to 15·3 hands.

A thousand required annually. Trooper 9th Lancers, bought in Ireland for £40 as a four-year-old; 15·2. Black gelding, shows a lot of quality, plenty of bone and nice forehand.

Author's note. There is only one class of cavalry – of the Line.

Figure 2 Household Cavalry (the 2nd Life Guards). Must be well bred and up to weight. A certain amount of action is necessary, and the horses must be good looking. Bought at a considerably higher price than Cavalry troop horses. Black, at four years old 15·3, at five years old 16 hands. This is a typical trooper of the 2nd Life Guards bought in Yorkshire as a four-year-old for £65. Photographed at six years, 16 hands high.

Figure 3 Royal Horse Artillery. Weight-carrying hunter type. Every horse in the gun team or not should be capable of taking its place there if necessary in an emergency. The same type is required right through.

For the Royal Horse Artillery a little more quality and pace required than for Field Artillery. Height at four years 15·2 to 15·3 hands, over four years 15·2½ to 16 hands. Figure 3 bought in Ireland for £42 as a four-year-old 15·2 hands.

Figure 4 Royal Field Artillery. R.F.A. leader. A bay gelding 15·3, thirteen years old. Can gallop and looks as if he ought to have spent his life as a hunter; short legs, deep through the heart and a good shoulder.

Figure 7 Royal Engineers draught horse. A bay-brown mare 15·3 hands, twelve years old, a useful sort.

Figure 8 Army Service Corps. A good stamp of slow draught horse, a short-legged bay gelding 15·2½ hands, eight years old.

Royal Engineers and Army Service Corps. Draught horses of the type known as the 'Parcel Vanner' are required. Must be able to trot with a good load but do not require as much pace as the R.A. remounts.

Height: Royal Engineers 15·2 to 15·3 at four years; 15·2½ to 16 hands over four years.

Army Service Corps, 15·2½ to 15·3 at four years; 15·2½ to 15·3½ at over four years.

Required annually for R.A., R.E., and A.S.C., 1,360 horses.

Figure 9 Mounted Infantry. Cob or Galloway class, quick and active and able to gallop fast for a short distance. Height: 14·2 to 15·1½ hands. Five years and over only taken.

The height taken is over the standard for polo (in those days 14·2 and from 1919 unlimited, author) so there are plenty of animals of the stamp and quality required. Annually 140 horses required.

M.I. cob 14·2½ hands and twelve years old. Nice short back and intelligent head. Has done seven years' hard work without a day's rest.

Figure 10 M.I. cob 14·1½ hands. A piebald nine years old.

Plates 79–81 Types of horses suitable for Army remounts, War Office 29th July, 1927. Photographs reproduced by permission of the Controller of Her Majesty's Stationery Office.

Age Horses are purchased between the ages of four and seven and a few at three years.

Colour A small number of white and grey horses bought for special purposes, but very light and washy horses are not suitable.

Suitability and soundness Only horses with good action are accepted. Entires, docked, unmanageable and vicious horses etc., are not bought. Soundness in eyes, wind and limb are essential.

Officers' chargers should be well-bred horses of the hunter type of horse, active, well ribbed up, short in the back with plenty of bone and good head and shoulders.

Types Two types are specially required, the cavalry or hunter type and the active light draught horse which can trot on.

The Household Cavalry trooper must have quality, be up to weight-carrying and be good looking. A higher price is paid for them than for ordinary troop horses. They must be black with a minimum height at four years of 15·3 and at five years 16 hands. (Not illustrated.)

Plate 79 Cavalry of the Line. Height at four years old not less than 15 hands or exceeding 15·2. At over four years, 15·3 hands.

The type of horse required is deep bodied, with a short back, well-sprung ribs of the hunter type, with substance, quality and true action.

Plate 80 Royal Horse Artillery. A well-bred 'ride and drive' horse, able to gallop in a gun team. Short in the back, deep through the heart, strong quarters to hold the gun in the breeching, plenty of bone and good and true action. Entails being able to move with cavalry.

Height at four years, 15·1½ to 15·2½, over four 15·2 to 15·3 hands.
Weight 1,200 to 1,300 lb (10 cwt to 10¾ cwt).

Plate 81 Royal Field Artillery, Royal Engineers and other light draught. This is the best type of light vanner, similar to R.H.A. but somewhat heavier; quality and pace are less important. Must be capable of moving at a fast trot over rough broken ground pulling a great weight. Height as for R.H.A.

Plate 82 Bodyguard of the Governor General of India, *c.*1806, believed to be a portrait of Lieut Colonel Francis A. Daniell by Sir R. Ker Porter. Presumably an imported horse, either from the Cape as were the chargers of General Sir Rollo Gillespie and Brig. General T. P. Vandeleur or from England.

Plate 83 Vedette of the 9th Lancers during the siege of Delhi in 1857. A contemporary water-colour by Captain Roger Upton of the Regiment. The troop horses were described as Arabs and Probyn's Horse took over 'a hundred Arabs from the 9th Lancers in 1860'. Reproduced by courtesy of the 9th/12th Royal Lancers.

Plate 84 Charger of an aide-de-camp to a Divisional Commander in India *c.*1871. The A.D.C. was Captain Michael Henry Saward, R.H.A., later General. From the collection of his daughter Miss Dorothy Saward by kind permission. The charger might have been a stud-bred, but this is uncertain. 'The hunting saddle was regulation for Staff': see Dress Regulations for Officers of the Army, 1857.

Plates 85a and b Two pictures by 'Ed. Durand', in 1884 to 1887 serving with the Boundary Commission which settled the frontiers of Afghanistan with its neighbours. Both from the India Office Library, by permission of the Secretary of State for Commonwealth Relations. They show the celebrated Turcoman horses, which were so prized in India before Russia stopped the export. They were used as stallions, as gun-team horses and as cavalry troopers.
a 'The Turcoman Goat Game.' Two teams have to chase a goat and catch him from the saddle.
b 'At Kirki, a Russian Advanced Post on the Oxus.' Shows four Turcoman horses with the characteristic head and neck as described by some writers and the Eastern or Oriental type saddle in this case derived from the Moguls.
     Summerhays on page 218 of *The Observers Book of Horses and Ponies*, considers there are very few of the breed left.

Plate 86 Arab charger, the property of Colonel Parr, later Major General Sir Henry Hallam Parr, ridden when in command of a Battalion of Infantry of the Line in 1894.

Plate 87 A grey Gulf Arab foaled 1925–6 and bought as a yearling. The photograph was taken at Poona in 1931 and two years later the pony was taken over by the Remount Farm at Saugor to be used at stud. Reproduced by courtesy of Mrs A. M. H. Westland, who owned the pony for a long time. She is shown riding Tiffin. This Gulf Arab shows but little if any difference from Plate 86.

Plate 88 Havildar of the Bikanir Camel Corps in 1898 with an officer and two camels in the left-hand portion of the photograph. Shows riding camels and the arrangement of saddles for two men. From the *Navy and Army Illustrated*.

Plate 89 Sowar, Mounted, of the 18th Bengal Lancers. From the *Navy and Army Illustrated*, 1897. Shows possibly a stud-bred trooper, a useful type of light cavalry remount. Note the single rein. The carbine bucket is the Mark III 1884 for the Martini-Henry carbine.

Plate 90 A trooper of Lumsden's Horse, a Volunteer unit raised in India for the South African War. The troop horse is presumably country bred.

Plate 91 A Waler from New South Wales. The photograph shows a Senior N.C.O. of the New South Wales Lancers in 1898.

Plate 92 A New Zealand Volunteer's mount of 1897.

Plate 93 The California Stock Saddle used by the North West Mounted Police of Canada from 1878 to 1919 and by the Canadian Contingents in the South African War of 1899 to 1902. From Turner's *North West Mounted Police*, Volume II, p. 449, published Ottawa, 1950, reproduced by permission of the Queen's Printer, Ottawa.

Plate 94 A troop horse of the Royal Canadian Dragoons, a Regular Regiment *c.*1899. British Army U.P. saddle. A typical good-class ride and drive Canadian remount of the type so much used by the Royal Artillery in the South African War.

Plate 95 Photograph of an oil painting by Captain Goodrich, then serving in Cape Mounted Rifles, of Lieut General Sir George Cathcart and his Staff on the borders of Basutoland in 1852 with an escort of the 12th Lancers. Pronounced by Cathcart, shown in front, as 'very lifelike', the painting shows the strong, upstanding better type Cape horse of the period. Sir George's charger 'Rifleman, is trotting and keeping all the others at a gallop.' From his *Correspondence*, published Murray, 1856, p. 353. Reproduced by permission of the Africana Museum, Johannesburg. See JAHR, Volume XLI, pages 208, 209.

Plate 96 A well-bred Basuto pony, 1900. From Miller's *Modern Polo*, 1902, by kind permission of Mrs E. D. Miller, O.B.E., J.P., and the Hutchinson Publishing Group.

Plate 97 Two typical South African ponies of the South African War period. These two were probably bred in the Transvaal, as they are ridden by two South African Republican Police of that Republic. But they could have been bred anywhere on the high veldt, in the Cape Colony, or the Orange Free State or Natal. The left-hand pony, head on, shows the narrow chest that was common. The other pony is up to far more weight than he looks to be.

Plate 98 A five-year-old black Argentine remount, 15 hands, cost £30, bought for the Natal Police just after the South African War. A very large number of these horses were bought for the Army during the War. They were not very successful and no more was this one. He pulled like a steam engine and knocked himself about so much that he was cast in 1908. By courtesy of Major A. A. Wood and Captain G. F. Court of the Natal Police.

Plate 99 A China pony 13·3 hands issued to the 1st Lancashire Fusiliers in N. China in 1937. Rider 5 feet 8 inches. By permission of Colonel P. Cleasby-Thompson, M.B.E., M.C.

Plates 100 and 101   100: Percheron Stallion bred in the United States of America. This is the type of horse used on common mares of the right stamp to produce the Field Artillery teams of the British Army from 1914 to 1918. He will have stood 17 hands, and his first cross with small Western mares of *c*.1,000 lb will have produced foals which would have matured at from 1,100 to 1,207 lb. These half-bred Percherons when put to clean bred stallions like the one in the photograph will have produced horses like the two in Plate 101. These are from drawings by Lionel Edwards, with whose permission they are reproduced, and should be compared with Plate 33. They show the same 'Yank' as landed in England and as despatched to France.

Plate 102   Egyptian Cavalry remounts 1896. Usually known as 'Syrians' or 'Syrian Arabs' (see in text). Issued to British Cavalry in 1884 and performed tremendous feats of endurance. They were all stallions, though these do not look it. The average height was 14 hands. They were bought in Syria and Lower Egypt and continued to be used by our cavalry up to the time of the final campaign against the Mahdists in 1898. They have been described as 'characterized by round chests, deep barrels, well ribbed up, short legs and plenty of breeding'. (See Burn, *Transport and Camel Corps*, pp. 272, 273.)

Plate 103   'Patterns of British Army Cavalry Bridles and Bits from 1660 to the Present Day' (1960), specially drawn by Harry Payne for the *Cavalry Journal*. These are described in detail in the section on bridles in Chapter Six.

Plate 104   His Majesty King George V, Colonel-in-Chief of the Scots Guards, showing the Regimental horse 'furniture' of modern times. Reproduced by gracious permission of Her Majesty The Queen and the Regimental Lieut Colonel The Scots Guards.

Plate 105   Shabraque belonging to Lieut General Sir John Taylor, used by him between 1825 and 1837, as a Major General, which he became in 1819. He had served in the 88th Regiment, the Connaught Rangers. Presented to the Staff College Museum by Field Marshal Sir Gerald Templer, K.G., G.C.B., G.C.M.G., K.B.E., D.S.O. with whose permission and that of the Staff College it is reproduced.

Plate 106   Shows the furniture used by Field Marshal Lord Hardinge. Reproduced by kind permission of The Queen's Own Royal West Kent Regiment.

Plate 107   Housing and pointed holster cap – green, trimmed with silver lace with red stripe – date from 1788. The rounded holster cap – red, trimmed with silver lace with two green stripes – dates from 1795, and is similar to the one shown in Plate 63. The plate is reproduced by permission of the Officer Commanding The Queen's Royal Irish Hussars.

Bibliography

Adams, John. *The Analysis of Horsemanship*, three Volumes, London 1799, 1805, 1812.

Adye, Major R. W. *The Bombardier and Pocket Gunner*. Egerton, London, 7th Edition, 1813.

Agriculture and Fisheries, the Board of. *Types of Horses Suitable for Army Remounts*. H.M.S.O. 1908, revised 1909.

Aide Mémoire to the Military Sciences, edited by the Corps of Royal Engineers in three Volumes, 1850–3. Many plates. John Weale, London.

Alderson, Lieut Colonel E. A. H., Royal West Kent Regiment. *Pink and Scarlet, or Hunting as a School for Soldiering*. Heinemann, 1899 and a second illustrated edition in 1900.

Aldershot Military Society, the Lectures of. Three Volumes 1888–97. Gale and Polden.

> Vol. I. G. Fleming (1833–1901) Principal Veterinary Surgeon 1883–90. 'The Physical Condition of the Horse for Military Purposes.'

> Vol. II. General Sir F. Smith (1857–1929) writing as Veterinary Surgeon Major. 'Saddles and Saddlery, Bits and Bitting, 1891.'

> Vol. III. Hayes, Captain M. H. 'The Horse for Military Purposes'; Veterinary Surgeon Colonel H. Thompson 'Our Military Horses', 1895.

> These Lectures are probably not well known. They were delivered by the leading veterinary experts of the period which covered the South African War of 1899–1900 and are of the greatest significance.

A.M.O.T. The Army Museums Ogilby Trust. Ministry of Defence (Army Dept.). The Trust Office have been responsible for a number of the sources listed here.

Animal Management, H.M.S.O. 1908, reprinted 1914.

Army Equipment 1864, Part IV, Military Train; 1865, Part II, Royal Artillery, H.M.S.O.

Army of Great Britain. 1862, 1865, 1886. Compiled by Captain M. Petrie. H.M.S.O. (In War Office Library.)

Army Historical Research, Journal of the Society for (JAHR), *passim* but especially Inspection Reports, Sumner's Articles on the Scots Greys and other Heavy Cavalry, mostly in Volumes III, xvi and xvii. But the General Index must be the guide for research.

Army Ordnance, Reports on Army Matters and on Miscellaneous Subjects Unconnected with Ordnance, Minutes of Evidence on Ordnance Commissions of Enquiry on Saddlery and Reports by Directors of Army Contracts, 1806–1900. These voluminous papers are to be consulted in the War Office Library. By the kindness of the Librarian and his Staff it is possible to extract a great deal of information as the indexing, if very full and difficult to follow, is comprehensive. Especially Volumes ix, xiv, xvii and xviii.

Army Service Corps, the Royal. Training, Part III, Transport 1911 and 1922. H.M.S.O.

Army Veterinary and Remount Services, 1939–45. H.M.S.O. 1961.

Army Veterinary Corps, a History of the Royal, 1796–1919, by Major General Sir Frederick Smith. Baillière, Tindall & Cox, 1927.

Army Veterinary Corps, *A Veterinary History of the War in South Africa*, by Major General F. Smith (as above). 1915.

Army Veterinary Services in the First World War: See Volume edited by Major General Sir L. J. Blenkinsopp, and Lieut Colonel J. W. Rainey, in Official History of the War. H.M.S.O. 1925.

Army Veterinary Corps, the History of the Royal, 1919–61, by Brigadier J. Clabby, Director of Veterinary and Remount Services. J. A. Allen & Co., 1963.

Arthur, Sir George. *The Story of the Household Cavalry*, two Volumes. Constable, 1909.

Artillerists Handbook of Reference, by G. Will and J. C. Dalton. Clowes & Co., 1876.

Artillerists Manual and British Soldiers Compendium, by Captain F. A. Griffiths. Woolwich, 1840. Printed by E. Jones.

Baily, Dep. Comm. General J. W. *The Otago Saddle*. Abyssinia 1867–8. Extracts from Reports on Field Equipments. Eyre and Spottiswoode, 1869. (War Office Library.)

Baker, Valentine. *Remarks on Organization of British Cavalry*. Longman, London, 1858.

Baldock, Lieut Colonel T. S. *Cromwell as a Soldier*. Kegan Paul, 1899.

Bannatyne-Allason, Major General R. 'Reminiscences of 40 years of Peace and War.' *Journal of Royal Artillery, 1923–4*, Volume L, No. 12.

Barrett, C. R. B. *History of the 7th Hussars*. Spottiswoode & Co., 1914.

Barrett, C. R. B. *History of the XIIIth Hussars*. Wm. Blackwood, 1911.

Bechuanaland Field Force, 1884–5; Confidential Report of Proceedings of. By Major General Sir C. Warren. London, 1885. War Office Library.

Bechuanaland Field Force, Regulations for. Cape Town, 1884.

Bethell, Lieut Colonel L. A. ('Pousse Cailloux'). 'The Silver Hand of Alexander.' *Blackwoods Magazine*, May, 1928.

Birkbeck, Major General Sir W. H. *The Remount Service*. H.M.S.O. 1918.

Bloodgood, Lida Fleitmann. *The Saddle of Queens*. J. A. Allen, 1959.

Bloodgood, Lida Fleitmann and Piero Santini. *The Horseman's Dictionary*. Pelham Books, 1963.

Bolton, Captain E. F. *Horse Management in West Africa*. 1931.

Brabant, Major General Sir E. V. 'Autobiography.' Typescript in Cape Town Archives.

Brett-James, E. A. *Wellington at War*. Macmillan, 1961.

Buckell, L. E. The Buckell Collection is now in the A.M.O.T., q.v.

Burgoyne, General (later Field Marshal) Sir J. F. *Military Opinions*, edited Wrottesley. Bentley, 1859.

Burn, Major D. B. *Notes on Transport and Camel Corps*. H.M.S.O. 1887.

Burne, Lieut Colonel A. H. *The Noble Duke of York*. Staples Press, 1949.

Burne, Lieut Colonel A. H. and Brigadier P. Young. *The Great Civil War*. Eyre and Spottiswoode, 1959.

Calendar of State Papers, Domestic, Charles I, 1628–9. Edited by John Bruce. Longman, Brown, Green, Longmans and Roberts, 1858.

Carriage Builders Journal, 1859, 1860.

Carter, Colonel W. H. (United States Army). *Horses, Saddles and Bridles*. Baltimore, U.S.A., 1902.

Cassels, Cmdr. S. A. C. *Peninsula Portrait*, 1811–1814. O.U.P. 1963.

Catalogues, Barnsby, J. A. (Sir Jabez Cliff & Co.), Walsall.
      Catalogue of Saddlery, 1892 and 1904.
      Bliss & Co., London 1904 and 1906.
      Brookes & Son, Walsall, 1904.
      Hawkins, J. H. & Co., Walsall, *The Equine Album*, c.1899, known to the Trade as the Saddlers Encyclopaedia.

Cathcart, Lieut General the Hon. Sir George C. *Correspondence*. Murray, 1856.

Cavalry Drill. H.M.S.O. 1898.

Cavalry Journal: *The Evolution of the Cavalry Saddle*, 1909, pp. 359–70. *Madras Cavalry*, 1927, p. 80; 1929, p. 580.

Champion and Wilton, Saddlers, 74 New Oxford Street, incorporating Messrs Whippy, Stegall & Co. 'Equipment Book', with sketches, 1895 to c.1940.

Childers, Erskine. *In the Ranks of the C.I.V.* Smith, Elder. 1901.

Christy, E. *Side Saddle Riding*. Vinton & Co. 1899.

Churchill, Rt Hon. Winston S. *My Early Life*. Odhams, 1947.

Clabby, Brigadier. See under Army Veterinary Corps.

Commissariat and Transport Corps. Exercises for. H.M.S.O. 1885.

Crookshank, Lieut Colonel C. de W. 'Prints of British Military Operations.' Adlard & Son and West Newman Ltd, 1921.

Cruso, John. *Military Instructions for the Cavalry*. Cambridge, 1632.

Curson, Dr H. H. Typescript List of Cavalry Regiments Posted to South Africa, 1796 to 1914, with the provenance of their remounts.

Cunynghame, General Sir Arthur. *My Command in South Africa, 1874–78*. Macmillan, 1879.

Denison, G. T. *Modern Cavalry*. T. Bosworth, London, 1868.

Dress Regulations for Officers of the Army, 1857, 1874, 1883. H.M.S.O.

Duhousset, Lieut Colonel E. *Gaits, Exterior and Proportions of the Horse*. London, translated from the French. 1896.

Engineer Training, Volume 1, 1929. H.M.S.O.

Field Artillery Service Handbook, Volume 1, 1883 and 1897. H.M.S.O.

Firth. *Cromwell's Army*, 2nd Edition. Methuen, 1912.

Fitch, C. G. *Queer Horses and Queer People*. Hurst and Blackett, 1947.

FitzWygram, Lieut General Sir F. *Horses and Stables*. London, 1869.

Fleming, G. (1833–1901; Principal Veterinary Surgeon 1883 to 1890). See under Aldershot Military Society.

Fleming, P. *Bayonets to Lhasa*. Hart-Davis, 1961.

Forbes, Major General A. *A History of the Army Ordnance Services*. Medici Society, 1929.

Fores. *Sporting Notes and Sketches*. 41 Piccadilly, London. 1887, 1888 edns.

Fortescue, Sir John. *History of the British Army*, 13 Volumes. Macmillan, 1899–1930.

Ffoulkes, Charles. *The Armourer and his Craft*, 1912.

Galtry, S. 'The Horse and the War.' *Country Life*, 1918.

Gilbey, Sir Walter. *The Great or War Horse*. Vinton, London, 1899.

Gilbey, Sir Walter. *Small Horses in Warfare*. Vinton, 1901.

Gilbey, Sir Walter. *Horse Breeding in India and England and Army Horses Abroad*. Vinton, 1901.

Gilbey, Sir Walter. *Horses Past and Present*. Vinton, 1900.

Goldsmid, Major General Sir F. J. *James Outram*. Smith, Elder, London, 1881.

Graham, Brigadier General C. A. L., *The History of the Indian Mountain Artillery*. Gale and Polden, 1957.

Grant, J. *British Battles on Land and Sea*, four Volumes. Cassell, 1891.

Grierson, Lieut Colonel J. M. *The British Army*. Many illustrations. Samson Low Marston, 1899.

Griffiths, Captain F. A. See Artillerists Manual

Grose, Francis. *Military Antiquities*. S. Hooper, London, 1801.

Hamilton, Colonel H. B. *Historical Record of the 14th (King's) Hussars*. Longmans, Green & Co., 1901.

Harrison, Colonel R. *The Officer's Memorandum Book*. Kegan Paul. 1881 edition.

Havelock, Major General Sir Henry Marshman. *The Three Main Military Questions of the Day*. London, 1867.

Hayes. See under Aldershot Military Society.

Head, Lieut A. S., Army Veterinary Corps. *The Wear and Tear of Horses during the South African War*. Printed at Pretoria, n.d. Reprinted for the Journal of Comparative Pathology and Therapeutics, n.d.

Hinde, Captain Robert. *The Discipline of the Light-Horse*. London, 1778.

Hogg, Brigadier O. F. G. *English Artillery, 1326 to 1716*. R. A. Institution, 1963.

Horton, Major J. *The Evolution of the Cavalry Saddle*. See under Cavalry Journal.

Hutchinson, G. S. *Machine Guns*. Macmillan, 1938.

Hylton, Lord. *The Paget Brothers*. 1790–1840. Murray, 1918.

Instructions in Military Equitation and in the Elements of the Field Movements of Cavalry (A.G.'s Office). Clowes, London, 1819.

Jackson, Lieut Colonel Donovan. *India's Army*. Samson Marston Low, 1940.

Jackson, Major E. S. *Records of the Inniskilling Dragoons*. Humphreys, 1909.

Jackson, Murray Cosby, Sergeant 7th M.I. *A Soldier's Diary in South Africa 1899–1901*. Goschen, 1913. Illustrated.

JAHR – See Army Historical Research, Journal.

Jessel, Colonel Sir H. M., Bart. *The Story of Romsey Remount Depot*. Abbey Press, 1919.

Jocelyn, Colonel J. R. J. *The History of the Royal Artillery* (*Crimean Period*). Murray, 1911.

Kane, Brigadier General. *System of Camp Discipline*. 1749.

Knötel-Sieg. *Handbuch der Uniformkunde*. Hamburg, 1937.

Krickel, G., and Lange, G. *Das Deutsches Reichsherr*. Berlin, 1889–92. Plates.

Lawson, C. C. P. *History of the Uniforms of the British Army*, Volumes I and II. Peter Davies, 1940 and 1941.

List of Changes in Warlike Material, Small Arms and other Military Stores. 1860–1912. Many plates. H.M.S.O.

Littauer, Captain V. S. *More about the Forward Seat*. Hurst and Blackett, 1917.

Long, Major General R. B.: Manuscript notes of. In the R.U.S.I. Library.

Longstaff, Major F. V., and Atteridge, Captain A. H. *The Book of the Machine Gun*. Rees, 1917.

Lucas, T. J. *Camp Life and Sport in South Africa*. Chapman Hall, 1870.

Lucas, T. J. *The Zulus and the British Frontiers*. Chapman Hall, 1879.

MacGuffie, T. H. (Ed.) *Peninsular Cavalry General* (Major General R. B. Long, see above). Harrap, 1951.

MacMunn, Major General Sir Geo. *Soldiering in India Today*. Journal of R.A. Institution, Volume L, 1934.

MacMunn, Major General Sir Geo. *Armies of India*, illustrated by Major A. C. Lovett. A. & C. Black, 1911.

Maguire, T. M. *Strategy and Tactics in Mountain Ranges*. London, 1904.

Maguire, T. M. *Guerilla and Partisan Warfare*. Rees, London, 1904.

Marling, Colonel Sir P. *Rifleman and Hussar*. Murray, 1931.

Manual of Artillery Exercises, Field. 1861, 1875 and 1883. H.M.S.O.

Manual of Engineer Training, Volume I. 1929. H.M.S.O.

Manual of Horsemastership, etc. 1937. H.M.S.O.

Manual of R.A.S.C. Training, Volume III, 1922. H.M.S.O.

Manual of Saddles and Sore Backs by Major General F. Smith (see under Aldershot Military Society). H.M.S.O. 1891.

Markham, Gervase. *The Soldiers Accidence*. 1625.

Marriott, Captain G. *Source History of the South African Veterinary and Remount Corps, 1939 to 1946*. Typescript, by courtesy of Dr H. H. Curson, South Africa.

Massé, Lieut Colonel C. H. *The Predecessors of the R.A.S.C., 1757 to 1888*. Gale and Polden, 1948.

Maxwell, Captain E. L. *The History of the XIth King Edward's Own Lancers, Probyn's Horse*. Guildford, 1914.

Miles, W. J. *Modern Practical Farriery*. William Mackenzie, 1895. Includes saddlery, harness, riding, etc., etc. Plates.

Military Artificers Handbook, 1899, 8th Edition, 1915, 10th Edition. H.M.S.O.

Military Train. See Army Equipment.

Navy and Army Illustrated, 1896, 1897, 1898.

Nevill, Ralph. 'British Military Prints.' Connoisseur Publishing Coy., 1909.

Newcastle, William Cavendish, Duke of. *Horsemanship*. 1667.

Nolan, Captain L. E. *Cavalry: Its History and Tactics*. T. Bosworth, London, 1853.

Olsen, S. J. 'The Development of the U.S.A. Army Saddle.' *Military Collector and Historian*, Spring Number, 1955.

Oman, Sir Charles. *Wellington's Army 1809–1814*. Edward Arnold, 1913.

Palmer, F. N. *More than Shadows: Biography of W. Russell Flint*. Studio, 1943.

Parr, Major General Sir Henry Hallam (1847–1914). *Recollections and Correspondence*. Edited by Sir Charles Fortescue-Brickdale. Fisher Unwin, 1917.

Parrino, Major M. F. *An Introduction to Pack Transport and Pack Artillery*. Queensland Publishing Coy., New York, 1956.

Parry, D. H. *The Death or Glory Boys*. Cassell, 1890.

Pembroke, Henry, Earl of. *Military Equitation*. 1761. 3rd Edition. Sarum, 1778.

Peters, Lieut Colonel J. G. *Treatise on Equitation, or The Art of Horsemanship*. Whittaker, 1835.

Philipson on Harness and Nimshivitch on Cape Carts. Stanford, 1882.

Pietsch, Paul. *Die Formations und Uniformierungs-Geschichte des Preussiche Heeres 1808–1912*. Volume II. Plates. Berlin, 1912.

Pocock, R. *The Frontiersman's Pocket-Book*. Murray, 1909.

Pomeroy, Major Hon. R. L. *History of the 5th Dragoon Guards*. Blackwood, 1924.

Prescott, H. F. M. *Spanish Tudor*. Constable, 1940.

Preston, Lieut Colonel the Hon. R. M. P. *The Desert Mounted Corps*. Constable, 1921.

Quarterly List: see under Vocabulary.

Queen's Regulations. 1844, p. 371. Horses of Cavalry. (The Cavalry Colonel's Charter.)

Record of the Expedition to Abyssinia, 1868, by Major T. J. Holland, Bombay Staff Corps and Colonel Sir Henry M. Hozier, 3rd D.Gs., two Volumes. H.M.S.O. 1870.

Reitz, Deneys. *Commando*. Faber, 1929.

Report of the Committee on the Supply of Remounts for the Army, 1902. A 726. H.M.S.O.

Reports on the Service Saddle, Egypt, 1882. 54/Gen. 39818/7712, 1882.

Rimington, Major General Sir M. 'Lecture before the Military Society of Ireland, The Horse in the Late War', 1902. Reprinted in Miller Maguire's *Guerilla and Partisan Warfare*. Rees, London, 1904.

Rogers, Colonel H. C. B. *The Mounted Troops of the British Army*. Seeley, Service, 1959.

Routh, E. M. G. *Tangier, England's lost Atlantic Outpost, 1661–1684*. Murray, 1912.

Royal Artillery Institution Journal, and Journals of the Royal Artillery, Volume LXXXIX, Volumes XX to LXXI, *passim* and 1962.

Shakespeare's England. Two volumes. Clarendon Press, 1916. Volume II, *Horsemanship*, by A. Forbes Sieveking.

Sherwell, J. W. Saddlers Company, 'Introduction to the London Saddlers Exhibition of 1892 Catalogue.'

Sidmouth, Major Viscount. 'Notes on the Remounting of the Madras Cavalry in the Days of the Company Bahadur.' *Cavalry Journal*, 1927 to 1929.

Sidney, S. *The Book of the Horse*. Third Edition. Cassell, 1878.

Sessions, H. *Two Years with Remount Commissions*. Chapman, 1903.

Soldier, October 1963, article on the R.A.S.C. 'Man, Mule and Mountain.'

'Statistics of the Military Effort of the British Empire, 1914 to 1920', Part VI, Remounts. H.M.S.O. 1921.

Stevens, Captain Henry. The Papers of Captain Henry Stevens, Wagon-Master-General to King Charles I. Edited by Margaret Toynbee. Oxford Record Society, 1961.

Stewart, Captain P. F. *History of the XIIth Royal Lancers*. O.U.P., 1950.

Stocqueler, J. H. *The Life of Field Marshal the Duke of Wellington*. Volume 1. London, 1852–3.

Summerhays, R. S. *The Observer's Book of Horses and Ponies*. 2nd Edition. Warne, 1953.

Swartz, A. (Staff Veterinary Surgeon, Royal Bavarian Light Horse). *The Horse*. Translated from the German by Principal Veterinary Surgeon G. Fleming, *c*.1891.

Theal, C. McG. *History of South Africa: Before 1795*. Three Volumes. London, 1897.

Theal, C. McG. *History of South Africa: After 1795*. Ten Volumes. London, 1908.

Thompson. See under Aldershot Military Society.

Thornton, R. W. *Origin and History of the Basuto Pony*. Privately printed, 1937.

Times History of the War in South Africa, 1899 to 1902. Samson Low, Marston & Co. Volumes v and vi, 1901–3.

Tomkinson, W. *Diary of a Cavalry Officer in the Peninsular and Waterloo Campaigns*. Swan & Sonnenschein, 1895.

Tract, Wehr und Waffen (Medieval Costume, Armour and Weapons, 1350–1450) by Eduard Wagner, Z. Drobna, J. Durdik. Translated by Jean Layton. Printed Czechoslovakia, 1957. P. Hamlyn, London, 1958.

Trew, C. G. *The Accoutrements of the Riding Horse*. Seeley, Service, 1951.

Tylden, Major G. *The Armed Forces of South Africa*. Africana Museum, Johannesburg, 1954.

Tyndale, Lieut Colonel W. (1st Life Guards). *A Treatise on Military Equitation*. Egerton, 1797.

United Services Journal, 1831. Part I, p. 396. 'The Letters of Sergeant Saddler W. Wisely, 1st Royal Dragoons.' H. Colburn and R. Bentley.

United Services Journal, 1864. Part III. Article on p. 329. Hurst and Blackett.

United States Army Pack Transport from 1944. Basic Field Manual, Animal Transport.

Vivian, C. *Lord Vivian: a Memoir* (1775–1842). Isbister & Co., 1897.

Vocabulary of Stores. War Office Quarterly List, 1860, 1863, 1864 and 1934.

Walker, Stella A. 'Fashion and the Horsewoman.' *Country Life*, 19.7.62.

Ward, R. *Animadversions of Warre*. London, 1639.

Ward, S. G. P. *Wellington's Headquarters*. O.U.P., 1957. The author is indebted to Mr Ward for the M.S. notes on Captain Scovell's portable forge of 1810.

War Office. *Types of Horse Suitable for Army Remounts*. H.M.S.O., 1927.

Wellington. *Supplementary Despatches and Memoranda of Field Marshal Arthur Duke of Wellington*. 15 Volumes. Edited by the 2nd Duke of Wellington, 1858 to 1872.

West, J. *Village Recorder*. Macmillan, 1962.

Whinyates, Colonel F. A. *From Corunna to Sevastopol, the History of 'C' Battery, R.H.A*. Allen, 1884.

Wilson, Lieut Colonel A. W. *The Story of the Gun*. R.A. Institution, 1945.

Wolseley, Field Marshal Lord. *The Soldier's Pocket Book*. Macmillan, 1869.

Wood, F. M. Sir Evelyn. *The Crimea in 1854 and 1894*. London, 1895.

Wood, F. M. Sir Evelyn. *Winnowed Memories*. Cassell, 1918.

Appendix

THE COLOUR OF A HORSE'S COAT

There have been various methods in the past of describing the colour of the hair which covers the entire body of the horse and mule and in reading old books one not infrequently comes on unfamiliar names applied to different variations of colours, especially of grey animals. There is also the difficulty that horses are apt to clip a different or slightly different colour from that which the coat is when left to grow.

The descriptions used in Bloodgood and Santini's *Horseman's Dictionary*, published in 1963, have been taken as standard for the present day. They differ widely in some details from the usage normal in the latter half of last century and there are also slight divergencies current in different parts of the English-speaking world.

There has been in the past a certain amount of disagreement as to the correct way of describing a brown horse. Sometimes what today are called bay horses are classed as brown; another point has been the use of the word sorrel. These terms will be listed in due course.

The British Army, in common with most other armies of which we have particulars, has always liked to mount units or parts of units on the same coloured horses. There has also been a marked tendency to mount trumpeters on greys, and kettle drummers on horses of as startling colours as possible; see the colour plate of the drum horses of the Household Cavalry.

For many years the British Cavalry were mounted on blacks, as the Household Cavalry still are.

With the exception of the 2nd Dragoon Guards, Queen's Bays (now the 1st Queen's Dragoon Guards), who rode bays from 1753 and probably earlier and the 2nd Dragoons, Royal Scots Greys, who rode greys and were described in 1702 as the Scots Regiment of White Horses, the first break away, in peace time at any rate, from the practice of riding blacks, was caused by the introduction of Light Dragoons, who rode horses of varying colours, often having each troop mounted on horses of the same one. This practice and that of mounting trumpeters on specially coloured horses was forbidden by Queen's Regulations in 1844, but continued in India for many years. Grey horses were naturally a stumbling block, as a man on a grey was a mark, whether consciously or not made no difference, to any enemy firing at the unit to which he belonged. Though the Royal Artillery sometimes had gun teams all on greys in India and in South Africa, this was obviously not desirable before the days of camouflage, as six limbers all with grey teams must have made a magnificent aiming mark. The once famous chestnuts of A Troop, Royal Horse Artillery, were a different matter and both Gunners and Sappers liked to have matched teams in guns and waggons whenever possible.

Generally speaking the old adage that 'a good horse is never of a bad colour' holds good, though few men who have passed all their lives with horses would altogether agree with it, and it is a fact that what are called 'washy' chestnuts are specially disliked as liable to be soft hearted. Whether this is really so it is impossible to say.

A list of colours, mostly as described by Bloodgood and Santini follows; there will undoubtedly be experts who will not agree altogether with the details given.

BAY A bay horse must have a black mane and tail and should be 'fox brown with more red than chestnut'. He can be distinguished from a brown by the fine hairs on the muzzle. Varieties are: bright, blood, mahogany, light sandy; and the French cavalryman, Lieut Colonel Duhousset, added cherry, golden, chestnut, maroon and vine-coloured as adjectives to precede the word 'bay'.

BROWN Duhousset included all browns in the above variations. The generally accepted description is that a brown horse varies from 'dark, almost black-brown to the colour of faded leaves'. The muzzle and the light areas inside the legs should be tan coloured. The Bavarian authority (see under references) gives as variations light, dark, dappled and chestnut.

BLACK A black horse should be of a shiny jet hue and can be rusty or dull black.

CHESTNUT Often described as sorrel, except in Australia, where the word sorrel means a roan, q.v In the U.S.A. the term sorrel is common, as it used to be in England. A chestnut should have a mane of the same colour as the coat or lighter. Varieties are bright gold, liver, mealy or red. Also golden, cherry and copper-coloured. A real golden chestnut is a most beautiful colour.

CREAM At one time creams were much in favour for band or trumpeter's mounts and till comparatively recently creams drew the State carriages in this country. There are Isabella-coloured as well as pale creams and the tail may be white or yellow.

DUN A dun usually has a black dorsal stripe and is considered to be a good hard-conditioned animal, much sought after when remounts are on issue. A black mane and tail are usually found with the stripe down the back. Also described as dead grey, yellow or buckskin, sand, mouse, or clay-bank colour.

GREY or GRAY Grey horses normally go white with age and vary from that colour, shading off into roan, q.v. A grey always has one parent of that colour. There are black-grey, dappled, iron,

dead-lead, flea-bitten (considered a very hard colour), nutmeg, slate, trout-coloured or clayey 'greys', according to the ideas of the individual naming the horse.

PIEBALD Black and white in large patches.

ROAN A difficult colour to describe. An inter-mingling of red, white and yellow or black, white and yellow hair. In Australia used of a chestnut, q.v. In South Africa known as skimmel and much liked. Roans, like duns and flea-bitten greys, are considered to have strong constitutions. Varieties are black, bay, red, or chestnut roan, also strawberry, blue or silver.

SKEWBALD Red and white in large patches, or brown and white. Both piebalds and skewbalds have been fashionable as drum horses. See colour plate, drum horses of the Household Cavalry.

Writing in 1895 the Director General of Remount Services, Major General H. Thompson, agreed that as a rule the darker shaded a horse's coat was the more stamina he probably had, and in *Animal Management*, the official handbook of 1914, it is stated that horses with a faded or washed-out appearance in the coat should not be selected as this indicates a general want of hardness. The author goes on to quote the saying, already quoted, that 'a good horse is never a bad colour'. He adds that the colours usually bought are bay, brown, black and chestnut; not so commonly seen are dun, grey, roan, piebald and skewbald.

The same book gives the markings as follows:

ON THE HEAD

Star A white mark more or less rounded in the centre of the forehead; may be large, small, irregular or faint.

Race A narrow white stripe down the face, usually in the centre, may be short, broad or faint. Also sometimes called a 'reach' or 'stripe'.

Snip A white mark between the nostrils.

Blaze A broad splash of white down the face. When very exaggerated the horse may be described as 'bald-faced' or 'white-faced'.

Upper-lip and under-lip Are the names used for white skin at the edges of the lips.

ON THE BODY

List, Ray and Stripe Are terms used for the dark lines seen along the back of some horses, all donkeys (see under 'Donkeys') and many mules, and apply to the same marks on the shoulders of the last two animals.

Zebra Marks Are the dark horizontal stripes at the back of the arm above the knee and across the lower part of the thigh. They are unusual in horses, but common in mules and donkeys. When on a horse they are called mule or donkey marks.

Saddle and Gall Marks Are white patches where the hair has grown over old injuries.

Animal Management Explains the colour flea-bitten grey as meaning that the coloured hairs in the coat are arranged in tufts all over the body.

Salmon Marks Seen particularly on Australian horses, are fine white lines of hair looking like a sort of wide-meshed network on the loins and quarters.

ON THE LEGS

White feet, white coronets, white pasterns or white fetlocks are all common. When the white comes just above the fetlock it is called a sock, and when higher a stocking or a white leg. If the white is 'in spots' it is called 'with spots'.

Black points Describes the hair on the lower part of the leg and the hoof being black.

There is an old rhyme referring to white legs on a horse:

One white leg, ride him for your life,
Two white legs, give him to your wife,
Three white legs, give him to your man,
Four white legs, sell him if you can.

Possibly this jingle was composed because white hoofs are not as strong as black!

REFERENCES

Animal Management, H.M.S.O. 1908, reprinted 1914.

Lida Fleitmann Bloodgood and Piero Santini, Major, Italian Cavalry, *The Horseman's Dictionary*, published Pelham Books, 1963.

Duhousset, Lieut Colonel E., French Cavalry, *Gait, Exterior and Proportions of the Horse*, translated London, 1896.

Swartz, Veterinary Surgeon A., Royal Bavarian Light Horse. *The Horse*, translated from the German by G. Fleming and published by Philip and Sons, London.

Manual of Horsemastership, H.M.S.O., 1937.

Glossary of Terms Used in this Book

AGED A horse over six years old, used in a general sense of a fully developed animal.

AMBLE or 'Pace' See under 'Paces'.

ARAB The oldest known breed of domesticated horse, believed to have been bred pure from *c*.630 A.D. Indigenous to Arabia, and used practically all over the world for crossing with other light breeds to give courage, intelligence, pace, endurance and handiness to horses used for war and for many other purposes under the saddle. The Arab has one rib and one lumbar vertebra less than other breeds and measures 14 to 14·3 hands in Arabia, and 14·2 to 15 hands as bred in other countries. An Arab weighs from 800 to 1,000 lb and the usual colours are grey, bay or chestnut. The head is usually dish-faced and the head and tail are carried high. The Arabs in breeding these horses laid stress on the female line.

ARCHES The curved front and back (pommel and cantle) of a saddle-tree. (Illustration: Plate 11.)

A.T. Animal Transport Cart, two-wheeled for a pair of animals.

BALANCE GIRTH See under 'sidesaddle'. A strap buckled on the right side of the cantle and running to the girth straps on the left side to preserve the balance of the sideways seat.

BARB A light type of saddle-horse found from Syria to Morocco, with a large amount of Arab blood, country-bred mares being the dams. Less shapely than the Arab and often smaller; usually possessing the stamina of the Arab. (See Plate 102.)

BARS OF A BIT The part of the bit passing through the horse's mouth.

BARS or Sideboards of a saddle The curved parts of the tree running along each side of the spine and joining the front and rear arches.

BARS, STIRRUP The metal attachments to the saddle tree to which the stirrup leathers are fastened. In some cases these bars have a spring release at one end.

BAY See under Appendix on Colour.

'BAYS' The sub-title of the 2nd Dragoon Guards, Queen's Bays, now the 1st Queen's Dragoon Guards.

BEARING REIN A rein running from the snaffle or bridoon to the pad or luggage saddle of the off horse of a harness pair to keep the horse's head in the correct position. (Plate 29.)

BIT The metal mouthpiece, either straight or with a short raised section in the centre, running through the horse's mouth and bearing on the jaws and tongue. The raised portion is known as the port, and the straight pieces on either side as the canons. On each end of the mouthpiece are fitted the cheeks on which the mouthpiece revolves. The metal of the cheeks above the bit are buckled to the bridle and the long straight lower portion carries the bit rein at the bottom, and in the case of the modern Universal Pattern elbow bit, the so-called snaffle rein at the top, level with the mouthpiece. (Plate 103.)

BLANKET, SADDLE Usually white or brown, should be made of thick material; size about 5 feet 5 inches by 4 feet 8 inches; folded to fit under the saddle, sometimes in as many as sixteen folds, to pad the saddle along the spine. The number of folds depends on the condition of the horse. A blanket can be used as a covering at night when it is called a 'horse blanket'.

BLINKERS Sometimes called winkers. Curved leather shields fastened to the bridle behind a horse's eyes to prevent him seeing behind him. Used, unnecessarily, in the Army until 1853.

BLOCKED SEAT The seat of a saddle made in one piece, wetted and shrunk on to the tree.

BOARD or Sideboard of a saddle See under Bars.

BRADOON or BRIDOON The name of a snaffle bit, usually jointed, when used with a bit as a double bridle. (Figure 22.)

BRANDING An animal bought as a remount is marked by burning through the hair into the skin with a red-hot iron, either on the thick part of the hind leg, on the shoulder, on the neck or on the hoof. When sold out of Government service the brand is usually cancelled in the same way.

BREAST COLLAR or BREAST A wide leather band going round a horse's breast in harness, instead of a shaped collar round the neck, to which the traces are fastened. Adjustable to different animals.

BREASTPLATE A strap round a horse's neck, fastened to the front of the saddle and between the forelegs to the girth. Prevents the saddle slipping back.

BREECHING In a set of harness the wide band going round a horse's quarters well below the dock on which the horse can exert his weight backwards and act as a brake on the vehicle he is pulling.

BRIDLE The head gear to which is attached the bit or bits by which the horse is controlled. (Plate 103; Figure 22.)

BUCK The action of a horse or mule when intending to get rid of a rider or a saddle. The animal leaves the ground suddenly with the head between the forelegs and has all four legs off the ground at once. Common in Western America and Australia, but also all over the world.

BUCKET Used to describe any leather or canvas case in which a long-barrelled firearm is carried on a saddle. Usually a so-called deep bucket takes the arm muzzle down; a shallow bucket takes it muzzle up, a lance bucket the butt only. In the case of a lance bucket it is strapped on the stirrup, in other cases on the Dees of the saddle.

BURS The continuation of the sideboards or bars of the saddle-tree beyond the front arch or pommel, usually fitted with Dees to take the holsters, wallets, or a front pack.

CACOLET Chairs or stretchers fitted one on each side of a pack-saddle to take wounded men in the sitting or lying position. Plate 49 shows both types fitted to camel saddles.

CANTER Correctly a pace of three beats, but also used of a slow gallop of four beats. A pace of nine miles an hour. In early nineteenth-century Cavalry Regulations called a slow gallop.

CANTLE The curved arch at the back of a saddle-tree. The cantle has been at times built up to give support and protection to the rider's loins. Plates 1

to 8 show variations and Plates 11 to 13, 17, 18 and 20 the so-called 'spoon' cantle.

CAPE CART A two-wheeled cart for a pair of animals used in South Africa, as described in the *Manual of Horsemastership*. The neck bar fitting is similar to that used on the limber. A.T. Cart, q.v. – a version of the same type.

CAPE FAN The 'Trade' name for the saddle, or more correctly the tree, known as the Colonial or semi-military saddle and by various other names. Presumably this tree originated at the Cape of Good Hope, though evidence is not forthcoming.

CAVALRY Included horse and in time Dragoons and Light Dragoons, q.v. All 'Cavalry' were mounted men carrying some form of *arme blanche*, and usually pistols as well, whose main purpose was to attack mounted, if necessary at the highest speed commensurate with maintaining a regular formation. From about 1660 in the British service Cavalry also carried some form of shoulder fire-arm, for use when dismounted for reconnaissance or any similar duties.

CENTRE PAIR or PAIRS The name applied to the pair or pairs of a team between the leaders and the wheelers.

CHAMBER OF A SADDLE The hollow space between the panels along the spine which, if they are correctly fitted, allows a current of air to circulate. With a packed saddle this chamber should be large enough to allow of three fingers being inserted under the cantle between the fans.

CHARGE The culminating point of an advance by a force of cavalry when attacking mounted. Made at the gallop, with the utmost possible speed during the very short final stage.

CHEEKS See under 'Bit'. The side pieces of the bridle are also called the cheeks.

CINCH Canadian and North American name for a girth.

COB A short-legged strongly built horse not over 15 hands. The Dragoon units of the Civil War period rode cobs, as did the Mounted Infantry on Home Service in the last quarter of the nineteenth century. (Plates 71, 73, Fig. 2, and 78.)

COCKTAIL A common expression for a horse with a docked tail. (Plates 23a and b, 62 and 63.)

COLLAR See Plate 29. A heavily padded leather case made to fit round a horse's neck to which are attached the traces by which the animal pulls a vehicle. See under Hames.

COLOUR or COAT of a horse or mule. See in the Appendix on the subject.

COLT A young male horse under three or four years old.

CORONET The region round the top of the hoof.

CRADLE The wooden or metal frame fitted on a pack-saddle to take various kinds of loads. The parts of mountain guns need specially designed cradles. Used roughly to describe a pack-saddle.

CROSS-TREE Another name for a cradle, specially used of an 'X' pattern saddle, as on page 180.

CROUP The part of a horse's back behind the saddle. Hence the French expression 'en croupe' for a person sitting behind the saddle, either on a pillion or merely on the horse's back.

CRUPPER The strap running from the back of the cantle, divided where it passes under the horse's dock, which keeps the saddle from slipping forward.

CRUTCH Another name for the support or supports on the front of a sidesaddle round which the rider passes a leg or both legs. Also called pommel or horn.

CURB BIT See under 'Bit'. The type of mouthpiece fitted with a piece of chain, fastened at each end, which fits into the groove under a horse's chin. (Figure 22.)

CURB CHAIN The chain described above. In the U.P. army bit the steel chain has nineteen links. Plate 65 shows this chain on the charger drinking. (Figure 22.)

CURRICLE A two-wheeled vehicle for a pair of horses of Regency days with the pole supported by a metal bar fastened to the saddles on the horses. See in the section under artillery harness.

DAM The female parent of a horse or mule.

DEES or Ds Metal loops or staples fixed on a saddle or parts of harness for attaching other parts or articles of equipment.

DIP An imaginary perpendicular line from the lowest part of the seat of a saddle to a horizontal line joining pommel to cantle.

DOCK The bony part of a horse's tail. Thus a horse is said to be 'docked' when a part of this bony structure has been artificially removed. See in section on 'Tails'.

DOUBLE BRIDLE See under 'Bridle'. Plate 84 shows a double bridle with very small snaffle (bridoon) rings.

DRAFT or DRAUGHT Used of any animal put to pull a vehicle or sled.

DRAGOON GUARDS Heavy Cavalry or Horse. The change of title in no way affected their role; see in text.

DRAGOONS From 1660 to c.1700 Dragoons were men drilled as infantry who rode cobs, q.v., and fought dismounted with shoulder fire-arms. From c.1700 Dragoons were armed as Cavalry and were used more and more in that role.

DRIVERS Usually the men, known as 'Drivers', who ride the near-side horses of a harness pair. But used of any man in charge of and controlling led animals, and used in both a military and civilian sense for those who sit on a vehicle and control a team by the use of long reins.

ENGLISH SADDLE Used by Sidney and by Bloodgood and Santini (see Bibliography) meaning the ordinary hunting saddle in use in England from at least as long ago as the early seventeenth century. Plate 84 shows one with holsters added. (Figure 3.)

ENTIRE An uncastrated male horse. Entires are not accepted as remounts in Europe, as they fight too much with other horses; but were common as troop horses in Egypt, India and South Africa at various times. It was considered, rightly or wrongly, that an entire had more stamina than a gelding.

FAN The continuation of the sideboards of a saddle behind the cantle, usually fitted with Dees to take a rear pack. Gave the name to the Cape Fan saddle.

FARM HARNESS A simple type of harness used in single draft in the nineteenth century and by the artillery from early days till c.1800.

FARRIER The 'tradesman' (blacksmith) who does the shoeing of the horses of a unit. Farrier Sergeant Major is the senior rank.

FETLOCK The lower rear portion of a horse's ankle joint.

'FIFTEEN BOBBER' The slang name for the remount loaned by the Government to officers between the two World Wars for 15s a month. The remount could be used for sport and was kept in good condition at no expense to Government.

FILLY A mare up to the age of three or four years, who has not been put to stud, is called a filly.

FLAP OF A SADDLE The leather sides over which the stirrups hang where the rider's legs go.

FOOT REINS Reins running to the stirrups of a Kettle-drummer (colour plate), used for guiding the Drum Horse.

FOREHAND The part of a horse in front of the saddle.

FOUR-IN-HAND Two pairs of horses driven with long reins from a vehicle.

FRAME Another name for the cradle of a pack-saddle.

FROG The V-shaped piece of horn between the angle of a horse's heels.

FRONT PACK Any form of rolled cloak, blanket, etc. etc., fastened across the pommel of a saddle over the holsters or wallets.

GAIT See 'Paces'.

GALLOP The fastest pace of the horse. The *Manual of Horsemastership* gives the pace as 15 miles an hour. A horse is capable of about twice this speed for a short distance.

GELDING A castrated male horse. In Europe geldings and mares only are taken as remounts.

GIRTH Broad or narrow bands of leather, cord or rawhide, fastened to a saddle on both sides of the tree underneath the flaps holding the saddle in place. The normal girth goes under the horse a hand's-breadth behind the foreleg. In the 'cowboy' type of saddle there may be a second girth going much further back.

GLANDERS A serious, highly infective disease of horses and mules affecting the bronchial tubes, lungs, glands and skin. Common in wartime, resulting in large numbers of animals having to be destroyed.

'GREAT SADDLE' Originally the saddle used by men in full armour. In a slightly modified scale, weighing as much as 60 lb, used in very limited numbers in the armies of the Civil War period and as late as 1664.

'GREYS' The Second Dragoons, the Scots Greys. See under Colour in the separate section.

GULLET PLATE A curved metal plate reinforcing the wooden pommel of a saddle.

HACKNEY In the eighteenth century a type of riding horse, with a well-developed capacity for covering long distances at a fast trot, was bred in the Eastern Counties and known as a Norfolk Trotter or Hackney. Usually got from thoroughbred sires crossed on selected local mares. In the nineteenth century became a highly specialized high-stepping trotting breed used for light harness work and much in favour as sires for artillery teams on the Continent.

'HAIRIES' The nickname for the horses of the light draft units, Royal Artillery etc., who were apt to have a good deal of hair on their heels from having been bred from cart-horse stock.

HALT The expression used of mounted troops when stationary, e.g. 'At the halt'. The word of command to stop troops when on the move.

HALTER A headstall of leather, rope, or webbing used for tying a horse up. Sometimes made to act also as the headpiece of a bridle.

HALTER CHAIN A chain attached to the halter for tying the horse up.

HAMES Metal rods fitting round the outside of the collar used in draft to which the traces are fastened.

HAND The lineal measure used for ascertaining a horse's height in Anglo-Saxon countries. Stated by Bloodgood and Santini to have been devised by Leonardo da Vinci. A hand measures four inches, and a horse described as 14·2 hands measures 4 feet 10 inches or 58 inches; measured perpendicularly at the highest point of the withers, i.e. in front of the saddle.

HANDLER The specially trained man in charge of a war dog.

HARNESS Plate 29 for double collar harness, shaft draft, Plate 31a and b for pole draft. Plate 32b for breast harness and Plate 44b for single harness should be of more use than verbal descriptions. Up to 1853 Universal Pattern harness was made of black leather, after that of brown.

HAUNCHES The hindquarters of a horse. The expression 'to pull a horse back onto his haunches' means that he is reined back until his hocks are right under him. The wheelers in Plate 35 are in this position.

HEADROPE A rope attached to the halter for tying the horse up.

HEEL The back portion of a horse's hoof or the raised portion at the back of a horseshoe at the two points.

HIGH MOUNTING Late eighteenth- and early nineteenth-century expression for a saddle of Hussar type with a high pommel and cantle.

HIGH SCHOOL or HAUTE ÉCOLE The training of a horse to execute a series of difficult and controlled movements at all paces. This practice, still in vogue, was much favoured at various times by officers of our own and various Continental armies for training chargers.

HINNEY The offspring of an entire horse and a she-ass or donkey. Often mistakenly called a jennet, q.v. Hinneys are comfortable to ride and are useful light draft harness animals.

HOCK The main joint of a horse's hind leg between the stifle and fetlock.

HOLSTER A shaped leather case holding a pistol, normally fastened as a pair, joined by a broad leather band over the pommel of a saddle and secured to Dees on the front of the saddle or on the burs, if such exist. In the past covered with 'holster caps' made of cloth or fur to keep the pistols dry.

HOLSTER CAPS See above.

HOOF The horny casing of a horse's foot. The sides are known as the quarters.

HORN The strong, high and narrow prolongation of the pommel in a Western American and Canadian saddle to which the lasso or lariat is fastened.

HORSE Any equine, stallion, gelding, mare or filly. More specifically a male.

'HORSE' The Heavy Cavalry of the British Army, renamed Dragoon Guards; see in text. By the early years of this century only the Household Cavalry were 'Horse'. See under 'Cavalry'.

'HORSEMAN' Used of a man who rides well; thus the Rough Riding staff of a mounted unit, who are concerned with the breaking of young horses should be capable of being described as 'Horsemen'. In the general sense a man who rides.

HORSEMASTER One who can get the best results out of a horse with a minimum of fatigue to the animal. One who therefore possesses the qualities of Horsemastership. Not necessarily a very good horseman.

HOUSINGS A cloth or skin, usually embroidered, going under a saddle and covering the horse's flanks. The housing was sometimes joined to the holster caps by a piece of leather going over the saddle.

HUNTER A horse capable of following a pack of foxhounds hunting a fox at full speed over a countryside with numerous obstacles which the horse must jump. Distinguished as heavy-, medium- and light-weight hunters. Plate 79 shows a heavy-weight hunter type. Plate 72 medium- and light-weight hunter types. The influence of the hunter type on British Army remounts can hardly be exaggerated.

HUNTING SADDLE See 'English saddle'.

IRON, STIRRUP A footrest, suspended from the saddle-tree, the use of which enables the rider to make the fullest use of his strength both to control the horse and manage his weapons effectively.

JENNET A small Spanish horse. The name is used incorrectly for a hinney, q.v.

JOWL or THROAT PLUME or ORNAMENT As the name implies, this is a piece of decoration hung from the bridle, swinging under the horse's throat.

KEHAILAN or KEHILAN Arabic for a pure bred horse, synonymous with the word 'thoroughbred' as used of English horses, q.v.

KNEE ROLL A leather pad running down the front of the flap of a saddle intended to prevent the rider's knee slipping forward. (Plate 1.) The knee roll is not found in modern military saddles.

LASSO or LARIAT A long rope of cord or rawhide used to catch a horse or other animal. The lasso was issued to a small proportion of men of mounted units during the nineteenth century for the purpose of using troop horses to assist in pulling vehicles which had stuck fast in difficult ground.

LEAD or LEADERS The front animal or animals of a team. The driver who rides the near-side leader of a gun had to be a highly skilled man. He was known as the Lead Driver.

LEAPING HEAD OF A SIDESADDLE See Figure 13b. The lower pommel is the leaping head or horn.

LEATHER, STIRRUP The flat strap used double, buckled to the iron stirrup and passing through the saddle-tree or attached to it in front of the upper part of a rider's thigh. Pierced with holes to allow of alterations in length.

LIGHT DRAGOONS Later Hussars and Lancers. A lighter form of Cavalry riding smaller horses, introduced in the mid-eighteenth century; see text. Lancers, introduced c.1816, were originally classed as Medium Cavalry which did not affect their use. The title Light Dragoon meant Light Cavalry as distinguished from Heavy.

LIMBER The two-wheeled cart fitted with shafts or a pole for two animals to which a gun or another limber is hooked.

LUGGAGE SADDLE Sometimes called a harness saddle or pad saddle. The small saddle not made to hold a rider; used in harness for horses not ridden.

MACCLELLAN PACK SADDLE Designed by Lieut Colonel G. P. MacClellan, D.S.O., in 1920 for the Mountain or Pack howitzer used by the Royal Artillery, both British and Indian.

MCCLELLAN CAVALRY SADDLE The U.P. American Army saddle from 1858 to 1947. (Plate 21.)

MANE The hair on a horse's neck.

MANÈGE An enclosed riding school or a piece of ground marked out with tracks, such as figures of eight etc., used for schooling remounts.

MARE A female horse over five years old.

MARKHAM SADDLE Introduced by Gervase Markham from France in the seventeenth century. Became the prototype of cavalry saddles in Great Britain until the early part of the eighteenth century. (Plate 1.)

MARKINGS Distinguishing marks of a different colour to that of a horse's coat of all sizes and shapes from the large markings on the body of some breeds to the small strips and white feet found on nearly all breeds.

MELTON MOWBRAY A town in Leicestershire where the H.Q. of the Remount Training School has been for many years. Situated in the heart of the finest fox-hunting country in Britain.

MOUNTED INFANTRY or 'M.I.' Picked men from infantry regiments trained like the original Dragoons to fight on foot. First raised during the second half of last century.

MOUNTED RIFLES The 'M.I.' of the Commonwealth Forces, raised and trained as mounted men.

MULE The offspring of a donkey stallion and a mare or filly, q.v. Mules do not reproduce their kind.

MUSTANG A loose term for Western American cowboys' ponies. Sometimes incorrectly applied to remounts from North America. More properly the wild horses of the Western American prairies.

NEAR SIDE The left side of a horse as seen by the rider. All remounts are mounted on the near side. Thus 'near-side stirrup', etc.

NIGERIAN or WEST AFRICAN HORSES See under the section on the subject. They might be roughly classed as offshoots from the Barb.

NOLAN'S SADDLE The British Cavalry saddle of c.1856 was commonly called by this name, though incorrectly. The saddle invented by Captain Lewis Nolan, c.1820–54, was slightly different and was used by Indian Cavalry from c.1862.

NOSEBAG A canvas bucket-shaped receptacle, waterproof when new, holding a day's feed of corn for a horse and slung from the saddle Dees.

NOSEBAND That part of the bridle or halter passing round the front of the horse's head above the mouth.

NUMNAH A thick felt or sheepskin pad used under a saddle, sometimes taking the place of panels. Adapted by the British Army from India.

OFF SIDE The right side of a horse as seen by the rider. Thus the right-hand horses in a gun team are the 'off horses', 'off wheeler', etc.

O.P. An old Universal Pattern of equipment, obsolete but still possibly in use.

'PACE' A very fast walk, the horse moving both legs on one side simultaneously (Bloodgood and Santini). Not an official pace.

PACES The *Manual of Horsemastership* gives the following rates. Walk 4 miles an hour. Trot 8 m.p.h. Canter 9 m.p.h. Slow gallop 12 m.p.h. Gallop 15 m.p.h. Unofficial paces are the amble, a four-beat fast walk which can be developed into the faster 'Pace'.

PACK-SADDLE A saddle specially made for carrying all types of arms, tools, equipment and materials used by the Army. Also fitted to convey wounded men; see under cacolets.

PAD Properly speaking, a saddle without a tree but usually with stirrups, girths and sometimes cruppers.

PANEL or PANNEL The padding or stuffing usually of horsehair, covered with leather, serge, or canvas fitted and fastened under the saddle-tree to prevent the latter rubbing the horse. Originally made in one piece to cover both sides of the horse. During the nineteenth century made in two pieces allowing a hollow space (see under chamber) along the spine. Panels can be fixed or detachable.

PEAK An old term for the high pommel of a saddle, sometimes spelt 'pique' from the French, hence 'demi pique' for a lower type of pommel.

PERCHERON The French breed of heavy draft horse, short backed and active, used in North America to breed the artillery horses used in large numbers by the Royal Artillery in France in 1916 to 1918. The origin of the Percheron is said to have been a mixture of Arab and Barb stallions with Flemish stock in the eighth century A.D. See Plate 100.

PICKAXE TEAM A combination of three leaders and two wheelers or two leaders and one wheeler. See also under unicorn.

PICKET POST A short pointed pole, once carried on the saddle, used to tie the horse to when unsaddled.

PILLION A small pad fastened behind and under the cantle of a saddle to take a rear pack in the late seventeenth and early eighteenth centuries. To ride pillion is to be taken up behind another man.

POINTS The extensions of the pommel of a saddle below the sideboards or bars. Usually fitted into pockets on the panels.

POLE A single long shaft running from the centre of the front of a vehicle between the two wheel animals. The end is attached to the collars or breast straps to allow the animals to act as brakes. In two-wheeled carts the pole is supported by a short pole attached to the collars or breast straps.

POLEBAR The light wooden cross-piece fastened to the pole of a two-wheeled vehicle and attached to the collars or breast pieces of the two wheelers. (Plate 31b.)

POLO A ball game, somewhat of the type of hockey, played by four mounted men a side. Played in India and first played in England by the officers of the Xth Hussars in 1869.

POLO PONY A fast very handy animal, originally a pony and considered as the most suitable type for Mounted Infantry.

POMMEL The front arch of a saddle, also called, peak, head, or saddle bow. Also used as a name for the crutches used on a sidesaddle to take the rider's legs.

PONY Any horse averaging 14·2 hands and less strongly built than a cob.

PORTMOUTH BIT The Universal Pattern bit introduced in 1902 and known as the Elbow bit.

POSTILLION The man riding one of a pair of harness horses was known as a postillion.

POSTING Riding like a postboy or postillion, i.e. rising in the stirrups in rhythm with the time of the horse's trot.

QUARTERS The hind part of a horse – the hind legs and buttocks.

REAR PACK The rolled cloak, valise, blanket, etc. carried behind the cantle strapped to it and to the fans.

REINS The long leather straps running from the bit in the horse's mouth to the hands of the rider or driver by which the horse is controlled.

REMOUNT The technical term for a horse bought for military service before issue to a unit. Used in this book as a synonym for an Army horse at any stage of his career.

RIG A male from which only one testicle has been removed; unsuitable as a remount.

RISING See 'Posting'.

ROUGH SHOE or ROUGH SHOD To rough shoe a horse is to fix projecting nails to the shoes to enable the horse to get a grip on frosty or slippery ground.

R.H.A. or ROYAL HORSE ARTILLERY. Batteries specifically organized to accompany Cavalry.

SHABRAQUE See in the section under 'Furniture'.

SHEEPSKIN See in the section under 'Furniture'.

SHOE, HORSE A metal rim nailed to the horn of a horse's foot underneath to preserve the horn from wearing away on hard surfaces.

SIDEBOARD The sides of a saddle-tree joining the pommel and cantle.

SILLADAR SYSTEM Under what was known as the Silladar system from 1858 to 1921 Indian Cavalry, except the three Madras Regiments, found themselves in remounts, arms, clothing and equipment from funds contributed by the rank and file. From 1864 fire-arms were provided by Ordnance.

SIRE The male parent of an animal.

SHIRE HORSE The heaviest English breed of horses. Probably descended from the Great Horse of mediaeval times. Used in breeding heavy draft horses.

SKID A wooden or metal shoe fitting under the circumference of a wheel, put on to lock the wheel and prevent it turning during a steep descent. In other words a brake.

SKIRT The small flaps on either side of the front of a riding saddle covering the stirrup bars.

SNAFFLE Called also a bridoon, q.v. The simplest form of bit. It can be a slightly curved bar used in harness, but the snaffle is usually a bit with a joint in the middle so that it can be moved up and down at that point, with a ring at each end for attaching the headstall of the bridle and the reins. (Figure 22.)

SPAN The South African name for a team of animals in draft.

SPOON The narrow high curved prolongation of the centre of the cantle to which the rear pack is strapped.

STALLION As 'Entire'. An uncastrated male horse.

STAYER A cant name for a horse with a capacity for keeping up speed for a long distance without getting unduly tired. One of the most vital characteristics of a remount.

STIFLE The joint of a horse's hind leg between the hip and the hock.

STIRRUP See 'Iron, stirrup'. The support for a rider's foot. Can be made of wood as in the Western American saddle.

STIRRUP LEATHER See under 'Stirrup'.

STOCK SADDLE Any type of riding saddle used by men working cattle, sheep or horses. The Northern American and the Australasian types are the best known and the Hungarian saddle was also a stock saddle.

STONE An English measure of weight used of the weight carried by horses. A stone is 14 lb.

SURCINGLE A narrow leather girth going over the saddle and under the horse.

SWINGLE TREE or SWINGLE Short pieces of wood fitted to take the ends of the traces. Either attached directly to a vehicle or to a longer swingle tree taking a short one at each end. Plate 39 refers.

TAILS The tail is the bony prolongation of the horse's spine. See in the section on 'Tails'.

TANDEM Two animals driven one in front of each other in harness.

TEAM Any number of animals over two, harnessed together.

THIGH PAD or BLISTER A padded piece of leather on the edge of the flap of a saddle used to give support to the thigh.

THILL or THILLER The early name for shafts, still in use in the nineteenth century in some parts of Great Britain. The horse in the shafts was known as the Thiller horse.

THOROUGHBRED A horse registered in the English General Stud Book (Weatherby's). A common term for a racehorse.

TRACES Thick straps, ropes or chains running from the collar or breast harness by which an animal moves a vehicle. Plate 39 shows both leather and chain traces.

TRAIL The continuation of a gun-carriage behind the breech of the gun which supports it in the firing position and is lifted up and hooked on to the back of a limber, q.v., in order to move the gun.

TONGA A two-wheeled cart for one or two animals used in India. Mentioned in the *Manual of Horsemastership*. The tonga, like the curricle, when used by a pair has the pole supported between the pad saddles of the animals.

TREE The solid, wood, metal or ivory framework shaped to the horse's back on which a saddle is constructed.

TROT A two-beat gait of the horse. For military purposes a pace of 8 mph used with the walk in a rapid approach march.

TUGS, shaft or thiller A short length of chain leading from the collar to a metal attachment on the shaft, which serves instead of a trace. Part of what is known as Farm Harness. Alternatively, a loop of heavy leather on a harness saddle through which the shaft passes.

TURCOMAN See under 'India'. Horses bred in Turkestan and used as remounts from *c.*1820 to 1880.

UNICORN A team with two horses in the wheel and one in front. The leader pulls from a swingle on the pole.

U.P. Universal Pattern. Used of any article of equipment in general use by the Army and sealed by Ordnance.

VALISE A leather or cloth container fitted to be strapped behind the cantle of a saddle to the spoon, if any, and to the fans.

WALER The generic name for Australasian saddle horses, in most cases bred from a thoroughbred sire and a light type of farm or ranch mare. Originally most of these remounts were shipped from New South Wales to India, hence the now generally adopted name.

WALK The slowest pace of the horse – should normally be at the rate of about 4 mph. Some horses can be taught to walk up to as much as 5 mph. If ridden by officers at the head of a column these horses keep the tail of the column at a jog trot, a most tiring proceeding for both horse and rider.

WALLETS The wallet replaced the holster and was strapped on the front of the pommel in the same way with a broad leather band connecting the two. Among other things spare rifle ammunition was often carried in the wallets.

WANTY A single rein for leading a horse in harness or under pack, but see also p. 198. In use by the Royal Artillery as early as 1766.

WHEEL or WHEELER The animal or animals immediately in front of a vehicle.

'THE WHEEL' of a gun team is the two horses harnessed directly to the limber, and the wheel driver is their rider.

WINKERS See 'Blinkers'.

WITHERS The highest part of a horse's shoulder coming immediately under the pommel of a saddle. The top of the perpendicular where the height of a horse is measured, in 'hands', q.v.

WOOLF or WOOF The seat of a military saddle. The expression occurs in Captain L. Nolan's *Cavalry* on p. 135.

WOOD ARCH The pommel and the cantle of the 'Hussar' type of saddle in use during the nineteenth century up to the 1880's by Regular Cavalry.

YAK Animal closely resembling the buffalo, used for pack and draught in Tibet in 1905. See in text under 'Bullocks'.

'YANKS' The slang name for the North American-bred light draft horses used in France and Flanders during the First World War in such large numbers.

YOKE Any solid attachment fitting on the neck of an animal from which traction is exerted. Usually a yoke means the wooden bar from which a bullock pulls.

Index

(The Index does not include the contents of the Glossary, nor the majority of the illustrations covered on pages 238–251.)